STRANGE
TIMES,
My Dear

STRANGE
TIMES,
My Dear

**THE PEN
ANTHOLOGY
OF CONTEMPORARY
IRANIAN
LITERATURE**

Edited by Nahid Mozaffari
Poetry Editor: Ahmad Karimi Hakkak

Arcade Publishing • New York

The publication of this book was made possible in part by a grant from the Open Society Institute. Translator's fees were supported in part with public funds from the New York State Council on the Arts, a state agency.

FIRST EDITION

Library of Congress Cataloging-in-Publication Data

Strange times, my dear : the PEN anthology of contemporary Iranian literature / edited by Nahid Mozaffari ; poetry editor: Ahmad Karimi Hakkak. — 1st ed.
   p. cm.
Translations from Persian.
ISBN 1-55970-765-8
1. Persian literature—Translations into English. 2. Iranian literature—Translations into English. I. Mozaffari, Nahid. II. Karimi Hakkak, Ahmad.

PK6449.E1S77 2005
891'.5508003—dc22   2004023527

Published in the United States by Arcade Publishing, Inc., New York
Distributed by Time Warner Book Group

Visit our Web site at www.arcadepub.com

10 9 8 7 6 5 4 3 2 1

Designed by API

EB

PRINTED IN THE UNITED STATES OF AMERICA

To Iranian writers everywhere

and to

Moez Nosrat Mozaffari
1946–2001

CONTENTS

PROSE: PART TWO

ACKNOWLEDGMENTS

PEN American Center in New York was the place of inspiration for this project. The occasion was a visit to New York by several Iranian writers in 1999, and a series of discussions with American writers about the difficulties of being translated (well) and commercially published in the United States. With professional dedication, human compassion, and much patience, many of the current and former staff and several PEN members helped nurture the far-fetched idea of publishing an overview of contemporary Iranian literature in the United States into a reality. Sincere thanks are due to Betty Fussell, Karen Kennerly, Michael Roberts, Larry Siems, Anna Kushner, Esther Allen, Linda Morgan, Christie Fountain, Siobhan Dowd, Jake Krielkamp, Diana Ayton-Shenker, and Elham Kalantar. Betty Fussell and Karen Kennerly spent many hours reading and editing the stories and poems with insight, wit, patience, and perseverance. The Iranian literary community cannot thank them enough. We are also very grateful to Ervand Abrahamian and Behruz Moazami for their guidance and support throughout the project.

We would like to thank Jeri Laber and the members of the Association of American Publishers' International Freedom to Publish Committee for their support and for their ongoing efforts in encouraging the publication of literature from other languages as well as in defending freedom of expression and publication wherever it is threatened.

Many thanks are due to the New York State Council on the Arts for awarding us a translation grant in 2001.

Leyla Ebtehaj was a close collaborator in reading, translating, editing, researching, and selecting stories. She provided invaluable help throughout the project. This book would not have been possible without her. Sara Khalili provided consistent and invaluable help, not only with her excellent translations, but also with biographies and the bibliography. Many thanks to Deborah Tall and Sholeh Wolpé for sharing their talents as poets and writers and providing excellent editorial assistance. Others who read and helped select stories, provided us with guidance in the selection process, or helped in various other ways were: Mohsen Ashtiyani, Reza Baraheni, Hamid Dabashi, Reza Daneshvar,

Leyli Dariush, Sheida Dayani, Kuross Esmaili, Massumeh Farmanfarmaian, Reza Farokhfal, Fahimeh Gooran, Farangis Habibi, Hushang Keshavarz, Mehdi Khorrami, Mandana Kolbadi, Frank Lewis, Farzaneh Milani, Jilla Moazami, Mahnaz Moazami, Nasser Mohajer, Azar Naficy, Matt Noel, Nasser Pakdaman, Nasrin Rahimieh, Frederic Ramade, Saba Ruhani, Faraj Sarkuhi, Sussan Shahabi, Goli Taraghi, Sholeh Vatanabadi, Natalie Willens, and Hura Yavari.

In Iran, Farkhondeh Hajizadeh and Shahriyar Mandanipur, themselves successful and busy writers and editors of journals, gave us invaluable help in the selection process.

Mahmud Dowlatabadi, Javad Mojabi, Mohammad Sepanlu, Simin Behbahani, Karim Emami, Farzaneh Taheri, Moniru Ravanipur, Payman Soltani, Pejman Soltani, and many others in the literary community provided valuable guidance, suggestions, and comments.

Many thanks are due to Abbas of Magnum Photos for saving the day. We cannot express enough gratitude and appreciation to our families, who were supportive and patient throughout the project.

Finally, We would like to express our sincere thanks to Richard and Jeannette Seaver and the rest of the gracious staff at Arcade Publishing. We are very lucky to have the opportunity to work with people whose courage, principles, and dedication we so deeply respect.

INTRODUCTION

We are writers. By this we mean that we write our feelings, imagi-nation, thoughts, and scholarship in various forms and publish them. It is our natural, social, and civil right to see that our writing—be it poetry or fiction, drama or filmscript, research or criticism, or the translation of works written by other writers of the world—reach the public in a free and unhampered manner. It is not within the capacity of any person or organization to create obstacles for the publication of these works, under whatever pretext these may be.

—The Declaration of 134 Iranian Writers, 1994

Literature is the question minus the answer.

—Roland Barthes

I don't know why, but every time I'd read a book, I'd end up wanting to fall in love.

—Seyyed Ebrahim Nabavi in "First Love"

In the last twenty-five years traumatic events—a revolution, a long bloody war, political purges, economic hardship, religious repression, and censorship—have taken place in Iran. Nevertheless, a cultural revival is occurring in literature, art, music, and cinema. Western audiences have observed only part of this surge of creativity through their recent fascination with Iranian cinema. Appreciating the breadth, creativity, and new directions in poetry and fiction has been more difficult, because this literature has not been available to the general reader in translation. What does exist in translation is mainly for academic consumption. Many writers and poets in Iran feel strongly that their work is not benefiting from the level of international scrutiny, appraisal, and criticism that makes any national literature part of world literature.

The PEN Anthology is a step toward remedying this situation by presenting a sampling, or, as best conveyed by the Persian word *gol-chine*—a bouquet—of some of the best poems, short stories, and excerpts from novels written inside and outside of Iran since the revolution of 1979. These stories and poems, written by over fifty men and women from three generations, were chosen by Iranian writers and critics themselves solely on the basis of literary quality and translatability. Political, social, or gender considerations did not influence the decision-making process. For the Western reader, this collection provides a window into a largely undiscovered branch of world literature that will we hope bring literary enjoyment as well as a better understanding of a rich and complex culture. It is our hope that this volume will also serve to awaken further interest in the more extensive translation and publication of Iranian writers and poets.

HISTORICAL OVERVIEW

Classical Persian literature is a mosaic of the elaborate poetry and prose (treatise and discourse) of the court tradition, mystical devotional poetry; philosophical and love poetry; epics, legends, and travel literature. For centuries, poetry prevailed over prose. In fact, the towering figures of Persian literature who have been translated and known in the West have been the major classical poets of Iran such as Ferdowsi (940–1020), Omar Khayyam (1048–1131), Sa'adi, (1220–1290), Mowlana Jallaleddin Rumi (1207–1273), and Hafez (1320–1390).

From the late nineteenth century to the middle of the twentieth century, Iranian literature underwent a vast transformation, partly because of contact with the West and Western literature and partly because of changes within the country. The most important internal stimulus for change was the modernist and antidespotic movement to transform Iran from an absolute monarchy to a constitutional monarchy. Although the Constitutional Revolution (1906–1911) did not ultimately achieve its long-term political goals of establishing a functioning parliament, the rule of law, and a lasting democracy, it did succeed in changing society in other fundamental ways. Educational reforms, the establishment of a vibrant press, and the growth of critical public debates about politics, religion, and society in the late nineteenth and early twentieth centuries gave intellectuals in the nascent middle class new channels to communicate with the population at large. The use of new genres and the employment of simpler language, as well as increased literacy rates, expanded the audience for literature, and turned writers not only into observers and critics of society but mouthpieces for the people. Writers began to use literature to communicate with one another and with readers about social and political issues and about backwardness, identity, and nationalism. Literature, including fiction and poetry, came to be regarded as an instrument for educating and enlightening the population. Much of Iranian literature became a *littérature engagée,* and thus began a long struggle between the successive dictatorships, each with their own forms of censorship, and the intellectual, literary, and artistic communities. During certain periods, when the power of the dictatorship and the censor waned—for example, from the abdication of Reza Shah in 1941 up to the CIA and British–backed coup against Prime Minister Mossadegh in 1953 is one instance—the literary community thrived, and larger numbers of people wrote and read and participated in the prevailing social discourses.

From the early 1960s, with the growth of the nationalist and leftist dissent against the royal dictatorship, the sense of political commitment and social responsibility of the writer as intellectual increased. The solid connection between "westernization" and "modernity" began to come under question by some writers and intellectuals, who felt that under the rule of Mohammad Reza Shah (1941–1979), the identity of Iranian culture was being undermined by the emulation of the West in most aspects of life (except, of course, democracy). Thus, many "nativist" and "nostalgic" works began to be written in the 1960s and 1970s. Many of these stories, essays, and poems reveal the gray area that exists between questioning the wholesale adoption of westernization on the one hand and questioning modernity in the form of idealizing and romanticizing ideology, tradition, or religion on the other. This literary and cultural movement also coincided with the growth of the leftist, nationalist, and religious opposition to the royal regime. Since poverty, injustice, and oppression of the many by the few became the main themes of poetry and prose, the period before the 1979 revolution has been called the high age of "committed" literature by literary historians. The state responded with stricter censorship, and by imprisoning, torturing, and executing political activists and writers. By the late 1970s literary events were indistinguishable from political gatherings, and poetry and story readings became opportunities for protesting censorship and repression.[1]

WRITERS, GENRES, AND THEMES

Undoubtedly influenced by translations of European novels such as Dumas's *The Three Musketeers* and *The Count of Monte Cristo,* and James Morier's *The Adventures of Haji Baba of Isfahan* in the 1890s, the first genres in fiction to succeed in attracting readers were historical novels and satirical portraits.[2] Many of the historical novels dealt with Iran's pre-Islamic history, or other themes of lost glory, and expressed the emerging nationalist spirit of the times. Satirical portraits were popular as a way to indulge in social or political critiques with less fear of retribution from contemporary political or religious leaders.

In 1921, M. A. Jamalzadeh (1892–1997) wrote the first collection of short stories in Persian literature entitled *Once Upon a Time.* These "realistic" stories are told using colorful elements of local culture both in the choice of language and in the depiction of characters. From the 1920s onward, novels, short stories, and poetry began to deal with more social themes, such as the problems of the village and the city, modernity, and women as victims of displacement.[3] Romances and adventures continued to be published in serial form in magazines.

The towering figure of Persian prose fiction for much of the twentieth century has been Sadegh Hedayat (1903–1951). He wrote short stories, novellas, and novels as well as nonfiction. His masterly satirical portraits of people from every social group, his depiction of the contradictions that exist in societies where tradition and modernity coexist, and his philosophical and psychological perspective, made him the best-known and most translated modern Iranian writer. Particularly notable is his experimental surrealist novel *The Blind Owl.* Most of Hedayat's work has been translated in English and other languages.

---

1. For example, the Ten Nights of Poets and Writers Program at the Goethe Institute in Tehran, October 1977.

2. Houra Yavari, "Modern Fiction in Persia" in *Encyclopedia Iranica,* ed. Ehsan Yarshater, vol. 9 fascicle 6.

3. According to literary historians, many of these works were influenced by European naturalists like Emile Zola. See *ibid.* p. 585.

Hedayat influenced generations of writers that followed, including Bozorg Alavi, Sadegh Chubak, and Ebrahim Golestan.

After 1953—the year of the CIA-sponsored royalist coup and the end of the short experiment with democratization in Iran—disappointed intellectuals and writers turned to new sources of inspiration for their work. American writers like William Faulkner, Ernest Hemingway, and John Steinbeck were read and applauded; Jean-Paul Sartre and Albert Camus also appealed to those interested in philosophical and political approaches to literature. Franz Fanon and other third world writers who addressed the various aspects of colonial domination were read, and their ideas were adapted to the Iranian situation. Socialist realism became a favored genre to explore social and political subjects. The lives of peasants and the urban poor, social injustice, cultural and political alienation were common themes in the work of Chubak, Behazin, Afghani, Al-Ahmad, Simin Daneshvar (the first female novelist), Mahmud Dowlatabadi, Hushang Golshiri, Ahmad Mahmud and Jamal Mirsadeghi.

The modernist poetry of Nima Yushij (1895–1960), Forugh Farrokhzad (1935–1967), Ahmad Shamlu (1926–2000) Mehdi Akhavan Saless (1928–1990), and Sohrab Sepehri (1928–1980) completely changed the form, structure, content, and language of Persian poetry from the early twentieth century. This topic will be addressed in Dr. Karimi Hakkak's introduction to the poetry section.

THE CURRENT STATE OF LITERATURE IN IRAN

Most writers supported and participated in the revolution of 1979, and enjoyed the brief period of freedom of expression that it brought. Before long, the religious factions attempted to consolidate their power by taking American hostages and launching a cultural revolution. Universities were first purged of all nonreligious elements, and then closed altogether. Political opponents were imprisoned, killed, driven abroad, and otherwise silenced. Sanctioned broadly by the West including the United States, Saddam Hussein attacked Iran in September 1980. Cities were bombed, and hundreds of thousands of people perished under rockets and chemical weapons. Despite facing repression and strict censorship from their own state, war with Iraq, international vilification from abroad, and dire personal financial circumstances, Iranian writers have resumed writing and publishing from the early 1980s.[4]

Today, two-thirds of Iran's population of 70 million is under thirty years old. One–half of the population is under twenty years old. Seventy-six percent of the population is literate. Deprived of different forms of mass entertainment, the readers in Iran are mostly young, residents of the larger and smaller towns of the provinces, and—judging from the letters sent to literary journals—an increasing number of rural people.

In spite of the censorship imposed by the strict religious ideology and by various organs of the state, the number of writers and poets has multiplied and literary magazines have flourished. Literature has begun to emerge from the private sphere and from the domain of the upper and upper-middle class to the public sphere, where many writers and readers from economically disadvantaged backgrounds are beginning to participate. A large body of feminist literature, written mainly but not exclusively by women, has also grown and flourished within this literary landscape.

A diverse and dynamic literary environment has emerged that, interestingly, cannot be characterized as an integrated movement with an overriding set of aesthetic principles. Writers continue to write in multiple genres and styles that range from social realism to complex psychological stream of consciousness to various styles of postmodern prose. As a body of work, this literature is often apocryphal, in the sense that the stories and poems tend to be sad, often allegorical and allusive, with different dimensions of meaning and interpretation. This can be attributed to the complexity of the psychological and practical realities and emotions that the writers are trying to convey through their work, as well as to the treacherous alleys of censorship that writers have to maneuver through in order to be allowed to publish.

Most of the writers are middle class and secular, nationalist and cosmopolitan, grappling with their perceptions of the problems of con-

---

4. Many writers made their living through teaching or writing for journals. A great number of them were purged from their teaching jobs, and journals were closed down.

temporary Iran and the world.[5] The revolution began as a movement against royal dictatorship and its wholesale acceptance of Western economic and cultural domination, and resulted in the adoption of a different homegrown system of repression based on a politicized religious nativism. Whereas before the revolution the state dictated everything related to politics and made Iranians feel like incomplete second-class Europeans, this regime crossed the boundaries into our innermost private spheres, setting laws and seeking to control (often by force) how we dress, eat, drink, engage in sexual behavior, think, and express ourselves. As the poet Shamlu put it in "The Blind Alley": "They smell your breath lest you have said 'I love you.'" The stories and poems presented here demonstrate the writers' acute awareness of the human condition in Iran and the world.

The body of literature is also, encouragingly, introspective and self-critical, nuanced, and, at times, nostalgic. Many writers explore aspects of Iranian history and culture to seek clues to explain the persistence of the power of religion, the ease with which those in power are able to manipulate the masses, the anatomy of patriarchy, and the savagery of war.

THE CURRENT SELECTION

Based on the suggestions and submissions we received, the prose selections are divided into two categories.[6] The first group is made up of writers who were already established and published *before* the revolution, and continued to write afterward. Most have experimented with different styles and subjects over the decades, but their preferred genres and themes were short stories or novels addressing power, corruption, class differences and injustices, the effects of dislocation, alienation, and the plight and weaknesses of intellectuals. In style, they range from Ahmad Mahmud, the social realist chronicler of war, poverty, and injustice ("Scorched Earth"), to Hushang Golshiri, the chronicler of

---

5. By "secular," I do not necessarily mean that they are not believers; I mean that they believe in the separation of religion and state.

6. Much of this categorization is for explanatory purposes only. Some writers from each group overlap with others and defy categorization in different stages of their writing careers.

doubt, uncertainty, and contradictions, whose writing is based on the premise that reality is ultimately unknowable ("The Victory Chronicle of the Magi"). Mahmud Dowlatabadi's "The Mirror" is an allegory of alienation in which the author departs from his previous social realist style that poignantly explored the oppression and dislocation of Iranian peasants and tribes in his previous works *Klidar* and *The Empty Place of Soluch*. Esmail Fassih *(Sorraya in a Coma)*, Hadi Khorsandi ("The Eyes Won't Take It"), Nassim Khaksar ("The Grocer of Kharzeville"), and Iraj Pezeshkzad ("Delayed Consequences of the Revolution") try to portray the different stages of the experiences of rupture, dislocation, uncertainty of identity, and exile that followed the revolution for many Iranians. In the excerpt by Taghi Modarressi *(The Book of Absent People)* we observe the writer locating and inscribing the self in place and time by delving into the realm of memory.

The second group is primarily made up of writers who began to write, publish, and be read after the revolution. This varied group addressed new and taboo subjects grounded in specific less ideological situations. Awareness of gender and writing from women's points of view permeate these works, as do critiques of patriarchy, marriage traditions, and poverty. For example, *Women Without Men,* "Satan's Stones," "Mahbubeh and the Demon Ahl," and "A Little Secret" all focus primarily or principally on the issue of gender and women's oppression. In the work of Shahrnush Parsipur and Moniru Ravanipur, we can readily observe a form of magic realism set in Iranian historical and regional contexts. Though both Shahrnush Parsipur and Goli Taraghi wrote before the revolution, their most important work was done in the years after it, and it is interesting to see the influence of Freudian or Jungian psychoanalytical perspectives on their work.

Some writers in this group are from the younger generation of writers who have rejected customary narrative rules and practices in their choices of genre, language, theme, and style. They believe that the complexities and contradictions of the contemporary world are best portrayed through ambivalence and through engaging the reader with possibilities of multiple readings. The word *postmodern* has often been used in connection with the unusual narrative techniques, nonlinear plots, and experimental approaches to time and space employed by this group. "Shatter the Stone Tooth" by Shahriyar Mandanipur is an example of this style, as is "White Rock" by Ghazi Rabihavi, who often writes about people marginal to society.

Both groups have certain traits in common, signifying the continuity of the literary tradition in the face of rapidly moving events such as revolution, war, and the profound social flux that follows. Complex structures based on metaphor are common in these stories, as are the practices of mixing realism and surrealism, and creating ambivalence and nuance with words and meaning. A concern with regional issues, dialects, and cultural characteristics is evident. The gender issue has assumed a very important place in almost every work of fiction in contemporary Iran. Problematic or unresolved processes and events in Iranian history appear and reappear in the stories, as if there is a desire to find the key to contemporary problems by revisiting the past. The 1953 coup, for example, seems to be in the text, or the subtext, of a large number of the stories that appear in this volume. The 1979 revolution itself and the Iran-Iraq War (1980–1988), with its widespread loss of life and destruction, are also recurring themes.

Finally, I would like to draw attention to the fact that these stories and poems reflect the diversity and hybridity of Iran and Iranian culture itself. Multiple cultures, languages, ethnicities, religions, and world views have coexisted in this land for thousands of years and continue to do so despite the shocks of traumatic events or the passage of transient ideologies. The cosmopolitan Zoroastrian gentleman in *Sorraya in a Coma*, the pious Muslim girl in "Ask the Migrating Birds," the *New York Times*–reading Jewish couple in "A Room Full of Dust," the gay couple in "White Rock," and strong women are all familiar figures in our cultural landscape despite the stereotypes of Iranians constructed abroad.

I mentioned above that most contemporary stories and novels have complex structures based on metaphor, a mix of realism and surrealism, and ambivalence with words and meaning. This is partly due to stylistic choices, but also partly due to the fact that being a writer in Iran has been a dangerous business. Novelist Esmail Fassih was only exaggerating slightly when in 1987 he wrote, "In the splendorous land of Iran, a good writer is a dead writer"[7] In the 1980s and 1990s, since

---

7. Esmail Fassih, "The Status: A Day in the Life of a Contemporary Iranian Writer," *Third World Quarterly*. 9, no. 3 (July 1987): 825.

most of the political opposition to the regime had been repressed, reduced to silence, driven out of the country, or killed, intellectuals, writers, and journalists were considered to be at the forefront of the struggle for reform and democracy. In fact, not since the days of the Soviet Union have writers, intellectuals, and journalists been such an important element in the movement for reform, and, as a group, such an object of wrath, repression, and vilification by the state. The methods of repression have included various levels of censorship, economic pressures, imprisonment, torture, forced public confessions, and even assassination. From about 1992 until 2000, several writers, intellectuals, and dissidents were killed by vigilante groups directly linked to the security apparatus of the Islamic regime. The subsequent swift and persistent national and international outcry against these "serial murders" gave courage to the men and women of the literary community to continue their struggle for due process of law and freedom of expression.

Ghazi Rabihavi's "story" about censorship quoted below gives the reader a graphic idea of how writers have had to cope with the demands of the censor:

> Once upon a time, an Iranian writer wrote a 179-page-long novel, and like every other Iranian writer, presented it to the Ministry of Islamic Guidance to receive a publication permit. Then, the writer waited. The book began with the following passage: *"She knew that once her husband had brought her a cup of coffee, she would feel better, like every other day. As she stood by the window, the wind slid gently over her brown arms, and her eyes were on the rising sun that was pulling itself up over the government buildings. It was a sunrise that was like a sunset."* After thirteen months spent climbing up the slippery ladder of bureaucracy, the Iranian writer finally managed to obtain an appointment with the director in charge of censorship. The director was just a head. His body was hidden behind the desk and it seemed to be reclining gently against something soft.[8] The head delivered the following speech to the writer: "Unfortunately, your book has some small problems which cannot be corrected. I am certain you will agree with me. Take these first few sentences . . .

---

8. Many government censors were injured and handicapped veterans of the Iran-Iraq War. As poet Ahmad Shamlu recounted, for many years the chief censor for cinema was a blind man!

nowhere in our noble culture will you find any woman who would allow herself to stand waiting for her husband to bring her a cup of coffee. OK? Well, the next problem is the image of the wind sliding over the naked arms, which is provocative and has sexual overtones. Finally, nowhere, in any noble culture will you find a sunrise that is like a sunset. Maybe it is a misprint. Here you are then. Here is your book. I hope you will write another book soon. We support you. Support you." Then the head slid back under the desk. [9]

While we are still on the topic of censorship, it must be pointed out that these are indeed strange times (my dear) not only in Iran, but in the United States as well. Recent rulings by the Office of Foreign Assets Control of the Treasury Department of the United States of America designated the commissioning, editing, or marketing of material written in Iran, Cuba, and Sudan as "prohibited exports of services" to enemy nations, unless a license was obtained from that department in advance. "Collaborative interaction" betweem a U.S. publisher and a writer from these countries was prohibited. According to PEN, the Professional/Scholarly Publishing division of the Association of American Publishers, the American Association of University Presses, and my own publisher Arcade, who joined together to file a lawsuit to change the regulations, this in effect meant that editors, translators, and publishers had to "seek a government license to carry on First Amendment–protected publishing activities or leave themselves open to criminal pentalties." In these days of the ascendance of transnationalism throughout the world, it certainly seems bizarre, if not downright shortsighted and irresponsible, to futher limit the already meager lines of communication and understanding between peoples with differing perspectives. Rules and regulations such as these infringe on the freedom of expression and discourage editors and publishers from considering manuscripts from abroad, further isolating the American people from other cultures and points of view. After the lawsuit was filed, the Treasury Department issued new regulations authorizing most of the publishing activities that were previously prohibited.

---

9. Ghazi Rabihavi, "With the Lost Words," reading in London, December 6, 1996, repr. in *Index on Censorship,* Spring 1997.

SELECTION PROCESS

To make the selection process as representative of the will and taste of Iranian writers as possible, I sent out scores of letters to writers, poets, critics, anthologists, editors of literary journals, and university professors in Iran and throughout the world requesting their input and participation in this project. I also made two trips to Iran, where I consulted with many people in the literary community. The criteria for selection were: high-quality prose or poetry, written and (first) published in Persian since the revolution of 1979. Cultural and linguistic translatability was also added as a condition, since the anthology was meant to be accessible to the general reading public in the Western countries.

The outpouring of response was heartwarming but daunting as well; as the rooms in my house became filled with piles and piles of letters, stories, books, and poems, some sent from remote towns and villages in Iran, I came to realize that making the selections fairly for such a volume would be extremely difficult. The literary journals sent from Iran and from various cities of Europe and the United States where exiles had settled gave testimony to a lively literary culture, and to raging debates among poets, writers, and critics concerning the current state of Iranian literature and the quality of this or that work.

I am sure that I shall not be able to satisfy everyone with these choices, but I have tried to consider as many points of view as possible in the selections that have been made. I have also solicited the help of many readers who are first and foremost lovers of reading and literature, and not privy to disagreements in literary circles.

Finally, I would like to point out that there were many more good stories and excerpts of novels and poems that could not be included for lack of space, translation, or permission problems. I deeply regret that the work of Zoya Pirzad, one of the best and most successful writers of this generation, and several other very gifted writers could not be published in this volume. It is my fervent hope that we will be able to publish a second volume in the near future and remedy these shortcomings.

N.M.

Prose

Part One

Mahmud I

Mahmud Dowlatabadi was born i
province of Khorassan, in 1940. A
his native village, he moved to Tel
working at a variety of odd jobs. In
traditional religious plays (*ta'zieh*) tl
tices that befell the Shi'a imams, an
conservatory and worked in the the
stories in *Desert Strata* and in 1970,
Shah's secret police, SAVAK, and sper   . . . 1970) in prison,
but continued to write and publish stories throughout the 1970s.

Dowlatabadi has gained his fame as a writer by portraying peasants, tribesmen, and workers struggling against injustice. Many of the
events in his novels have been inspired by real events. He is one of the
most prolific and respected writers of contemporary Iran.

His two most important novels, *Klidar* (1978–1983*)* and *The
Empty Place of Soluch* (1979), were published after the revolution. *Kli-
dar* is a saga of the men and women of the tribes and villages in Khor-
rassan and their clashes with the government in the 1940s. *The Empty
Place of Soluch* focuses on the decline of village life in the 1960s.
Dowlatabadi has also written many other stories and novels, including
We Are of the People Too and *The Spent Lives of Old People*.

Written in 1995, "The Mirror" is from *Seven Men, Seven Stories*,
published in Tehran by Rahiyan-e Andisheh Press in 1999.

et crossed the mind of the man walking down the street should remember it had been fifteen years since he had at himself in the mirror. Neither did he have any reason to re- that it had been nearly as long since he had heard himself laugh. And he certainly would not have remembered that he had lost his identity card, had it not been announced on the radio that all "dear citizens" must renew them — that the expiring cards should be mailed in right away, so the new ones could be sent out within the requisite four weeks. After the announcement, the thought had crossed his mind to look for the old one: it was then that he remembered he had lost it.

But the only way he was able to figure out that it had been thirteen years since he had lost it was to remember that the last time he had had to deal with his identity card was some thirteen years ago (or was it thirty-three years ago? — at a much earlier time, on a historical day); he had put the card in the inside pocket of his raincoat so that he could, for the first and only time in his life, go to the polling booth, show his identity card, and have it stamped on one of its pages. Since then, there had been no reason for him to remember where he might have left the card or wonder if he had lost it. Now another historical occasion had arisen, one that once again required the use of his identity card; and it was lost. At first he thought he might have left the card in the pocket of the raincoat, but it wasn't there. Then it occurred to him that perhaps he had put it in the safe, but no . . . it wasn't there, either.

He walked down to the end of the alley, boarded the bus, and went straight to the Personal Records Office. Once at the Office, he was not given a clear answer, so he went back home; but when he got home, he remembered that — apparently — he had been told to get his neighbors to attest to his identity in writing and bring it in as proof. Yes, that was it. That was what he had been told. But how to formulate the citation?

He sat on the chair in front of his desk and pulled out a pencil and some paper. Well . . . it had to read, "We, the undersigned, testify that the identity card belonging to Mr. _____ has been lost without a trace." Using a calligraphy pen, he made a clean copy of what he had written, left the house, and went straight to the grocer's where he did his weekly shopping. But the grocer, not wanting any trouble, said he did not know his name, because up to now, it had never crossed the grocer's mind to ask. "Especially since you yourself have left a blank on the citation where your name should be!"

Yes, that was right.

He should have gone directly to the dry cleaner's first, because he'd been having his suit and shirt cleaned there every year for New Year's, and he would have been given a receipt. Yet — although the dry cleaner had a powerful memory and was able to recognize all his customers, if not by name then by face — he could not place the man! He said he was sorry, rarely had he had the pleasure of meeting him. "Could you please give me your blessed name?"

Please! This is too much.

"Or at least a receipt. The problem will be solved when you bring in one of our receipts, which you undoubtedly have at home."

Yes, the receipt. There, on the piece of paper, they noted one's name, the date the clothes were brought in, even the number of items. But the receipt . . . why should a customer keep the receipt after the clothes have been picked up? No, that wouldn't work.

Where else, to whom could he go?

To the bakery. The bakery was in the same row of shops. He bought his bread there every week. But what time was it now? The baker's assistant was sitting on the floor against the wall, resting. "We're finished baking for the day, sir."

So the man turned back and walked home along the wall, holding the piece of paper he'd torn out of a school notebook.

Standing behind the window in his room, he stared for a while at the algae floating on the surface of the pond, but he couldn't remember anything. Then, by dusk — or perhaps it was already evening — it occurred to him that he should head back to the Personal Records Office with his pockets full and bribe the man in charge of the archives to set aside an hour after work to help track down his identity card. This, at least, was a possibility, wasn't it? Yes . . . why not, after all, shouldn't it be?

He reached an agreement with the old man, who was smoking cheap cigarettes out of a long cigarette holder held at the corner of his mouth, that they would go down to the cellar and look through the archives. It was perhaps an hour or so after they had their afternoon tea that they went down and began their search. The man who had lost his identity card had been smart enough to bring along a pack of cigarettes and a box of matches he had bought on his way to the Office. That way, it would not be a problem if they had to hang around the archives after hours. Once there, the seriousness with which the old man rolled up his sleeves and peered into the cabinet files from behind his thick glasses assured the man that he would not leave the archives department disappointed — especially after he himself began to help and gradually became familiar with the files.

After they had gone through the letter *A,* the old man straightened up, asked for another cigarette, and took the *B* files out of the cabinet. "What did you say your blessed name is?" he asked.

"I didn't say," the man replied.

"Yes," said the archivist, "I believe that you did tell me your name, and your family name. It was when we were in the teahouse."

"No, no, no . . ." said the man.

"How could you possibly not have said anything?" asked the archivist.

"No, no, no . . ." said the man.

"Well," said the archivist, taking off his glasses. "It's not too late. There are many more letters to go through; you can tell me now."

"Strange, isn't it?" said the man. "I've been wasting your time. I apologize. I forgot to tell you what the real problem is. I . . . no matter how hard I try, I cannot remember my own name. I haven't heard it for a long while. I thought maybe . . . maybe I could get hold of an identity card?"

"Of course," said the archivist, putting on his glasses again. "Of course, there must be a way. But why do you insist that you must —"

"No reason," said the man. "No reason at all. Just like that . . . Why don't we forget the whole thing? Why does it matter, anyway?"

"Whatever you wish," said the archivist, "but I can also understand the problem of forgetfulness and senility. I myself have suffered from it from time to time. Still, there are ways, if you insist on having an identity card."

"What ways?" the man responded quickly.

"It costs a little," said the archivist. "If there are no real problems, there are solutions. I know someone who does this kind of work. I can take you to him. But it's your decision, and you have to make up your mind right away: if we are going we must get there before dark."

The two men left the Office and turned into the alley that led to the main street, and from there caught the bus to the neighborhood the archivist knew like the back of his hand. The building was long and low, with a slight bend in its facade, like the sheath of an old dagger. An old man, wrapped in a cloak and sitting in front of the shop, greeted the archivist and showed him and his customer to the back of the shop, where, walking past rows and rows of old or used objects, he led them straight to an alcove hidden behind a dirty curtain. He pulled the curtain to one side and opened an old chest. There, he showed the men a huge pile of identity cards.

"It depends," the archivist said, "it really depends on what kind of identity card you want. These days it's very common for people to lose their names, or their identity cards, or both. Now, what would you like to be? A king? Or a pauper? We have everything. Only the rates are different. Even there, we'll take into consideration your circumstances. Some people shut their eyes and pick a card, like in a lottery. It all depends on what your taste is. Where would you like to have been born? Where would you like to have been raised? What occupation? What face or image would you like to have? Everything is possible. Will you make your own choice or shall I draw a lot for you? If it's to be lottery style, you could draw the identity card of an officer, an iron merchant, an automobile showroom owner, a landowner, a business owner, or a government contractor. You should not worry at all. This is perfectly normal. For instance, this bundle of cards marked with an *X* are for Special Services, but I don't think they would suit you, given your age. This other bundle is for the media — for instance, giving you a permit to publish a weekly paper or, let's say, to produce a television program. As for your name, what would you like your name to be? Hassan, Hossein, Buzarjomehr . . . ? A name from the *Shahnameh*? It all depends on what kind of name you like. What kind of name do you like?"

The man who had lost his identity card remained silent and thoughtful for a few minutes, then said, "I have troubled you. Still, if it's no problem, could you please look around and find me an identity card of someone who has died? Is that possible?"

"Nothing is impossible," said the archivist. "That is even cheaper."

"Thank you, thank you."

As they stepped outside, the old shopkeeper had started to cough as he stood up, looking, it seemed, for the long hook with which to pull down the shutter. In between coughs, he was telling the two customers standing by the counter to come back tomorrow "because there was no electricity at the back of the shop."

And . . . the thought crossed the mind of the man who had lost his identity card that he had not laughed for some thirteen years. And now that he had begun to laugh, he suddenly felt that his teeth were peeling away, falling out, dropping down along his legs and landing on the tips of his shoes. He also felt that, one by one, a piece of his jaw-bone, an eyelid, his fingernails, were falling off his body. It occurred to him that perhaps it was time for him, if he did get home and did walk into his room, to go straight to the mantelpiece and take one look — one last look — at himself in the mirror.

— *Translated by Hossein Shahidi*

Hushang Golshiri

Born in Esfahan in 1937, Hushang Golshiri grew up in the south of Iran in the city of Abadan. Returning to Esfahan to pursue his education, he graduated from the University of Esfahan with a degree in Persian language, and became a teacher. He began to write and publish fiction in journals in the late 1950s. In the 1960s he established *Jong-e Esfahan,* a literary journal, which quickly became celebrated as the most important journal published outside the capital. His first collection of short stories, *As Always,* was published in 1968, followed by his most successful and famous novel, *Prince Ehtejab.* About the decadence of the ruling class as seen through the memories of a dying prince, it was made into a popular movie in 1974, directed by Bahman Farmanara. Golshiri was arrested and imprisoned after the film was shown because his criticism of the prince was construed as an attack on the Shah's regime.

Other works published before the revolution include *Kristine and Kid* (1971), *My Little Prayer Room* (1975), and *The Shepherd's Lost Lamb* (1977). After the revolution, he published *The Fifth Innocent* (1980), *The Armory* (1983), *The Story of the Fisherman and the Demon* (1984), *Five Treasures* (1989), and *Mirrors with Doors* (1997). Golshiri was an able critic and a tireless teacher of literature and writing. Many among the young generation of writers today participated in his writing seminars and workshops. He died in the year 2000, at the age of sixty-three. Two of Golshiri's novels, *Shazdeh Ehtejab* and *Christine and Kid,* are currently being translated and will be published in English.

"The Victory Chronicle of the Magi," written just after the revolution, is a complex rendition of the experience of the common man and his ultimate betrayal by the revolution. Golshiri deliberately weaves contradiction, rumor, and ambiguity to show how the meaning of revolution and being revolutionary shifted as the popular movement to remove the Shah became more and more controlled by Islamist factions to become another form of repression. With the interesting, ambiguous usage of "we said" and "they said" Golshiri introduces different voices and perspectives, and shows how people cling to their perceptions of shifting realities, often believing what they want to believe rather than registering the tragic facts.

A note of explanation about the title: *Pir-e Moghan* — the old Magus, or the elderly Zoroastrian tavern keeper — is a frequently used image in classical Persian poetry, particularly the poetry of Hafez. The old tavern keeper represents wisdom and sincerity and honesty, in contrast to the hypocritical followers of religion, who profess belief and piety, but lie, cheat, and hurt others.

THE VICTORY CHRONICLE
OF THE MAGI

Finally, we started doing it, too. The windows of the cinema had already been broken. People had thrown a couple of rocks and the large panels of glass had shattered into tiny pieces. When we couldn't find anything better to break, we smashed the neon signs above the doorways. The banks had tight security. A couple of cops were always there, with revolvers and G-3s, though no one could imagine them shooting at a bunch of ten- or twelve-year-old kids.

The rocks made it through the metal security bars and grrrring . . . The glass shattered all over the floor. We were doing okay up to this point. Only a few of us got hurt. A boy holding a slingshot — the son of Hassan Agha the cloth merchant — got shot right in the middle of his forehead. The taverns and the statue of the Shah in the middle of the main square were still untouched.

But we couldn't bring ourselves to do it. We knew most of the tavern keepers; we greeted them in the street. Besides, they were just regular people, like us, in a small town like ours with a single park, a few recently planted trees, and some rundown benches used mostly by retired people. In the late afternoon, the fountains around the four corners of the square were turned on, and the benches filled with older men holding canes and wearing felt hats.

It wasn't till the Moharram mourning days when finally two taverns — and they weren't even open for business — got their windows smashed.[1] After that, we felt we could do whatever we wanted. We began with the Majidiyeh tavern. Customers fled as soon as we showed up and made some noise. We passed the liquor bottles from one person to the next, like they were bricks, and broke them on the edge of the curb.

Ali Agha was screaming: "Why are you breaking them, you infidels? You could have told me to close my shop." He grabbed one of

---

[1] Moharram is the first month in the Arabic calendar. For Shi'a Muslims, the first ten days of this month are mourning days because they commemorate the Battle of Karbala and the martyrdom of Imam Hossein, the third imam and the Prophet Mohammad's grandson, in 61 A.H. (683 C.E.).

us: "Hassan, my boy, why don't you tell them to stop? Don't let them ruin me."

Suddenly someone — I don't know who it was — punched Ali Agha in the face, smack on his bony nose and black teeth. Ali Agha had just been saying to him: "Why you? Just last night you were . . ."

Ali Agha's nose and mouth were covered with blood. He knelt down by the gutter overflowing with booze and wine, and sobbed.

So for a couple of days, this is all we did. But Barat's tavern was still open for business. Even when they brought in a flatbed truck and pulled down the statue in the middle of Shah Square with a lot of pomp, not one person threw a good-for-nothing rock at Barat's full length window panels.

Barat was one of us. He was from our town. He was an old hand at this sort of battle. He'd even been to prison. He'd brought the eighteen-wheeler truck himself. Some people tied a rope to the horse's hoof and started pulling it. They began swinging at the base of the statue with pickaxes. But the horse was still standing on two hooves. When Barat jumped out of the truck, we made way for him, clasped our hands and hoisted him to the top of the base. Then he managed to crawl up one of the horse's legs, grab the tail, and sit behind the rider. Pulling himself up the rider's arm, he managed to slide over and sit on the horse's mane. He undid the shawl he wore around his waist and let it hang down. Someone tied a hammer to it and Barat hoisted it. At last, he stood up. He held on to the rider's arm with one hand, and raised the hammer in the other hand. He turned around and looked at us from up there. And we, so many of us, as far as the eye could see, were standing and looking at him. What could he do with a hammer?

Barat turned around, lifted the hammer, and brought it down hard on the rider's nose. There was a spark but the nose didn't budge. He pounded again, and again. From the other side of the square, armed soldiers began to pour out of a side street. The news traveled from mouth to mouth till it reached the statue where Barat was. He continued to pound, but the nose remained just the same. He started to hammer away at the brim of the hat, hitting it again and again. But now we weren't looking at Barat anymore. We stepped aside to make way for the soldiers, and we watched them as they raised their guns and aimed at our foreheads. For sure, Barat had seen it too. He yelled out: "Hurry up, give me the cable!"

We stretched out the towing cable and tied it to Barat's shawl, which was still hanging down. We heard gunshots as a shower of bullets passed just above our heads. The crowd heaved backward and swung back into place again. With the next round of bullets, the crowd stretched out, spilled over, and poured into the back streets. Now the guns were pointing at the statue. Two people had fallen at the base. They were the men who had climbed up to hoist the cable. But Barat was still there. His back was to the rider as he sat astride the mane, holding the bridle in one hand and the towing cable in the other. He leaned over to put the cable around the horse's leg, which was raised up to the blue sky. The soldiers started to move. By now, we could just hear their footsteps since we, all of us, were hiding, here and there, in the bend of an alley, in the gutters lining the streets, and in the few stores that remained open on the square.

That's when we heard Barat's voice. We heard him yell: "Come on, move it!"

The commanding officer was now aiming his gun at him. Barat slid down the horse's mane and yelled again: "Pull!" The cable tightened around the horse's leg. The soldiers crouched down and aimed at the truck's tires. But it was already too late. The horse and its rider had begun to tilt. They leaned over, and when they finally collapsed, the entire main square shook, and the water in the four fountains of the square spilled over the edges.

The soldiers stood up. The crowd crouching in the gutters stood up, too. It all happened in one instant. We had seen that statue since we were kids, and now as the dust settled, we could see that it was gone — the horse erect on two legs, neighing; the rider, with his military cap, forever holding the horse's bridle, forever galloping, no more. The base was now empty. And there, in the middle of the square, lay the head of the rider, wedged in the stone pavement. The horse's four limbs were pointing at the sky and trembling as though the animal was alive. The limbs shook, then seemed to search the ground for a firm footing, as if the horse was attempting to rise up, get the rider back on the saddle to hold the bridle, so that it could neigh and rise once again on its legs.

We, all of us, emerged from the back alleys, jumped out of the stores, driven forward onto the streets, looking at our hands, our empty hands, when we saw Barat. He was standing there, on the base of the statue, his chest bare, and he was holding his shirt in his hand, his other hand on his waist. He was dancing and twirling his shirt over his head like a handkerchief, and he was shaking his lower body. No, the statue would not rise again. It had been toppled and the rider's nose and hat were stuck deep in the pavement.

We said: God is great!

We said: Death to the Shah!

We said: Long live the people!

And we began to dance. We danced like Barat, with or without a handkerchief, holding each other's hands. It was finally over. The war was over. And the soldiers who were pointing guns at us were now only pretending to fight. We danced and we walked. Wherever we saw people bent over weeping, we grabbed their hands and twirled them around. If they pulled their hands away to wipe a tear, we kissed their half-open mouths. We knew the Shah wouldn't come back.

Suddenly we heard a shot. Where did it come from? The soldiers were facing us though their guns were at rest. The commanding officer was just holding his hat in his hand. Who was it, then? The base of the statue stood empty. Barat had been shot. The soldiers were looking at us, showing us their empty hands. They stared at one another to see who had fired the shot. Suddenly, a shower of rocks began. The soldiers huddled together. Holding on to their guns, they began to retreat. Then, it was them again shooting, and they were not shooting in the air. They were aiming at us. A few of us fell, but we couldn't stretch out and pour out into the back streets. Some of the soldiers stopped, put down their guns, and tossed away their hats. They were weeping.

The rest were running, under a shower of rocks, toward the military vehicles that had begun to move.

Barat had collapsed right there, at the base of the statue. He was covered with blood. We picked him up. He just said: "My arm." It was his right arm. It was broken, and blood was gushing from his shoulder. We lifted him up and ran through the passage that people opened up for us.

That was the kind of guy Barat was. He was one of us, an old hand at resistance, and very headstrong. When they had to operate on him, we all lined up to donate blood: the line we formed went around the hospital and all the way up Majidiyeh Street. And on the day they released him, we all went along to bring him home, with much pomp and celebration. His tavern was closed and we didn't want to him to go there. We said: "Stay home. Stay till your arm heals." He said: "It will heal."

The bone in his arm had been shattered. It was in a cast. But Barat was not one to stay put; after a couple of days, he undid the bandage around his shoulder, and the next thing we heard was that he was heading back to his store, with a pot under his arm. He even managed to open the metal gate with his left hand. We loved him. We didn't want him to get into trouble. We went over and asked: "Barat, what are you doing?"

He said: "What do you all do at night, huh? Go home before the sun sets and coop up like chickens?"

We said: "Barat, the Shah is gone. Isn't that enough?"

He said: "I was fourteen when I saw them smash his nose with a sledgehammer. I was a member of the party's Youth Organization.[2] My father was a party member, too. I saw with my own eyes how they tied the cable to his arm and pulled it with a truck."

We said: "This time he is gone for good. Now the people of Tehran are armed. They are not fighting with empty hands. Our young people are no longer dependent on others; they can stand on their own two feet."[3]

He said: "Yeah, I've heard it, too. Sadduq's son told me. He also told me that as you were on your way to fight, a van drove alongside, and over the loudspeakers they kept saying that no jihad had been declared. Here you were, ready to fight and push the Royal Guards back, and they kept telling you, over loudspeakers, 'People, these people are SAVAK agents, move away from them.' "

We said: "You weren't even there. You were in the hospital. We went and took over the SAVAK building.' "

He said: "Yes, I know, but when was that? By the time you got there, they had already burned all the documents or taken them away. You dilly-dallied so long that those bastards managed to escape."

We said: "They wouldn't let us."

He said: "Who wouldn't let you?"

"The counterrevolutionaries."

---

[2] Indirect reference to the Tudeh, or Iranian Communist Party, in 1953.
[3] The Tudeh Party was dependent on the Soviet Union.

"What counterrevolutionaries? You guys are supposed to be the counterrevolutionaries. Haven't you heard the radio? You, all of you, are counterrevolutionaries."

"What about you, with this pot of yours, and with your bottles of liquor?"

He said: "Look in here and see what my wife cooked." He lifted the lid of his pot. Warm steam wafted out. It was filled with dolma, stuffed grape leaves, light green in color and arranged neatly all the way to the top. They sure would hit the spot. He picked up the chairs, which had been stored over the tables, and set them down.

He said: "Well, why don't you take a seat?" And before we could do or say a thing, he had wiped the table clean, placed four slender glasses before us, along with four plates, spoons, and forks.

We said: "Dear Barat, don't you understand?"

We pointed to the street. People were walking by, staring at us.

He said: "You mean *this* was the problem?"

"No."

"Then what?"

"Well, when we were smashing the windows of the cinemas, we weren't really thinking of the cinemas. We were attacking vulgarity, and those who perpetrate it. And when we were throwing rocks at the windows of the banks, we had no grudge against the glass itself, or against the bank employees. We —"

"And what came of it?"

"What about the statue? Have you forgotten?"

He adjusted the sling around his cast as if to remind us, and said: "Didn't I just say that the statue was toppled once before."

"This time he won't come back."

He took a bottle out of his pocket and filled four glasses. He said: "I have no bean salad to offer you.[4] You'll have to forgive me."

All four of us turned and looked toward the street. We couldn't start drinking openly, not like this. Just a few days ago, we had heard about someone getting flogged, the religious punishment for drinking. Eighty lashes. We thought maybe Barat hadn't heard about it.

We said: "They give lashes. They've already flogged several people.

---

[4] A popular snack made from cooked beans, onions, and parsley consumed while drinking arrack or vodka.

Right there, in public. They made them lie down on the ground and flogged them."

He said: "I know. They have to do it. The Commander of Resisters Mohammad did the same thing. He carried out the sentence himself, with his own hands. I am sure that you have read Hafez:

> *They shut down the taverns, O God, do not let it be.*
> *For they shall open the door to deceit and hypocrisy.*

"They always start with this cursed drink, too. And before you know it, they won't even allow us to bury Ferdowsi in our cemeteries."[5]

Things hadn't gone that far yet, though some were saying that Ferdowsi's poems were being eliminated from textbooks.

We said: "It isn't that bad. It's different now."

He brought the pot over. As he placed the hot green dolma on our plates, he asked: "What's the difference?"

We didn't know.

We knew we would make matters even worse if we argued that now you can't stone someone to death, you can't collect blood money, or carry out retributions. Barat was a fun-loving man, a spiritual, down-to-earth man. He was familiar with Rumi's poetry. When he lost his office job, he opened a bookstore. They shut it down. They arrested him. He couldn't keep his mouth shut. He'd said: "If I open up a tavern, they'll leave me alone."

We said: "Man, you should be ashamed of yourself."

He said: "In this dark and dreary town, we're all looking to find a cozy place, a simple spot with no frills. Well, I have found the place. Even if it's only my friends from the office who are my customers, I could still make a living."

Eventually he opened a tavern, though he was no tavern keeper. His food was first-rate, and he wouldn't serve liquor to just anyone. He could always spot the SAVAK agents.[6] He would say: "After all, that 'Mother of All Evil,' drinking, has its own set of customs; you must respect its traditions. Look at our history; people have never gone to

---

[5] National poet Ferdowsi's poetry is used on graves. Hakim Abol-Ghasem Ferdowsi Toosi (940–1020 C.E.) wrote the famous epic history of Iran, *The Shahnameh*, in verse.
[6] The Shah's secret police, SAVAK.

taverns merely for the pleasure of drinking. When our poets write of wine and of the cupbearer, they mean the fight against deception and hypocrisy."

If anyone got drunk and rowdy, Barat would ask him to leave. He would say: "Either you sit down and drink quietly or you go to some other place." Whenever we went there, he would set our table before we even said a word. He knew what each of us wanted. He knew how much drink we could handle. He wouldn't serve us beyond our limits. And when a stranger came in, he kept an eye on him, and would warn us to watch what we were saying. For those of us who had passed through Barat's filter, it no longer mattered whether we had money or we were broke, we'd still go in for a chat and a sip of what Barat called "Mother of All Evil."

He didn't drink himself. He never drank with the customers. He always said: "If I were to drink at every table, I'd be smashed by the end of the evening." But sometimes, late at night, he'd close the gate halfway. Then, he'd bring over to our table his own bottle and his food. He'd fill his glass and say: "Cheers!" And we would say: "Cheers!" in return. He'd raise the glass to his lips and down it in one gulp. We'd offer him a spoonful of yogurt. He'd tap our hands in a gesture of gratitude, and eat it. He'd wipe his long mustache with the back of his hand, and recite the famous line from Hafez:

That bitter elixir that the Sufi called Mother of All Evil
Is sweeter to us than a virgin's kiss.

We said: "Dear Barat, everything you say is true, but we still don't want to end up in trouble because of this 'Mother of All Evil' you give us. It's not something worth standing up and fighting for."

He said: "But we can't go back to those dark, dank wine cellars run by our Jews in the old days. Nor can we go back to sitting on stone benches, while Turkish and Tajik cupbearers serve us wine, as our classical poets describe.[7] And besides, even if we wanted to make our own wine, where would we get the vats? And in what cellar would we do it?"

---

[7] During much of Iran's history, wine and liquor could not be made or served by Muslims. Jewish and Christian minorities specialized in making alcoholic beverages and ran the taverns.

We said: "That's what everyone is already doing. Go and look around. If you manage to find a single handmade pressure cooker made in Najafabad, we'll buy it from you for three times the going price. Nowadays, when you go to the grocer's to buy some raisins, he says to his assistant: 'Boy, go get a vat from the back room for this gentleman.'"

He said: "Then you are all practicing hypocrisy. I told you, this is how it begins. As the poet Khayyam would say, when we hide who we are, and pretend to be something else, we accept to be shamed and humiliated. Once that is done, we are easily manipulated. What do you think Reza Khan did?[8] He just said, 'Make your hats a little less tall, and shorten your gowns, yes, just a bit. That's all.' And when we did it, when we agreed to do it, hypocrisy became a part of our nature, and began to dictate our actions. If a ruler is ruthless like the Il-Khanid, Holaku Khan, we become submissive like Khajeh Nasir, the learned man. If a ruler is like the Seljuk king, Malek Shah, we become his instrument, like his grand vizier, Nezamolmolk."

He went to the shelves across the room and brought back a bottle. He opened it with his teeth, picked up a glass with the hand that was in a cast, and poured himself a drink. He put the cap back on the bottle, and came back toward us, holding his glass. He walked heavily, dragging one foot.

He said: "Do you know that for more than twenty years I went every single year, on the anniversary of Mordad 28th, down to Shah Square. There would be large crowds there, and I wanted to yell at them, 'Listen, people, we did pull him down once before. We did make him run away.' But I could see that no one remembered. Maybe they'd never seen it, or even heard about it. They'd all stand around the square and listen to the military march."

We said: "Didn't you always tell us that if ever the bastard left you'd shut down this place, never touch another drop of the stuff, and you'd even make your daughter wear a scarf?"

He placed the glass on the edge of the table, and stroked the beard of one of the fellows — I don't remember whose it was. In those days, there was only one of us who had a beard.

---

[8] Reza Khan was the first Pahlavi king. He came to power through a coup d'état in 1925 and was forced to abdicate in 1941.

He said: "So, now you have started growing a beard, too?"[9] He picked up his glass and took a sip.

He said: "Cheers!"

We didn't say "Cheers!" in return. He bristled like a cat and glared at us. He reached out and picked up two glasses between his index finger and the thumb of his left hand. He downed both in one gulp, and dropped the glasses into his pocket. Liquor was dripping from the tip of his mustache. He didn't bother to wipe it with the back of his hand, the way he used to when he came to sit at our table late at night. He bent over, drank the two remaining glasses in the same manner, and dropped them into his pocket.

He said: "Well, that's done. I was the only one who drank. Now, how about some food? You still eat, don't you?"

So we did eat, though the bottle remained right there in the middle of the table. We couldn't say a thing. When five more customers showed up, we felt relieved. We knew them. They were fun-loving people. As soon as they sat down, Barat brought them a bottle and five glasses, and he poured for all of them. Then he went to prepare five plates of dolmas. We knew we no longer belonged here. Barat returned to their table. He asked: "Where is the bottle?"

We looked over. Their table was empty. Not even glasses to be seen. They were holding them in their hands, and they all stared back at him. He shouted: "I said where is the bottle of arrack?"

Someone pointed under the table, behind one of the legs. Barat bent down and picked the bottle up. He placed it back in the middle of the table.

He shouted: "Either you are man enough to risk the lashes, or you can go home and drink in your own back room. And after you've rinsed your mouth, you can take your prayer beads and go out to greet people with a pious look on your face."

They stood up, wiped their mouths, and threw some money on the table. Barat walked over, his foot dragging behind. He grabbed one of them by the jacket with his hand which was in a cast. He stuffed the money back in his pocket, and said: "You know I never serve the Mother of All Evil to those who don't deserve it."

---

[9] Growing a Muslim-style beard in those days was a sign of identifying with the religious factions.

So we left, too. We went looking for a vat and a cellar. We could no longer sit openly at one of Barat's tables, and let him bring us drinks, along with bread, cheese, and herbs, or beans, and yogurt with shallots. He had always poured us the first glass himself. Yes, we had to leave Barat, although we did worry about him, and with good reason. Later on we heard that he'd been attacked one evening and beaten up. But Barat wasn't easily intimidated, and he continued to carry his pot under his arm. And if a "deserving" person showed up, he'd place the bottle on the table, and pour him the first glass. Then, he'd pour one for himself, too, and wipe his mustache with the back of his hand.

Things got much worse. Even for those of us who were now drinking homemade "Mother of All Evil," in a storage room or in a cellar: a quick drink followed by a spoonful of yogurt or a bite of pickled cucumbers, that's all. We had so many problems ourselves that we forgot all about Barat. They announced that all women had to wear the veil.

Mohammadi said: "I told my daughter, 'Look, dear, some people hope to create discord among us with things such as scarves and chadors. They want us to fight each other. Then, they can come back and put us on the rack again. Don't you remember what happened in Chile? Go and read about it. See how their women prevented the revolution from taking root.'"

Of course, this was good for our pockets: all we needed to get for our wife and daughter were a scarf, a pair of pants, and a loose shirt. All the beauty salons were shut down. Sadduq's daughter went and got her hair cut short, like a boy's. She said: "During the demonstrations in Tehran, at first there were only people like us. The supporters of the Shah didn't dare to come and demonstrate under a shower of stones, a shower of bottles. It wasn't till the second and third day that we started to see women with makeup. And the clothes they wore! That's when we said: 'No, this isn't for us. They can have it,' and I got my hair cut short."

We too would go to shout: "Death to America."

Hassan Agha, the cloth merchant, said: "What do you think imperialism looks like? It's this sort of thing, these frills. Who cares if there are no more cinemas? I didn't lose a loved one so that they bring back the same old movies. And what do I need music for?"

Hasan was in mourning. We were, too. Sometimes in the late afternoon, on a Thursday, we'd get Akbar Agha, "Magic Fingers," to come over with his sitar. We'd prepare food and drinks, and Akbar Agha would play softly. And once in a while, he'd let himself go and begin to sing in a scratched and husky voice a well-known line from Hafez:

Drink wine secretly, for they will punish you.

We would say: "Akbar Agha, we beg of you, not so loud."

Later, we would rinse our hands and mouths, and be done. What did we need Barat for? We just said, "Death to America," and kept going. And when some new drinking fountain appeared on the street corner, dispensing "sacred water," we'd say: "It's okay, some people believe in such things. In the old days, maybe only an old woman would have stood here, holding on to it, wailing and begging for help. Nowadays many more people are like that, they even have to wait in line. Well, this too shall pass. So what if a couple of bookstores get attacked, and ransacked, and they even pile up the books in the middle of the streets and burn them. They'll print them again. They'll write them again." And we told our friend's uncle: "Can anyone prevent changes from happening? Can anyone reverse the course of time?"

"Yes, as you can see for yourself."

"In the short run, but . . ."

He'd shout: "Change requires instruments, requires knowledge. When you destroy these things, you can even return to the Stone Ages."

Nonsense, this was all nonsense. What a shame, to have vocal cords and yet speak with the voice of another.

When his son was arrested, Sadduq came to us and said: "Didn't I tell you?"

"Well?"

"I saw it myself. They broke all his bones with their sticks. These people are riffraff. I didn't recognize a single one of them. They're bringing them in from other places."

"It will be all right."

"What will be all right? They say that someone threw acid into a woman's face. They say that a girl got attacked with a needle; they injected her with something and now her arm is paralyzed."

"These are rumors. The counterrevolutionaries are spreading rumors. Don't you remember what they said about the people who set fire to the Rex Cinema?"

He said: "They don't need to give precise instructions. They say, 'Films lead to corruption; cinemas are centers of corruption, dens for infidels.' And someone, one of their most fervent devotees, is bound to think, 'This is a jihad.' So, he pours gasoline around the theater and strikes a match, and the enemy's fortress — and all its belligerent infidels — turn to smoke and disappear into thin air. Now, what should you do? Should you grab this guy by the collar? No. I say, you should grab that idea by the collar."

We said: "There are those who want to prevent the fight against America, and for this revolution to become victorious.[10] They want the blood of all our young people to go to waste."

He said: "Revolution? This is more like vomiting one's guts. Like taking a knife and sticking it into your own belly, then pulling out your innards and crying out, 'Come and see.'"

There you have it: this is our intellectual, our Western-educated fellow. There are times when you would like to stretch him out and beat his precious bottom with a stick.

Sadduq was upset. He said: "They won't even give visitation rights. They've thrown my boy in prison along with the SAVAK agents, can you believe that?"

We said: "It's a revolution; it has its ups and downs. It is not going to get fixed in a day or two."

Well, this is how it was. Soon, there was just one bookstore left, and it carried only books by Shariati and Al-e Ahmad, or books like *The Rays of the Quran, The Path Taken.*[11] There was also just one cinema left: it had been confiscated from its previous owners, and now it played censored movies from Tehran, which had been cut so many times that in the end you could no longer tell what they were about. As for television, they only showed documentaries. The number of newspapers was

---

[10] In the early months and years of the revolution, there was a widespread fear that the United States would again plot a coup against the popular uprising and bring the Shah back, as happened in 1953. The Islamist factions used this fear to force veils on women, disarm and eliminate the secular opposition, and consolidate their power.
[11] Shariati and Al-e Ahmad were intellectuals who advocated using Islam as a mobilizing force to fight dictatorship and imperialism.

down to just a few, and all were following the same line, one just like the other, as if they'd all been printed in the same shop.

Then there were the doors and walls, and they had been painted and written over so many times, you could no longer tell what they said. And besides, how many streets did we have? All together, six main streets, and a couple of narrow lanes with small dried-up trees on either side. There was also a park and two squares. The retired people would still come and sit on the old benches around the square and look at the fountains. A green cloth was now wrapped around the base in the center of Imam Square.[12] We went there with Sadduq.

We said: "You see it's not there, that neighing horse, with the rider who seemed to want to gallop forever. It's no longer up there. We should be patient. It's a struggle, but we should not despair. We should not despair over things."

Sadduq said: "All that's left is religious mourning and weeping. Why don't we just say, 'Long Live Death! Long Live the Graveyard!' and get it over with?"

His son was still in jail for distributing newspapers. Not even his mother had been allowed to visit him. They had told her: "Go away, Mother, and thank God that we have not sent him to the firing squad yet."

Some time later, Barat showed up again. We had totally given up on him. They had broken the sitar of Akbar Agha "Magic Fingers." Barat's cast was gone and he grinned from ear to ear. As he sat down, he said: "Well . . ."

We knew what he wanted to say. In fact, he was saying it with his eyes. Sadduq was there, too. He didn't let on that he understood. He answered: "Well, what?"

"Why don't you come?"

"What? We should come there so that you put a bottle right in the middle of our table?"

"No, it's finished. All that I had is finished. And you know that I'm not the kind to deal in contraband."

"Could it be that you are afraid of religious punishment, of lashes?"

"Maybe."

And then he said: "I only serve food, all sorts of things. And the students are coming, too. It gets crowded. Be sure to come." He got up.

---

[12] Previously, Shah Square.

He was still grinning. He had come to his senses. We stood up. He hadn't reached the door yet when he turned around and came back toward us. He pulled a sealed bottle from the inside pocket of his overcoat, and placed it in the middle of the table. He said: "I almost forgot that I'd brought this."

We were all stunned. We had pretty much put it out of our minds, and now, it was right there in the middle of the table. One could get the homemade stuff, but it wasn't any good. Besides, it was different when you're sitting at a café table, drinking out of those slender glasses, with a big bowl of beans and angelica power in the middle. Sadduq would peel a cucumber, slice it, and place it around the plate of feta cheese and fresh herbs. Then, you'd hold the slender glass between your thumb and forefinger and say: "Cheers!"

"Cheers!"

"To your health."

"To yours."

And you'd take a sip of the chilled and bitter "Mother of All Evil," and as it burned your throat, your lips, and your tongue, you'd welcome the next sip, along with the brittle and salty aroma of a slice of salted cucumber.

We said: "Have a seat, what's the hurry?"

We felt awkward with the bottle sitting there. We all dug into our pockets to contribute. He said: "This one is on me. I had a few left over; I thought you should have your share." He bit the end of his mustache, sucked on it. Then he left, dragging his foot, the same way he always came in or went out.

We thought of calling Akbar Agha, "Magic Fingers." He was heartbroken, and this would make him feel better. These sad and fearful songs have come to us over the years because of such times. We talked about recording Akbar's voice, how his music had to survive. We would just make it a condition that he should sing in a low voice. But Akbar Agha didn't show up. We were told that he was sick, that he didn't feel up to it.

Later on, we started getting our weekly supply. Barat would bring our ration, and say that it was the last of it. And he'd take our offering — the same price that he had paid for it when he had bought it himself — and he'd leave. Sometimes he would sit and have a couple of glasses. When he got warmed up, he would begin complaining again.

Then, for a couple of weeks, he stopped bringing it, so we went to see him.

He said: "You see, there isn't any left."

He had removed the bar, but we had already heard about that. In place of the colorful shelves with all their "Mother of All Evil," there was now a straight wall covered in wallpaper with a flower pattern, and a framed picture. There was also a notice, written in his own good handwriting: "No Alcoholic Beverages Served Here."

It was rumored that he had closed the place for a week and had changed everything by himself.

When the food was brought out, the leg of lamb and eggplant stew, the feta cheese with the small radishes, the yogurt with cucumbers, and God knows what other concoctions, we didn't feel much like eating. He came and stood by us, very dignified but smiling. As he chewed on the ends of his mustache, he said: "Eat. Wasn't this your problem, a few shelves? Now they're all gone. I don't even have a single bottle left. And, as you can see for yourself, I haven't had any drinks myself, either."

He brought his head forward so that we could smell his breath. He hadn't been drinking. We ate, bit by bit, but it was hard to swallow.

He said: "You can't eat? It won't go down? But see, others are eating, just as they ate in those days, and on Mordad 28th,[13] when they'd go to Shah Square, cracking melon seeds, and listening to military marches."

He shouted to his waiter: "Boy, turn on that radio, turn it up." No. He was going too far.

We said: "Please, Barat."

He said: "Maybe you've come for your ration?"

We had gone for our ration, but if there wasn't any left, so be it.

He said: "I know you, because I know myself. We believed any old back street, any means that could lead us to our political and social lala-land, would do. The main goal was to get there, take over the power, get political sovereignty. And we thought that once we achieved that goal, these things — our hypocrisy and our daily flip-flops — we'd take them off like so many borrowed clothes, and toss them into the trash bin of history. But now we realize that history has no trash bin at all. Nothing gets thrown away."

---

[13] Anniversary of the 1953 coup d'état that returned the Shah to the throne.

We said: "Barat, will you let us eat our damned food in peace?"

He said: "These people have taken some students.[14] One of them said, 'I'll execute you; if you have not committed a sin, then you will be a martyr and go to heaven; and if you have, well, you'll get what you deserve.' Do you people understand? We deserve it."

We said: "We shouldn't pay any attention to him. Let him babble." And he babbled. He talked and he talked — about cheating in the elections, the slaughter at Qarna, Turkoman Sahra.[15] Then, finally he left.

Well, after all, this is a revolution, and counterrevolutionaries are not sitting idly by. Whorehouses have been attacked and set on fire. Pictures of one of the executed smugglers are distributed, as if to say, "We told you so!"

You can tell from their shoes, their tattered pants, who we are dealing with. We say: "Well, mistakes can happen, but what about the torturers?"

Oh, it made us feel so good: people had gathered around to see the picture of executed General So-and-So. What a crowd! We were climbing over each other's shoulders.

But the counterrevolutionaries don't miss a beat. They're saying: "Yes, first they killed just a few, to be able to kill whomever they please later on." And they distribute a picture of executions and firing squads. It is probably a fake, and how skillfully done! They're saying: "See how they wrap their faces?" The faces are wrapped in Arab shawls, their backs are to the camera, and guns are held up. Counterrevolutionaries are lined up, facing forward, blindfolded, their hands untied; they're standing there, without even the support of a wall or a post behind them.

They say: "You see that corner?"

We say: "Yes, we do. It is a package, something white lying on the ground."

They say: "They must have brought that guy on a stretcher. His leg's broken because he's been shot. They executed him lying down."

They keep circulating pictures. And each time they do, someone is down on the ground. Another one and another one. It seems as

---

[14] Islamist militia.

[15] These events took place shortly after the revolution. The slaughter refers to the attempts by Islamist revolutionary guards to put down the tribal rebellion for autonomy of the Turkoman areas.

though, in this firing squad where all the heads are wrapped in Arab shawls, some are firing shots just for the fun of it, one after another; an hour later, still more. And then, there's an enlarged picture.

We said: "Maybe it is a movie." It really is like out of a movie. Otherwise, how could a person stand like that, erect, blindfolded, with hands untied, facing the firing squad? And, since they are aiming at his chest, how can he continue to stand, not bending toward the firing squad, not shouting or saying anything, though his hands and mouth are free? And finally, there's a picture of the man who fired the finishing shot. They have plastered this one on the walls. What stature! Clad in white, with boots and gloves, one hand on his waist, bending over to fire the finishing shot.

We say: "This is a Hollywood actor."

They say: "Yes, we also believe that he is an American; or maybe an Israeli."

Nonsense. It is all nonsense. Sadduq says: "By the way, did you read about the man and woman who were stoned for adultery in Kerman?"

We say: "There you go again!"

"The religious judge said it."

He digs into his briefcase for the newspaper to read the protocol:

"First, the person should perform an ablution. Then it is recommended for the adulteress to repent and put on her own shroud, with her own hands. It mentions that the adulterer should get buried in the ground up to his chest and everyone should cast a stone upon his face. I heard that one of them died after ten minutes and the other after forty minutes."

We say: "Please, don't make us vomit."

Slowly we eat, but the food won't go down. Our stomachs are twisted into knots.

He says: "Apparently, the foreigners have filmed it and shown it on television around the world." We feel sick to our stomachs. As one friend's uncle would say, it feels as if our guts are coming up into our throats.

Sadduq says that they made his son run with his eyes shut.

The boy said: "They keep running after me, and hit me on the forehead, and there is the sound of a gunshot."

First, it was a game. The boy thought it was a joke. They had made him run again, and again, and the gun barrel had hit his forehead and, bang, they had fired. And then again, they had made him run, till finally he couldn't run anymore.

He said: "Dad, I threw up." He had fallen to the ground and thrown up.

We say: "But, dear Sadduq, do you have to do it, too? You see that they've surrounded us with all the radios and propaganda. They're exposing our insides to the world, and then you come and sprinkle salt on the wound?"

Sadduq said: "I beg your pardon. I didn't want to say these things. I just remembered it."

But do you think Barat would understand? He had turned up the sound of his radio. We didn't go there anymore. We didn't even think about it. We had seen so many guts, stomachs, and innards in the newspapers. We had carried so many mutilated people on our shoulders that we had forgotten all about "Mother of All Evil." So many pictures, endless news. But will the young people let go? They don't understand. They are inexperienced. Severed hands, cut-off legs, pictures of graves. So much death! A woman is wailing on a grave, and next to her, the wide-open black eyes of a girl who is staring, staring at us. Death is so cheap now, like they are giving it away. Like they have placed the television camera in the cemetery, and they have given the radio microphone to the ones who read the prayers in the graveyards of the world. And when you get up in the morning, it is like you have been sleeping with the dead.

On Fridays, with heavy heads, with an acrid taste of flesh in our mouths, and the smell of camphor under our noses, we would go and sit on the old benches in the square and look at the fountains. And then, we would go to the Friday prayers. We would stand in line, shout slogans, perform our prayers more or less, and run into some friend or acquaintance. Until one morning, when a van came with a loudspeaker. It said: "Hurry up." It said: "Come, let's go."

They were going to flog someone. The van circled the square. An eight-wheeler truck appeared. They had stretched the condemned person on a bench on the truck. Two men were holding his legs and two his arms. Another, with an Arab shawl wrapped around his head and face, was standing above him, whip in hand.

It was Barat. He was half-naked. We ran toward the truck. A large crowd gathered. They said: "Last night, they stormed his house, searched everywhere, even split open a couple of walls. They didn't find anything. Then, they went to his store. When they split open the wall in the front, God knows how many bottles they found."

When we reached the main square, we saw the eight-wheeler at the fork in the road, with a line of bearded young men surrounding it. The van continued to circle, reciting Quranic verses and shouting slogans. We shouted slogans, too, and climbed over each other's shoulders. Women were holding babies in their arms. Men, even old men with canes, had come. Little boys had climbed the little trees. Sadduq said: "Let's go over there, on that platform!"

We did. We took a peek. The first blow was struck with the whip. It was the man with the shawl wrapped around his head and face. Barat had raised his head and was looking at the people. The whip struck a second blow. A woman lifted her child over her head. It was an infant with a pacifier in its mouth. It was looking out and sucking on the pacifier. The man struck again. A little boy held on tight to my leg. He wanted to come up. There was no room. We held him up. He wasn't even ten years old. He was sucking on his lip and with his two big black eyes, staring. He struck again. Barat just looked, as if he were counting the people's heads, one by one, the heads of all of us, old and young, even the child who was held up by the woman. We shouted a prayer. He struck again. This time, someone else was hitting. He had not wrapped his head and face. He lifted his arm as far as it would stretch, the whip swung in the air, in that blue sky, and descended. This one was an expert. He knew how to hit. This is how you should hit! You fling your arm so that it comes down heavy, and then you jerk your arm back just as the whip reaches the skin. It takes a lot of practice. If you hit as they usually do, it is not very painful, but if you jerk it, jerk your arm suddenly, it's like fire. You can embed the whip in the skin. It takes a lot of practice. Later, you will be able to hit so well that, with only a few strikes, pain will reverberate to the marrow of his bones, and the fellow will begin to cry out. It is necessary. A corrupt member of society must be surgically removed, severed, and thrown into the trash bin. Then no one will ever dare to hide all those bottles for himself, as rations for fun-loving people. The villain! The cursed man had no doubt kept them for himself, or to sell at a high price.

The infant with the pacifier in its mouth was watching. The

woman herself couldn't see. The baby was chubby and healthy, with big eyes. It was heavy. It could see. You jerk your arm and with all the weight of the shoulder, the arm, the wrist, and the hand, like a stone falling from the sky, you hit heavily, and then suddenly, you jerk back. Barat was not looking anymore. We couldn't hear what he was saying. We didn't even hear him say "Ouch." The woman said: "Sir, for God's sake, tell me what are they are doing."

We said: "His head has dropped down."

She asked: "What is he doing now? What is happening to his face?"

We said: "His head is down. We can't see. His hair is covering his face."

He was foaming at the corner of his mouth. They struck again. Another was hitting. Four people hit, each one's share was only about twenty lashes. They were now hitting with their faces uncovered. Why hide? Then they took him away. The crowd went to prayers. We went to prayers, too. We performed our prayers with all our hearts. In his first sermon, the Friday Imam spoke of the necessity of repentance, then about the necessity of torment in the next world. He spoke about the Desert of Resurrection, about the day that is fifty thousand years long, when we must stand in a long line, shrouds on our shoulders, under the bright sun, a sun as red as a basin of blood. And the ground will be hot, hotter than molten copper. We will stand barefoot, all in a row. We will stand for fifty thousand years, until it is our turn.

We performed our prayers with all our hearts.

In the afternoon, our friends did not come. We were to have a get-together, simple and casual, just a chat and some tea. They didn't come. Sadduq called and said: "Aren't you ashamed?"

"Ashamed? Why?"

He said: "All of us, we should all be ashamed."

We should be ashamed? Why, and before whom? The whole world was focusing its cameras on us, as though there had never been a Vietnamese girl in flames, or as though they had never lynched any blacks in their own states.

Sadduq doesn't understand. He says: "You are a real fool!" And he hangs up. Sadduq is prejudiced, he is too nervous, and he has no patience or perseverance.

I called the rest of them. They wouldn't answer the phone, or else I was told that they had already gone to bed. Early evening, someone called me. I couldn't figure out who it was. He said: "Listen. I know where they ditched the bottles."

I said: "Why are you telling me?"

I hung up. There were more calls. I said: "Don't answer." I said: "Turn on the television and listen to the news." The phone rang again. It was my friend's uncle.

He said: "Did you hear?"

I said: "What?"

He said: "Someone called. They said that the tractor driver had been told to take all those bottles and dump them somewhere. He put them in his tractor and took them out to the fields."

I said: "Well?"

He said: "They say the tractor driver has said, 'I went and dug a hole, and dumped them all in there and covered them with dirt.'"

I said: "Good. This is what they should have done. Did you expect them to give them to you, or to me?"

He said: "Don't you get it? The guy has said, 'I dug somewhere where the soil is soft. And I covered them with a layer of dirt.' He has said, 'If they find out, if they get wind of it, it will be a waste.'"

I said: "My good man, in the midst of all these problems, how is this any concern of yours?"

He said: "I am going, and I know the place."

How they tempt you. Like the cursed Satan, they constantly get under one's skin. Maybe Barat himself had started this commotion. I thought I should go and see. You can't just sit around. I looked out of the window. I saw a couple of people walking by a wall, holding oil lamps. I picked up mine, too. My wife asked: "Where are you going?"

I said: "I'm going out for a little while."

She said: "But the streetlights are on."

I said: "Some streets are not lit, you know."

And I went out. A couple of back streets farther, I saw someone. I didn't know him. His lantern was lit. We nodded. He asked: "Do you know where it is?"

I said: "No."

"They say it's toward the mountain, by the foot of the mountain. He ditched them under a tree."

"Which one?"

"I don't know."

When we got out of town, we saw others with lights, walking in twos and in fours. And many were ahead of us. They all were going there. We walked faster. It was cold. We hadn't brought overcoats. A jackal was howling somewhere. Soon, there were more than twenty of us. And more were coming from behind. Someone said: "Where is it?"

I said: "Someone probably knows."

We walked in groups; we teamed up and walked faster. One or two people had brought small shovels. Why shovels? The bottles will break. But we didn't say anything. We kept going. Behind us, people kept popping out of back streets. There was such a chill in the air. We pulled up the collars of our jackets, moved the lantern from one hand to the other, stuck our numbed hands into our pockets, and went on.

Someone said: "They will soon find out about it. We've got to hurry."

We should have stopped, even gone back. Cursed be Barat! But our legs walked on, out of our control. Or was it the smell of the soil, the smell of the old rotted leaves, that drew us — as if we were walking between the clay walls of a cellar? Once in a while, a dried-up bush would appear before us. Or someone would say: "What a sky!" Indeed, what a sky it was. We had forgotten. The same old stars, as if you were observing them from the Maragheh Observatory: there was Scorpio, and Virgo, and Libra. The constellation of the Bear was there, so big. There was also the smell of trees, the smell of damp earth.

We saw the black silhouette of the trees in the thicket from a distance. The lights ahead of us assembled, and became fixed like a ring of fire. Bent over silhouettes circled the fire. We quickened our pace. Long shadows were cast on the ground. There was jubilation. Were they saying something to each other in a strange language? We ran. When we arrived, we saw them kneeling around the fresh earth, as if bowing down in prayer. But their hands were pushing the earth aside. We dug, too. We sunk our fingers into the earth and pushed aside the soft earth on which dew had set. We said: "God bless his soul for having thought of everything."

And we laughed. Someone was about to dig with a shovel. We said: "What are you doing, my good man?" We pulled the earth fistful by fistful and if we came across a rock, we handed it back to those standing behind us. Someone said: "Ouch!"

He pulled his hand out, and put his bleeding finger to his mouth.

Then he dug some more into the dirt. It was a broken bottle. Blood was dripping from his muddy hand, but he was laughing. We said: "Well, there it is, right there, but we shouldn't be hasty. The mud and earth must be pushed aside carefully, the broken bottles passed from hand to hand."

But we were hasty, because we could smell the sharp scent of that "bitter, keen, light, delicious, rose-hued elixir," as if we stood in the cellar when clay lids were removed from the tops of a thousand vats. Someone said: "I found it."

He stood up, holding something smeared with mud between his two bloody and muddy hands. He kissed it and handed it over to others to kiss. Someone opened the bottle with his teeth and he drank, and wiped his mustache with the back of his hand. There was more. We dug, and as we scraped the mud from the neck of those treasures buried by that crafty conniver, we handed it to those behind us, and dug again into the mud. We didn't even say "ouch" anymore, and if a hand gave us an offering of a sip, we wiped our mustaches with the backs of our hands. Someone from the back shouted: "Dastardly is he who takes it home. It should all be finished here, right here."

He was drunk. He was bending over us, searching our pockets and underarms. We said: "Go home. If you can't handle it, why do you come?"

Then, there was only mud and broken bottles. And we wiped our hands on our laps or whatever was on our shoulders, and wrapped our bleeding hands with a piece of torn shirt. And there, in the middle of the field, we gathered in groups, sitting on the earth with a light in the middle. Someone had even brought pickled cucumbers, just a few, to counter the bitterness. After each sip, we bit off a small piece of cucumber, and handed the rest over so that others would also have a taste. Someone said: "No thanks, the earth is our salt."

Who was it? Where was he? And to which circle did he belong? We did not know. Then, we heard the voice of Akbar Agha "Magic Fingers," with the same old, tired voice, coming from somewhere among the people who stood in a circle around the few lights. He started to sing in a husky voice, we didn't know what song. Then, suddenly he raised his voice and sang out loud:

The heart, the heart does not long for grassy meadows, it does not.

And we chanted: "It does not!"
He sang:

It does not long, does not long for strolling among the flowers, it does not.

And we said: "It does not!"

The heart, the heart does not get along with us, it does not.

"It does not!"

Let this heart bleed, for it does not have fortitude, it does not.

"It does not!"
He had risen up, as he was singing. We rose up, too, dancing, hand in hand, or else placing a hand on each other's waists, and stomping our feet. Suddenly, shots rang from a distance, from the town. Come on over. Akbar Agha "Magic Fingers" continued to sing. We couldn't hear what he was singing. Someone said: "Put the lights out, hurry up, or they'll see us."

We bent over, but we couldn't do it. We looked at our bloody hands, and we couldn't. Akbar Agha "Magic Fingers" was singing a *ghazal* by Hafez:

Even though the preacher of the city . . .

He was singing in a full voice:

Learn to be a libertine and be generous, for it is no virtue
To refrain from drinking, yet reveal no trace of humanity.
The grand name of God will be your saving grace,
For by disguise and tricks the demon cannot become Solomon.

We could no longer hear the shots. All we heard was the voice of Akbar Agha "Magic Fingers," as we stood around the lights, bottles in our hand. They got closer. When Akbar Agha "Magic Fingers" finished the song, he started to sing it again, and we joined in. They had arrived. The sound of their machine guns and G-3s wouldn't let us hear the song anymore. They were firing into the air. They stood in the dark, and we couldn't see them. Someone was reciting a Quranic verse, in eloquent Arabic. When they stepped into the circle of light, we finally saw them. They had wrapped their heads and faces with Arabic shawls. They squatted, one knee to the ground, and aimed the barrels of their guns toward us. Only one of them was standing, holding a whip in his hand. Akbar had stopped singing. He was sitting. We were also sitting, all of us.

They said over a loudspeaker: "We must flog them, all of them. Start from one end, and even if it takes us till the Day of Resurrection, so be it." They stretched out one of us. Two held his legs and two his arms. They spread a black cloth over his head, gathered the ends of the cloth, and stuffed it in his mouth. And they began to hit. No one made a sound. Then, they sat on the ground, with their shawls wrapped around their heads and faces. They formed a larger circle around our circle, on the edge of the light of our lamps. All we could see was their eyes. And we all waited with our backs to the old stars, waiting for them to grab our two legs and stretch us out, laying us side by side, humble and down to earth, to await our turn. And until it was time for us to receive the Islamic lashes, we took the neck of the bottle in our mouths, and sucked on the last drops of bitter "Mother of All Evil." And drunk, we put our heads and faces to the ground, on the cold, dew-covered dirt, our ancestral earth, and we waited.

— *Translated by M. R. Ghanoonparvar*

Ahmad Mahmud

Ahmad Mahmud was born on December 25, 1931, in the southern city of Ahvaz. In his youth he worked as a day laborer, driver, and construction worker. Later he was arrested and imprisoned for his leftist political views and activities. He first began publishing short stories in magazines in 1959. Other collections followed: *The Sea Is Still Calm* (1960), *Uselessness* (1962), *A Pilgrim in the Rain* (1968), *The Little Native Boy* (1971), and *The Strangers* (1972).

The Neighbors appeared in 1974 and gave him immediate status as a novelist. Seven years later he published *The Story of One City* and the following year *Scorched Earth*. These three novels comprise a continuing saga set in the southern oil province of Khuzistan during three important periods: the days of nationalization of oil in 1951, the aftermath of the coup d'état that brought the Shah back to the throne in August 1953, and Iraq's invasion of Iran in 1980.

In the 1990s, Mahmud published two collections of short stories and several novels: *The Visit* (1990), *The Familiar Tale* (1991), *Zero Degree Orbit* (1993), *The Living Man* (1997), and *The Fig Tree of the Temples* (2000). Ahmad Mahmud died of respiratory failure on October 4, 2002.

The excerpt, part of the first chapter of the novel *Scorched Earth,* describes how, in the damp heat of late summer, the normal lives and routines of ordinary working people were shattered by Iraq's invasion of Iran in 1980.

Excerpt from
SCORCHED EARTH

These are the final days of summer. I'm still groggy from my afternoon nap. Damp heat shrouds the city, weighing on my every breath. I turn off the air conditioner and head into the courtyard. Sunlight has drawn up past the wall. Saber is sitting on the edge of the garden next to the fountain pool drinking tea. Mina is watering the petunias with the hose and their fragrance fills the courtyard. I squat next to the shallow pool and slap two palms full of water on my face. I hear Mother's voice; she's sitting on the porch tending the samovar.

"Do you want some tea?"

"Pour it for me in a large glass, Mother."

Mina lets go of the hose, takes the glass, and hands it to me. The sparrows have gathered in the thick lotus tree in the middle of the yard and are making a commotion. Around dusk, the sparrows swarm the lotus, turning it into a mass of shimmering gray. I am sipping the tea and staring at the goldfish in the pool when I hear Saber's voice,

"You slept a lot today."

I had slept for four hours. It's six o'clock. Mina sweeps away the red petals of the bougainvillea and the green and yellow leaves of the lotus tree, then hoses down the tiles of the courtyard. Branches of bougainvillea cover the entire eastern wall of the house. The bright flowers seem to twinkle in between the deep green leaves of the plant.

Sunlight is drawing past the roof when Shahed comes through the door. He has a folded newspaper under his arm.

"What's in the news?"

He offers me the paper

"There's something going on at the border."

I take it. Saber gets up and comes toward me, and Shahed squats on the edge of the porch to get tea. On page two there is an article about Iraqi tanks taking position at the Iranian border. When Saber sees it he begins, "Well, if this is true, why isn't anybody saying anything?"

I take my eyes from the paper and look at him. "Who? And who's supposed to say what?"

His broad forehead wrinkles up. "The government, our leaders, the president . . . I don't know . . . the people in charge."

"And what are they supposed to say?"

Saber takes the newspaper from my hand. "You can't just bury your head underground about things like that. This rumor has been going around for ten or fifteen days now!"

Shahed takes his glass of tea, gets up, and comes toward us. "It's not a rumor anymore. By now everyone knows Iraq is up to something at the border . . . everyone but the people in charge."

Mina is standing next to Saber with the broom in her hand, reading the paper.

"You think he'll dare attack?"

Shahed scratches his broad bony chin.

"He might. With the mess we're in, it doesn't take much courage. All it takes is being a bastard."

Saber folds the newspaper and hands it back to Shahed. "If you think about it, this is the best time for Iraq to attack us."

"Right now? Why?"

Saber turns to Mina.

"To destroy the revolution," he says calmly. "To topple the regime. If he attacks, all of Khuzestan is under his knife. Khuzestan . . . and its oil!"[1]

Mother gets up from the teapot and comes to the pool to wash and get ready for the evening prayers. Shahed puts the empty glass on the edge of the garden

"But they've got it all wrong this time!"

I go inside to get dressed. I have dinner plans with some friends at the club, but I'm not in the mood. Instead, I think I'll go see Mohammad the barber. I'll get a haircut, take a walk for about an hour, and return home in time for the news.

Sunlight has pulled away completely from the rooftops, and the streetlights are on. The bakery is empty. Majid the food vendor is sitting by a big pot of rice pudding on the cobblestones next to the bakery, doing nothing in particular. A mellow breeze from the Karun River is pushing back the mugginess, and the air is cooling down.

---

[1] Khuzestan is the oil-rich southern province of Iran that borders Iraq.

I pass by Asad's bike shop. Amu Haidar is sitting next to the store smoking a water pipe. He waves at me. "How are you?"

"Very well."

"What's new?"

"Not much, pretty good all around."

A bit farther down, some young men are standing on the sidewalk, talking. I pass by and hear fragments of their conversation: "Iraq can't do a damned thing!"

"That's just a slogan. You're talking out of your —"

"No I'm not!"

"Oh yeah? We'll see. Once they . . ."

I pretend to light my cigarette and stop to hear the rest.

". . . when they attack, we'll all have to put our tails between our hind legs and run . . . and hand over Khuzestan!"

"Why are you so pessimistic?"

"It's not pessimism. The guys who came back from Bustan have even seen their tanks."

I slow down.

"They can't do a damned thing!"

"Sure, if we're prepared. But what preparation? Where? I haven't heard . . ."

I drift away. It's dark. There's no one in the barbershop. I look around. Mash-Mohammad is standing on the corner next to the pushcart, eating cooked fava beans. I wave to him. The bean-seller is busy pumping his gas lamp. Muhammad waves back at me. He drinks the juice from his bowl, empties the remaining favas in his hand, and scuttles straight toward me.

"Hi!"

"Hi, Mash-Mohammad, how are you?"

"Pretty well. You're late this time . . . your hair's getting long." He opens his fist, full of favas. "Here."

"Thanks, Mash-Mohammad."

"You don't want any? It's really good. Well, then . . . please, come in."

I sit on the chair. Mash-Mohammad shoves the last favas in his mouth and washes his hands.

"You weren't in town, right?"

He is taking a towel out of the drawer and shaking it open.

"Yes, I was."

"Well, why haven't you been by? There's a forest growing on the back of your neck!"

He ties the towel around my neck. Through the mirror I see his small television set behind me. It is no wider than the span of two hands. Mash-Mohammad looks at the clock and takes the comb and scissors,

"What have you heard?"

"About what?"

"The Iraqi soldiers."

I play dumb to figure out where he's coming from.

"What about them? Has something happened?"

The scissors are ringing.

"'Has something happened?'! They say twenty Iraqi divisions are taking up positions at the border!"

I'm surprised.

"Twenty divisions!"

"I heard it from Sheikh Ta'imeh. You know who he is."

"No."

He takes his hands off my head and looks at me in the mirror.

"You don't know Sheikh Ta'imeh? He's one of my customers. He's the Sheikh of Susangerd. The one who owns a pickup truck."

The scissors ring once again, and he keeps talking nonstop.

"You must know him. You've seen him here hundreds of times. He was here yesterday, saying that the Iraqis have set up camp at the border. He said that at night they light up the sky with signal flares, get on their boats, and come over to our side through the reeds of Hur al-Azim to reconnoiter. He said they have huge tanks, each the size of a refinery!"

I look at Mash-Mohammad's pockmarked face through the mirror. His short hair is the color of wheat. When he talks, his gold teeth flash at you.

"Cut it short?"

"Just a little."

The comb scratches my scalp.

"Their spies are everywhere."

"Iraqi spies?"

"Of course, the Iraqis . . . damn! It looks like you're totally out of it."

"No, no. I'm listening!"

"They say that the spies ride around on motorcycles and figure out distances that way."

Mash-Mohammad smiles. Pockmarks have almost eaten away his eyelids. His eyelashes seem to have been burned off, and he has the typical cauliflower ears of a veteran wrestler. Mash-Mohammad used to be a champion wrestler when he was young. And what vigor he had, too!

Mohammad the mechanic comes in.

"Greetings!"

"Greetings."

I shake his hand, seated.

"How are you?"

"I am well."

Mash-Mohammad asks, "Got any news?"

Mohammad the mechanic lets go of my hand. "About what?"

"The Iraqis."

Mohammad the mechanic hesitates for a second. "No . . . not much more than anyone else. I heard the newspaper even had something about it today."

Mash-Mohammad pauses. "The newspaper? See, what did I tell you? Sheikh Ta'imeh saw the tanks with his own eyes. He was here yesterday and said —"

Mohammad the mechanic cuts him off. "How late are you open, Mash-Mohammad?"

"Why do you ask?"

"I want to go somewhere and come back."

"Sit. I'll be done in a second."

"If you're open till nine, I'll go and come back."

"I am, but sit down and wait for a minute."

"I don't have time to sit."

"Where are you going?"

"I need to buy some flowers and candies. It's my cousin's wedding. If you're open till nine, I'll come back."

"It's up to you, but by the time you finish a cup of tea, I'll be done."

Mohammad the mechanic shuffles a bit and sits. Mash-Mohammad sticks his head out the door, comb and scissors in hand, and calls out: "Three teas, sugar on the side, extra strong."

He then turns the TV on to a Basra television station.[2] I look at

---

[2] Throughout the south of Iran, the signals to Iraqi television stations can be picked up, particularly from the bordering towns.

the fuzzy screen in the mirror. Mash-Mohammad fiddles with the set to try and make the screen clearer. Mohammad the mechanic starts to speak. "It won't get any better than that, Mash-Mohammad. Don't waste your time."

"Why wouldn't it get better? I get great reception every time."

"That's only when it's muggy and humid."

"Even with the northern winds, I have good reception."

The screen does not clear up. Mash-Mohammad grumbles and leaves the TV set for the comb and scissors. A woman's meaty face fills the screen. She is singing a song in Arabic. She is so made up that I can almost smell the oils and odors of her makeup, and shudder with disgust.

The waiter brings the tea. Mohammad the mechanic points to the television and asks the barber, "You like these programs?"

Mash-Mohammad pours the tea in the saucer and blows on it. "What else can I do? My only entertainment is tea with sugar cubes, and belly dancers!"

Mohammad the mechanic says, "It doesn't take much to make you happy."

Mash-Mohammad the barber pours the tea down his throat and says, "There isn't much else going on." And then he combs my hair and looks at me in the mirror. "Do you want some cologne?"

"No, I'm fine."

He holds the mirror behind my head.

"Looks great. Thanks."

He unties the towel from my neck. I leave the shop and turn onto Khomeini Street to stroll down White Bridge Street. The kids are raising a storm in front of the Islamic Bookstore. They're buying schoolbooks. Their voices blend together.

"He doesn't have the biology book!"

"He doesn't have geology, either!"

"Did you get the pens?"

"Yeah . . . but I still need six hundred-page notebooks."

The days go by so fast; it feels as if summer started only two weeks ago. The schools will open in a couple of days, and life will shake off the sluggishness of summer, and the bustle and excitement of young boys and girls going to school will give the town another feel. Khomeini Street is lit up like daylight. People swarm; automobiles inch along slowly in a chain.

In White Bridge Circle, a milky white car — decorated for a wedding — has jumped the median and crashed into the streetlight. People are surrounding the car, laughing and making wise cracks. The scents of fragrant stock and petunias have filled the square. A group of men and women are sitting on a blanket on the grass in the middle of the square drinking tea. People think they are so entitled. As if it's their own house, they have lighted their samovars and are just lounging around in the middle of the public square.

The bridge itself is not crowded. I lean on a pole and light a cigarette, looking at the Karun River. What a flood. For the past couple of days the water level has risen two meters. Motor boats crisscross the river and speed toward the Naderi Bridge and back. A group of people are standing on the bank for their turn to ride the boats. I get dizzy from staring at the water and turn my eyes to the skyline. The lights alongside the Karun are on. Under some of them, kids are playing soccer. Farther down, under another streetlight, girls and boys have surrounded an ice cream cart, eating ice cream. The end of the Karun is buried in darkness.

I hear the sound of a train. I turn and look at Black Bridge. The train shakes the bridge as it passes. There is no light on the island in the river. More than half of the island and its tamarisk trees are buried under water. In the northeastern part of town, the open flames of the refinery have turned the sky blood-red. With a final glance at the motorboats and their front lights breaking the water, I start walking. I decide to stroll across the bridge, then go home.

Behind me two men are walking and talking. They are talking about Iraq and the Iraqi army at the border.

"I think this is one big joke."

"I don't. I think it's deadly serious."

"You mean you believe Iraq might actually attack Iran?"

"Why not?"

"It's not feasible. The people of Khuzestan can take all of Iraq by themselves!"

I stop, lean on the railing and look at the men. They're both middle-aged, maybe a bit older. One of them is wearing white shirt and pants — very clean-cut — with sleeves rolled up and hair combed.

"You are not considering an important factor, which is that our military has thoroughly imploded."

The other guy is wearing a gray shirt and a dark red tie. "But the military is secondary right now."

The man in white is holding his hands behind him, twirling the big yellow beads of a rosary. "How so?"

"Simple! Peoples' militias . . ."

They walk away. It seems the few lines in the newspaper have gotten people worried. I hear the sound of a motorcycle screeching by. A light cool breeze caresses the Karun. The sky is clear and full of stars. I stop at the western end of the White Bridge, next to the juice stand in Three-Girl Garden.

"What would you like?"

"Carrot juice, please."

Under the streetlights, on the edge of the grass next to the flower beds, people are filling the seats and benches and drinking juice. A traveling ice-cream vendor weaves through the crowd. Farther away, on the edge of the pool in the middle of the garden, a young couple is sitting and eating ice cream as their child plays with a little red and blue plastic ball on the grass.

"Your carrot juice."

"Thank you."

I light a cigarette, twirl the smoke in my mouth, and take a long sip, slowly sucking the juice from the cup. The two men in white and gray walk around Three-Girl Garden and pass me by on their way to the juice stand. They are still talking about Iraq and the army and the people's militias. The air has cooled down. Together, the scent of the grass, the scent of the flowers, and the scent of the night are exhilarating. The glimmering lights on the high ceilings of White Bridge seem like icicles suspended from the sky.

I am blinded by a pair of car lights at the edge of the park. Then the lights turn off and by the time my eyes get used to the dim light, Ahmad emerges from the car. Hoori and Reza stay inside. Ahmad goes to the juice stand. "Three glasses of apple juice."

I call over to him and he comes toward me.

"Oh . . . you are here? Hello!"

"Hi . . . how are you?"

"Well, thank you."

Ahmad calls Hoori. They get out of the car and little Reza

waddles and stumbles toward us. Hoori is right beside him, guiding his steps. She smiles. "What are you doing here?"

"Nothing. I have nothing else to do, so I'm just taking a walk."

"You aren't here checking out the girls, are you?"

"Oh yeah, right!"

Ahmad takes the three glasses of apple juice and comes over.

"We were on our way to your house," Hoori says.

I take Reza from her arms.

"It's still not too late, let's go together."

In the house, there's a discussion going on. Basra television has been showing the capture of an Iranian border post. As if he has been personally insulted, Shahed pulls in his chin, inflates his chest, and waves his big hands in the air.

"Pimps . . . as if they have conquered the Khaybar fortress of Arabia. They keep on showing the takeover of the Provisions Register of the local army company."

Mohsen, who has just finished his military service, is sitting on some cushions at the far end of the room.

"They also captured a jeep and a machine gun," he says bitterly.

I take the glass of tea from Mina.

"How did they capture it?"

Mohsen is chewing the end of his thick black moustache.

"How should I know! Basra television was showing it."

Ahmad pours his tea in the saucer, blows on it, and holds it to Reza's mouth.

"What a time these bastards have picked!"

"You didn't say what 'Provisions Register' means," I say.

Saber takes a big drag on his cigarette.

"It seems they overran this border checkpoint and found a small notebook, which apparently had the account of the food and provisions for an army company. The bastards have been holding it like a trophy and beating their drums to it."

It seems to be getting serious; it's not just rumor anymore. If the newspaper is right and if Sheikh Ta'mieh was telling the truth . . . plus, if the Iraqis have indeed stationed their tanks on the border and have even attacked a checkpoint . . . tomorrow they'll probably attack others, and then . . . God have mercy on Khuzestan! We'll be on the front lines!

On top of the normal drowsiness after a big lunch, the drone of the air conditioner is making me sleepy. I'm trying to take a nap, but the neighborhood kids are raising hell in the alleyway. They have so much energy, these damn kids! Heat and cold make no difference to them — even at noon, in this muggy heat, they keep going. My eyelids are getting heavy when a ball hits the window, jolting me awake. I have a good mind to get up and shout down at them. I barely make it up, however, before I sprawl down again, exhausted. I light a cigarette and flip over to rest my chin on my hands. The possibility of sleep has gone, but the drowsiness lingers. Saber knocks on the door

"Are you awake?"

There's a quiver of excitement in his voice.

"Yes."

He opens the door and says in a rush

"They've hit the airport!"

The fatigue rushes out of my body. I spring up.

"Where did they hit?"

"The airport!"

"What are you talking about?"

"Iraqi planes have bombarded the airport!"

"Where did you hear that?"

I turn on the radio.

"Some friends called me."

"Friends? Did you hear anything yourself?"

"Me? No! I was in my room. We're too far from the airport."

The radio announces today's news. I ask Saber, "If they have hit Ahvaz airport, then why isn't the radio saying anything about it?"

"They just hit it. A couple of minutes ago. I guess it takes a while before the news gets to them."

"It takes a while?" I put out the cigarette. "How come we heard about it so soon, then?!"

I get up. I want to make myself busy. I feel as if I have lost something, as if there is an errand that I've forgotten.

"Where's Shahed?" I ask.

"Sleeping. He took a nap after lunch."

I call Mina to bring me the phone. Mohsen passes my room quickly on his way out the door.

"Where are you going?" I call out to him.

He's in a rush. "I'm going out to see what's going on."

"If this news is true . . ." Saber says.

Mohsen closes the door behind him. Mina brings the phone. Saber lights a cigarette. I've barely had a chance to plug the phone in when it rings.

"Hello?"

It's Ali, my cousin.

"Have you heard?"

"You mean about the airport?"

"They've hit the airport tower."

"Were there any planes on the tarmac at the time?"

He doesn't know. I hang up. The radio is broadcasting the international news. I turn the knob to find another station with the news, but there's nothing. I get up, dress, and leave the house. It's a few minutes before three o'clock, and it's hot. The whole city seems to be shaken. This time of day the streets are usually quiet, but today people couldn't stand being inside once they heard about the airport. They walk the street aimlessly. In front of stores, men and women gather and listen to the news. It's just ordinary news, as if nothing has happened to Ahvaz airport. A car passes by and the driver shouts

"We're at war!"

This is serious. I wander aimlessly around town. I get to Mama Rain Circle and head toward the coffeehouse. I stop by the public water pump to wash my face and cool down. Three young men are sitting and chatting in the shade by the wall of the café. They are talking about Iraq and the bombing of the airport and the fact that the radio announcer is acting as if nothing has happened. I fill my mouth with water and gargle, listening.

"You begin to think that with this silence, they are being traitors to this country! Otherwise, why wouldn't they say anything about it?"

I look at them. One of them looks very familiar. I think he is a student from the College of Philosophy at the university.

"They've almost wiped out the airport . . . and not a word on the radio."

One of them is skinny and tall, and, with his legs crossed, he retorts, "If it were any other hellhole, they wouldn't only inform people about the events, they'd actually use the mass media to instruct and lead."

The philosophy student, whose most visible characteristic is his thick curly hair, rubs his hands together and says in a voice filled with protest and sadness, "Silence, silence, silence."

After cooling down, I sit on the coffeehouse bench. The owner, who is called Mehdi the Pauper, comes out and hands me a glass of tea.

"You've heard, of course."

I nod. "Yes, I've heard."

The radio in Mehdi's store goes silent for a second, and then a politician begins to speak. His voice is completely calm. One of the young men asks Mehdi to turn up the volume, and he does. The sound of the radio is filling the square. Rostam Effendi is sleeping inside the café. Kal Shaban, the neighborhood grocer at the other side of the square, comes out of his store and looks over in our direction. The politician is saying that Iraq has unilaterally transgressed the Algiers Accord and that today, a few minutes after two in the afternoon, Iraqi planes attacked our nation and bombed the airports of Tabriz, Hamedan, Dezful, Ahvaz, and Tehran's Mehrabad airport.

One of the young men pushes the meaty part of his fist into his forehead and says in a muffled voice, "Bastards!"

Dumbfounded, Mehdi the Pauper listens to the radio. Rostam Effendi gets up, comes over, and squats at the café door. The official asks people to remain calm and then, his voice a crescendo of excitement, says that our people will defend their revolutionary nation and will repel the transgressors.

I am concentrating on the radio when a voice says, "It's finally started!"

I turn my head. It's Mohammad the mechanic, just back from work. His black eyes are tired and his curly black hair is a mess.

At dusk, the streetlights do not come on. People are pouring out of their houses. Radios are blasting. The Iraqi attacks have united the people. People, friends or not, greet one another. The word on the street is about resistance and beating back the enemy.

"We'll crush him like a snake!"

"We'll bury all the Iraqis in one grave!"

"Who'd have thought that Saddam would have the guts!"

"This doesn't take guts, it takes stupidity!"

"He had to invade — our revolution has shaken up Iraq!"

"It has shaken up the whole region!"

There is no sign of worry on anyone's face. The darkness of night flows in the streets. Car lights are off. In Khomeini Street — usually bright as daylight — there is not even the flicker of a candle. A mild mugginess has taken over the city. People have covered their doors and windows. The supporting pillars of White Bridge are enveloped in the mist rising off the Karun, and the bridge, in the dark of night, seems to hover in midair. The motorboats are bobbing alongside the flooded river. The hollow, fearsome sound of the Karun River seems threatening at night. There's no one on the banks.

I am sleeping on the roof when I jolt awake to the roaring thunder of an airplane.[3] It's early in the morning. The sun hasn't yet risen. Shahed jumps off his bed and hoists himself up to the top of the staircase. He shades his eyes with his hands, looking east. Everyone is now awake. I get out of bed. The coolness of dawn is blending with the light mugginess of daybreak. I look down at the street from the edge of the roof. I hear Baba Rahman's voice:

"It was a plane, right?"

I turn toward the other roof. Baba Rahman's forehead, eyes, and nose are visible over the wall.

"I think it was . . . Yes, it *was* a plane!"

Shahed jumps back on the roof.

"They've hit around Silu! There's thick smoke . . ."

The words have barely left his mouth when the plane approaches again and passes right over us. It's so loud that my knees turn to water for a quick second. Shahed covers his ears and squats. I think of the radio next to the bed. I turn it on and tune to the Ahvaz station. Sirens start wailing. People are gathering on their rooftops, shading their eyes with their hands and looking in the direction of the plane. The radio asks people to go in their cellars until the air raid is over. Saber, his eyes still full of slumber, murmurs, "Air strikes!"

As the sounds of antiaircraft guns are heard from the western part of the city, Baba Rahman calls me, "Wait . . . look over there!"

---

[3] Most houses in Iran have flat roofs, and in summertime many people move their beds or mattresses to the roof to sleep in the fresh air and keep cool.

At Silu, a thick smoke rises, tears apart, and disintegrates into the east.

The sun is pulling up. On Ahvaz radio, the announcer asks people to pay close attention to the different sirens, and then they set off the yellow alert. I take the radio and go downstairs. Mother has set up breakfast on the porch. Saber takes the tea glass from her.

"Mother, from today on, we have to live in the cellar."

Mother is calm. "God will protect us. Whatever He wills . . ."

Saber says, "That's right, Mother, God will protect us. But we still have to live in the cellar." The siren is still on the radio as Saber continues, "Take all the appliances and furniture to the cellar. The refrigerator, too."

I don't know what time Mohsen had left this morning, but he comes back in a rush. "The local guys have formed a group!"

Shahed is putting on his shoes to go to work. "A group?"

Mohsen wipes the sweat from his forehead and sits on the edge of the balcony. "Yes, a group. To fight Iraq. Since last night, there are already two groups of ten to twelve kids . . ." Mohsen takes the tea glass from Mother. "Hojjat's group had eleven people."

He takes a sip of the tea, and continues, "Babak's gang, too, is up to nine people!"

"Hojjat? Abdollah the carpenter's son?" Shahed says.

Mohsen swallows more tea. "Yes, Abdollah's son."

Shahed lights his cigarette. "But he's so wimpy!"

"Maybe . . . but he has a head on his shoulders. The other kids respect him!"

Shahed heads out.

"Good-bye."

"Good-bye."

He hasn't reached the door when the red siren goes off; he pauses a second and looks back at us. Saber calls him. "Come back . . . don't leave now . . ."

The antiaircraft batteries start in again. Shahed looks at his watch, his ear cocked to the sound of the guns. Mohsen goes upstairs to the roof to have a look. Shahed shuffles about a while. "I should be off. I'll be late to the office." With which, he pushes out his motorbike and closes the door. The airplane can still be heard in the distance. Mohsen stretches his neck over the wall of the roof. "It looks like they've hit Campelu!"[4]

With that, I peel off my seat and hurry up the stairs. Saber doesn't move a muscle. Once on the roof, I pull myself up onto the ledge above, which supports the staircase. In a few spots around the western part of the city, clouds of dust are rising. The airplanes can be heard. I look at the sky. Not even one shred of cloud. The sound of antiaircraft machine-gun suddenly roars like thunder. It's from the Island. Overnight, it seems, they've put up antiaircraft guns on the Island, alongside the bridges, in fact throughout the city.

Baba Rahman is still on the roof. This time, he's standing on a stool, with only his head and chest visible from our side. I hear the voice of the old man. "Looks like there's really going to be war!"

I jump from the ledge down onto the roof. Baba Rahman's son calls out to him from their courtyard, but the old man keeps standing on the stool looking at the sky. I move slowly over to him.

"That's right, Baba Rahman, the war has started!"

Baba Rahman's red gums peer through his toothless grin.

The news of tanks creates a lot of confusion. It's ten o'clock in the morning. Suddenly word spreads that over two hundred tanks have pulled to within ten kilometers of the city. They have crossed the Azadegan Plains and are approaching. Suddenly the whole town turns into mayhem, like a bees' nest on fire. Movements are hurried. Words smell like fear peppered with anxiety, resistance, and flight.

"Who says the tanks are coming?"

"Who? The radio!" someone shouts.

"Did you hear it yourself?"

"Get a grip on yourself, man!"

"Everybody in the city has heard."

"More than two hundred!"

"Two hundred!"

An old man is leaning against a wall, drenched in sweat and hyperventilating. He pounds his head with his fist and murmurs, "We've nowhere else to go. All our life, our honor, our work . . . and now we'll be on the streets!"

_____

[4] A section of the city of Ahvaz.

A retired colonel, with one foot in the grave and a pair of scorpion tails for a mustache, takes his binoculars and breathlessly goes up to his roof, grumbling, "This isn't some backwater. Just two hundred tanks? Is the army dead?"

Offices close. People pour into the streets and build barricades with sandbags.

Two nights ago, Basra television announced the fall of Dabb Hardan. Now, at night, everyone watches Basra TV. They showed us how their soldiers had poured out of military trucks, stood in tight lines and gunned down the whole city, then dispersed into the town and killed everything — even the cats and dogs — with their Kalashnikovs.

Everyone in town has their radios turned on. The rhythm of revolutionary anthems and military marches has filled the city. The military march fades away for a few moments as the radio announcer declares that all schools will be closed. But the kids have left school already and started making Molotov cocktails. The voices of young people are everywhere.

"Hey, Asad . . . MOVE!"

"You . . . yes, I'm talking to you, Morad . . . take Jaber and Amir and go find some jars, bottles, empty bottles."

"Ghazal . . . yeah you, Ghazal . . . get some soap . . . run . . . Now!"

"And don't forget the grater . . . the grater!"

Kids are stopping cars, adding to the frustration of the drivers.

"What the hell are you doing?"

"Gasoline!"

"What do you want to do with my gasoline?"

"Even a liter is enough!"

"For heaven's sake, I don't have a hose!"

"It's all right, we do . . ."

Doors get pounded. Kids, sweat dripping from their faces, haul bags full of empty bottles. Gas canisters, soap boxes, and cans of burned cooking oil weigh down on their shoulders. The effort is getting more intense and widespread. Gasoline lines grow longer by the minute

"Thirty liters . . . that would get me to Khurramabad."

"Are you running away?"

"Running away?"

"Why are you in such a rush?"

"Listen, Mister, I have to get my kids to a safe place!"

Again, the antiaircraft rockets; and then, the sound of a plane explodes like thunder. Everyone leaves their cars and lies flat on the medians and sidewalks, looking at one another in disbelief and shock.

"Did you get burned?"

"No . . . but I think I twisted my ankle."

"Check it out . . . you might have been shot!"

Workers — blue- and white-collar — are building barricades. From Zeitoon to Zand Street, from Kianpars to Shilangabad, from Golestan and Bustan to Chaharshir. The black market in gasoline is booming.

"I just want ten liters."

"That'll be a hundred tomans a liter!"

"A hundred tomans?! Buddy, I hope you are praying for your own soul . . ."

"Oh, yeah?! Then go wait in the gasoline lines till grass grows under your feet . . . and maybe even get shot for all I care!"

Handcarts, trucks, and pickups rush sand from the Karun to all parts of town. Everyone's wet with sweat. The sun is blistering. There is not even a trace of a cloud.

An old man is standing in front of the construction site on his property. He's holding a dented shovel in his hand, guarding his pile of sand from anyone who gets close. Kids laugh and taunt him. He is foaming at the mouth, chasing them, panting and cursing.

Women, kids, boys, and girls go house-to-house collecting empty bags. Next to the barricades kids are shoveling sand into the bags.

Homes are abuzz. Everyone is gathering their goods.

"Father, why are you rolling up the carpet?"

"Didn't you see what they did in Dabb Hardan?"

"Yes, but . . ."

"There's no 'but' . . . they have no mercy for anybody . . . they're burning down everything!"

Voices overlap.

"Mother, empty that rice sack!"

The mother turns around in confusion.

"Where . . . where I am supposed to empty it?"

"I don't know . . . on the floor . . . in that pot."

As kids pound on the doors, voices come from inside,

"What's all the noise?"

"Auntie . . . soap . . . give us all you can!"[5]

"They took it already . . . I swear my own kids took everything I had!"

Bottles of Molotov cocktails are standing next to the barricades, on roofs, alongside walls. The images from the fall of Dabb Hardan have put hatred in everyone's heart.

"We'll counter aggression with aggression!"

"We'll break their legs!"

"Over our dead bodies . . ."

"If they set foot in this city we'll burn them alive!"

Buses, minivans, and passenger cars are filled with young and old on their way to the military base.

"Get in!"

"Where to?"

"The base!"

"What for?"

"Weapons!"

The roar of motorcycles cracks like a storm and fills the streets. Boys and girls, two, three, even four to a seat, are driving toward the base for weapons. Mohammad the mechanic appears for a second and then hurtles like a meteor down the street. Wind blows his thick hair and makes it look even bigger. Young people with G-3s and Kalashnikovs arrive at the barricades and load their weapons.

"Who's that guy . . . the redhead?"

"Nezam, the ironsmith."

"Mash Safar's son?"

"That's him. He's the son of Mash Safar the ironsmith."

"Who's the other one . . . the dark guy?"

"Qasem the bricklayer."

"And the tall one?"

"You don't recognize him?"

"He looks familiar."

"He's a schoolteacher . . . he's formed a group with his students."

In front of the giant gates of the military base, it looks like Judgment Day. People are screaming. Everyone wants a weapon. The

---

[5] Soap is used to make Molotov cocktails.

soldiers are holding guns and placing their sweat-filled bodies between the people and the walls of the garrison. Every time a new group arrives, the voices get louder and the crowd, pressed into each other, drive toward the garrison like a wave.

"Give us weapons!"

"Guns!"

"Machine guns!"

"RPGs!"

"I've served already . . . armored division . . . give me a tank!"

Voices are rising like the sound of the sea before the storm breaks, a roar that sinks fear into your heart. Sometimes a resonating voice overtakes the noise and rises above it, drives towards the garrison, and echoes like a wounded bird hitting its flailing head against the wall.

"Who is going to protect the city?"

"The tanks are coming!"

"We're fed up with this incompetence!"

"Give us weapons!"

"Please be quiet and listen to me!"

The voice of a young officer soars from a loudspeaker. "We thank you . . ."

"Give us weapons!"

"I beg you, please allow me to speak!"

The sound of the crowd disintegrates. The voice of the young officer — which now has a pleasant tone — calmly and patiently emerges from the loudspeaker: "We thank you . . . the captain has ordered me to thank you and ask you to return to your homes. I beg you, please remain calm. Do not lose your heads. Be confident that the army will protect the city. Know that the Ninety-second Armored Division alone can go all the way to Baghdad. Please have faith. The only thing that . . ."

The voice of a young man standing at the front of the crowd rises. "If the army is protecting the town, why did the Iraqi tanks . . ."

Suddenly, the young man's voice is drowned out by the blast of gunshots fired into the air.

The young officer yells into the loudspeaker. "Don't shoot!"

A few soldiers rush to the far end of the garrison wall. All heads turn. It seems some people have been trying to climb the walls. The young officer's voice rises again from the loudspeaker.

"If you try to make trouble for us, you will only hurt yourself . . . you will impede the defense of the city . . ."

People pull back from the wall. A voice emerges from the crowd: "We won't leave until you give us weapons!"

The voice of the young officer again: "If it becomes necessary, we will arm every resident of the city . . . but give us a chance . . . I beg you, return to your homes . . ."

Some young people drive endlessly back and forth on their motorcycles, arms raised, guns aloft. People cheer and applaud.

The news of the fall of Hamid Army Base explodes like a bomb.

"With all its fancy defenses?"

"Its barricades!"

"All those big cement blocks!"

"How can this be possible?"

"There is no 'how,' brother. It fell!"

An old man, rubbing his calloused hands together, is shaking his head.

"Our pride, honor . . . gone!"

And then he stares in humiliation and says under his breath,

"Iraq . . . ? Damn!"

Rumors crawl like lice over people's bodies.

"In Susangerd they have raped women and girls!"

"They've looted all the stores and houses!"

"Looted?"

"And shot all the men!"

"Bastards!"

A young girl, fuming like incense on embers, screams, "Some of the Sunni Sheikhs are cooperating with them!"

"Damn them!"

"They say that Sheikh Shonar is now the ruler of Susangerd!"

"I don't believe it!"

"Believe it, brother."

"Damn them!"

When the MIGs arrive, people scuttle toward the bomb shelters, or lie down on the sidewalks behind columns, under staircases and behind the sandbags piled high in every street in the city.

Traffic is completely out of control. There are no traffic police at the intersections. The city's cars are the color of the desert: people have covered them with mud to hide them from air strikes. Now, without anyone teaching them anything, people are gradually learning confrontation and resistance. Bakeries close one after another, and the lines at the ones still open grow by the minute. At high noon, when even camels are forced off their feet, workers in the bakeries stand in front of the hot ovens to make bread, sweat pouring from their faces. Before long, they are standing in a puddle of their own sweat.

Two consecutive explosions rock the city. Rumors spread that the square in front of White Bridge has been hit. People charge up to their roofs, shading their eyes, looking at the mountain of dust rising from the square. The dust mixes with smoke and flames and finally threads apart and disappears. People leave their roofs and pour back down into the streets. A man arrives on a bicycle.

"They're killing . . . killing . . . massacring!"

The bicycle rides away and voices mix.

"They've destroyed the whole square!"

"They were aiming for the White Bridge!"

"God knows how many people were killed."

"They say eleven."

A man on a motorcycle sputters toward the crowd and pauses in front of the people.

"Eleven people!"

Voices mix into the mellow hum of the motorcycle. The biker roars from the depth of his chocked throat: "All the bank employees are under rubble. God have mercy on them!"

"Damn them and their fathers!"

In the distance, ambulance sirens can be heard. The biker pushes the gas. The motor explodes into life and away he flies.

"There were people killed in the square!"

"And they say thirty, maybe forty, were injured."

Now, when the MIGs come down and break the sound barrier, we lace our fingers behind our heads and hold our forearms against our ears. Spines stretch, knees weaken, legs give out, and you are forced to sit. "Phantoms" follow the MIGs. All the glass doors and windows shatter. We haven't had time to tape the glass. In one night, tape has become scarce. The building trembles. Dust falls from the brick ceiling of the cellar. It has now been two weeks since we started living in the cellar. It is October 8. Yesterday they pounded the railroad. Just as the train was about to pull out, with people milling about in the station saying their farewells, a bomber dipped around the Municipal Building, flew on its side, and, before anyone could move, pounded the station, the control room, and the overpass.

Now all trains leave from Karun Station.

— *Translated by Kouross Esmaili*

Esmail Fassih

Esmail Fassih was born in Tehran in 1935. After finishing his secondary education in Iran, in 1956 he studied in the United States at Montana State College, where he obtained degrees in science and English literature. Upon his return to Iran, he worked as a translator for the Franklin Institute and the National Iranian Oil Company. In 1963, he became a full-time employee of the National Iranian Oil Company and moved to the southern city of Ahvaz to teach at the company's Institute of Technology.

In Ahvaz Fassih began to write fiction, publishing his first novel, *Raw Wine,* in 1968. During a leave of absence from his job, he studied at the University of Michigan, where he got his master's in English language and literature. Back in Iran, he settled in the southern city of Abadan to teach at the Abadan Institute of Technology.

In the 1970s Fassih published a novel, *The Blind Heart,* and two collections of short stories. His 1980 novel *The Story of Javid* is based on the real life of a Zoroastrian man during the Qajar dynasty and *The Winter of '62* is about the horrors of the Iran-Iraq War. His novel *Sorraya in a Coma,* published by Zed Press in Iran in 1985, has been one of the most successful post-revolution novels.

The excerpt from *Sorraya in a Coma* was translated by the author. With as much humor as possible, the story depicts the anguish, insecurity, and confusion that surround lives disrupted by revolution, war, and emigration.

Excerpt from
SORRAYA IN A COMA

Late autumn, 1980, a cold Tuesday afternoon, around two o'clock, Tehran . . .

At the open access to the west bus terminal, on the northwestern outskirts of Azadi Square, peddlers, vendors, and passengers mill about in the dust and diesel fumes, the honking, the jumbled noise and shouts, "Liver . . . Mmm! Two tomans a skewer!" "Sandwiches, Agha![1] Fresh egg sandwiches!" "Move on, Agha!" "Beans! Baked beans!" "Shahsavar oranges!" "Sweet buns!" "Out of the way, you!" "Winston cigarettes, Agha!" "Biscuits!" "Hamburgers! Sausages!" "Handbags, Agha!" "Move your bags, Father!" "Woolen socks, hats, gloves!" "Fresh tea!" "Agha, move on! Move aside, Mother!"

Some have spread out their wares on an upturned drum, a cardboard box, or piece of cloth on the ground. One sells *barbari* bread and cheese; another *lavash* bread and boiled eggs. An old man sitting in a corner sells plastic packets of dried seeds, almonds, pistachios, chickpeas and raisins, dried figs, and mulberries.

The new makeshift terminal's interior is a shapeless, undefined space, with no buildings, no facilities, not even a wall. Inside, it is still just a taken-over lot. But buses heading for the north and northwest of Iran, and even for Turkey and Europe, all start from this point.

To the north, under the blue sky and fat white clouds, rise the clean snow-covered Alborz Mountains. Closer, a cluster of tall, multi-story buildings, dusty gray and white, huddle together like dingy monsters modeled on New York's skyscrapers; these supposedly residential units are now stranded, unfinished, worthless, useless, and empty under the autumn wind, behind the terminal. In the foreground, scattered around the lot are tarpaulin tents, each representing a bus company or travel agency, and in every corner, "cooperatives" have sprouted. Behind the tents, coaches unload and reload passengers.

The crowd milling around are mostly from the provinces, or are

---

[1] *Agha* is an honorific term for men, roughly equivalent to Mister.

war refugees, or just people like myself, driven from their homes for one reason or another. There are homeless Turks, Lurs, Kurds, and Khuzestani Arabs, pouring into Tehran or leaving it. Where I enter the terminal, to one side, several dusty-bearded soldiers in crumpled uniforms are drinking tea. Three Kurds in baggy trousers, wearing paramilitary jackets and their traditional polka dot turbans, are resting in a corner smoking Winston cigarettes. An Arab from Khuzestan sits in a corner apparently with his mother, wife, and six or seven children, doing nothing, their faces empty.

I find the tent representing the TBT bus company, now "Cooperative No. 15." There is even a bivouac counter in a corner with a cardboard sign: "Passengers to Istanbul." The counter is almost deserted. I find somebody and hand in my ticket. Without even checking it, the man ticks off my name on his list. I have no luggage as such to hand in, so he allows me to keep my small suitcase and handbag. The door of "the coach" — a well-worn Deluxe Benz 0302 — is open, and the driver and his assistant are loading luggage onto the roof, but it is not ready for boarding. A tall man, with a soft curly beard, fine mustache, and a round white fur hat, which gives him a holy Zoroastrian look, has a pile of luggage and is haggling with the driver.[2] One of the larger suitcases has burst open, and he is trying to tie it up with rope. I help him, then lift it and the other pieces, onto the roof; he thanks me. Then I wander around, light a cigarette, and wait.

Just then the Red-Alert siren sounds from the airport across the road. Almost immediately the nationwide two o'clock news, on the radio in the little TBT tent, is interrupted by the now familiar monotone warning: "Attention, attention! The sound you are now hearing is the Red Alert or the Danger Warning, it means an air raid is about to take place. Leave your place of business and go to shelter!" The Red Alert is then broadcast. No one pays much attention. Except for a few jeers and grumbles, more or less everyone goes on with what they are doing. After two months of war with Iraq, the people in Tehran are hardly very excited by these mostly false alarms.

---

[2] Zoroastrianism is the first monotheistic revealed religion. Founded by Zarathustra around 500 B.C.E., it became the official religion of various Persian empires and was the dominant religion of Iran until the Arab invasions in the seventh century. *Ahura Mazda* is the Zoroastrian term for God.

The tall gentleman with the beard and mustache strolls up and stands by me. He has stashed away his luggage, but is still loaded with bags and parcels, blankets, and assorted cushions. He, too, has lit a cigarette.

He shakes his head. "Red Alert!"

"Yes."

"I don't think they'll hit, Jenab, eh?[3] What is your excellency's opinion?"

I do not answer.

"They've probably seen something on their radars, no?"

"Probably."

"Or perhaps an unidentified object has been reported?"

"All finished with your luggage?" I ask.

"Yes. Are you by any chance traveling to Europe by TBT?"

"Coach to Istanbul." I turn and toss my half-smoked cigarette aside, retreating into my own thoughts.

"What is your point of destination?" he asks.

"Paris."

"Are you a French resident?"

"No."

"How did you, er, get an exit permit in this chaos?"

He simply won't give up, so I briefly tell him about my niece's accident in Paris and the ensuing troubles. He volunteers no information. "So," he says, "your excellency's heading for Paris?"

"Supposedly."

"You're not married, are you?"

"How did you figure *that* out?"

"Ah! I'm an expert on faces and characters. I have spent a lifetime in the public relations department of the national airlines."

"I see."

"Have you had lunch?" he inquires in a friendly tone.

"I had a little something at my sister's place."

He looks around the terminal. "Looks like there are no restaurants or anything around here."

"I saw some liver kebab and egg sandwich stands by the entrance."

"Oh God, no!"

---

[3] *Jenab* is an honorific term, roughly equivalent to *sir.*

The siren has been cut off.

My companion says, "Let's go . . . By God almighty, let's get out of this nowhereland."[4]

The Arab woman sitting quietly in a corner just shakes her head in silence, steadily beating herself on the head.

We walk slowly back to the bus, and as there is nowhere to sit, we stand and wait. Curly-beard continues complaining about the state of things in Iran.

"How did *you* get an exit permit?" I ask him.

"My passport has a Pakistani permanent residency stamp. My mother's there. I sent my passport over, she fixed it."

"I see."

"I've got a valid U.S. visa, too. My ex-wife, my son, and my daughter are there, in Virginia and Los Angeles; according to their laws, they grant asylum to emigrants with political or religious insecurity. They fixed it for me."

I do not understand what exactly he means by "religious insecurity."

We finally get on the coach around midafternoon, and the driver starts the engine. The migrating Zoroastrian-looking gentleman and I are seated next to each other, he by the window and I in the aisle seat. Before sitting down, he arranges a couple of blankets and cushions under and around him. "If we can't travel by 747 jumbo, let's at least travel in comfort!" Opposite me in the aisle sits a young woman, and a not-so-young, tubby little fellow who is apparently a student in Germany.

Before we take off, the driver welcomes each and every one of us with his typical Azerbaijani kindness and good humor. In front of him, and ranged around and above his windshield, is an assortment of tiny pictures, curtains, tassels, artificial flowers, mottos, a radio, a box of tissues and other odds and ends. Between a portrait of the Imam Ali, and a snapshot of the driver's little son, is a poem printed in fine Persian script: "A night at home, and a hundred on the road/Oh, fatherless Benz where doth thou lead me on?" He calls out, "I introduce myself: Ladies and Gentlemen. I am Abbas Agha — Abbas Agha Marandi — at your service. Anything you need, you need at all, let me know. And this here is my helper, Hussein Agha — ditto for him. By his holiness,

---

[4] "Nowhereland" is a Persian euphemism that means a very unpleasant, unruly place.

Imam Ali himself, the first Shi'ite imam, the king of men, I hope the trip goes nice and smooth for all the ladies and gents. So, to Mohammad and his descendants, *Salavat!*"[5]

All the passengers loudly chant the *Salavat.* Curly-beard, too, raises his voice, but he turns aside and laughs. Abbas Agha Marandi calls for a second, a third, and even louder *Salavat* for the leaders of Islam and for our dauntless fighting soldiers.

After armed Revolutionary Guards have checked the bus and the driver's papers at the terminal's only exit point, the Benz 0302 finally starts the journey.

Ten kilometers up the main highway, Abbas Agha stops to gas up. A long line of vehicles, stretching over two or three kilometers, is lined up at the filling station. Passenger-carrying coaches are exempt from lining up for fuel, so Abbas reverses slowly to the head of the line. About ten minutes later the refueling is complete.

Meanwhile, my traveling companion, who says his name is Vahab Soheili, tells me about his many years service with Iran Air, how he had recently been kicked out of his job, how on several occasions they had "barged" into his house and confiscated many of his books and albums, and how he had been kept in Evin Prison for a month and a half, before it turned out that he had committed no crimes, and so was released without a trial. His wife, his ex-wife, and his offspring were either in England or in the United States, his mother was in Karachi, and his late brother's four sons and daughter were in Germany.

Looking around, it seems that nearly all the passengers are in the same position. Except for me and one or two of the students, the rest have gathered up their belongings and are leaving for good. Soheili, for one, is bidding adieu to his motherland, and says he has packed even the pumice stone in his old bathroom; Dr. Kiumarspur, a microbiology Ph.D. from America, is going to join her husband in Paris. In a none-too-rigid Islamic headcovering, she is breast-feeding her baby, which is probably a game in itself, for apart from this, her only concern is flirting with the tubby student bound for Germany.

Dusk has fallen when we come out of the filling station. About half a kilometer farther up the highway, a little pickup truck has been

---

[5] *Salavat* is the traditional praise prayer to the Prophet Mohammad and his family. It is usually said in chorus.

hit and overturned. Seventy or eighty kilos of onions are scattered over the road. The driver, an old peasant, squats by his vehicle and the onions, his head in his hands, as if dazedly wondering what do. Traffic whizzes past, left and right, nobody caring about him. The scattered onions, the overturned truck, and the old man are a hilarious laughing matter for most of the passengers.

Two hours after nightfall, Abbas Agha Marandi pulls up in front of a large coffeehouse outside Takestan city limits, "for supper and saying of prayers." Several other buses are parked there. Most of our passengers rush to buy dinner tokens from the coffeehouse proprietor, who is already helplessly crowded with customers. Soheili is in front of me.

"Jenab Aryan," he says. "They only have rice and *khoresh gheimeh*, lamb stew and kebab. What should we do?"

"Whichever. Both are fine," I reply.

"The *khoresh-geimeh* is certain to be full of fat. And God only knows where the kebab meat came from!"

"Take it easy, Agha Soheili."

"I don't see any dogs around here, by the way . . ."

I chuckle. "Even if it's crickets' chitterlings from the Moghan Desert," I said, "I'm eating it."

Soheili laughs. "In that case, if I may so trouble you . . . you wouldn't happen to have a hundred tomans or so change?[6] If you could lend it to me, a thousand thanks. I only have dollars and pounds left. We'll settle what we spend later."

"Of course."

"Dinner's on me!"

"I'm most grateful."

"Tea or soft drink?"

"Tea's fine."

"Well, then — two kebab *barg*, two teas, two yogurts. How's that?"

"Perfect."

I hand over a hundred note and Soheili gets tokens for food and yogurt. While, bag in hand, he goes to "clean up," I get the food at the

---

[6] In Iranian money, ten rials are equal to one toman. Currently, roughly eight hundred tomans are equal to one U.S. dollar.

crowded kitchen door. Loaded with kebabs, country bread, yogurt, and onions, I find an empty place in a corner.

Soheili comes over. We sit down to eat. The kebab is not at all bad. The rice, too, had it been steamed long enough, would have been fine. Two peasants come and sit down next to us, with a rice and *khoresh geimeh* — they don't just eat it, they make passionate love to it, their faces at kissing distance to the plate. They scoop up the food with a chunk of bread, and stuff it in their mouths; some stays in, some escapes to the loving bosom of the plate. They lick their fingers. They have nothing to do with spoons and forks. Between plate and mouth exists a spirit of unity and of intimacy. Soheili eats his white rice with a fork.

"I'm going from Istanbul to Karachi by Pan Am," he says.

"I see."

"How are you getting from Istanbul to Paris, Jenab Aryan?"

"I have an Iran Air ticket, but . . . I'll just have to wait and see."

"Iran Air doesn't have a flight now, does it? Iran's airports are shut."

"That's right. They have a contract with Turkish Air, which apparently flies Iran Air passengers."

"Is your ticket full-price?" he asks.

"No. Forty percent discount."

"Are you a government employee?"

"Oil company. In the south."

"Could I see your ticket?"

I show it to him. "No-cash-return and nontransferable," he says. "But I've got friends in Istanbul who'll fix it for you. If they have a new contract to fly Iran Air passengers, we'll fix it. How long are you staying in Istanbul? It's a very beautiful city."

"I'm not planning to stay. I'll get moving the day we arrive — if I can."

"You are worried about your niece?"

"I must get to her hospital as soon as I can."

"What about your own leg? You have a limp. Were you hurt in the war?"

"It's nothing. I tripped over a bottle of Coca-Cola."

He laughs. "If I may say, God bless you, good man. I hope that with our lord Ahura-Mazda's help, all will turn out well for you and your niece, and everything will come to a good and happy ending right there in Paris!"

"I don't know . . ."

We each light a cigarette. A boy brings us tea.

"What happened?" he asks.

"What?"

"To your niece."

"We don't exactly know. In the letter we had, and the few telephone calls to my sister from Sorraya's friends in Paris, we've been told that she was bicycling back from a friend's house. Apparently the roads were slippery. She fell turning a corner."

"And has brain damage?"

"Apparently."

"How long ago?"

"She's been in a coma for two or three weeks now, I think."

"God. As simple as that?"

"Yes . . . as simple as that."

"How old is she?"

"Twenty-three, twenty-two."

He shakes his head. "How strange . . ."

I sigh. "Yes. A fifty-year-old banana like me survives in war-torn Abadan, and in the battle areas, comes through the palm tree plantations, gets on a dilapidated motor dinghy by night, traveling over a hundred kilometers under heavy bombing and shelling to Bandar Mahshah. A twenty-two-year-old young woman falls from a bicycle in the suburbs of Paris . . ."

"There's no sense in anything in this world, is there, Jenab Aryan?"

"No . . . apparently there isn't, Jenab Soheili!"

"And now, you're going there to take her back to Tehran?"

"Well, not while she's still in a coma, of course, but my sister does want me to bring her back to Tehran eventually."

"Well, Lord willing."

"You said it."

"Don't lose hope. Ahura-Mazda himself is the resolver of ills."

"Thanks."

Around ten in the evening we board the bus again and move on. This time the passengers are mostly silent, and soon almost everyone is asleep. The good Soheili arranges all kinds of cushions and blankets around and under himself. I like this: he pampers himself and is excellently organized, too.

"Bless you, Jenab Aryan, if you would be so kind as to hand me that cushion up there, a thousand apologies. I really have put you to immeasurable troubles tonight." He places the little silk cushion against the window, so that if his head rolls in his sleep, it should come to rest against something soft.

Outside, everything is dark; the coach moves on, groaning. Soheili is soon in the Seven Golden Slumbers. I cannot sleep. Although I have taken my medicine, I feel dizzy, my head aches as if things keep spinning round inside my skull. I look out. In the darkness the night seems silent, and the earth calm. But not within me. The silent night and the calm earth are out there. Or under little Soheili's little silk cushions. Or perhaps it has slipped and fallen out of the window. It is the kind of night when the passenger is the bus, and the bus is the night, and it is the night that moves. It is the Jalal Aryan night. A man, almost fifty, teetering this year between life and death. When he walks, he looks like the late Charlie Chaplin — in slow motion. His face is the cross section of a full-frontal view of something between the long-armed Shah Ardeshir and the inventor of carrot jelly. When he breathes, his chest sounds like an asthmatic pig. Apart from all this, he's healthy, handsome, and gorgeous.

At three in the morning, we arrive in Tabriz. Empty streets everywhere; cold, windy and drizzling. Abbas Agha pulls up in front of the local TBT bus terminal. A couple of new passengers board here. The Tehran passengers are mostly still asleep. Only Dr. Kiumarspur takes a child out to pee by the gutter. Tonight, her biology Ph.D. is worth nothing. Under the glow of the streetlight, her gold bangles and the arc of her son's urine make the same spectral array of colors.

At daybreak, we pass through the clean steppes of western Azerbaijan, and head toward the Bazargan border. It is freezing outside, and daylight grows slowly. The steppes and the hills are bare, but it is beautiful when the first wide rays of the sunlight appear. In the plains, single ghostlike trees stand out here and there. The hills are empty. From time to time, a bird soars, spreads its wings in the strong wind blowing from Russia, rocking like a small dinghy in a storm. It reminds me of Sorraya.

We arrive in Maku in the early morning hours. Abbas Agha stops again, and we refuel. Maku seems to have turned stiff with cold, looking shrunken and wan. Even its main street, with its low stone-front buildings, shops and houses carved into the mountain, seems more empty and diminished than ever. In this ungodly dawn hour, the people are lining up, with empty cans for kerosene, standing rigid in lines, or sitting sleepily, or dozing. There are other lines, at the baker's, at the grocer's, people waiting for bread, foodstuffs, or some other rationed items.

I swallow my morning ration of medicine with a glass of water brought for me by Abbas Agha's apprentice. After a while, Vahab Soheili — who is a fine sleeper — begins gradually to stir at my side. I am not in the mood to talk, but there is no stopping Soheili's lingual engine.

"Top of the morning to you, Jenab Aryan."

"Salaam."

"*Sabbah-Kum-Allah . . .*"[7]

"Knock it off, Agha Soheili!"

He laughs. "Any idea where we are?"

"Just past Maku."

"Then we can't be very far from the Bazargan border."

"We're supposed to be arriving there around seven-thirty, eight."

He looks at me. "Morning dose, going down the hatch there?"

"Morning dose, down the hatch," I answer.

"What are those long, orange pills? Aren't they Gaverine?"

"That's right, Gaverine Rx. Three a day."

"Dilutes the blood and regulates the body's salt. Yes, it's the best kind. My brother took the very same pills after his first heart attack. They kept him alive for years. You know something else, don't you, they must have told you. If you take these pills, then NO alcohol. Gaverine and alcohol don't mix. They're fatal enemies."

"Yes, they've told me," I say. And I remember, too, my promise to Farangis.

Then Soheili says, "Jenab Aryan, bless your little hand, would you be so gracious as to hand me down that little black bag up there?"

*   *   *

---

[7] Arabic greeting.

At about eight o'clock, we come into the Bazargan border installations. A dozen or so other passenger coaches and over a hundred trucks and cars have already parked in front of us.

The Bazargan transit building is a big, old single-story edifice, with only one narrow Dutch door now open, but controlled by Islamic revolutionary guards. Hundreds of travelers are crowded in front of it. There is no sign of the regular police force. Only a few boyish *hezbollahi* youths, quiet and polite, with G-3s and Uzi machine guns dangling from their shoulders, are assisting the passengers and attending to what has to be done. It is clear that one must wait for hours, perhaps even days, before getting through the rigamarole here.

The good Soheili is awake now — very much so. Like the other passengers, he has come out of the coach, but is silent and worried. He is busy gathering his pile of suitcases and packages together. Abbas Agha Marandi and his apprentice have just finished unloading all the baggage. Abbas Agha collects all our passports, and taking them, along with his own papers, somehow pushes his way through the mob and into the half-door. Orders are for all of us to carry our own baggage and belongings into the transit hall. A bearded, middle-aged man shouts out through the narrow doorway: if anyone has any extra currency, or gold, or any other valuable objects with them, they must be handed to the customs authorities and get a receipt. Otherwise, if anything is discovered, it will be confiscated, and the passengers turned back. The Iranian world travelers, who used to cruise abroad so elegantly in the years of the Shah's regime, with so much pleasure and in luxury, are now waiting, silently, like deaf mutes. Not a peep out of anyone. All they want is to get out, somehow, anyhow. It is an emergency situation. The men are no longer "gentlemen," they are "brothers." The women are no longer "ladies," they are "sisters." The people are in batches and groups. "Iran-Peima Bus Company passengers, come forward. Mihan-Tour passengers, get back there!" Dr. Kiumarspur, with her baby in her arms, stands next to me. The German-bound student has abandoned her, and gone off to care for his own. She looks worried and at a loss, probably because of her jewelry. Her baggage is scattered everywhere, in bits and pieces. She sighs. "Have you read that book by André Gide," she asks me, "*The Narrow Door*?" She's glancing at the guarded half-door.

"No, I haven't."

"He says, 'Try and enter through the narrow door.'"

I smile at her. "You don't have that much luggage. Brother Soheili is the one who's going to have to try awfully hard. . . ." I glance at Soheili behind me.

Soheili does not laugh. He simply shakes his head. However, he is looking cool and experienced.

"Gide doesn't mean baggage," Dr. Kiumarspur says, "he means resurrection."

"I see."

"One of my sisters was a university professor, she's now on the government blacklist: 'Exit Forbidden.' Another sister's in prison, we've had no news of her for months."

After two hours, it's our turn. We somehow squeeze past the mob swarming in front of the tiny door for no reason, save perhaps anxious haste to get into the transit hall. We spend a good deal of time passing on Soheili's numerous pieces of luggage hand-to-hand. At last, we all get in.

It is a large lobby, ending in a corridor leading to yet another hall. A gloomy hush suddenly reigns here. There are several lines. One for retrieving the passports. One for body search. Another for luggage search. Another for handing in valuable objects, and another for going out and into the transit hall on the Turkish side. I stand in the small passport line.

A boy with a scant fuzz of a mustache on his upper lip, and sensitive green eyes, is seated behind a very large table, with an Uzi machine gun on his lap.

"The reason for your trip abroad?" he asks.

I explain.

"Are you traveling alone?"

"Yes." In my hand, I have a signed copy of an official memo, on government-printed stationery with the letterhead of the Ministry of Petroleum, National Iranian Oil Company, the Islamic Republic of Iran. The Tehran Committee Caring for the Problems of the Employees of the War-Struck Territories, Abadan and Khunin-Shahr, instructed the deputy authorities of the passport office to render what emergency help the aforementioned (i.e., me) may need.[8] The deputy oil minister has acknowledged the note. I show it to the "brother."

---

[8]The southern city of Khorramshahr was so devastated by the Iraqi invasion that it came to be called Khunin-Shahr, or Bloody City.

"What was your position in the oil company?"

I tell him.

"Who did you say issued your exit permit?"

I mention the name of the deputy minister who signed my permit from the Oil Ministry.

"Why didn't the minister himself sign it?"

I inform him that the oil minister is being held a prisoner of war by the Iraqis.

He hands me back my stamped passport. "Go on, brother."

"That's all?" I ask.

"God be with you."

The lines for body search lead to two booths, one for the "brothers" and another for the "sisters." After that the passengers move on to the luggage-checking lines, stand by their things, and shove them gradually forward. In the body-search booth marked "Brothers" is a slightly built boy no more than seventeen or eighteen. Standing before me, he is almost like my child. Without looking at anything, he begins to feel the lining and shoulder seams of my jacket, crushing them in his hands, asking the same questions about the reason for my trip, my occupation, who I am traveling with, etc. He reminds me of Seyyed Matrud's retarded boy back in Abadan. Only this boy is plucky and alert. While he gives my shoe a through inspection, tapping the heel, he asks, "How are you? Well?"

"Oh, not bad." He himself seems tired and dry. "How are you doing, yourself?"

He does not answer me, he just lowers his head.

"You do a thorough job," I say. "But I noticed one point."

He does not pay much attention, just glances at me dubiously. "What point?"

"It's not that I mean to criticize the brothers' work, or anything. But I've noticed that people who come out of the body-search booths go straight to their baggage. They could take something out of their cases and put it in their pockets. Don't you think it would be better to do the body search after?"

"We're terribly crowded," he says, scratching his head. "We're making some changes here . . . going to have a new corridor built. . . ."

He does not search the other shoe. "Off you go."

"That's all?"

"God's hand be with you."

I thank him and come out. Soheili is next in line. His face is the color of dried mustard. I could guess why. Even his mustache seems to have suddenly grown grayer and is standing on end.

"Do they search thoroughly?" he asks.

"Thoroughly as you could wish," I assure him.

He gives up his place, leaving the line, and heads back toward his luggage. He changes his coat and shoes. (In Istanbul, he tells me he had 38,000 pounds worth of travelers checks and thousand-dollar bills sewn into the lining of his coat and shoes.) I join the luggage-search line, and because my lone suitcase is skimpy, and the money I am carrying is within the legal limit, I get through more quickly than most. I enter the transit hall. Dr. Kiumarspur is arguing with the Hezbollah brothers at the customs desk, for they have taken all her gold and jewelry and given her a receipt. She is fuming, all in vain.

In the main transit lobby a large, U-shaped counter turns across the hall. The door on this side of the counter opens to Iran, the one on the other side, to quote Abbas Agha Marandi's Azerbaijani accent, to "Turchish" soil.

I do not see Soheili anywhere until noon, when finally he enters the Turkish transit hall through a side door. Not only is he now back to his normal color — he is positively glowing. Obviously, he has sneaked through whatever it was he had with him. This, however, is only the beginning of our trouble with the Turkish officials, who seem to enjoy their own signs of order or discipline. For a start, they have kept everyone waiting, saying the inspector in charge has gone to make a phone call. Also, there is no electricity, because of a power cut. (Iran supplies the electrical power for both halves of the border and customs facilities.) Of course, the Turks blame this on Iran, saying Iran's juice is gone, and find this very ludicrous. They talk and joke about it in Turkish, laughing merrily. Next, when the official inspector arrives on the scene, the first thing he says, and is translated for us, is that everyone should have had cholera vaccinations on the other side of the border.

The Iranian passengers, who have just been through the twelve tasks of Hercules with the Islamic Republic officials, raise their voices in shouts of protest, demanding to know why no one had told them about this cholera business beforehand. The Turkish inspector is unmoved. Passports *must* have cholera vaccination stamps. The only exceptions are those with International Vaccination Booklets. This is a recent order. Harsh discussions follow, but the Turkish inspector remains adamant. He has the passports in his hand, and he waves them in the air, saying they must go back and be stamped with cholera inoculation stamps, or else. My passport is there, too.

"I'm not going back!" Dr. Kiumarspur declares.

"Wild horses wouldn't drag *me* back," Soheili says. "They should have told us this before." Then he booms in English at the Turkish official, "You should have notified us on the other side! You should have declared. . . ." I had not heard this voice of his on the other side of the border.

"How doltish this lot is," Dr. Kiumarspur says. "They're even worse than us!"

"It's not right. It's not fair!" Soheili cries. Everyone joins him, throwing in some insult. But it is no use arguing with the Turkish official.

I step forward, take the passports, and having commissioned Soheili to keep an eye on my little suitcase, I head back toward the Iranian side of the border. Asking as I go, I manage to locate a little booth at the far end of the corridor, where I find the Iranian quarantine officer, sitting in the dark, smoking. I explain the problem to him. Even before I open my mouth, he seems to understand. This, apparently, is nothing new. He takes the passports — there are fifteen or sixteen of them — opens them all to the next-to-the-last page, and lays them in a pile. Then he begins stamping them in rapid succession. He is a plump, sick-looking man of forty or so, and in the dark little room, he seems even more unreal than his actions.

"These passports," he mumbles, "will never contract cholera!'

"They probably won't," I agree.

"Here you go." He hands me the batch.

"Thanks, Doctor!"

"Ha! Bon voyage!"

When I emerge once more into the light of the transit hall and distribute the passports among their owners, it turns out that they have all been stamped upside-down! This does not matter, however, and everyone laughs, because now a new dilemma has come about. It is twelve-thirty, and the Turks have closed up their side of the lobby, and will not reopen till two-thirty. The officials have all gone out to lunch. The doors at the end of the hall are closed — padlocked and chained.

So, we just wait another two hours doing nothing, behind the locked doors of the Turkish transit lobby. Most of our passengers are gathered behind the chained doors. A few are spread out on the ground, busy eating. Some offer fruit and nuts to one another. One group sits on the counter, filling out forms. Dr. Kiumarspur's baby is asleep in the arms of the student, who is sitting cross-legged on the floor. The woman herself, her eyes red from crying, is also sitting on the floor, exchanging Turkish lire, German marks, and French francs with another student. I sit next to Soheili, beside his mountainous pile of luggage, and light up the last of my old Oshnu cigarettes. I do not ask how he managed to get all that luggage through, or, if he had any money with him, how he got that through. Being well traveled, and having spent a lifetime working for the national airlines, in close contact with customs officers, and having been the director of numerous excursion tours, has obviously had its effect.

"Do sit down, Jenab Aryan," he says. "Be patient."

"Yes."

"At this moment, we are actually nowhere. Neither in Turkey, nor in Iran." He says this with delight.

"Congratulations," I say.

"People without a country . . ."

"Dear Agha Soheili, we are in the Bazargan border transit hall," I declare. "Between Iran and Turkey."

"No. Neither here . . . nor there. People without a country, in this mad world. We're all dangling . . . in nowhere, I swear."

"For the love of God, Jenab Soheili — don't get philosophical!"

"No, I implore you, it's true! This is our situation, exactly. The whole country, the whole world, is in a sorry, confused state."

"In two hours, the Turkish officials will come back and open the doors. Then your excellency can walk to freedom and be on your way to Karachi and then Washington, D.C. In a week's time, all this will be just a memory for you. You will joke about it at cocktail parties."

"They're opening up in *two* hours?"

"Apparently."

"What do they eat that takes two hours?"

"Dolmas!"

Soheili laughs. Taking another cigarette from his pack of Winstons, he lights it with a gold lighter, which he was hiding up to now, I have no idea where. Then he offers me a cigarette, too. I tell him I just finished one.

"When we arrive in Istanbul, I must send a cable to my son in London," he says. "Tell him to send me a money order, that sort of thing — I have none, at the moment. I'm indebted to you, too, Jenab Aryan. I also need something for the expenses of my journey to Pakistan."

"I was under the impression that you had dollars and pounds left."

"Oh, in the bank, yes!"

"I see."

"I shall tell my son in London to send a money order immediately."

I do not know whether he is saying all this really for me to hear or for others.

"I thought you said your son was in L.A."

"That's my *own* son, this one's my wife's son from her first marriage."

"I see."

"Believe me, Jenab Aryan — he's more sincere and more faithful and more loyal than my own son. He's a petroleum engineer. Worked in London for OPEC. Now he's working for Saudi Arabia."

"Who's the one in Virginia, then? I thought you said *he* was your wife's son from her first marriage."

"Oh, no. That's Robert, my son-in-law. He's American, he married my daughter in Tehran. She's an IBM computer technician."

"Oh, her name's Virginia?"

"No, her name's Firuzeh. Robert's working with his brother-in-law now, that's my own son from my first wife."

"I'll have that cigarette now, if you don't mind."

He laughs, extending the pack toward me, "Have I given you a headache with all my talking?"

"No, but my stomach's rumbling like crazy."

"I do happen to have some *gaz* and some pistachios at the bottom of one of these cases, somewhere. Allow me . . . I'll be most happy to, eh, open them up and . . ."

"No, no, please! We'll be out soon, we should be able to get a bite to eat somewhere"

It's almost four o'clock when the last of our passengers leaves the transit hall on the Turkish side. I expect now everyone to be as tired and hungry as me, but suddenly the entire busload is restored, lively and jovial. The luggage has been reloaded, tied up, the coach is ready. In the rearview mirror, I see Abbas Agha Marandi's beaming face as he releases the handbrake. He wastes no time with *Salavat*. He speaks only to say there's a big restaurant two or three kilometers up the road, which has food *"and everything!"* and almost all the passengers applaud loudly. They know he means booze.

At dusk, having eaten, rested and refreshed, we resume the journey, moving on through Turkey. It is cold again, and the sun sets rapidly, dying away into the horizon. I do not feel we are in another country; the noises and clatter in the coach are exactly the same as before, and the passengers are the same passengers. The steps and the hills are still naked, and the landscape seems to be the continuation of the hills and valleys on the other side of the border. The same birds seem to shudder in the heavy wind.

Soheili is now very much livelier and jauntier. He has taken out a piece of paper and is counting up the expenses he and I have shared, and for which I have paid; supper, lunch, and other expenses, all of which he adds up. He writes in English, neat figures, in fine handwriting. He then divides the total by two, and takes out an amount of Turkish lire from his wallet, handing it to me. I do not want to take any money from him, but he insists, saying all must be made fair and square. When I put the lires in my wallet, he asks, "Whose photo is that? Your sister's?"

He's a born snoop!

"No, it's Sorraya."

"Oh. She's very lovely I hope to God she'll get well, soon."

"I hope so."

"Who's paying for her hospital expenses? Does she have insurance?"

"Honestly, I don't know. I'll have to look into that when I get there. Apparently, the students are insured for as long as they're at the university, but Sorraya finished her studies three months ago. She was waiting to fly back when the war broke out and airports were closed. And then this came up."

"What will you do if she's not insured?"

"Pay right out of the old pocket."

"Do you have money, there?"

"No. Nor does my sister. We'll have to work something out."

"It's not easy now, sending money."

"I guess not."

He remains silent for a short while, then: "I expect your sister wanted very much to come along on this trip herself."

"She couldn't."

"They didn't give permission? Why? Didn't you have a hospital certificate?"

By God, he is nosy.

"Yes, but they only allow one person to go."

"Why didn't your sister go herself? I don't mean to be inquisitive."

"My sister has sciatica, she's partially bedridden."

"Did you say her husband's passed away?"

"Yes, he was a doctor in the oil company. He had a stroke and died."

"Goodness me. The world is a road to pass, Jenab Aryan."

"So it is."

The student bound for Germany passes round some baklava, giving me a reprieve from Soheili's tireless questioning. We spend the night in Erzurum sleeping in the tiny Heylun Hotel, with no shortage of night noise and bugs. Soheili and I take a twin-bed room, in which the radiator pipes sound like the entire Ottoman cavalry charging through. The establishment is a four- or five-story building, with narrow wooden staircases and wide, shapeless rooms. Whenever someone passes through the corridor or up and down the stairway, the building reverberates like the Great Armenian Massacre, but I take my pills and I think I sleep some five hours.

The next morning, after a small breakfast, we start out. The students going to Germany, Dr. Kiumarspur, who was heading for Paris, and several other passengers have left us to catch their planes.

All that day we travel through the Turkish mainland, spending the second night in Ankara, in a hotel not much better than the Erzurum

Heylun. The third day we still travel on. Everywhere the land is very much like Iran — bad roads and bare trees. The small towns and villages are beautiful but trampled in mud and poverty.

The steppes are empty, the vast orchards weather-beaten. Army trucks, soldiers in full battle gear, fill the roads; they stop the coach every few kilometers and make a complete inspection. Everything from their helmets down to their boots and their strange weaponry is American-made. Sometimes, near larger cities, the coach's progress is slowed down because the trucks and tanks obstruct the traffic, the long barrels of their guns jutting out, covered with tarpaulin in the rain.

It's a long, very tiring bus journey from Tehran to Istanbul, but every few hours, whenever it suits Abbas Agha Marandi's fancy, he makes us stop and gives us a rest. He is a free and jolly spirit and I like him more and more. I wish I knew what he had left behind him in Tehran, what sort of a life he led, and I wish I could make him my guest sometime, buy him a bottle of something, somewhere. "One night at home and a hundred on the road forward — Fatherless Benz, to where doth thou lead me on?"

But within three days he gets us all the way from Tehran, tired and travel-weary, to the furthermost tip of Asian Turkey, and across the Bosphorus to the European side of Istanbul.

It is just after nightfall when we get off the coach at the Istanbul TBT bus terminal, in a busy section of the city, surrounded by hotels of all sizes. One by one, the passengers fade away into the misty Istanbul night. Soheili and I, still in the spirit of the journey, come to a small hotel near the terminal where the owners are pleasant, friendly, and humorous, like most Turks. When they learn we are Iranian, coming all the way from the Islamic Republic at war, they treat us with kindness and sympathy, giving us a "good" room with two "nice" beds.

The room is, in fact, a little larger than a telephone kiosk. After a brisk shower, however, the only thing I care about is a good, long sleep.

— Translated by the author

Simin Daneshvar

Considered to be Iran's first female prose writer, Simin Daneshvar was born in Shiraz in 1921. She moved with her family to Tehran, where after the death of her father she worked for Radio Tehran and the newspaper *Iran* to support her family. Daneshvar received her doctorate in Persian literature from Tehran University. In 1948, she published *Extinguished Fire*, inspired by the works of O. Henry, the first short story collection by a woman writer in Iran.

Daneshvar spent two years (1952–1954) as a Fulbright scholar studying with Wallace Stegner at Stanford University. Upon her return to Iran she became a professor of art history at Tehran University. In 1961 she published another collection of short stories, *A City Like Heaven*, and her novel *Savushun* — the first novel ever written by a woman in Iran — in 1969. Told from the viewpoint of a woman, *Savushun* is about the effects of the Allied occupation in World War II on Shiraz and surrounding areas. Many of the major themes of modern Iranian history and society — foreign occupation, the situation of women, tribal politics, and the condition of peasants — are touched upon in this important novel, which has been translated into English in two versions: *Savushun,* translated by M. R. Ghanoonparvar (Mage Publishers, 1990), and *A Persian Requiem,* translated by Roxane Zand (George Braziller, 1992).

Daneshvar continued to write after the 1979 revolution. Her collection, *Whom Should I Greet?* was published in 1980. She then began work on a trilogy, the first two books of which were *Island of Bewilderment* and *The Dazed Camel Driver,* both novels about the revolution and how the lives of various social groups, including intellectuals, were affected by it. She is currently at work on the last volume of the trilogy, *The Mountain of Bewilderment.* She is also an accomplished translator of English, including works by Chekhov, Shaw, Hawthorne, Schnitzler, and Saroyan. Daneshvar was married to Jalal Al-Ahmad, the famous Iranian social critic and writer. She lives in Tehran.

Her short story here deals with the life and death of a young girl in Islamic Iran. It was first published in a collection by the same name, *Ask the Migrating Birds,* in 1997.

ASK THE MIGRATING BIRDS

I was dreaming that my mother had a dream about me, and I was present in it myself, playing out the events in her dream in person. True, it defies all logic, but should we weigh all things in life on the scale of logic? My mother could see the hand brandishing the scissors approach my head. Shorn hair littered the floor. My file was tucked under my arm.

As I was going up the stairs, the head teacher shouted out, "Hey, you! Pull up your head scarf!"

"Ma'am," I replied, "there aren't any men in our school. Even the janitor is a woman. The doorway's screened by a heavy curtain, and the door's closed, too . . ."

"You little slut of an orphan!" the head teacher thundered. "Do as you're told!"

"I'm not an orphan, I've got a mother," I countered. "What's more, I've got a dear brother who's just back from the war front and has his handgun on the mantelpiece!"

"You wait till I show you —" she menaced.

The geometry teacher was telling us in class, "Two parallel lines will never converge unless God wills it."

"God is 'plus infinity,' and two parallel lines can converge in distant infinity," I said.

"Bravo!" said the geometry teacher.

"The roundness of the earth helps too," I added. I wrote down the formula for it: God is equal to plus infinity ($+ \infty$), and the devil is minus infinity ($- \infty$). The geometry teacher came up to the blackboard. She sighed, and wrote:

"There is only One who embodies Unity and merges with it." She then asked, "What is a number?"

"Sentences made up of 'ones' that are bound together." I added, "God is that 'Only One' who stands alone. More alone than anyone or anything else."

One of my classmates quipped, "Satan could be God's only soul mate."

"Absolutely not," replied the geometry teacher, "unless, just for your sake, we change the formula in the following way: God equals plus minus infinity. In that case we *should* recite Nasser Khosrow: 'If you were not plagued by a pebble in your shoe, why did you have to create the Devil?'"[1]

Before long the bell rang. Why had the head teacher rung the bell before class was up? After all, she knew that we would only remain glued to our seats, listening with heart and soul to the geometry teacher.

I don't know whether in her dreams my mother went over the image of my mind, which was spinning like a top. I knew myself why I had suddenly been so reminded of God and Satan. But my mother hadn't been with me in the geometry teacher's class, had she? I was thinking, what did God think about before the Creation? I was asking myself: Can Satan really be God's only soul mate? So why did He create the Archangels, then? The proverbial Archangels who came 'knocking at the alehouse door'? I heard the knocking myself. I saw the two parallel lines converge together in distant infinity. I, who had had only paper flowers grow in the garden of my life. Did other flowers grow and I didn't notice? Proud trees, uncaring tarmac. Bright green vegetables and red button radishes in the shop opposite our home; bougainvillea or oleander flowers — were the oleander meant to poison and petrify the head teacher?[2] My corpse on the street tarmac, white sheets flapping on the neighbors' rooftops, the screech of the siren, migrating birds in the sky — were they all just waiting around to appear in my mother's dream?

On the rooftop, I could see birds following their leader as they migrated. The leader fell. Perhaps it had been shot, or maybe it was exhausted, or both. I heard the gunshot. I had placed my brother's

---

[1] This is a line from a famous poem by Nasser Khosrow, a poet and writer of the fifth century, addressing God and raising the question of the source of evil. To have a pebble in one's shoe is akin to having something up one's sleeve in English.

[2] Here the writer presents a clever play on words with the Persian names of bougainvillea and oleander flowers. Bougainvillea is literally called *gol-kaghazi* or "paper flower" in Persian, alluding to the fact that the flowers look like brightly colored paper. In the text, the writer uses deliberate ambiguity when employing the terms *gol kaghazi,* meaning the actual flower bougainvillea, and *gol-e kaghazi,* "paper flower," as an image of the innocent, unfulfilled life of a young girl. Oleander is *khar-zahreh* or "donkey poison" in Persian. In fact, oleander is a poisonous plant that can kill any animal that ingests it. Here the writer uses the image of the flower to invoke its poisonous attribute, to suggest a state of shock from fright (*zahreh tarak*) for the sadistic head teacher.

handgun behind my neck. I was gripping the handle so hard that after the shot, my brother couldn't manage to pry it out of my hand, no matter how hard he tried. He was sobbing. "Why am I bothering my darling sister? A burial is painful, with or without this handgun."

The migrating birds were chirping. They zigzagged, and sometimes formed a circle. It was as if they were trying to choose a leader. I rose from my corpse and took flight until I reached them. They chose me. They selected a fellow traveler for me, too, and resumed their triangular flight formation. Where were we flying to? Perhaps we were flying toward infinity, or heading to the nowhereland. But I remember we first passed over the greengrocer's vegetables. The greengrocer was sprinkling water over the vegetables and button radishes.

We were lining up to go to classes after prayers. The head teacher grabbed my arm and pulled me out of line. The two of us stood in front of the others. The head teacher removed my head scarf. First she chopped off the middle part of my hair with a pair of scissors. Angrily, just like that. My head probably looked like the African continent, or like the shape of our own country. The shorn parts were the deserts.

"Jeer at this stubborn girl!" she ordered the children.

Not a sound escaped a soul. I could hear some of my classmates mumbling.

"Get your scarf back on, you worthless wretch!" the head teacher said. I didn't do it, so she did it for me. But she knotted the scarf so tightly under my chin that I nearly gagged. She took me to the school office. The principal was breast-feeding her baby. She didn't look up. Her gaze was fixed on the baby's earlobe. An earlobe that looked like a freshly unfurled spring bud.

The head teacher asked the registrar for my file.

"Has she got herself into trouble?" the registrar asked.

"I have run out of ideas what to do with all of them!" replied the head teacher. "The principal has turned this school into a second home for herself. She even does her washing up at school. She has her breakfast at school. And she has the janitor do her grocery shopping."

Searching for my file, the registrar asked, "You still haven't said what offence this girl is guilty of?"

"Disobedience. Blasphemy, too. The geometry teacher doesn't bother to lead them on the path of righteousness. I heard it with my own ears — she read out to them that there are pebbles in God's shoe, and then this girl said Satan is God's friend. I've already reported it. The theology teacher, too. I'll take care of her as well."

"But this girl is in her last year," said the registrar. She added a few words about my cleverness and my good grades, and about the final exams, but by then the head teacher was swearing that she would take care of her, too.

The head teacher thrust my file under my arm and said, "You are expelled. As a lesson to the others here. Have your mother and father come to the school tomorrow to see me."

"But I already told you I have no father." Then I asked, "So you spy on us behind classroom doors, and what's more you overhear incorrectly and report incorrectly on us. I never said Satan is God's friend. The geometry teacher and the theology teacher didn't blaspheme, either."

"Shut up!" she shouted. She picked up a ruler from the office desk and went at my head, face, and shoulders with it. I kicked her anklebone with the tip of my shoe. She nearly passed out on one of the chairs. The registrar handed her a glass of water and quietly told me, "Off with you, now. She has a problem that goes back thousands of years."

I hadn't blasphemed. I just didn't know that the solitary fast on the third day was a compulsory one.[3] I didn't even know it was possible to be secluded on the third day. If I had known it, I would have cloistered myself in the paper-flower garden of my mind and would have let weariness befriend me instead of Satan. I even told the theology teacher so. The theology teacher laughed and said, "Child, where on earth did you learn such big words?"

I abandoned the migrating birds. I told them to fly ahead in a straight line, that I would catch up with them soon. The birds said, "We will never fly without you." I said to them, "Go with my fellow traveler instead." They said, "We will rest by the spring and take water. This, too, is a kind of fountain of life." My fellow traveler said, "You as well thirst after this fountain of life."

I asked all of them, "Can you wait for forty years?"

"We can wait a thousand years for you to come," they answered.

"Forty years is only the shortest of waits for God," I said.

---

[3] These are the details of religious practice regarding compulsory fasting.

The classroom window was open. I went in. My classmates looked up at the ceiling. The theology teacher cut short what she was saying and stared ahead. I don't think they saw me. No, they hadn't seen me. They had placed a pot of bougainvillea flowers on my empty seat. I perched on my classmates' head and said, "You are the Queen of Sheba and a stork will transport you to Solomon."

They didn't hear my voice, either, but both the theology teacher and my companions seemed to be listening to a message they didn't understand or know from where it came. Suddenly the head teacher opened the door and walked in. The children booed her.

"Why do you blame me for what happened?" she said.

"You can't fill up the ditch you've just dug," said the theology teacher. "But if you're determined to dig graves, at least go for a proper plot for yourself instead of standing in the ruins." She picked up her notebook and bag as she was leaving the classroom, and said, "Good-bye, children. There's no place for me in this high school anymore."

And now I was sitting on the rooftop by the drainpipe, waiting for water. The neighbors' white sheets were flapping in the wind. The sky was so pristine it was as if angels had licked it clean. Or maybe it was as pure as a freshly bathed person, someone who had just done their ablutions . . . the sun had grown so large the whole horizon gleamed. A cool breeze was stroking my wings. The earth beneath us was bright. Perhaps the earth was festive or celebrating something. The fields were lush and green. As green as the greengrocer's greens in front of our house. The bougainvillea flowers had opened up and their perky bright blooms reminded me of red button radishes. But I couldn't figure out why I was craving peaches or figs. It was possible to swoop down to a fig tree and peck at the figs. But none of us had warped beaks. I could hear my mother's voice saying that no one gave anything out for free, not even figs.

In the early evening the stars came out. I recognized my own star. It burned out and fell, and we found ourselves flying over a graveyard.

My mother was asking my brother in her nightmare:

"What do you wish for? I'm prepared to give up my life to get you whatever your heart desires."

"I only want my sister."

My mother sprinkled rosewater on the tombstone. My mother's tears, and those of my brother, mingled with the rosewater. I could hear their wailing, and I kept shouting:

"Don't go! Don't leave me by myself!"

But I knew there could be no reply to my shouting. I knew that we migrating birds would continue to fly toward infinity, with moon-beams penetrating our wings to touch the feathers of our bosom.

— Translated by Roxane Zand

Hadi Khorsandi

This is what Hadi Khorsandi wrote when asked for a biography:

When I was born I was two years old. In those days due to high death rates and high birth rates, it was customary to keep the identity card of a dead child for the next child to be born. So if I say I am 60 years old, you may be confused. Am I really 58 or 62?

I was born in Khorassan, near the city of Mashad, in the town of Fariman beside the famous Fariman sugar factory. My father worked at the factory, and my mother said that when I was two, I fell into the factory pool. I am not sure if I was 4 years old at that time or if I was just born. In any case, I know it was me who fell into the pool and not my brother because, according to my mother's account, the child who fell in the pool was rescued from drowning. It had to be me.

I received my elementary education in Iran. I received my secondary education in Iran. (I say them separately to make my educational résumé appear longer.) I was uninterested in literature as a child, but I liked religious and Quran studies. Now, I don't know why, the situation is quite the reverse.

I began my profession as a satirist when I was 18 years old and have continued until today. That is why I still can't make my mortgage payments.

Khorsandi has been the editor and writer of the satirical journal *Asghar Agha* since 1979. His other publications include *The Ayatollah and I,* published in English by Readers International in 1984, *The Iranian Verses,* and *The Essays of Sadegh Sedaghat.* He was the recipient of the Hellman-Hammett Award in 1995, which was established in 1990 by the executor of the estates of Lillian Hellman and Dashiell Hammett to help "writers all around the world who have been victims of political persecution and are in financial need."

THE EYES WON'T TAKE IT

It happened five years ago. A smuggler led us to New Zealand, saying it was the only possible destination left. We said it would be all right if it were near Sweden, as we had relatives there. The smuggler replied that New Zealand was a bit farther away, but it was the only country that admitted refugees. We gave our consent. He first took us to another country, possibly the Philippines, and from there he led us to New Zealand. Before we boarded the plane, he collected the remainder of our cash, telling us that having cash with us would cause problems. His other piece of advice was that we should tear up our passports and flush the bits and pieces down the lavatory. There were four of us. He strongly urged all four of us to get rid of our passports.

On board the plane, my companions went to the toilet one by one and tore up their passports. But for me, my passport was too near and dear to get rid of. I had protected it everywhere as part of my body; how could I get rid of it just because the stupid smuggler told me to?

I resisted. We were approaching New Zealand when my companions told me once again to get up and tear up my passport. One of them quarreled with me, saying that I was ruining not only my own chances of being granted asylum but theirs, too. He told me that if we did not comply, our Iranian nationality would be discovered and we would all be returned home.

I went to the toilet. I was very upset. How could a sane man tear up his own passport? How could he destroy the proof of his identity, his nationality, and his trustworthiness? But on the other hand, our aim was not to be identified. I took the passport out of my pocket. Good-bye, my passport! I tore it up into smaller and smaller pieces. I was not kind to it. I was even cruel, as if confronting an enemy, as if wanting to tell my companions: "Here you are. Are you satisfied now or shall I tear it up into even smaller pieces?"

The cover was hard. My friends had given me a small razor blade for the purpose of cutting it up. I did so. I cut it up into smaller and smaller and yet smaller pieces, as if I was doing something very important.

The toilet bowl was full of the bits and pieces of my unfortunate passport, but my hand would not move toward the handle. No, it was not easy. I was looking at the bits and pieces of my identity, my respectability. My hand felt as if it was about to pull a trigger and send a bullet through my head. I put all my strength into my eyelids and closed my eyes. Next, I grabbed the handle and flushed the toilet. The sound of rushing water made me feel that all my belongings were being flooded away. My eyes closed, but I could not visualize how the bits and pieces whirled around the bowl and went down.

When I opened my eyes, a few bits and pieces were still there. I flushed the toilet again — with cruelty, with violence. The water and, with it, the remaining bits of my passport whirled and whirled . . . and so did my head. Water was breaking up their resistance and taking them with it.

I was about to leave the toilet when I felt someone was calling me from inside the bowl. Was I imagining things? I had a look. A pair of eyes was gazing at me. I felt that these eyes were calling me. They were my own. They were the eyes of my passport photograph that had not been torn up properly. Although they were tiny, they looked huge to me. They were talking to me: "Is this your affection and your loyalty? You are just leaving us here to go away without us?" I was frightened. Then I felt ashamed. Then I was frightened again. Then I felt ashamed again.

The eyes moved around on the water of the toilet bowl but would not go down. They were gazing at me. They were talking to me. They were saying: "You just dump us down the drain? Great! Go ahead, leave us! And good luck! You've shown how much you care. Go on, you save your own skin and flush us away!"

I was really frightened. I was panicking. The eyes were getting bigger and bigger. They looked as big as my own. I was holding some toilet paper. I formed it into a ball and threw it at the gazing eyes. I felt a pain in my own eyes. I heard somebody or something saying: "If you had a revolver, I suppose you would shoot at me!"

I flushed the toilet again, this time as hard as I could. The water whirled around and around. It took away the compressed toilet paper but not the eyes. Water moved them upward and they were stuck on the metallic surface of the bowl. Damn! What was I to do? I looked at them. They looked sad. They were begging me not to leave them alone.

Water was dripping from them in such a way that they appeared to be weeping. I sobbed. I had tears in my eyes. In addition to tears, there was a flow of sweat from my forehead and into my eyes, which prevented me from seeing clearly. I was about to bolt out of the toilet when they called me again: "Where are you going, you coward?"

I was horrified. I took out my ballpoint pen and with the tip of the pen moved the remaining bit of the photograph, making it fall into the water. I flushed the toilet again. With a lucky strike, the little piece was now upside down, so the eyes could no longer see me. I thanked God. It is good to be a believer. I felt relieved. There were no longer any eyes. There was just the whiteness of the back of a bit of an old photograph. Whatever it was, it whirled around and kept going down — like a man in a whirlpool. Two pairs of eyes were no longer gazing at each other. But I could still hear the moaning of the other pair. It was refusing to go. It was screaming. It was swearing at me. It was trying to stick to the bowl's surface.

But it was taken away.

To make absolutely sure, I flushed the toilet once more and stepped out triumphantly.

— Translated by Lotfali Khonji

Nassim Khaksar

Nassim Khaksar was born on January 1, 1944, in the southern city of Abadan. Upon receiving his teaching certification from colleges in Esfahan and Hamadan, he taught in villages in the Abadan and Boir Ahmad region of southern Iran until his arrest for political activity in 1968.

Khaksar began writing fiction in 1966. He writes short stories, novels, plays, poetry, criticism, and travel literature. Two collections of his short stories, *The Grocer of Kharzeville* and *Between Two Doors,* have been published, as well as his novel *Windmills and Lashes.* He has also published a collection of plays, *Under the Roof,* and an account of his travels to Tajikistan. A number of his stories and plays have been translated into German, English, French, and Dutch.

Obliged to leave Iran after the revolution, Nassim Khaksar currently lives in Holland. Since he began his life in exile, his has been an articulate voice for the experiences of millions of Iranians who had to adjust to life in unfamiliar lands. He has been particularly adept at demonstrating the feelings of disassociation, loss of language, and the inability to express oneself and one's feelings that accompany the experience of exile.

"The Grocer of Kharzeville" was published in a collection of the same name. The fragmented sequence of the narrative, its disunity as exemplified by patches of thoughts and memories woven into reality, its fixation on language, all reflect common traits in the literature of exile, in effect mirroring this painful experience.

THE GROCER FROM KHARZEVILLE

The old couple's bedroom was right next door to mine on the second floor. But they spent most of their time on the first floor, where they would watch TV until the last show and then come upstairs. I had been renting the upstairs room from them for about four months. They were easy to get along with, and the old man knew a little Persian. I had found the room through the college in town that offered courses in Middle Eastern languages — Turkish, Arabic, and Persian. People who had studied there for at least two years could rent out a room to foreign students from Turkey, Iran, and the Arab countries; by doing so they could get a little practice in speaking these languages. Of course, the old man was past the age when he actually wanted to practice speaking Persian. All the same, he didn't mind the chance to remember the few words that he'd learned from Saadi's *Golestan*.[1]

In the beginning, about once every two weeks, they'd call me and I'd go downstairs to join them when there was a good show on TV. Then I'd chat a bit with the old man as we watched the program. And sometimes I'd play a few games of chess with him.

One time we were playing and I was winning every game. Even though he was desperately trying to win, the old man kept losing. He just didn't have any skill at it. After I had won another three games, I realized he was getting pretty upset. When we started the fourth game, I decided to let him win no matter what. I can't remember now, but I think he played so poorly that he didn't give me a chance to lose — after all, I had to play so that the old man would really believe I had lost.

I do remember, though, that by the fifth game I started getting really annoyed and irritable. The old man was acting cocky, and he

---

[1] Saadi Shirazi (ca. 1213–1293) was one of Iran's greatest classical poets. One of his two principal works, *The Golestan* (The Rose Garden), published in 1258 and translated to English in the eighteenth century, was one of the texts commonly memorized by students of Persian literature and in Persian language classes.

kept bragging about the glories of European democracy. Maybe it was my imagination, but in all honesty it seemed he was going too far. I remember in the middle of all his chatter he also started boasting that in his youth he had been an expert chess player. In fact, the best, a master of all the moves.

It was hard challenging him on European democracy. My English wasn't good enough, then, and I had this habit of using Persian slang phrases that, when I was forced to translate, came out sounding ridiculous and comical! And the old man would always insist, no matter what, that I explain exactly what I had just blurted out. I couldn't help it, I took my revenge in the chess game: since he was on his high horse, I checkmated him. He was so startled his glasses flew off his nose and his fat face turned beet red.

After that, the old man didn't invite me to watch TV for a while. The old woman also turned a little cold toward me. And, you know how it is in this country: unless neighbors (even close ones) have got specific business, they don't see one another sometimes for months at a time. The old man and woman were true-blue Dutch: once they withdrew you couldn't even get them to look at you! For one whole month they boycotted me; the only times I saw them were when I bumped into them twice on the stairs.

They would wake up late, and on days when the old man didn't work they would walk in the nearby forest for a few hours. And when they were home, they would sit in the living room and draw the curtains. One Sunday evening I was overwhelmed with loneliness. I had spent the whole week in the house. I couldn't even take my lonely walks because of the cold, the snow, and the storms. All week I sat staring out the window. The snow had covered everything. My new knee-high boots — the ones I was so surprised were so cheap — failed on me the very first time I wore them out in the snow. Water leaked in from every possible seam. The boots got so waterlogged that after even a short walk, it was as if I wasn't wearing anything! Anyway, it didn't matter. Even if I had the best boots in the world, where could I have gone with all that rain and snow? Waking up very early in the morning, I would light up a cigarette on an empty stomach and tune in to the BBC News. When the news was over, I'd sit by the window and think.

The world of an exile is a strange one. At first you think it's just you and your backpack — your four shirts, two pairs of socks, a suit, two pieces of underclothes, a towel, and an electric shaver. Then for a while it's all about finding a place to live: you get a small room, a desk, a lamp, and a notebook, then a few books — half in English, half in your native language. Little by little it starts. You see yourself, and realize that you have a whole history you've left behind. You begin to remember, one memory after another. And suddenly it dawns on you that the being that sits here is really an empty space whose whole existence is floating around somewhere else. Stunned, you find yourself gazing at both people and things.

You see everything but at the same time you see nothing. The pain penetrates to your bones; you feel you're cursed. Damn it, remembering the past has no boundaries — any phrase, any word, triggers yet another memory. Nothing you do brings any relief. At first, a shot of booze eases the pain, but after a week or so you start to dislike the liquor and beer. A long endless road looms ahead.

Maybe it was all of this — and fear — that kept me imprisoned in my room for a week. It's strange that I didn't get sick — develop an ulcer or a nervous disorder. I used to think, during one of those nights, that my heart would just stop beating of its own volition. I even went so far as to leave my door open, so that the old man and the old woman would find me quickly before my body started decomposing and smelling to high heaven. But nothing happened. Each morning I would wake up fine, healthy, and in one piece. During those few months, I didn't even catch a cold and I eventually stopped thinking about death.

Finally one day the old man spoke. "How are you?" he said.

And without hesitation I blurted out, "*Gooze peecham!*"[2]

He laughed and repeated it with difficulty, "*Gooze peecham?* What does that mean?"

I was stuck. How could I translate this? Secretly, I cursed all the Middle Eastern language professors. If they would only teach a few pages from Hedayat's *Alaviyeh Khanum* instead of two or three hundred pages of Saadi's *Golestan,* the task before me would be so much easier![3]

---

[2] *"Gooze peecham,"* translated literally, means "I am wrapped up, or twisted, in farts."
[3] Sadegh Hedayat (1903–1951), a major modern Iranian writer, is famous for his use of colloquial language in his novels and short stories. His short novel, *Alaviyeh Khanum,* was written in 1933 and is full of episodes of juicy colloquial cursing.

I decided to demonstrate. I pulled a tissue from my pocket and sat on it. Then I made a farting noise with my mouth. I pointed down, indicating the noise came from below. Then I stood up and crumpled up the tissues and explained, "You have to wrap that sound up in the tissue."

"What for?" he asked, still laughing.

I said, "First, tell me: did you understand or not?"

"Yes, you have to wrap up the fart in a paper tissue."

"Is this how your Persian-English dictionary would translate and make sense of *gooze peecham*?!" I asked.

Completely astounded and confused, he replied, "Huh, how weird."

"It's an expression. When somebody doesn't feel well, this is how they answer," I explained.

"So, in other words, you're annoyed that I asked you."

"No, not at all," I said. "It's just an expression that describes a feeling."

"That's really strange. No matter how hard I try, I can't connect the two," he said.

"It's a little surrealistic," I said.

"Uh-huh."

It sounded as if he finally got it. In any case, I let it go.

I kept vacillating whether or not to go downstairs. Before finally deciding, I swore to myself once more that if he set up the chessboard, I would let him win. I would gain nothing by shutting myself out of this possible place of refuge. I was tired of talking to myself. Afternoons, when it would usually get foggy outside, it was really hard to look out the window. The gloomy dark green pine trees would appear and disappear in the fog like ghosts, and when I'd talk to myself it felt as if I was talking to a ghost. It was really hard to accept that I was now talking to ghosts. Maybe it was too soon, but when I thought I was talking to a ghost and accepted it had come to this, I started to cry. I cried the way you cry when your heart pounds and a power within makes your fingertips burn.

Hadn't I always been the one on the offensive? Hadn't I spent my whole short life running? Never looking back or wondering what is, what was, or what will be? The flame in my heart warmed me. With only a bouquet of wildflowers in my hand and the shining sun above, I would boldly recount the tales of my journey. And this was what was so difficult to accept. I knew it was still too soon — that there was still something that made my fingertips explode with impatience.

I took my cigarettes and my lighter and went downstairs. As always, the sitting room door was closed, but I could hear the sound of the TV. I knocked.

From inside the old woman said, "Yes?"

I had learned that this meant to come in. I opened the door. The old lady didn't move, but the old man got up.

In Dutch, he said, "Hello. How are you?" I shook his hand.

"How are you, Mama?" I asked the old lady.

The old lady liked to be called Mama. She laughed and asked, "Was your room warm last night?"

I'd become very sensitive to this kind of inane question and answer, but I refrained from answering. I hadn't traveled thousands of miles to care if my room was warm or not. Under my breath, I cursed the whole world and myself, but outwardly indicated nothing. I didn't want to screw things up.

"Very warm," I said and cut it short. The old lady seemed pleased.

"Will you have tea or coffee?" she asked.

"Coffee, please."

And so I sat down on the sofa next to the old man. There was an American film on television, but the hero was Italian and spoke English with a heavy accent.

The old man started telling me about a new roof design he was working on for a building. He had already told me he was an engineer specializing in roofs but every time he told me about his work he would emphasize again that he was an expert in roof design. "I was better than everyone." I was listening to him, but watching the TV out of the corner of my eye. It wasn't a bad film. The man was a fanatical socialist and the woman, a feminist, and they didn't get along. Caught between them was a sad little child who broke your heart. The old man noticed that I was paying attention to the TV.

"There are a lot of feminists in this part of the world," he said.

The old woman put my coffee down. "Milk?" she asked.

"Do they drink coffee with or without milk in your country?" the old man asked.

It was one of those stupid questions that drive you crazy.

But I had no choice.

"We drink it all kinds of ways," I said.

I think I said this in a way that made the old man think. His chin began to quiver and he said, "I don't understand. . . ."

"With milk, sugar, and sometimes with nothing . . . sometimes with crying, sometimes with tears. It's our misfortune, you know," I said.

"You're upset today, aren't you?" the old woman asked.

"No, I swear I'm not. Here they drink coffee with milk and there are a lot of feminists. There they drink coffee without milk and . . ."

I cut myself off. To go on about this would just make me angrier. I picked up my cup and said, "Mama, the coffee you make doesn't need milk or sugar. It's delicious as it is."

The old lady laughed and laughed and looked as if she wanted me to repeat it all over again. But the old man still sat there staring at me and frowning like a brooding hen.

"How about a game of chess?" I asked.

The old man looked as if he was remembering his losses. He rubbed his forehead and said, "I've got a headache. I worked hard today. I'm not feeling too well."

"That's okay," I said. "Another day."

"Yes, he's not feeling very well today," the old woman said.

They're banding together to prevent another chess game, I thought. I leaned back on the sofa pillows and lit a cigarette. I'd lost track of the film on the TV, but it looked as if the man and woman were still fighting. They were walking in the rain, trading blows, after which the woman stalked off alone. The man stood for a while and then started to follow her, trying to get her to come back to the house. The woman wouldn't and kept shouting. They were both soaked to the skin. And then I remembered the child.

"The design I gave the office today is wonderful. Perfect," the old man said.

"Can't you mail the design in so you don't have to go all the way there and back?" I asked.

"I couldn't! As the engineering specialist, I definitely have to be there," he said.

"You're right," I said. "Usually engineering specialists have to be there. Otherwise no one can figure out their drawings." I pronounced "engineering" carefully and he really loved it.

"You're absolutely right," he said, and added. "Anyway, I'm used to traveling. And Germany isn't very far from here."

"It's not bad in the spring and summer, but it isn't great in the winter," I said.

"You know how many kilometers I've driven so far?" he asked.

"No! But I bet it must be a lot."

"I was twenty years old when I started to drive. I've driven five hundred thousand kilometers!" he said.

The old woman gave the old man an approving look. He got up, picked up an album from the bureau and showed me pictures of the cars he had driven — a Volkswagen, a Fiat, and a Toyota.

"BMWs are the best," he said.

"How many kilometers did you drive with this one?" I asked.

He pulled his chin into his chest and thought a little. Then he said, "A hundred fifty thousand kilometers."

I said, "If you had been driving a straight line, you would have been halfway to the moon."

He laughed and I felt sorry, but I don't know for whom, him or me.

A few days ago, when I was sitting in the Eastern languages library, a small dark handsome Bengali fellow appeared. He looked at the Persian books for a while and then came and stood above me. He said in English, "Excuse me, are you Afghani?"

"What difference does it make?" I said. "Right now, we're stuck in this dump."

My words must have struck him as being a bit harsh. He pulled himself together and stepped back. I regretted my words. I thought: he's like me, homeless.

"Do you smoke?" I said, and offered him a cigarette.

"No, I don't," he said, adding, "I'm looking for someone who speaks Persian."

"What's the problem?" I asked.

"My name," he said, pausing. "I mean my family name is Chunie. I wanted to know what it means in Persian."

I wasn't thinking of anything bad yet and I said, "It corresponds to *chand*, which means how many. *Chand* expresses an amount; *chun* expresses a condition."

He looked baffled. "That's strange," he said.

"What's strange about it?" I asked.

He grinned a little shamefully and asked, "Doesn't it mean . . . doesn't it refer to something else?" Hesitantly he pointed to his ass.

Finally I understood. For once, I said to myself, you tried to act like an adult.

"You mean *kunie*?"[4]

"Yeah," he said.

"Well, the kids in the street in the south of the city sometimes say *chunie* instead of *kunie*, but you're here and they're there — there's no connection."

"Sometimes some of the Dutch professors at the school where I study tease me," he said.

"What do you do?"

"I teach sociology," he said.

"Why did you come here? Did you have to? You should have stayed home."

"They pay well here and the environment is better, too," he said.

This really annoyed me and I felt spiteful. I said, "Are you sure your name isn't *Kunie*?"

"No!" he said and puckered his lips and said, " 'Chunie!' " and then he repeated, "It's really strange!"

I looked down. The Bengali stood there nervously rocking from side to side then said, more to himself than anyone else, "I'm surprised that foreigners pronounce my name like that. 'K' and 'Ch' really do sound different."

"Maybe they don't like you," I said.

"Maybe," he said. Then he abruptly turned the pages on some of the books and left.

* * *

---

[4] *Kun* is a colloquial term meaning ass; *kunie* is a derogatory slang term referring to homosexuals.

When the old man realized I was deep in thought, he said, "Okay. I'll play one game, but only one."

"Great," I said and cleared off the table to set up the game.

The man and woman in the film were still in the rain, tired of the stupid and meaningless fight they were still having. The woman had her hand on the man's shoulder as they walked back to the house.

The old man sat down at the table and we drew pieces. He got white. As soon as he moved his first piece, I realized he was starting to play crazy again. But I had made my decision. I followed his lead and played like him. He was so absorbed in the pieces that if you didn't know better and hadn't seen him play before you'd think he was unrivaled. He moved his pieces like a general who was ordering his soldiers about on the field. I let him take a few of my pawns. When he saw he was ahead, he lifted his head and asked, "Whiskey or wine?"

"Whiskey!" I said.

"Me too," he said.

"It seems your headache is better, no?" I asked.

He stared at the chessboard and didn't answer. His wife, who was sitting on the other side of the room, said, "I'll get it," and got up and went into the kitchen. I could hear the sound of the cabinets opening and the glasses being taken out.

He moved a piece. "Now it's your turn!" he said.

I took a quick sip from my glass that the old lady had put on the side of the board and hit one of his men. After thinking a little, the old man moved his queen in front of his king, so that I could have checked him with my bishop. I thought it might not be a bad idea to shake him up a little after having lost my pawns. But when I went to move my bishop, I realized I was checked myself. I don't know how his rook got in front of my king. Bad luck, I guess. I had been checked for some time and now I wanted to check somebody else. When I thought about it later, I couldn't believe it had really happened. But it had. I was stuck in a bad way. I could still make a few more moves, but I couldn't break out of it. Being in check is painful. You can't move forward and you can't move back. You've made a stupid move and you have to face up to it.

Exactly like my life situation. What was the use? With whom can you share the bitterness of these moments? Who can you tell that your heart is breaking, piece by piece? And that you can hear it crumbling?

One day you'd say, how nice it is to be with one's people and share their whispers. You'd say, see how you spoke out loudly? But the stream that leads to the river that leads to the ocean always flows with a whisper. Then when you understood the meaning of a whisper you understood why a rock tolerates years of wind, storms, and sun, and then remains forever. And you felt the roar that was concealed in life. You accepted to be a whisper; to slowly whisper the silent pain of your heart to yourself and others as if you were reading the alphabet. You lived life as if it were a journey that passed through interlocking doors. You wove a colorful shirt from the laughter of children and hung it in the blowing wind. You lighted a small lantern with the small stream of hope from those you loved until the sun, little by little, shone its glorious light. But behind all of this, little by little, a hand was weaving its own nightmare.

"It's no use," I said to the old man. "I'm checkmated."

"Huh," the old man said as if he were waking up from a deep sleep, leaning over the board for a better look.

"Really?" the old woman said.

Suddenly realizing what happened, the old man gave out a winner's hoot and extended his hand to me.

"Yes, with the bishop's move, you're done." He motioned to the old woman to come over and see my losing board. The old woman got up.

The film also seemed to be ending. The man and woman were sleeping in one bed, but each with very different dreams. In another room, the child played all by himself with his lifeless dolls. I got up, too.

"Where to?" the old man said. "You haven't finished your whiskey."

"Later, another time. I'm really tired," I said.

As the old man, swollen with pride, described his victory to his wife, move by move, I left and climbed up the stairs to my room.

The room was cold and empty, and the oncoming dusk made it even more depressing. I didn't dare look out the window at the pine trees. But when I sat down on the bed, I saw a red light in the street that was glowing strangely in the fog. It looked just like an eye that had been crying all day. From above my bed I pulled out *The Travel Memoirs of Nasser Khosrow* and opened it to this passage:

And from there my brother, Ghollam Maki Hindu, who accompanied us, and I entered a village named Kharzeville. We had few provisions. My brother went to the grocer to buy some food. Someone asked, "What do you want? I'm the grocer." My brother said, "Anything you have, since I'm a stranger just passing through." But everything my brother asked for, the grocer said he didn't have. So from then on, whenever someone spoke like this, we said he must be the grocer from Kharzeville.[5]

I set aside the book and closed my eyes.

— Translated by Leyli Shayegan

---

[5]Nasser Khosrow was an important eleventh-century Iranian philosopher and poet. His most famous prose work is *Travel Memoirs,* an account of his journey to Egypt.

Iraj Pezeshkzad

Born in Tehran in 1928, Iraj Pezeshkzad was educated in Iran and later in France, where he received his law degree. When he returned home, he served as a judge in the Iranian judiciary for five years prior to joining the Iranian foreign service. In the early 1950s he translated the works of Voltaire and Molière into Persian and began writing short stories for magazines. His writings include the best-selling comic novel *Uncle Napoleon,* as well as *Haji Mam-ja'far in Paris,* and *Mashalah Khan in the Court of Harun al-Rashid.* He has also written several plays, short satirical stories, and various articles on the Iranian Constitutional Revolution of 1905, the French Revolution, and the Russian Revolution. *Uncle Napoleon,* which was made into a popular television series before the Islamist revolution, was published in an excellent English translation by Dick Davis (Mage, 2000). Pezeshkzad is currently working as a journalist.

"Delayed Consequences of the Revolution" was published in the collection *Rostam Solatan* (Los Angeles: Nashr-e Ketab, 2000), and was written when Pezeshkzad went into exile after the revolution . It is a hilarious depiction of the pomposity and emptiness of some of the members of the Pahlavi-era elite.

DELAYED CONSEQUENCES OF THE REVOLUTION

We were a more or less well-suited group of four or five people, and we spent our free time together. As time went by, each one went on in a different direction and I was left alone. I suffered through a few difficult, lonely months. Reading, writing, watching television, visiting doctors, ingesting medications, and the management of the internal affairs of the household can fill up quite a lot of time. But somehow it isn't enough. The particular desire to converse — which is indeed an essential need — remains unrequited.

What I actually mean is conversing in the Persian language, which is for us an absolute necessity. If we don't say "Yes, no" in Persian several times a day on a daily basis, we get a sore throat. Of course, there are foreign languages too, but we have no use for them. Basically, we can work with foreigners if we have to, but we can't really socialize with them. We don't share any common memories; besides, trying to explain the simplest situation to them puts you out of breath. I mean that if you want to explain something to your compatriot in your own language, you can use five or six words and get the meaning across, but to explain the same thing to a foreigner in another language, you'll need to employ at least fifty or sixty words. For example, if a foreigner asks you:

"How did Mr. Ali X get so rich all of a sudden?"

Then you have to respond:

"Mr. Ali X had bought a million meters of land in the outskirts of Tehran at five *shahis* a meter many years ago.[1] Then he invited a member of the Very Powerful Upper Crust Elite of the country to participate in this deal, and thus, as a result of the exertion of That Person's influence, the definition and designation of the city limits were expanded, so that Mr. Ali X's land came to be included within it. And

---

[1] Unit of Iranian money from long ago, virtually worthless today; 100 *shahis* equal one *rial*; 100 *rials* are equivalent to one *toman*. Roughly eight hundred *tomans* are equivalent to one U.S. dollar according to present exchange rates.

since, on the one hand, during those years people were coming into Tehran in droves from all parts of the country and the demand for land substantially exceeded the supply; and because, on the other hand, the rise in the price of oil put a lot of money into the people's hands, the price of Mr. Ali X's land increased from five *shahis* a meter to two or three hundred *tomans* a meter. As a result, he very quickly became rich."

Now, with the aid of a few upward and downward movements of the eyes and eyebrows, you can convey precisely the same story to your compatriot in your own language in a just few words:

"Oh, yes! One million meters of desert land outside the city limits, now *inside* the city limits thanks to the power of His Highness. Oh, yes! Quite obvious."

It is even possible to use fewer words while getting your meaning across by placing more emphasis on the vowels and consonants when you're saying "Oh, yes!": "Ooooh yessss! God's vacant land now within city limits by way of His Highness!"

Anyway, I was left alone, with no audience, and I was getting desperate. Quite coincidentally, during those very days I was watching a television program on psychology, and they were saying that these people who walk around in the streets talking to themselves mostly do so because they're alone and don't have anyone to talk to. Such possible effects of loneliness terrified me. So I began to eye some groups of my fellow countrymen in exile who got together in cafés for a few hours on certain days. By chance I ran into one group that included a number of pretty eminent people, one of whom, it turned out, I knew. He offered me a place to sit at their table, and so the bait worked. I was delighted to become a part of this gathering. Since almost all of them had held prominent positions in the former regime, in private I'd refer to them as "VIPs": there was a former government minister, a former provincial governor, a former senator, a former ambassador, a former protector of the shrine, a former secretary general, a former high eminence, etc.[2] My eagerness to become a part of this group stemmed from my deep-seated interest in history, and I suspected that socializing and conversing with such living icons of the history of our nation over the last fifty

---

[2] "Protector of the shrine" refers to the traditional title Nayeb o-Tolieh, bestowed by kings on their relatives or supporters ostensibly to protect the holy Shia shrines, but also to maintain political control of economically important religious centers.

or sixty years would be a veritable gold mine for me. But I soon encountered certain obstacles and problems that distinctly detracted from the advantages of their company.

The first problem was enduring the constant redundancy. Redundancy in conversation is not unexpected among people of a certain age. But when the distance between repetitions shrinks from every three months to two months to every month and even to once a week, then it gets really enervating. Redundancy is annoying not only in quantitative but in qualitative terms as well, because, as versions of the same story changed and evolved, a dulling effect took place, and the recounted matter began to lose all credibility. Besides, sometimes this would lead to irksome arguments as well. Rampant as repetition was among this group, usually those present ignored the divergences in the same narrative. Once in a while, though, some younger, more meddlesome member of the group would make the speaker face up to it.

For example, the protector of the shrine's story of the ceremonial annual dusting of the Holy Shrine created a commotion. The protector of the shrine was recounting for the nth time:

"Oh yes, I remember that one day, during the dusting ceremony of the shrine, a golden chain with a cross, like the ones that Christians wear around their necks, was found. It turns out that on that same day Her Highness Princess Ashraf had come to the shrine to observe the ceremony . . ."

At this point, one of the aforementioned younger, meddlesome members said:

"Sir, I think it was Princess Fatemeh who was present at that ceremony."[3]

The protector of the shrine snapped at him in anger:

"If you were there, then you tell the rest of the story!"

Although the meddlesome man was right, and all of us had heard the story of Princess Fatemeh's participation before, and although Mr. Meddlesome was perfectly capable of finishing the story in detail, still, those present took the side of the protector of the shrine. Nodding heads and rolling eyes opted for the presence of Her Highness Princess Ashraf, and the younger man fortunately conceded.

---

[3] Ashraf and Fatemah, names of two of the Shah's sisters. This "story" refers to a rumor that one of the Shah's sisters had converted to Christianity.

But interference in the general's story led to harsher objections. The general took every opportunity to tell the story of how he quit smoking cigarettes. Sensing a wisp of smoke in the café or hearing a cigarette name brand would launch him into the story:

"I used to smoke two or three packs a day. One day, His Highness Shahpur Gholamreza said, 'Come my good man, make the effort. Once and for all, make the decision like a soldier and quit smoking.'[4] I immediately crushed the pack of Winstons that I was holding in my fist with such force that the box and the cigarettes were reduced to a pulp, and I never touched another cigarette again!" As he was mimicking the act of crushing the cigarette box, the general's eyes shone with a spark of power and courage, reminding the observer of that famous scene from World War II when Marshall Zhukov, after the capture of Stalingrad, described the crushing of the German Eighth Armored Infantry Division and the capture of Marshall Von Paulus. Lately, as soon as the general would begin to say, "I used to smoke two . . ." everyone would quickly clear up the table in the vicinity of the general's hands, because in recounting the moment of box-crushing excitement, he would grab whatever was on the table and squeeze it hard. The last time we didn't take this precaution he squeezed the ambassador's medicine box so hard that several of his medications were decimated.

Now consider what happened one day when another meddlesome character jumped into the conversation at the sensitive moment of the crushing of the box of Winstons, and, interrupting the general, said, "But the last time you said the cigarettes were Kents . . ."

The general was livid. He began to bang on the table with his fists. Fortunately, His Eminence saved the day by reciting a short poem about Great Men and their Will of Steel:

If Willpower is the cause and motive
A mere ant is capable of becoming Solomon.

In any case, aside from these occasional incidents, there was a kind of a gentleman's agreement among the members of the VIPs not to pick on one another's penchant for redundancy and on the discrepancies between different versions of their stories.

---

[4] Shahpur Gholamreza, one of the Shah's brothers.

Another kind of problem came up once in a while when someone pointed out the unfortunate correlation between various illnesses and symptoms discussed and the age of the gentlemen present. The members of the VIPs, may they be spared from jealous eyes, had all lived long lives. The majority of them had been born during the Qajar dynasty.[5] Those born during the reign of Reza Shah — who abdicated the throne close to sixty years ago — were the youthful minority.[6] Nevertheless, all physical ailments from weak eyesight and cataracts to hearing difficulties, hair loss, high blood pressure, arthritis, rheumatism, and even hernias were considered to be the consequences of the revolution and life in exile. If anyone dared to suggest the correlation between these ailments and their advanced age, they would be deeply offended. And when that someone left, they would call him a good-for-nothing windbag.

In socializing with the VIPs I am often reminded of Mrs. Afagh Saltaneh, who attributed all the ills of the age to Tehran's terrible climate, and in praise of Tabriz's good climate she would say:

"When I was in Tabriz I would walk for kilometers and kilometers without a problem. In Tehran, when I walk a few steps I have to sit down for a rest. In Tabriz, I would have two huge servings of kebab and rice, and I'd be hungry in a flash. Here, I have a little chicken leg and can't seem to digest it for the rest of the day. This is all because of Tehran's terrible climate."

What this lady forgot to mention is that she returned to Tehran from Tabriz after her husband's death *sixty years ago.*

I should also add that the VIPs were very careful to make note of who else, besides themselves, was suffering from "consequences of the revolution." So, during the time I socialized with them, I admitted to a few ailments that I wasn't actually suffering from to create sympathy for myself. In addition to this, they made me pretend I was deaf, too. This is how it happened. His excellency was practically deaf, so that if he wasn't sitting right in front of the speaker and looking at his lips, he thought no one was talking and would begin a new conversation. No one dared tell him about this problem to his face, so they thought that one of us would pretend to be deaf, and the others would try to convince

---

[5] The Qajar kings ruled Iran from 1796 to 1925.
[6] Reza Shah was the first king of the Pahlavi dynasty, and ruled from 1925 to 1941.

him of the benefits of hearing aids. Then maybe his excellency would get the point, too. They dillydallied in deciding who should pretend to be deaf until one day they put me on the spot and made me accept the task. At the end of the next café gathering, as I strolled away with his excellency and he asked me a question, I put my hand behind my ear, and asked him to repeat his question. His face lit up, and he said, "Well, well! So you are hard of hearing, too! Like me! Damn this revolution and all that it did to us. Actually, my own hearing problem happens to be quite negligible."

Alas, this little plot did not solve the problem of the VIPs. His excellency did not begin to use a hearing aid, but instead began to use me as one. Whenever he couldn't hear something, he would yell at the speaker, "Please, speak louder, for *his* benefit!" (He meant me.)

As a result, as if I didn't already have enough defects, I acquired a reputation for being deaf as well. From then on, ignoring the circumstances that led us to this point, the other participants in the group would address me with ear-splittingly loud voices.

Of course, as we know, loss of memory and muddle-headedness are "consequences of the revolution," too, and have nothing to do with age!

Occasionally the "consequences of the revolution" became unbearable for this revolution-stricken crowd and the aforementioned "gentlemen's agreement" would abruptly expire.

The secretary general had joined the group quite recently, and for the second time he brought up the matter of his great courage in standing up for the interests of our country: "On the day that the cabinet discussed in the presence of His Majesty the Shah the matter of the ratification of the judicial exempting of American military personnel from Iranian law, I dissented. His Majesty said to me, go ahead, sign it, the defense interests of the country require us to give this advantage to the Americans. I told him that I wouldn't put my signature on this document even if my hand were to be chopped off!"

Suddenly, the general cut him off. "*Excuse me!?* You have already mentioned this before, and I was polite enough not to pick up on it. I just want to remind you about the time that you and I were both in the waiting room of Niavaran Palace, waiting for permission to meet with His Majesty, Your Grace had to go to the bathroom every five minutes.[7] One of these times I happened to go to the bathroom, too, and we ran into each other. I asked you, 'Do you have a prostrate problem like me?' And you responded, 'No, no, it's a matter of nerves. Every time I have to meet His Majesty, the sheer fear of His Formidable Presence weakens my bowels.' Now I want to know that if you were such a twisting, trembling bundle of nerves from the idea of *meeting* His Majesty, how did you summon up the courage to speak that way to him?"

This reminder offended the secretary general to the point that he yelled, "Are you saying that I'm lying?!"

"No, but with the passage of time and the problems of exile . . ."

The secretary general stood up in protest and fury and left without saying good-bye. He never came back. We just heard him growl under his breath as he left, "Once a SAVAK snoop, always a SAVAK snoop!"[8]

Among the malignant consequences of the revolution was the impromptu and somewhat retarded inclination of his excellency the ambassador toward Persian poetry and letters. Perhaps the only occasion when repetition is not irritating, and is in fact pleasing, is when beautiful poetry is recited. But his excellency, recently harboring claims to be an expert on Rumi, and having duly delivered a couple of speeches on the subject, had accumulated a considerable number of nonsensical, indeed, trashy poems in his memory, and insisted on repeating them under any pretext. Unfortunately I remember this one:

> O Eyelash, mend the needle,
> Thread it with a strand of hair,
> For my broken heart still needs a few stitches.

Or this one:

> My bones are burning to ashes from the agony of separation,
> On the day I die, I regret that I'll disappoint the dogs in your alley.

---

[7] Niavaran Palace, the main residence of the ex-Shah.
[8] The previous regime's secret police, SAVAK; the acronym translates to State Information and Security Organization.

Sadder still, he recited these pathetic poems emulating the wistful tones of Miss Roshanak, the famed announcer of the pre-revolution radio program on poetry and music.

Among the last "consequences of the revolution" that I witnessed before I split with the VIPs were the mutual infirmities of the governor and the general. These two discussed their painful knee joints and their respective remedies so often that even the others would raise their voices in protest. One day his eminence, who is essentially a snoop, announced that the "knee pain" of the governor and the general is nothing but an agreed-upon code to cover up their *real* infirmity, and that he had discovered this fact by chatting up the governor's brother.

According to his report, for some time now the governor and the general had been keeping each other informed in private about the results of remedies they each pursued to strengthen their constitution and restore the powers of their youth. Together they would experiment with any new medicine they chanced upon. Accordingly, the general had given the governor a bottle of root of rosemary oil from Arabia, and the governor had provided the general with a quantity of ground rhinoceros horn from Malaysia. The story seemed credible enough with regard to the general, who, having recently remarried, was dyeing his hair and mustache. But the governor?!

In any case, as a consequence of this scoop, at our next gathering, regardless of anything else that was being said or done, every member of the group was keeping one ear tuned to the private conversation between the governor and the general, who were discussing their "knee pain" in the corner as usual.

The governor was asking about the effects of I don't know what medicine. The general shook his head and said softly, "No. It had no effect. I mean, when I get up in the morning, I think I have the energy, but as I take the first step, I realize no, I don't. The problem is still there, and my legs are weaker and more feeble than ever. The other day, I decided to bite the bullet and give it a try. But before the first step, my knee gave out. One of my friends was there, who very kindly warmed and massaged my knee. I really appreciated it, but alas, it didn't work at all. But tell me about your acupuncture cure. How is that coming along?"

"It is going nowhere, General. Of course, I have to go for ten sessions. I've only gone five times."

"Do they put the needles on the knee itself, or around it?"

"On the knee itself."

"And the needles are hanging on the knee for the entire hour?"

"Yes, unfortunately."

From the general's contorted, repulsed expression, and the use of the word *hanging,* one could surmise that the "needled member" was a more sensitive part of the body than the knee.

The image of the respected be-needled governor made me want to laugh out loud. I raised my head to exchange my suppressed laughter through meaningful looks with the others. Instead, I saw the members of the VIP not exchanging looks of mirth, amusement, or derision, but rather exchanging glances of sympathy and compassion. Like the compassion for a fellow soldier who will not lay his weapon down even if he has run out of ammunition, who will strive to keep the flag of resistance raised until his dying breath.

After all these events, I decided to review the balance sheet of the past few months in which I tried to escape from loneliness by mingling with others. The result was not good. I had escaped one consequence of the revolution — my loneliness — only to get entangled in a host of other "consequences." I had harbored hopes of speaking a few words of Persian, which hadn't materialized, either, because the VIPs didn't give one another a chance to speak, never mind a timid newcomer like me. Actually, two or three of them spoke loudly at the same time, at all times.

To ingratiate myself to the VIPs and to be accepted into their circle, I had pretended to suffer from many of their afflictions, which had a decidedly negative effect on my morale. I was now considered, among most of my compatriots, to be deaf.

In the realm of poetry and letters, instead of listening to the singer Shajarian's beautiful recitations of the poetry of Hafez and Sa'adi, which I used to do in times of solitude, I had to put up with the ambassador's recitation of the endless lamentations of an aged lover pining in shame about not being able to offer his burnt bones to the dogs in his lover's lane.

In the realm of politics, I had to ignore hundreds of books and articles and theses analyzing in depth the causes and consequences of the Iranian Revolution, and instead listen to a bunch of conspiracy theories about the machinations of foreigners responsible for everything going wrong in my country.

In the realm of compassion, I was reduced to feeling sorry, not for the true victims of the revolution, but for the victimized "knees" of two so-called sufferers. Most important, I had thought that associating with this group would link me directly to the main actors of the living history of my country, but instead all I witnessed was a disastrous mangling of history.

Considering this balance sheet, I abandoned this group of VIPs and their post-revolution symptoms to the grace of God and returned to consequences of my own change of heart. Now, in my solitude, I fervently appreciate sound health and peace of mind.

— Translated by Nahid Mozaffari

Taghi Modarressi

Taghi Modarressi was born in Tehran in 1931, and graduated with a degree in medicine from Tehran University in 1959. He moved to the United States in 1959 to do further training in psychiatry at Duke University and later, in Canada, at McGill University. Modarressi became an American citizen in 1977. A practicing psychoanalyst, he wrote fiction in his spare time, producing his first book, *Yakolia and Her Loneliness*, when he was still a medical student. His novels published in the United States, *The Book of Absent People* and *The Pilgrim's Rules of Etiquette,* were written in Persian. Later, he translated them into English. He died in 1997, leaving his wife, the novelist Anne Tyler, and two daughters.

This excerpt is composed of the first two chapters of *The Book of Absent People.* As the reader will note, Modarressi believed in the concept of "translation with an accent"; in other words, he felt that the cultural flavor and linguistic idiosyncrasies can, and indeed should, be maintained in translation.

Excerpt from
THE BOOK OF ABSENT PEOPLE

CHAPTER 1

Three nights before he went to Ghaleh Bagh, my Khan Papa Doctor sent a message to come see him later in the library. After I got the message, I went out to the balcony and looked down into the courtyard. Maybe he would appear and walk around the flower beds and inspect his crossbred roses one by one. With finicky care, he would clip the withered blooms and throw them into the green plastic pail he'd bought after New Year's. He would hold the fresh blooms between his fingers and draw back and study them with the Heshmat Nezami pridefulness.

But in the courtyard not even a bird was flying. It wasn't dark enough to turn on the lights yet. Only one lamp burned weakly in the entrance hall of the library. I was about to give up when he appeared from the direction of the orangery. He wore his white coat. He was busy with some idea, and he paid no attention to his surroundings. I ran to the opposite side of the courtyard. When I reached the sealed room of his first wife, Homayundokht, God forgive her soul, I put my hands behind my back and, walking parallel to my Khan Papa Doctor, goose-stepped like a soldier. As we reached the end of the courtyard, I raised my chin. I slapped my bare heels together hard and shouted from the depths of my throat, "Ten-SHUN!"

He noticed, but he continued walking. From his expression, it was clear he was displeased but not out of temper. He only threw a taunting, sidelong glance at me, as though to ask when I planned to give up my childish ways. For heaven's sake, I was twenty-three years old; when was I going to pull myself together and find a job worthy of me like most of the Heshmat Nezamis and enter the society of respectable people? Finally I drew up and yelled, "At eee-ase!"

He glared at me. He chewed a tip of his salt-and-pepper mustache. Close up, his face looked haggard and depressed. His white coat was gray with charcoal. With his sooty hands, he might have come from one of those whitesmith's shops where they enamel copperware. He gave off a smell I couldn't identify. It was something like a mixture of caraway seeds and potter's clay. He narrowed his eyes, and in an undertone asked, "Rokni, do you hear something far, far away?"

I said, "No, I don't hear anything, Khan Papa Doctor."

"Listen carefully. See if you do."

I listened for a moment. Then I turned up my palms and said, "I swear by the Lord of the faithful, I don't hear so much as a fly. I only wondered why you wanted to talk to me."

He gestured for me to leave, saying, "First I have to wash. Come to the library in half an hour and I'll tell you."

Then he disappeared in the darkness of the orangery. I thought to myself how old age had changed his character. He behaved more like the Sardar Azhdari side of the family. He had become pale, melancholy, loose-lipped, and talked a lot of nonsense. His words would have sounded like gibberish even to a monkey.

As I was heading toward my room, I pricked up my ears and listened to the mysterious sounds of our old house. In my mind, I heard the flapping of a handful of wild birds.

When I entered the library, I was surprised. There were hardly any books on the shelves. The rugs had been rolled and they were leaning against the pillar near the dais. The floor was cluttered with cardboard boxes, bundles of old magazines, and lithograph books. He had found most of those books in the Shah's Mosque bookstores, in dusty storerooms that had never seen the light of day, and he'd spent a great deal of money on every one of them. Some of them were sent to him from India, Turkey, and Egypt — books about alchemy, botany, the summoning of spirits, and secret societies; books with strange Arabic titles like *Treasures of Secrets, Gardens of the Horrified, Meghdadi's Secrets of Numbers,* and *The Deleted Beginning.*

The twenty-pound dictionary lay open on his desk, next to the lamp with its shade from the Naser ed din Shah period. The lamplight yellowed the page with a circle the size of a palm. A cigarette butt that had just been stubbed out was smoking in a china ashtray. The ashtray was a high-heeled shoe that my Khan Papa Doctor's father, the late Heshmat Nezam, had brought for his wife, the Lady of Ladies, as a present from his last trip to Austria. Now, why he had brought an ashtray for the Lady of Ladies, who wouldn't even touch a cigarette to her lips, was beyond anybody's comprehension. We didn't dare ask Khan

Papa Doctor about it, either. He wasn't the type to put up with any curiosity about the past.

I looked around at the walls and doors. Nothing had changed in that house for a century. Anyone else in Khan Papa Doctor's place, with his position and influence, would long ago have built a chic, new-style house on Pahlavi Street and put two of the latest-model cars in the garage and married a modern European wife. But my Khan Papa Doctor insisted that nothing should change in the house of his forefathers. The photographs of the late Sardar Azhdar and the late Heshmat Nezam still remained on the walls behind the dais. The only new ornament in the library was Khan Papa Doctor's own full-length photograph above the mantel, the one that he'd had taken in his youth before his marriage to Homayundokht, God forgive her soul — wearing a wool Cossack hat and his military uniform, with a cape on his shoulders and his hand on the hilt of his sword. He was staring at a corner of the veranda as if he'd been called unexpectedly. His expression revealed a sort of absent-mindedness that was seldom seen on the face of a Heshmat Nezami. I stepped forward and stood in front of his photo. It came as a surprise. I said, "Good Lord, how much he takes after his late father! They're like two halves of an apple; they don't differ by a hair."

Steps approached from the hall behind me. I turned, shifting the paper tube I carried. It was Khan Papa Doctor. He was standing in the middle of his office doorway, slowly taking off his surgical gloves. He was still wearing a white coat, but this was a clean one, starched and ironed. From beneath the hollow arches of his eyebrows he fixed me with his gaze — a cold, magnetic, penetrating gaze that made him look distant and unreachable. I thought he might finally have decided to start talking about his marriage to his first wife, the late Homayundokht, God forgive her soul.

He came closer, with easy, sauntering steps. When he reached the center of the library, he threw the rubber gloves on his desk. He took a cigarette from a drawer and lit it with the gold lighter he'd brought from Germany. He blew into my face the voluminous, dense smoke of his first puff. He sat calmly in his chair, leaned back, and looked at me. Maybe because I was in a weak position, maybe because I was nervous, I smiled foolishly. I unrolled my sketch on the desk and said, "Here." With a snap of his thumb, he flipped cigarette ashes into the late Heshmat Nezam's ashtray. He said, "Here what?"

I said, "I made this for you."

I showed him the sketch of the legendary bird Simorgh. He stubbed out his cigarette, leaned forward, and examined the sketch. He became absorbed and ran a finger around the outline of the bird. When he reached Simorgh's wide wings, he looked up and said, "These are flames, aren't they?"

I said, "What do you mean, flames, Khan Papa Doctor?"

"They say it burns up and then a thousand chicks will rise from its ashes."

"That's a phoenix. This one's Simorgh. Simorgh of Mount Ghoff. When it spreads its wings, the sky turns blue. When it opens its eyes, the sun or the moon shines."

I stretched out my arms like two wings, as if I were Simorgh circling the sky on my own, revolving and sightseeing and harming no one. My Khan Papa Doctor frowned and set aside the sketch. He stood up and started walking among the bookshelves with his hands clasped behind him. There were a few old books remaining. He lifted them off the shelves, dusted them, and put them in cardboard boxes. He was distracted and paid me no attention. I took my life in my hands and asked, "Didn't you send a message for me to come to the library?"

He paused and nodded. "Have patience," he said.

"Are you pleased with my sketch? Do you still say painting and sculpting won't make my bread and butter? Do you still think I'm wasting my life?"

"Rokni, stop this foolishness," he said. The tone of his voice had changed. His words echoed through the empty library as if he were talking in a Turkish bath. He gestured for me to sit on the leather chair in front of his desk. Without a care in my head I sat down, hoping he wanted to talk about Homayundokht, God forgive her soul. In recent weeks he had been behaving as though he was searching for a confidant. As though, finally, he was tired of thinking about Homayundokht, God rest her soul, and of all the events in the past. As though he wanted to open a conversation. But I knew I should watch myself. I should stay alert and act rational so I wouldn't annoy him. He set his heavy fists on the desk. He leaned forward and said, "I want to tell you something very important. Listen carefully."

I said, "All right, Khan Papa Doctor. Whatever you say."

He was silent. He looked disheveled, and the Heshmat Nezami

confidence had gone from his eyes. The lamplight carved deep lines in his face so that he seemed awesome, like Boris Karloff. In a hushed, intimate tone he said, "Rokni, this afternoon I stopped practicing medicine. I've examined my last patient and lanced my last boil. Do you hear me?"

Humbly I said, "I'm listening."

He said, "Today is the last day of the month of Khordad. Isn't it?"

"Yes."

"I want to go to Ghaleh Bagh and look after my herb garden. I want to get away from here and spend all my time discovering an anticancer medicine. In ancient Iran they had a cure for cancer that's lost now, it's gone . . ."

With a stroke of his hand he emphasized "gone." He pushed the dictionary toward me and with a palsied finger showed me pictures of wormwood, Mary's palm, Roman anise, and sweet marjoram. "The cure for cancer is among these plants. There are secrets in these herbs that nobody knows. Nobody understands them. Only the ancient Iranians guessed their uses. They knew long ago that the cure for cancer is not in the knife. You have to get to know cancer to uncover its mystery and halt it."

His eyes glittered. He looked at me triumphantly. Then he went to the next room and brought back a few small sugar pouches. These pouches were filled with the herbs he'd grown. He held one of them above my head and ordered, "Smell it, Rokni. See what kind of mood comes over you."

I said, "What is it, Khan Papa Doctor?"

He said, "Never mind. Put your nose close to the pouch and breathe deeply."

I rose from the leather chair to a half-standing position. I closed my eyes. I drew in a breath and waited for the effect. All of a sudden, in that hundred-degree summer heat I felt a kind of damp, sticky chill raising goose bumps on my arms. I thought, What if he wants to poison me? What if he's gone mad? Though this kind of personality change is very rare among the Heshmat Nezamis, anything is possible. It's the Sardar Azhdaris who have passionate dispositions. At around age thirty the hereditary melancholia afflicts their minds; their deaths occur on Thursdays that are even-numbered days of the month on the lunar calendar.

My Khan Papa Doctor said, "How are you feeling, Rokni?"

I said, "I don't know how to describe it for you."

"Aren't you getting dizzy?"

It's true, I was. I said, "Oh, my Lord, yes. My head is light as cotton, a puff of cotton. I'm spinning like a pinwheel. But I feel fine; there's nothing wrong with me. How cool it's turned in the library! Look how hollow and distorted the furniture has grown. What air, what cool and pleasant air — chilled and thin and brittle, just like a sheet of glass."

He said, "Prick up your ears and see if you hear the sound of singing far, far away."

I said, "Oh, my Lord, yes. How clearly I hear it, Khan Papa Doctor! Someone is singing far, far away. Oh, my Lord, that's not it. Someone is whistling. How well he's whistling, too! Like my cousin Masoud who used to go to the head of the alley every evening and lean against the lamppost and whistle for the neighbor girls. Do you remember, Khan Papa Doctor?"

He said, "Of course I remember."

I said, "Do you remember Homayundokht, God forgive her soul? After thirty-odd years, do you still think of her?"

I was speaking without fear now. I was picking up speed. I remembered the picture taken in Petersburg of Homayundokht, God forgive her soul, with her Dear Daddy, the late Mirza Yousef — the white shawl around her naked shoulders, and her pitch-black hair tossed and spreading on the lilac-white skin at the back of her neck, her swooning gaze turned to the sky. The photographer's backdrop shows a gray jetty in a stormy, raging sea. They have put a rattan chair in front of waves that are foaming at the mouth and tearing at their chains, and on the chair they've set Homayundokht, God forgive her soul, who is no older than thirteen.

My Khan Papa Doctor was taken aback by my question. He couldn't seem to think of an answer. I insisted: "Well, Khan Papa Doctor? What are you worried about?"

He set aside the sugar pouch. He sat down and said, "You puppy dog! This meddling doesn't become you."

I said, "Why not?"

"I asked you here so we could talk about your half brother Zia." I was thunderstruck. I hadn't expected this. I opened my mouth but couldn't speak. He grumbled, "How come you've stopped talking?"

"You swore you'd never utter the name of my Khan Brother Zia," I said.

In protest, he raised both hands and said, "There has to be at least one person who will look after our business, who won't allow that inheritance we gathered with our heart's blood to get lost. When I go to Ghaleh Bagh, who will there be to care? The Sardar Azhdaris? Like hell they will. You, Your Excellency? You've always got your head up your ass. Who's left, then? Obviously, your Khan Brother Zia. He may be stubborn as a mule, can't tell up from down, acts like a donkey, but he's a Heshmat Nezami. He gets things done, and he doesn't allow anyone to stick it to him."

It dawned on me that our lives were changing, that there was more here than met the eye. I stammered, "It's eleven years since we've seen a trace of him. We don't know where he is. May God cut my tongue off, cut it off, but what if he's deceased?"

He lowered his head in his hands and reflected. "I've thought of that myself. Some people say he's been executed. Some people say he's at large, has changed his name, is driving a truck in the south. Others say he's still in prison. But I know he's alive. It's been proven to me, and I don't give these rumors the attention I'd give a dog."

I said, "How has it been proven to you?"

He broke into a chuckle and said, "Maybe you won't believe this. I've seen him in my dreams. For two weeks now, I've dreamed about him regularly, every night, Rokni. All my dreams are the same. It's as though once again we've gone on that trip to Nishapur. In front of the house, there's a carriage parked. It's New Year's and the late Homayun-dokht is straightening your Khan Brother Zia's sailor suit for the traditional visits to relatives. Then there's a knock on the door. When I open it, Big Cousin Mirza Hassibi pokes his head from the carriage. I put your Khan Brother Zia in the carriage. I sense that the late Homayun-dokht is watching with anxiety. I feel uneasy and I tell myself, Well, she's a mother; she has the right; she can't part with her child. I want to take your Khan Brother Zia off the carriage and give him to her, but the carriage starts moving. Big Cousin Mirza Hassibi motions for us to come aboard. What are we waiting for? I point to the late Homayun-dokht and shout, 'Mirza, Mirza, we can't, we can't . . .'"

He fell silent. He lowered his head and stared into my eyes. "Do you remember Mirza Hassibi?"

"No."

"It's been a long time since I've seen him. He seldom shows himself. I have no idea where he is. You know, Rokni? It's as if everybody's gone. But there's something in the Heshmat Nezamis that will last forever. It only has to be looked after and protected. Your Khan Brother Zia, with all his obstinacy, would never allow these things to blow away. He'll come back. You must search for him. You must ask this person and that. Masoud was saying that on his trip to the south he saw your Khan Brother Zia. He knows something about him. Recently, Masoud himself has been invisible. That cuckold never keeps his feet in one place. Otherwise, he could find your Khan Brother Zia, even if it meant pulling a few strings. After all, Masoud's a Sardar Azhdari. The Sardar Azhdaris always have their hands in every bowl of henna."

"People say Masoud's in smuggling now," I said. "He goes to Kuwait. He smuggles back American suits, cigarettes, suede vests, and jeans."

My Khan Papa Doctor put on his reading glasses. From behind the lenses his eyes appeared wider and more watery. He stood up and came over to me. He set his hands on my shoulders and looked at me with an expression of discouragement. He shook my shoulders and said, "Now, wake up. You ass, the world is washing away and here you sit with your dreams. From now on, no more playacting. Nothing's going to be helped by those weird masks you put on your face, or those artificial beards. We don't have much time. We can't take our family lightly. It's a pity, Rokni. Listen to me. It's a pity."

He straightened and turned to leave the library.

"Was that all you wanted to talk to me about?" I asked.

He nodded. "That was it."

I said, "What about the story of Homayundokht, God forgive her soul?"

He didn't answer. With shuffling steps, he left the library. I turned my head, and through the window I saw my mother, my Bee Bee, and my half sister Iran following after my Khan Papa Doctor like a pair of pull toys.

I felt tired. The cool, dusty smell of the sugar pouch was still in my nostrils. The furniture in the library looked alive and uncanny. Everything was hunting for an excuse to unlock its tongue and share a confidence with me. But the silence continued, and the only sound was the grinding teeth of a solitary mouse, sawing away at the dark of the night behind the empty bookshelves. It was clear I had to look for Masoud.

CHAPTER 2

After the last few years, facing Masoud didn't much appeal to me. But in spite of all our childhood fights, we couldn't break our ties completely. It seemed to be our destiny that either I search for him or he for me. Even the plays we used to stage were based on that. He always played characters whose underhandedness my own characters relied upon; yet at the same time these characters couldn't get along. If I were the late Shah Sardar Sepah, he was Sardar Sepah's prime minister, Sayed Zia. If I were Shah Anushirvan the Just, he was the Shah's grand vizier, Buzar Jomehr the Wise. Then we got our high school diplomas, went our separate ways, and didn't see each other till the middle of last fall, when his head emerged from the water and, everywhere I went, he grew in front of me in the street like a weed. He wanted to talk, but I didn't give him the chance.

One time in Sarcheshmeh, I exploded, "Masoud, I don't have time to talk! I like to walk in the street alone." He answered, surprised, "Didn't you promise we'd go south together and find your Khan Brother Zia?"

"That was a few years ago. Now I don't feel like it. Get yourself another traveling companion."

"You Heshmat Nezamis are never in the mood for anyone. You put on a high hat for everyone."

I didn't answer. I ducked into Lazarian's and slugged down beer until the tiredness left me and I felt better and was sure Masoud was gone. Then, through the foggy window, I caught sight of him. He had turned up the collar of his raincoat. He had stuffed his hands in his trouser pockets, and from his half-open mouth the steam of his breath was twisting and knotting in the cold, wet air of autumn. With barely contained hunger, he fixed his sunken eyes on me. I waited till he glanced away. Soundlessly, I slipped through the back door and lost myself in the narrow alleys behind the mosque. I was free of him. When I reached the Curb of Shemiran I saw him again, standing under the lamppost in front of the Women's Hospital. In the dark of the night, he was whistling. He was whistling in the Scale of Shur, and as soon as he saw me he stopped. As I passed, he leaned forward and said, "How are you, Rokni? Are you feeling all right?"

I said, "Not bad. It's getting late. I have to find a cab and go home."

He said, "Never mind about me, but don't you want to come visit my Dear Daddy? He asks about you all the time. He says, 'Where is Rokni?'"

I said, "Give my regards to Uncle Abdolbaghi. Tell him I'll come see him very soon."

Then I set off again in a hurry. From a hundred paces away, I heard his whistling begin once again. He was whistling the Chekavak Corner of the Scale of Homayun. When he reached the Bee-Dad Corner, he started twittering like a nightingale — a constant, massaging twitter that polished the wet street. I felt guilty. Maybe I shouldn't have acted so cold and distant.

It occurred to me that night that much of the split between the children of Heshmat Nezam and the children of Sardar Azhdar was meaningless; it was all a masquerade. There'd been fifty years of bad feeling between Agha Heshmat Nezam and Agha Sardar Azhdar over the late Prime Minister Vosugh el Doleh's concessions to the British. It started at the festival of the thirteenth day of the New Year, when everyone had gathered at the family cemetery. They were busy with chitchat when Agha Heshmat Nezam descended from his carriage in his military uniform and went straight to the late Sardar Azhdar and shouted, "Honorable Brother! I wish our honorable late father could stick his head out of his grave and see that Your Excellency is putting this country in the hands of foreigners for a lousy ten thousand tomans! Agha, what do you feel attached to? What is important to you?"

People say that, because of his deafness, the late Sardar Azhdar didn't hear a word the late Heshmat Nezam said; but then the late Agha Ass Dass Dolah whispered something in the late Sardar Azhdar's ear that split the two brothers forever, as well as the brothers' children. You could see this split in the random photographs Mirza Hassibi had taken of their weddings, their funerals, and the thirteenth days of the New Year. In one corner the two sisters, Great Pride and Superior Venus, the first-ranking grandchildren of the late Sardar Azhdar, sit on openwork metal lawn chairs in the middle of their inherited courtyard. Each of them clutches a nosegay in her fist and gazes so hard at the camera that her eyes are widened. Their late father, Agha Ass Dass Dolah, with an unturbaned head, a Yazdi robe hanging aslant from his shoulders, leans on his cherry cane and admires the two sisters from a distance with a poetic smile. A little farther away, the late Aunt Lady Najafi and her insane husband, Sayed Kazem, the owner of *The Book of Divine Graces,* sit next to the samovar. All around them, Heshmat Nezamis and Sardar Azhdaris and Hamedani Sadats are swarming like ants and grasshoppers. And behind them Homayundokht, God forgive her soul, with her head bare, in her white lace gown, is stretched on the lawn under the walnut tree examining her fingernails. Aunt Lady Badi Zaman, the interpreter of the Quran, employed by Radio Tehran, with her hair cut *à la garçon* and her French cap and broadcloth suit and black tie that make her look like a classroom monitor, has drawn herself up as if to deliver her Friday night sermon. At the left, the Heshmat Nezami ladies are gathered and their gazes, full of pity, fall upon the giddy, coquettish face of Homayundokht, God forgive her soul. It seems they might at any moment move their lips and express their regrets that the daughter of Mirza Yousef had set herself on fire in front of relatives and strangers and her own little daughter Iran, all because of an insignificant quarrel with her obstinate, military husband.

Even now, after some thirty-odd years, they still talked about it as though it had happened yesterday. They had never given any thought to the children of Homayundokht, God forgive her soul, and used to melodramatically describe the onion and garlic of that story in front of my Khan Brother Zia and my sister Iran as though those two were deaf and couldn't hear them. Not only my Khan Brother Zia, who understood a good many things, but even my feeble-minded sister Iran grasped what they were saying. When you looked into Iran's face it would occur to you that still, after some thirty-odd years, she was staring at that scene with the eyes of a three-year-old child. As long as she lived and breathed, her gaze would be branded by that scene. It carved a vacant space around her with an invisible chisel and created in her face a contradiction of childishness and age, of thickheadedness and shrewdness.

But what about my Khan Brother Zia? No matter how I remembered him, I still couldn't imagine what went on in his mind. In the photo, he looks distant and apologetic. He is sitting on a stool. He has placed one heel on his knee. He leans his elbow against a pillar, tilts his head in the hollow of his palm, and fixes his eyes upon a corner of the sky as though he were about to start singing. The entire background of sky is black except for the corner that my Khan Brother Zia is watching. That corner is yellowed like votive candles, like congealed beads of fat on a bowl of soup. It seems he wants to open his mouth and tell me something but his tongue is tied.

In my heart I said, Oh, God, what's wrong with me? I can get moving and go look for him and ask for clues from this person and that. Eleven years is a long time, but still I have him in mind. A handful of memories and cluttered images rushed into my head. I stood up and left the library.

Since it was late in the evening, I abandoned the idea of calling Masoud. There was no hurry. Maybe tomorrow he would come to the School of Art, or I would run into him in the street. I felt he was loitering somewhere near me. He was passing shadowlike among the trees. I was sure I would find him eventually. Either he would search for me or I for him.

In the courtyard, my Bee Bee sat next to Iran watching television. They were broadcasting news of killings and a bomb explosion in the bazaar. There wasn't a trace of my Khan Papa Doctor. No doubt he'd gone to his office again, or perhaps he was inspecting his crossbred roses in the garden. Then I noticed that Iran's eyes were on me. She was genuinely looking at me. At the same time there spun, behind her pearly and unchanging gaze, a moving pattern of dreams and thoughts and feelings. I bent down and whispered in her ear, "Iran-jun, do you hear my voice?"

I thought she did. From the way she was looking at me I felt she could see me better than anyone else could. She was screwing questions into me with her drilling gaze. She was asking strange questions I knew the answers to but couldn't explain. My Bee Bee noticed. She turned her head and looked at me curiously. I raised my shoulders, as if confessing to this clumsiness. She poured me a glass of tea and put the sugar bowl in front of me. I said, "Bee Bee-jun."

She said, "Now what?"

"Has my Khan Papa Doctor talked to you, too?"

"Of course."

"What did you say?"

"Your Khan Papa Doctor will do what he has to. Maybe you can't see his purpose now, but you will later. There's a time for everything."

"I'm afraid that hunting my Khan Brother Zia won't have a happy ending."

She smiled and said, "Rokni, you with your natural gifts will succeed at whatever you tackle. You're not an ordinary person."

"What if I can't find him?"

"Don't let them discourage you. Don't listen to the Sardar Azdaris. It's not important to them. They say, 'Shit on the grave of the world.' They say, 'Seize the moment.' But you're not bitter and pushy like them. Go after your brother. It's God you should rely on."

I bent my head and started to drink my tea. A fairy lamp was burning in the vestibule. The servant, Zahra Soltan, was sitting on the bench in front of the kitchen, rubbing her swollen knees with goat lard and sarcocolla. In that old house, everything had the look of something left behind forever, like the cloth bundles in the dressing room of a Turkish bath. Even the walls were longing for movement, and the building seemed about to uproot itself and take off.

I stood up and started walking. I looked at the tiled wall in front of the basement. The late Sardar Azhdar had brought those tiles from Ghom, but after he was removed from office and retired, he couldn't pay for them. The Sardar Azhdaris circulated a rumor that the Agha's enemies were jealous of him, that it was they who put the banana peel under his foot and made a scandal of him. As his son-in-law, Agha Ass Dass Dolah, said, "They forced the old man to face the wall."

Anyone could testify that the late Sardar Azhdar's sleight of hand and magic shows were much more interesting than those of the most famous magician of his day, Mirza Malkam Khan. The late Sardar Azhdar put a pearl-handled revolver in a sugar pouch and attacked it with a sugar hammer till it was completely shattered. Then, with two of his pen-shaped fingers, he held the sugar pouch in midair and, like Mashd Abbas the bonesetter, he caused the broken pieces to be reassembled in the presence of His Majesty, the Mecca of the Universe himself. He took the revolver from the sugar pouch, whole and untouched, and put it on the blessed palm of His Majesty.

The Mecca of the Universe could not contain his delight. Unexpectedly, he jumped from his seat and embraced the late Sardar Azhdar and kissed his cheeks. He gave him a hat wound around with a scarf, a cashmere cloak, curly-toed shoes, and a robe of honor. The Mecca of the Universe made all the members of the Humanity Society envious. They started ridiculing the late Sardar Azhdar, saying he wasn't worth the smallest fingernail of the stupidest student of Mirza Malkam Khan. Then they invited him to repeat his magic show in a cabinet meeting. The old man was over eighty. He didn't catch the scent of trouble. He didn't know they'd rubbed soap on the soles of his feet and dampened his know-how, his magic skills.

Aping Mirza Malkam Khan, he came one hour later than the appointed time. All the ministers took their watches from their vest pockets and showed them to the late Sardar Azhdar, asking the reason for his delay. The late Sardar Azhdar, swollen with pride and haughtiness, smiled contemptuously and said that there was no delay. He said it was better for the gentlemen to toss their watches into a toilet and instead buy a Lari rooster to wake them every dawn for morning prayers with its cockle-doodle-doo. To demonstrate his claim, he threw all the hapless watches into the famous sugar pouch and attacked them with the sugar hammer. He hit them without ceasing. When he had finished the job, he used every trick and skill he knew for a full three hours, trying to reassemble the watches. But each time he opened the sugar pouch, sweat covered his forehead as he saw all those broken bits of glass, those bent and crooked gears and loose springs. He was about to collapse when the prime minister, the Lord Amin o Soltan, set His Excellency on his donkey with the help of the footmen. They put the order of removal from office underneath his arm and sent him home.

A few years later, the fall of Vosugh el Doleh's Cabinet added insult to injury, and the late Sardar Azhdar never set foot outside his house again. He also stopped reading the books by Flammarion and summoning the spirits, and he did no work. But four days before his death, he was struck again by the urge to stage his magic shows and jugglery. He took the notorious sugar hammer from under his mattress and went running to the orangery. He found the statue of His Majesty which he had set in front of the rose garden many years before. With his sugar hammer, he broke it to pieces. When he had finished, he threw the sugar hammer in the middle of the rose garden and went straight to his bed. He pulled the edge of the quilt over his nose, and until Thursday, which was the day of his passing, he didn't say a word to anyone.

In the dark, I realized that I had arrived in front of my Khan

Brother Zia's room. They had sealed it, just as they had sealed the room of Homayundokht, God forgive her soul. In the hundred years since the time of the Martyred Shah, it had become a tradition for our family to seal the rooms of those among us who were unfulfilled prisoners of the earth — those who, to quote Agha Ass Dass Dolah, had "untimely hid their faces behind the veil of dust." The glass panes in the door of my brother's room were dark and opaque. Nothing inside was visible. I put my hand on the door and got a surprise. The door was open. They had broken the seal. Surely this was by order of my Khan Papa Doctor. It was impossible to break the seals of those rooms without his permission. Maybe he wanted to let me know indirectly that he was allowing me inside his private life. Maybe he wanted to make a confidant of me, just for himself.

When I entered the room of my Khan Brother Zia, a strange smell hit my nose — a smell like an old water house, or a pool that had recently been drained. It was as though someone you couldn't see was living there. I turned on the light. The closet door was half open. Inside, my Khan Brother Zia had thumbtacked a picture of himself and Mademoiselle Sonia. Mademoiselle Sonia wore her canary-yellow cloak. My Khan Brother Zia had on his military officer's uniform — no doubt the same uniform whose price he had extracted from my Khan Papa Doctor. What a production he had made over that uniform! No matter how he approached the subject, my Khan Papa Doctor's answer was always the same: "What do you want from me, Zia? Any sane and sensible person would first go through compulsory military service and then think of buying an officer's uniform."

My Khan Brother Zia was furious. He ran to the library. He brought Khan Papa Doctor's money box to the veranda, but try as he would, he couldn't open the lock. Then, somehow, he found the sugar hammer of the late Sardar Azhdar, and he flung himself at the box with that. Bronze powder and black enamel flew everywhere, but the lid wouldn't open. He went to the library and came back with the pearl-handled revolver. He held the revolver to my Khan Papa Doctor's belly and forced him to unlock the box. Without a trace of embarrassment or shame, he took a fistful of bills from the box and stuffed them into his pocket. When he was through, he hit the street and didn't even shut the door behind him. My Khan Papa Doctor was so angry that if you'd stuck him with a knife he wouldn't have bled.

The officer's uniform is very becoming to my Khan Brother Zia. It suits his tall body. He rests his elbow on Mademoiselle Sonia's shoulder and holds his officer's hat between his fingers. He is smiling his famous smile at the camera. Behind them, the statue of the Angel of Liberty is stretching toward the sky, and behind that the statue of Baharestan.

As I opened his desk drawer, I saw his old album. Pictures of his favorite movie stars from his high school days were pasted into it — Ingrid Bergman, Greer Garson, Gregory Peck. In the middle of the album was another picture of Mademoiselle Sonia that I hadn't seen before. She is wearing a knitted angora blouse. She turns her head over the curve of her shoulder and smiles a lovely, self-possessed smile. Her face shines with cleanliness, as though she's just come from her bath. Underneath this picture, my Khan Brother Zia had written in his broken handwriting:

> To you who trust and love me,
> To you who are pure and honorable,
> To you, the guest of my empty days.
> Zia

The pictures on the last four pages had been removed. In their places, dark gray squares were left like a row of vacant windows open to the autumn sky. At the bottom of the final page, my Khan Brother Zia had scrawled a verse from Rumi:

> Is there anyone insane enough not to go insane?
> Anyone who sees the head constable and doesn't
> duck back in his house?

When I first saw my Khan Brother Zia in Mademoiselle Sonia's sports car I couldn't believe it. I said, That's not my Khan Brother Zia. It's some stranger who wants to mold himself in my brother's image. I couldn't believe that, after all the critical and sarcastic remarks the others had made, he would pick up Mademoiselle Sonia and bring her to our house for the New Year's visit. For a full three months my Bee Bee and Khan Papa Doctor had been talking about him every night at dinner. My Bee Bee begged and insisted, but my Khan Papa Doctor stood his ground. He swore he wouldn't let Mademoiselle Sonia enter our house.

"That little Polish slut isn't worthy of us. She's ten years older than that thick-necked boy. A Heshmat Nezami could never get along with an older wife, especially Zia, who doesn't even kowtow to God."

My Bee Bee said, "Doctor, all this mischief is just because he's young and without a wife. He doesn't have anyone to look after him, to pull him together."

My Khan Papa Doctor said, "Miss Asiah, try to imagine that this boy is basically not ours, that we never had him to begin with. Imagine that there is no Zia, that he has perished."

My Bee Bee said, "Doctor, I beg you in the name of my ancestor the Prophet, stop talking this way. It's unlucky."

I was petrified. What had happened? What incident had taken place? Why didn't Mademoiselle Sonia leave my Khan Brother Zia alone?

Mademoiselle Sonia was sitting behind the wheel, and it was she who drove the sports car down the narrow alley. She drove as slowly as if she were conveying a bride. As they passed me. Mademoiselle Sonia's perfume filled the air and a few men came out of the grocery store to watch. My Khan Brother Zia was unperturbed. Content and in good humor, he puffed on his cigarette. The sunlight spread everywhere and the gentle spring breeze sprinkled the fragrance of tulips and hyacinths.

They parked the sports car in front of our house. My Khan Brother Zia opened the car door for Mademoiselle Sonia. His eyes fell on me and he raised both arms. I rushed toward him and threw myself into his embrace. He lifted me from the ground and spun me around in a full circle. He said, "How're you doing, silly little Rokni?"

I said, "I'm fine, Khan Brother Zia."

He showed me to Mademoiselle Sonia and said, "This is that silly little Rokni I told you about."

Mademoiselle Sonia beamed a beautiful smile that made dimples in her cheeks. I knew who she was immediately, but I was too shy to let on. She herself started the conversation — actually, she opened her purse and took out a Nestle's chocolate bar and gave it to me. I accepted it, and she folded her arms and looked her fill at me. My Khan Brother Zia cupped a hand under my artificial beard and asked, "Who are you now?"

I said, "I'm the ex-Prime Minister Sayed Zia. I've struck a deal with the British, and with your permission I also plan to make a small and useful coup d'état."

He didn't say a word. He only grinned. He reached into the backseat of the car and brought forth a musical instrument. "Well, Mr. Sayed Zia, this is for you," he said.

I asked, "What is it?"

"It's a mandolin."

He pretended to play it. I said, "I don't know how to play a mandolin."

He lost patience. He threw up a hand and said, "It's an Italian mandolin; playing is easy. Practice till you learn."

He gave me the mandolin, and I started running through the courtyard. I reached my Bee Bee, who was on the veranda reciting the shopping list to Zahra Soltan. I said, "Bee Bee, Bee Bee!"

She said, "What is it, dear?"

I said, "Here you sit idle, and my Khan Brother Zia has brought Mademoiselle Sonia for the New Year visit."

My Bee Bee slapped her face and said, "Oh, my dear father! Your Khan Papa Doctor is going to raise havoc. In a moment it will be Resurrection Day."

My Khan Brother Zia stood in front of the vestibule and yelled, "O Allah! O Allah! Where are the inhabitants of this house?"

Fearfully, my Bee Bee pulled her veil over her head. She said, "Agha Zia, we're honored by your visit. May there be a hundred such New Years! What a surprise that you remembered us."

My Khan Brother Zia set a gift box on the ground and hugged my Bee Bee. Then he introduced Mademoiselle Sonia. My Bee Bee stretched an indecisive, clumsy hand from her veil and shook Mademoiselle Sonia's hand. Like the two ends of a seesaw, they gave each other repeated and exaggerated bows.

As we started toward the library, my heart filled with anxiety. I was praying this wouldn't end in scandal.

In the library, my Khan Papa Doctor was offering a box of Yazdi baklava to Mrs. Motlagh and her daughter Farideh. With nervous smiles, they declined. Then Mademoiselle Sonia entered. She unbuttoned her cloak, opened it, and took it off. As my Khan Papa Doctor caught sight of her, he set the box of baklava on the table. He put on his reading glasses and examined her. Then his eyes fell on my Khan Brother Zia, who had just come in. A smile appeared on my Khan Papa Doctor's face. He asked, "Is that you, Zia?"

My Khan Brother Zia put his gift box on the telephone table and approached him. They threw their arms around each other and gave each other long, hearty kisses on both cheeks, as though they'd been awaiting this moment for thirty years without a wink of sleep. Then my Khan Brother Zia turned around and introduced Mademoiselle Sonia. Mademoiselle Sonia gave a sweet, flirtatious smile. She held out her hand for my Khan Papa Doctor. Exactly like a German general, my Khan Papa Doctor clicked his heels, bent, took Mademoiselle Sonia's fingertips, and kissed the back of her hand. Such a European gesture from him was unprecedented; I couldn't remember ever seeing him exhibit so much etiquette. We were all astounded. None of us moved from our places. My Khan Papa Doctor broke the silence and said, in the accent of a Tehran hoodlum, *"Bonjour, mademoiselle!"*

Mademoiselle Sonia tossed her cloak onto the arm of a heavy chair, and with her sweet smile she answered in Persian, "You're very well, Agha. You are honored, Agha. Me wish you a happy New Year."

My Khan Papa Doctor was surprised. He raised his eyebrows with delight, he drew himself up on tiptoe and threw admiring glances at Mademoiselle Sonia and all those present. He sat down next to her and started talking in formal Persian. "This person, both on his own behalf and on behalf of the other members of the respected Heshmat Nezami family, sends you and all your respected Polish relatives good wishes for this auspicious, ancient, traditional celebration. From the time of antiquity, it has been a tradition in our country to pay homage to plants, light, and the health of the body. In other words, just as the Western world grants importance to money and material matters, we the ancient Iranians granted, are granting, and will continue to grant importance to religious principles, ethical values, the love of humanity, the care of foreigners . . ."

He pronounced each word and stretched it out so Mademoiselle Sonia could understand its significance. At the end of every word, he marked time with his hand for emphasis. He went on and on and on, and his speech grew more and more complicated. It grew so complicated that he couldn't even pay attention to Mrs. Motlagh and Farideh.

Mrs. Motlagh tried not to show her discomfort. With an artificial smile, she observed the conversation as though listening to an invisible radio. Farideh sat sideways on her chair, her back half turned to my Khan Brother Zia, and with a pouting glance she searched the bookshelves for something.

My Khan Papa Doctor suddenly stood up. He rubbed his hands together like a Park Hotel waiter and said, "How about a drink before lunch, in honor of this auspicious and ancient occasion?"

Without waiting for a reply, he offered his arm to Mademoiselle Sonia. Mademoiselle Sonia tossed her golden hair and burst into high-pitched laughter. She took his arm, and with much pomp and pride both of them went to the dais. My Khan Papa Doctor opened the corner cupboard and brought out the late Heshmat Nezam's special bronze cordial service. He pressed a ramrod in the pitcher, and drink started pouring into crystal glasses from six tiny faucets around the base. He was about to offer one of the glasses to Mademoiselle Sonia when my Khan Brother Zia said, "First let me show you this gift, and then we'll drink to our health."

In a low voice, my Khan Papa Doctor said in my Khan Brother Zia's ear, "I've been to Europe and I'm familiar with European customs. The rule is that first you offer drinks."

In the middle of all this, Mrs. Motlagh and Farideh suddenly stood up and said a hasty good-bye to everyone. My Khan Papa Doctor asked, "Why so early? Stay for lunch."

Mrs. Motlagh answered, "Some other time, God willing, Mr. Doctor. We have to go other places, too, to pay our New Year visits."

They left the library in a hurry. With their departure, my Khan Papa Doctor completely forgot about everyone but Mademoiselle Sonia. He lifted two crystal glasses. He gave one to her and kept one for himself. They clinked their glasses and drank to the health of Poland and ancient Iran. Out of joy, he put his hand under Mademoiselle Sonia's elbow and led her on a tour of the bookshelves and told her things that were impossible to hear from a distance. When they arrived in front of the gramophone of Homayundokht, God forgive her soul, he cranked it up for Mademoiselle Sonia and put on Badi Zadeh's "Fall Is Here" and made her listen with silence and attention. Then, to show that he was mindful of Mademoiselle Sonia's Western tastes, he changed the disk and put on one of Nelson Eddy and Jeanette MacDonald. As soon as the tremulous, screamlike twitters of Jeanette MacDonald began to rise, he grinned and again lifted his glass to the health of ancient Iran and Poland.

My Khan Brother Zia had already opened the gold wrappings of his gift. Inside was a blue velvet box. He took the box to my Khan Papa Doctor and lifted the lid. The box contained a complete set of silver knives, spoons, and forks. My Khan Papa Doctor glanced at them in a perfunctory way. He waved his hand and said, "Well, well, God bless you, it's a delight to my eyes. What a service! What a beautiful service! Give it to Miss Asiah so she can hide it in the closet."

Then he put his hand on Mademoiselle Sonia's shoulder. "I myself, before the war, imported a silver service from Germany. You are Polish and have been to Europe, you know better than I. The services they used to make in those days, the days of Germany before the war, were very different from what they make now. The one I imported was made by the Schultz factory, which was regrettably bombed by the Allies later. No doubt you know that whatever was worth anything got bombed by the Allies."

My Khan Brother Zia dropped his gift box on the table. He took my hand and pulled me out of the library. He said nothing to me, and I wouldn't have dared ask him anything. Under the warm, dizzying spring sunshine, he sat on the veranda railing and looked out at the flower beds, in which a wide variety of pansies was freshly planted and fertilized. I sat next to him and busied myself with playing the mandolin he had brought me. Through a window I could see my Khan Papa Doctor and Mademoiselle Sonia dancing in the center of the library, and Mademoiselle Sonia's yellow skirt puffed with each whirl like a canary's ruff. I was struck dumb; I couldn't think of a way to start my Khan Brother Zia talking. Finally I took courage and said, "Khan Brother Zia, it's a long time since I've seen you. I've missed you very, very much."

He threw a sidelong glance at me that made me anxious. He took a cigarette from his silver case and lit a match with a stroke of a thumb and carelessly held it to the cigarette. Suddenly he screamed and jumped up like a firecracker and threw the match to the center of the courtyard. He had burned himself, and he was shaking his fingers with pain. It struck me how much he resembled Homayundokht, God forgive her soul — especially as she appeared in the photo taken during the last year of her life.

She is more mellowed in this photo than in the earlier ones. With her checkered veil spread on her shoulders, with her sleepy, tired eyes, she holds her head high in resignation. Her face is laced with premature lines, like cracked antique china. The lines create a kind of paradoxical mood — not exactly weary and yet not exactly fresh. No longer does she wear the witty, gay expression she used to have in the years before the Third of Pisces Coup d'État of 1921. She looks determined and serious, as though she listens to no one and her business is separate from other people's.

My Bee Bee came out to the courtyard and asked my Khan Brother Zia, "What happened, Agha?"

My Khan Brother Zia said, "Nothing much. I burned my thumb."

"Shall I bring cold water and soap to stop the pain?"

"No thank you. It'll get better on its own."

"Please come in, then. Lunch is ready."

We went to the telephone room. A tablecloth was spread on the carpet. There was vegetable pilaf and fish for lunch. They had seated Iran at one corner of the cloth and placed before her a copper bowl of rice and fish. She picked up handfuls of rice and stuffed them hurriedly into her mouth, as though she couldn't wait. I couldn't understand why my Khan Brother Zia paid no attention to her. He rested his hand on the pillar of a molded plaster niche and stood waiting. My mother looked worried. She opened the door to the veranda and called her husband, "Doctor, Doctor!"

My Khan Papa Doctor's voice rose from the library. "What is it, Miss Asiah?"

"Lunch is ready. Please come."

After a few minutes, I heard Mademoiselle Sonia and my Khan Papa Doctor laughing in the hall. They entered together, tipsy and sweating. My Khan Papa Doctor begged Mademoiselle Sonia to occupy the head place at the table. Then he caught sight of Iran. He pulled himself up and asked my Bee Bee, irritably, "You have brought her here for what purpose? Tell Zahra Soltan to take her to her room and let her eat lunch there."

My Bee Bee said, "Doctor, Iran's not interfering with anything. She doesn't bother anyone. If she sits here with us and eats her lunch, what's the harm?"

"Miss Asiah, don't you see we have a guest — a stranger and a foreigner?"

Suddenly, my Khan Brother Zia stood up and opened the courtyard window wide. Then he came back and gathered the corners of the tablecloth, and with one shake he threw the tablecloth and all that was on it out the window. He gripped the wrist of Mademoiselle Sonia, who looked baffled, and he dragged her out across the courtyard. He heaved her through the street door and slammed it shut behind him.

My Bee Bee had become as pale as chalk and was trembling like a willow. It was obvious that the doggish temper of my Khan Papa Doctor had surfaced. Blood rushed into his face, and anger made his eyelids puffy. He shook his finger at my Bee Bee and said, "Never again let that mule into this house. Don't ever let me see that miserable face of his. If he sets his foot in this house again, I'll make sure that the biggest piece left of him will be his ear."

My Bee Bee caught her breath and said, "Doctor, for heaven's sake."

"Call me Doctor Snake Venom. Call me Doctor Pain and Illness."

"Don't say such things. He's your son, Doctor. He'll do himself some harm. Then you'll be sorry."

"Let him; it's one dog less."

Then, without eating lunch, my Khan Papa Doctor left the telephone room for the library. He locked the door behind him and pulled the shades down.

I hid; I didn't want anyone to notice me. Without deciding to, I went to my Khan Brother Zia's room. They hadn't sealed it yet. Inside the room, I stood in front of his closet mirror and looked at my own face; I don't know why. It seemed to me that my face with its tall and drumlike forehead, the round head, the bladelike nose, was a reminder of an animal violence — the boar claw that suddenly scratches.

I asked myself, now, what I was hunting in that room. On what business had I come? If I were going to find my Khan Brother Zia, I would have to hit the alley outside the old house.

This is the scene that seemed to appear in my mind: a patch of wet, heavy clouds rises before me. Somewhere far away, behind the Elburz Mountains or in the middle of the highway to Chalus, a thunderstorm is wetting the northern forests. In the dust of the storm I see the square black body of a carriage. The carriage driver is bent over, whip in hand, protecting his face from the wind with his sleeve. When he arrives in front of our house, he pulls back on the reins. He glances at my Khan Brother Zia, who is standing at the door in his sailor suit. As soon as my Khan Brother Zia sees the driver, he bursts out crying. The driver says, "Little Agha, this is not the time for crying. Hop up and let's go. Miss Homayundokht, your Bee Bee, has had something happen to her. We're going to take her to the holy shrine in Karbala."

My Khan Brother Zia swallows his tears and asks, "Then where is little Iran?"

"Your sister is feeling upset. We have to bring a doctor for her. When we bring him, he'll write a prescription and make her healthy and fat. Then you can see her, too."

They lift my Khan Brother Zia from the ground and place him in the carriage. The driver's whip snaps and the carriage moves away. As it fades into the dust and the whistling of the wind, the driver keeps turning his head and looking at my Khan Brother Zia with the filmed, malicious eyes of a beggar.

All my family used to say that I was an imagining person, that I believed whatever came to my mind. It was true. Eleven years ago, in fact, I imagined that I saw Homayundokht, God forgive her soul. It was when I was standing in front of the old fig tree. I looked through the dirty, cobwebbed windowpane into the room of Homayundokht, God forgive her soul. I tried to make out the details of the alarm clock that her Dear Daddy, the late Mirza Yousef, had brought her from Petersburg. In the darkness, I couldn't see very well. I could just discern the vague, borderless outlines of the dolls that she herself had knitted with her own hands and arranged on the mantel with such artistry and good taste. A big copy of *The Queen of Birds* hung on the opposite wall. The Queen of Birds held her palms together and turned her passionate, innocent gaze upon the sky. And what pearl and emerald necklaces she wore on her white crystal neck, and what diamond and topaz rings on her slender hands! A paragon of beauty, popularity, and virtue.

Now, my family says this is just more of my showing off, something to make me seem dramatic — a self-indulgence, like my habit of talking as if I were reading from an ancient tale — but the truth of the matter is, that night eleven years ago I was inspired to take the hurricane lamp from the niche, climb the stairs, and go to the rooftop. In the middle of the stairs, I was overcome by the sensation of a presence. I felt goose bumps and a cold breeze on my skin. A few steps higher stood Homayundokht, God forgive her soul, with a green umbrella in her hand. I couldn't believe it. It knocked the wind out of me. For a twelve-year-old boy to be granted such a privilege? She wore a white lace gown and she raised the umbrella over her head and looked at me intensely. I gathered my voice and asked, "Homayundokht, is that you? Are we asleep? Are we awake? Where are we?"

She didn't answer. Just like a new bride who has painted her face with seven brushes, she went up the stairs and I followed. On the rooftop, we saw the sky decorated with half a million stars, dazzling our eyes. She beckoned to me. When I stepped forward, the smell of her lavender perfume made me giddy. She put her hand inside her glass bead purse, took out the dark mirror of the Master Assar, and held it up so she could watch the world with the eyes of a painter. What a strange mirror! All around it was enamelwork and jewel-studded patterns. And how elegantly Homayundokht, God forgive her soul, held its silver handle with those fingers which, in their satin gloves, looked white as snow! I told myself, Oh, my God, who am I to be in this royal court? She conveyed to me that I must seize the moment, that the nightingale had no more than an instant to sing. I didn't understand. I thought she wanted me to sing a song. I started singing, "Portrait maker and painter of china, go and see the face of my beloved . . ." She listened and didn't shift her gaze from the sky. When I stopped, she smiled regretfully. I sensed that we had lost our chance and would have to endure until our next turn. She spun her green umbrella over her head and disappeared in the dark.

Who knows? Maybe, after eleven years, our next turn had finally arrived.

— Translated by the author

Prose

Part Two

Shahrnush Parsipur

Shahrnush Parsipur was born in 1946 in Tehran. She received her B.A. in sociology from Tehran University in 1973 and studied Chinese language and civilization at the Sorbonne from 1976 to 1980. While holding a variety of office jobs, she began her literary career with the publication of the novel *The Dog and the Long Winter* in 1974. Her highly successful *Tuba and the Meaning of Night* was published in 1989, followed by *Women Without Men,* in 1990. Over the years she has been arrested and incarcerated three times by two regimes in Iran.

Parsipur's novels and short stories demonstrate her concern for, and belief in, the open discussion of the oppression of women, and the problems of gender and sexuality in a male-dominated culture. Her bold style, her discussion of real social problems, and her use of surrealistic and, on occasion, mystical images, have prompted some to call her a proponent of an Iranian magical realism.

Her most important novel, *Tuba and the Meaning of Night,* is the story of several generations of Iranian women and their experiences with the different configurations of oppression through much of the twentieth century.

Parsipur fled Iran and now lives in the United States. She has published eight works of fiction, including *Tea Ceremony in the Presence of a Wolf, Blue Wisdom, Heat in the Year Zero,* and *To Sit on the Wings of the Wind,* as well as her *Prison Memoirs.* Some of her works are banned in Iran. She was the recipient of the first International Writers Project Fellowship from the Program in Creative Writing and the Watson Institute for International Studies at Brown University.

These excerpts are from *Women Without Men,* which tells the stories of several women from different backgrounds and life experiences who come to question their situation, and thus become marginalized by the society at large. The open discussion of taboo subjects such as virginity, rape, and male violence against women prompted the authorities to arrest and imprison Parsipur and her publisher shortly after the publication of this book.

Excerpts from
WOMEN WITHOUT MEN

MRS. FARROKHLAQA SADRALDIVAN GOLCHEHREH

Farrokhlaqa, age fifty-one, still beautiful and immaculately groomed, was sitting on a comfortable American rocking chair on the terrace. It was the middle of spring, and the smell of orange blossoms filled the air. From time to time, Farrokhlaqa closed her eyes and concentrated her entire being on the fragrance. She thought that if her father were still alive he would be sitting in the corner of the yard changing the soil in the geranium pots. Her father had died ten years ago, but it was as if he had just died yesterday. Two days before he died, he had said, "Daughter, take care of yourself. I don't know about this man."

Farrokhlaqa forgot the fragrance of the flowers for a moment. The memory of her father was so strong that it overshadowed everything else. Involuntarily she covered her face with her hands. She wanted to escape the memory of the dead and the overwhelming sadness that it brought.

Golchehreh was in the living room. He was standing in front of the antique mirror, tying his tie. Part of the yard, the terrace, and Farrokhlaqa as she rocked gently back and forth were reflected in the mirror. Golchehreh extended the two-minute task to half an hour so that he could keep his wife under surveillance. He didn't want to look at her face-to-face. Every time he looked her in the face he could only smile with contempt. He couldn't help it. He didn't know why he felt such loathing whenever he looked at her. In fact, when he was far from her, or could watch her unobserved as he did now, he liked her. More than anything or anyone in the world. But whenever he had to face her, the old hatred welled up in him again. It was a thirty-year-old feeling.

Farrokhlaqa stretched, extending her arms wide and arching her back. She felt ecstatic. She recalled Vivien Leigh in *Gone with the Wind*. In one of the bedroom scenes she had stretched the same way. Whenever she thought of Vivien Leigh, she thought of Fakhredin Azad. Her first memory of him was at the prince's party at Shemiran Garden.

Fakhredin had just returned from America. He had brought back slides and photographs of America to show everybody. The pictures of New York were so strange. Farrokhlaqa later went to New York three times, but she could never see the same New York that she had seen in those photographs. In her mind, it was all Golchehreh's fault. If she had gone to New York with Fakhredin, she would have seen that strange New York. But Golchehreh wasn't the one to show her that New York. All he did was eat breakfast in the hotel restaurant and spend the day sitting on a couch in the lobby until Entezami came and took them to a restaurant, a movie, or a show.

Golchehreh had finally finished tying his tie and was looking for a reason to remain standing in front of the mirror. It occurred to him that if he shaved, he could remain there for another half hour. He went to the bathroom, filled a bowl with warm water, and brought it with the shaving brush, the shaving cream, and a bib to the living room and began to shave.

Farrokhlaqa was patiently waiting for Golchehreh to finish what he was doing and go out. Since he had retired, every evening he would go for a walk for a few hours, read the newspaper and get a cup of coffee in a café, and then return. And every day his wife waited patiently for him to go so that she could feel energetic and move about freely. Whenever he was in the house, she would lose her ability to move, and she would hide in a corner. She had a thirty-two-year-old habit of not moving. She had gotten used to immobility. She knew only this, and she knew instinctively, that when Golchehreh went out, mobility and happiness would come to her. She used to be happier, since Golchehreh would be at work every day for at least eight hours, although he would come home for lunch and a nap. She had more energy to move back then. Sometimes she even sang. With his retirement she was deprived of this happiness. He was not only at home more often, but he was also annoying. It never occurred to him to fiddle with the flowerpots or adjust the grapevines or do something about the mosaics in the party room, which were falling off the walls. He was always wearing his pajamas, lying down on the sofa or on the floor to sleep, or teasing Farrokhlaqa with his pale and tasteless humor.

She said, "You should shave over the sink. You're getting the carpet wet." Golchehreh's heart beat with joy as he swirled the shaving brush around in the water.

"Shut up!"

Farrokhlaqa bit her lip. She turned to face the yard. She didn't have the patience to answer him, although words were whirling explosively around in her head, trying to get out. But she held her breath. Fakhredin returned. He always came at times like this and saved her.

That night, the first night that she and Fakhredin met, he had come to her. She heard him say, "Vivien Leigh!"

Farrokhlaqa turned. Fakhredin was looking at her. She could still remember his mouth. Although she later kissed those lips many times, that first memory of them was unique. They mysteriously pressed together as if to conceal his perfect white teeth.

"Who, me?"

"You, the delicate little sister of Vivien Leigh, such an amazing resemblance."

She wanted to look at him out of the corner of her eye, over her left shoulder, a habit that she had inherited from her mother. She knew that she looked good when she did that. But before she could even turn her head toward her left shoulder, she lost her nerve. She was like a frightened bird. Fakhredin smiled.

"Farrokh, believe me, you become more and more beautiful every day. How is it possible?" She was nervous and alert.

At that point she was able to look at him out of the corner of her eye over her shoulder, and say, "It's been ten years."

"Since I last saw you? How could that be?"

"Then where did you see me?"

Fakhredin patted his chest and said, "Here. Why did you get married?"

"I shouldn't have?"

"Did you have to?"

She was shocked. She had never promised him anything. When he went to America she was thirteen. She couldn't remember having any feeling for him. But at that moment, she thought that there could have been something.

"That's life. Everyone gets married."

"And you? How can such a beautiful woman get married? You had absolutely no right to get married. You should have given the whole world the opportunity to see you."

Farrokhlaqa laughed softly. His manner of speaking was funny. He must have been annoyed by her laugh. But he wasn't annoyed, and came closer to her, and said, "You should always wear blue, it looks good on you."

At that moment Golchehreh showed up, more than a head shorter than Fakhredin, with that stale laugh and skeptical gaze that had been bothering her for four years. Fakhredin said, "I was just talking to your wife about *Gone with the Wind*. I saw it before I came back to Iran. It was one of the first nights that it showed. You can't imagine how much trouble it was to get a ticket. I got in line at five in the morning. I was telling your wife how much she looks like Vivien Leigh, the actress in the movie."

Golchehreh simply said, "How interesting!"

His smile, as always, was full of resentment. It was a smile of defeat. He was smart enough to realize that he somehow fell short of Fakhredin. Fakhredin said, "If it comes here, you should go see it. It's the greatest masterpiece of the cinema. And the most expensive movie ever made."

That night they went home in her uncle's car. Golchehreh sat silently the whole way, out of respect for her uncle. They said farewell politely at the entrance to the alley, and they walked slowly, side by side, toward the house. Farrokhlaqa was thinking the whole time that in an hour he would be asleep and she would have time to think before she went to sleep. Golchehreh had not been in good form that night. In the alley he began to make nasty remarks about the "silly movies" about which that "pathetic guy" had spoken. About the stupid pictures. About that goofy hat that he had brought and put on everyone's head and taken pictures of them one by one. He had even taken a picture of Farrokhlaqa. Farrokhlaqa said with loathing, "Shut up!" The only advantage in saying this to Golchehreh was that it would make him shift his complaining to someone else. Now he left off on the "pathetic guy" and turned to her blue dress, saying how ugly and tacky it was, and how everybody had hated it.

He went down to the cellar and brought up a watermelon, and at two in the morning started to eat it, forcing her to eat it with him. She had been putting up with all this nonsense in the hope of having half an hour to let her thoughts wander before going to sleep. After eating the watermelon, he decided to fiddle with the radio, switching from the Berlin channel to the London channel to the Moscow channel to see what was going on in the world. Then, at three o'clock in the morning, he finally went to bed, and of course before going to sleep he wanted to have sex. She put up with this too, and then, at four o'clock, he decided to take a shower and pray, something that he did every now and then. From that night on, her heart was filled with loathing for him.

Golchehreh had finished shaving off his beard. Now he was slowly collecting his shaving things. He didn't know why he was procrastinating so much that day. It was as if he were waiting for something but didn't know what. The doorbell rang, and Mosayyeb went to the door. Farrokhlaqa waited patiently to find out who had come and what they wanted. Golchehreh came to the entrance and stood by his wife. Farrokhlaqa turned and looked at him for a moment. One look was enough for both of them to confirm their mutual hatred.

Golchehreh said abruptly, "Next month you'll be fifty-one years old. You have reached menopause, Farrokh dear."

Farrokhlaqa looked at him silently. His smile, as always, was derisive. Finally she said, "Listen, Sadri, if you think I'm going to put up with your jokes even for one second, I won't."

"I wasn't joking, dear. Menopause is not a laughing matter."

Farrokhlaqa took a deep breath. Mosayyeb returned with the newspaper and placed it at her feet. Then he said he was going to Karaj to buy meat from Nasrallah for Friday's party.

Farrokhlaqa said, "I wish we had a garden in Karaj."

"Do you think that after menopause you can still enjoy a garden?"

As she glanced at the front page, Farrokhlaqa said, "Are you pining for a plump young woman to walk behind your coffin? Is that why you say such things?"

"Maybe. But my queen will not allow it."

"Fine, go find yourself a maid. You are really vile."

Absentmindedly, she started to read the newspaper. Golchehreh took it from her. She stared at the yard. Mosayyeb put on his coat and shoes and went to the door. As he passed by the garden pool, he asked, "Do you want anything else?"

"Get some fresh green almonds, too, if you can find them."

Mosayyeb left without responding. Golchehreh was sitting on the windowsill fiddling with the newspaper. Farrokhlaqa thought, God, why doesn't he leave? She wanted to continue her fantasies.

She remembered the day when they had gone to meet Fakhredin's American wife. She had arrived six months after her husband, with their two boys, Teddy and Jimmy. How strange those names had sounded. She would never forget how anxious she was that day. She curled her hair and put on a white dress with blue flowers. Golchehreh laughed at her as she put on powder and lipstick and braided her hair. She spent a lot of time trying to get the seams of her pantyhose straight. At the last moment she spun around in front of the mirror. Everything seemed fine, but she hadn't seen the other woman yet. She had never seen an American woman before. But at least she had seen *Gone with the Wind* with Vivien Leigh. She was not inferior to her, although she didn't see any resemblance. But if Fakhredin said there was a resemblance, there must have been one.

Fakhredin and his wife were staying at Sarim Mirza's house until their own house in the northern part of the garden was ready. The American woman was standing at the entrance of the five-door living room when they arrived, shaking hands with all the guests. She couldn't speak to anyone. She just smiled. She was an extremely tall woman, with blond hair and hands covered with freckles and veins. Her eyes were so light that they seemed colorless. If you looked closely, you could see that they were blue, and Fakhredin was fond of the color blue. Farrokhlaqa shook hands with her and entered. There was a full-length mirror in the room, before which she stood and looked at herself. She stared for a while at her own dark eyes and the blue flowers on her dress. Fakhredin appeared behind her in the mirror, and asked, "Why did you get married?"

People had asked him the same question. But what a strange effect it had on her. The man was staring at her in the mirror, and Farrokhlaqa noticed that he was pale.

"This white dress with blue flowers looks really good on you." He hurried over to his wife. That night, the whole night, he and Farrokhlaqa kept running into each other. It was as if a force was pulling them together.

Years later, on the moonlit terrace in the prince's garden, she told Adileh Rif all about that night. Adileh was a good woman. She tried to understand. She thought that a woman had a right to love, and that love was worthwhile. She criticized Golchehreh's behavior. At that moment, Farrokhlaqa's older daughter and Adileh's son were walking around the garden. Rumors were circulating, and Farrokhlaqa knew that there was something between Adileh and Shazdeh. So she was telling her all about what happened to her, to loosen Adileh's tongue. It worked. Adileh cried and told her everything. "Eight years have passed, eight strange years," Farrokhlaqa said.

"So throughout the war you were in love. Good for you!"

Farrokhlaqa yawned and stretched. "Eight years of war."

Golchehreh was angry for no reason. "When a woman reaches menopause, do her feelings change?" he asked suddenly.

"I don't know, Sadri."

"They must. That must be why every man has the right to marry several women, so that he doesn't always have to put up with a woman past menopause in his bed."

"Perhaps."

Golchehreh was thinking about a woman he had known, who had also been called Farrokhlaqa. She belonged to the war years. She was a Polish woman who didn't know Persian, and Golchehreh had called her Farrokhlaqa. She worked in a bar. Golchehreh used to call her Farrokhlaqa and she would laugh. She couldn't say the name properly, and it sounded funny to her. When the war was over, the woman said, "Farrokhlaqa go back Europe." Then she laughed. The next week, she wasn't in the bar anymore.

Golchehreh asked, "If I go and get another wife, you'll get angry!"

Farrokhlaqa didn't respond. She went back to looking at the garden. She recalled the last time she saw Fakhredin. They were in his house. They were in a room with the door closed and the curtains drawn. The room was dark, and his eyes shone in the darkness.

"I have to go home and take care of my children," he said.

Farrokhlaqa began to cry.

"I'll come back, I promise."

When the war was over, his American wife returned with Teddy and Jimmy. She was emotionally disturbed. One night at a party, she shouted, "You're all crazy!"

She was probably drunk, or perhaps she just couldn't take it anymore. Ten days later, she took her children and went back to America.

Farrokhlaqa didn't know why, but she knew that Fakhredin would not come back.

He didn't: Five months later he was killed in an automobile accident. Farrokhlaqa was left with her own problems and Golchehreh. There were children, but they were busy with their own lives. They grew up and left home so fast that it was as if they had never been born.

Golchehreh finished the newspaper and put it down, waiting for her to ask for it so that he could say something else about menopause. Actually, he had just come across this word for the first time three days ago, and he had a feeling that it would upset his wife. She said nothing, and Golchehreh got bored. Finally he asked, "You don't want the newspaper?"

The woman held her hand out without a word. Golchehreh gave her the paper. She took the paper and lit a cigarette.

Golchehreh said, "You shouldn't smoke. Especially at your age, and in the middle of menopause."

"Why don't you go for a walk? You used to go every day."

"Maybe I don't feel like it today."

She regretted her question. If he knew that she was happy when he went out, he wouldn't go out anymore.

She said, "You're right, it's better for you to stay home."

"I'm going out now."

He stood up. But for some reason, he felt he had to stay. It seemed as if something was about to happen. He walked over and stood before her in a daze. For a moment he thought that perhaps, after thirty-two years, he no longer needed to look at her with that smile. In fact, for some time he had known that he used this smile as a defense against her strange beauty. He knew that if he had not smiled that way, he would have been like a dead man to her by now. He knew that she must not, even for one moment, know how much he desired her. But now, all of a sudden, he had an urge. He wanted to look at her, just one time, the way he had looked at the Polish woman when he called her Farrokhlaqa. But now she had reached menopause. Her eyes were no longer rebellious. She no longer had any dreams at night. She went to bed early and even snored sometimes. Maybe he could look at her naturally now, without derision.

"Farrokhlaqa, dear."

She trembled. He had never spoken to her that way. He always said "Farrokh" with that smile. She looked up. There was no derision in his eyes; he was looking at her kindly. Farrokhlaqa was frightened. She was certain that he was planning something. She thought, what if he kills me?

She punched him hard in the stomach. It was like a pillow. He wasn't ready for the punch. He tripped over one leg and tried to regain his balance with the other, but lost control and fell down the terrace stairs. She stood in front of the chair for a while. She didn't dare look down the stairs. He didn't make a sound.

Three months later she was sitting on the chair wearing black. She was thin and weak. She did not like the house anymore. Mosayyeb brought a message from Mr. Ostovari, the realtor, saying that if she wanted to sell the house, she should not forget Ostovari. Farrokhlaqa, bravely and without reflection, told Mosayyeb to tell Ostovari to sell the house for her on the condition that he use the money to buy a garden in Karaj. Ostovari started looking for a garden.

He found a garden by a river.

Mrs. Farrokhlaqa Sadraldivan Golchehreh sold the house, bought the garden, and moved to Karaj.

ZARRINKOLAH

Zarrinkolah was twenty-six years old and a prostitute. She was working in the New City at Golden Akram's house.[1] Akram had seven gold teeth and was also called Akram Seven. She had been there since she was a child. At first she had three or four customers a day. She was tired of working. She had complained to Akram several times, and was yelled at and eventually beaten, until she shut up.

Zarrinkolah was a cheerful woman. She was always cheerful, whether she had three or four customers a day or thirty. She even turned her complaints into jokes. All the women liked her. When they ate lunch, Zarrinkolah would start joking and dance around the table, and the women would die laughing.

---

[1]Shar-e Now, or New City, was the name of the red light district in Tehran before the revolution. It was burned down by the Islamists during the revolution.

Several times she intended to leave the house, but the women wouldn't let her go. They said that if she left, the house would be dead. Perhaps all the women encouraged Akram Seven to beat her. Zarrinkolah never really intended to leave, for if she left this house, she would have to go straight to another house. Once, when she was nineteen, she received a marriage proposal and had a chance to leave. The suitor was an ambitious construction worker who dreamed of becoming a mason, and who needed a hardworking wife. Unfortunately, before they could decide what to do, someone cracked open his skull with a shovel during a fight.

Although she complained sometimes, she had accepted her fate. But now, for six months, she had not been able to think clearly. The problem had started one Sunday morning when she woke up.

Akram had shouted, "Zarri, there's a customer, and he's in a hurry!"

There weren't many customers early in the morning. Usually just a few who had stayed over from the night before and had the urge in the morning. That Sunday morning Zarrinkolah thought, So a customer has come. So what. She wanted to shout, "So what?" but Akram Seven yelled, "Zarri, I'm talking to you. I said a customer has come."

She left her breakfast and angrily went back to the bedroom, lay down on the bed and opened her legs. The customer entered the room. It was a man without a head. Zarrinkolah didn't dare scream. The headless customer did his business and left.

From that day on, all of the customers were headless. Zarrinkolah didn't dare say a word about it. They might say that she was possessed by a demon. She had heard about a woman possessed by a demon, who would start shrieking at eight o'clock every night. For a while this scared away the customers until they kicked her out of the house.

Zarrinkolah decided to sing every night at eight o'clock, so that she wouldn't shriek like that woman. She did this for six months. Unfortunately, she couldn't carry a tune. A guitar player said, "You bitch, you don't even have a voice, you're giving everybody a headache." After hearing this, she went into the bathroom every night and sang there for half an hour. Akram Seven ignored it. After all, Zarrinkolah took care of thirty customers a day and was still cheerful. She was always cheerful.

Then they brought an innocent young girl to the house. One day Zarrinkolah took her into her room and said, "Kid, I have to tell you something. I have to tell somebody. I'm afraid I'm going crazy. I have a secret that's making me miserable."

The girl said, "Everyone has to tell their secrets to someone. My grandmother used to say that the poor Imam Ali, who couldn't talk to anybody, used to go out into the desert, put his head in a well, and pour out his grievances."

"That's true. Now I'm going to tell you. I see everyone without a head. Not the women. The men. They're all headless."

The girl listened kindly. She asked, "You really see them all without heads?"

"Yes."

"Okay, so maybe they really don't have heads."

"If they really didn't have heads, the other women would notice."

"Well, that's true. But maybe they all see them without heads, but like you, they don't dare say anything about it."

So they agreed that whenever Zarrinkolah saw a headless man she would let the girl know, and if the girl saw a headless man, she would let Zarrinkolah know.

Zarrinkolah saw all the men without heads and the girl saw them all with heads.

The next day, the girl said, "Zarrinkolah, maybe you should pray and make a vow. Maybe then you'll see the men with heads."

Zarrinkolah took two days off work and went to the bathhouse. Instead of going to the public section as she usually did, she went to a private room so that she wouldn't have to talk and joke with the other women. She hired a bath worker to scrub her back. She washed herself from head to foot. She ordered the bath worker to scrub her three times. The bath worker scrubbed until Zarrinkolah's skin was raw. But she wasn't satisfied that she was clean enough to pray.

The bath worker finally broke down crying and said, "You poor woman, you must be crazy."

Zarrinkolah paid the bath worker well so that she wouldn't tell anybody about her, and asked her how to perform ablutions after sexual pollution.

When the bath worker left, Zarrinkolah performed ablutions. She did it fifty times. Her entire body was burning from the chafing of the sponge.

She intended to get dressed and go to the shrine of Shah Abdulazim, but she had a sudden urge to pray. She decided to pray naked, but she didn't know how to pray. She decided that if Imam Ali was so sad that he went out into the desert to pour out his grievances to a well, it would be all right for her to just repeat his name as a prayer. She prostrated herself in prayer, naked in the bath, saying, "Ali Ali Ali Ali Ali Ali Ali Ali Ali Ali . . ."

As she was saying this she began to cry. She cried and called out to Ali. Somebody knocked on the door, and then banged on it. She came out of her ecstasy, and asked, sobbing, "Who is it?"

It was the bath attendant. She said they wanted to close up the bathhouse.

Zarrinkolah put on her clean clothes and gave her dirty clothes to the attendant. She went out and walked to the shrine of Shah Abdulazim.

It was nighttime and the shrine was closed. She sat outside in the yard and cried quietly in the moonlight.

In the morning when they opened up the shrine, her eyes were swollen shut. She stopped crying, but did not enter. Her body felt like a piece of straw. She ate breakfast in a diner. She asked the owner, "If a person wants to drink cool water this time of summer, where should she go?"

The owner looked at her puffy eyes with pity and said, "Karaj isn't bad."

There was nothing in her face to show that she had once been a prostitute. She had become a small woman of twenty-six with a heart as big as the sea.

She went to Karaj.

— *Translated by Kamran Talatoff and Jocelyn Sharlet*

Moniru Ravanipur

Moniru Ravanipur was born in the southern village of Jofreh in 1954. She grew up in Shiraz, and received a degree in psychology at Shiraz University.

Moniru began her writing career with the publication of a collection of short stories, *Kanizu,* in 1988. Her first novel, *The Drowned,* was published in 1989 and brought her recognition as a serious writer whose innovative style, structure, and subject matter distinguished her from other writers. Many of her themes deal with the village culture of southern Iran where she was born. She portrays the people's way of life — their customs and superstitions, their poverty and hardship — in a way that is both real and fantastic. Ravanipur often weaves local histories, myths, and superstitions into her stories.

Her second novel, *Heart of Steel,* deals with the trials and tribulations of a modern woman writer in Tehran and employs experimental methods in style and technique. Her latest work, *Nazlie,* was published in 2003.

Moniru Ravanipur is among the most prolific and respected post-revolutionary Iranian writers. She has been successful in the treatment of the complex subjects of tradition and modernity, juxtaposing elements of both, and exposing them in all their contradictions without idealizing either.

This story is taken from the collection by the same title, *Satan's Stones,* first published in 1991. It is the chilling account of a young woman who returns to her village and discovers that she is suspected of sinful behavior and must be forcefully "examined."

SATAN'S STONES

The sputtering red minibus let her off at the roadside and continued its way to the northern villages. A wind, biting and cold from the north, beat the desert sand against her face and legs. Sheltering her face with her hand, she huddled up and set out toward the village, shrinking away from a wind that whipped about her shoulders.

She passed through the large white Satan's stones that were scattered about for some distance around the village. No one knew in what distant time or with what enormous power Satan had thrown them into the desert. The shrieking of the wind swirled in her head, and a whirlwind seemed to be attacking the village. Like an old djinn with disheveled hair, it hid everything from view, a djinn who, with a voice unintelligible and frightening, sometimes calm and sometimes howling, was casting spells. Distraught and demented, when the spells did not work, it threw dust and debris into the air.

As she remembered distant fairy tales of childhood, a smile rested on her lips, and to relieve her legs from the driving sand, she stood in the shelter of a rock and gazed toward the village. The whirlwind swirled around her and the rock, as though it did not want her to reach the village. Maybe it was strong enough to lift her and the rock and toss them somewhere far, far away, turning her into a rock — a white rock — and when a camel driver's children would pass it with their caravans, they would turn their faces away and, under their breaths, whisper a prayer.

She huddled against the rock and covered her ears tightly so as not to hear the terrifying sound of the wind, so she would not know whose fate was being sealed, or whom the stones were entreating to restore their original forms. She thought of the days when she was no more than a child, when the wind would peep through the cracks in the windows and doors into the darkness of the room. Her mother would say: "They are sighing. Satan's stones are sighing, and when they have atoned for all their sins, you will see that the desert is full of people — men and women."

She had come unannounced to make everyone happy. When she left, she hadn't known it wasn't like school, that she could return six months later to this very village she loved, where she could stay for two weeks. How quickly the time had passed in Shiraz, with its paved streets and countless trees — here this road was still rocky, full of Satan's stones and the wailing of wind.

She peeked out from behind the rock. The whirlwind had released her and the rock. Unruly, spouting spells, it had headed west. It did not seem to have accomplished anything.

She clutched her bag firmly. Passing through the white stones, she set out toward the village. A biting cold wind hit her face. The ground was frozen, and the uncommon chill of this midwinter month had cracked the small stones. The wind blew into the palm grove near the village, and she could see the gnarled branches bending in every direction. The old djinn goes to the middle of the palm grove sometimes. It tugs at the tresses of the palms so they won't give their crown of fruit to sinners during the date season, so that if they eat one, every single date they eat will ignite in their mouths. She drew near the first house — still mud brick! — with low doors and small windows, whose frames were only big enough for a head, unlike those open windows in Shiraz . . . in houses and classrooms . . .

She looked at the blue door of a mud brick house and saw that it was still there — that very sign put on the door of Setareh's house at night. A djinn who is the protector of the village smells sin, and at night it marks every house where the smell of sin is concentrated. And who had ever seen this djinn?

Setareh, wearing a long orange dress, her black hair falling over her breasts, with kohl-lined hazel eyes, opened the low blue door. It was as though she had been waiting for her, waiting for her, and maybe through a crack of a window, as always, guarding the rocky path.

Setareh's face lit up with a broad smile, and in the middle of the biting chill and the distant sound of the wind she cried: "Hello, Maryam . . ."

Two years had passed since the djinn who watched over the village had seen the shadow of a heavy cloud over Setareh's house and appeared in the old matron's dream. The old matron, who was the village matriarch, had pointed to the sky in broad daylight with five henna-dyed fingers; there wasn't a single cloud. As punishment for loving a stranger, Setareh had been forced to come to this house — a house far from other houses. Two years ago, she had a house near the village square and lived with her mother. The stones that pelted the door and window of Setareh's house day and night, and the way the village women shunned her, drove her old mother to bed. Three days after the old woman's death, Gholam the Gendarme — who dropped by the village once every two months in a gendarmerie jeep — packed Setareh's things to take her to the city. Although she didn't love him, Setareh married him and settled down in this small mud-brick house.

It had been a long time since Gholam the Gendarme had dropped by the village in the gendarmerie car for a ten-day stay. Setareh always stood behind the window — the closed window — and watched for the dust her husband raised in the distance as he came to the door.

Setareh's friendship and congeniality were evident in the glow on her face and the sound of her voice. But she seemed to be afraid that someone would see her — see her talking with Maryam. She did not come out of the doorway; she stood right there, both hands on the doorpost, and smiled.

"Hello, Setareh! How are you? How is your son?"

"He's fine, kind of you to ask — but how about you? How have you been?"

She was in a good mood, but she watched everything around her. She was afraid that the village matron, the old woman who smelled everything and seemed to be everywhere, would see her. How many times had the women been forced to sit in the village square and ulu-late toward Setareh's house? Even Mother had joined them; they had taken her by force.

"Are you finished with school?"

"No, Setareh, it doesn't end that fast. It will take eight years."

"Eight years is a whole lifetime . . ."

Setareh had not gone into the village in a long time. Every Thurs-day she went around the mud-brick houses to reach the graveyard and say a prayer over the graves of her dead. If it weren't for Gholam the Gendarme with his rifle, and the bullets he had fired in the village square, the old matron could very well have had her paraded naked through the streets in front of everyone; she could have had her long black hair shaved off.

No one wanted to confront the old matron. It was she who had advised Mother not to send her to the port city. Mother had said: "She's not going to a strange place — it's her uncle's house." If it weren't for Maryam's uncle, who had lived in the city since his return from military duty and taken a wife from the port city where his children were educated, Maryam would never have been able to go to the port city and then to Shiraz.

Setareh's eyes sparkled. She leaned her arm, covered with bracelets, against the door and seemed to be searching for something to keep Maryam, to draw her toward the house. And if she went into the house? She was frightened. She looked all around her. No one was there — only the whistling wind blowing dust and debris.

After a long time, Maryam's uncle had come to the village with a bundle of souvenirs to talk with the old matron; her eyes had gleamed. Mother gave her lunch every day, and the other houses hosted the old matron every day, to ensure that food would remain plentiful on their tables; that, with her blessing, no one would get sick; that the rain would fall on time; and that the dead would rest in their graves.

Maryam had to leave. She had to break off this familiar, friendly exchange. She said good-bye and set off. The soles of her feet were freezing. A rough, abrasive wind beat against her face. A cow mooed in the distance. She had wasted too much time. She should not have stayed so long . . . Now she wanted to get home faster, to sit in a warm room beside a brazier full of charcoal and listen to the sound of a potato baking in the coals.

She reached the village square. The cold had blackened the familiar old tamarisk, and the tall narrow trunk of a palm with no top sank into the ground like an iron post on the left side of the square. The barefoot children rode stick horses made of palm tree branches, their cheeks red and their noses running. In a corner of the square, a small whirlwind played with dust and debris.

As she came nearer, the children stopped playing one by one and stared at her. She stretched out her hand to pat a little boy on the head. The little boy ran, and the others backed away on their wooden horses. A window facing the square opened, a woman put her head out and called: "Sardar, Sardar, come home!"

Maryam waved at the woman. She saw the woman's frozen, disgusted look, saw her back into the house and slam the window shutters closed. Maryam was stunned. It was Zoleykha. Why didn't she acknowledge her greeting? Maryam saw two other windows open, saw frowning women call their sons, look at her sourly, and slam the shutters.

This is where she used to play. Her childhood years were spent in this very square. And now she stood in the middle of it, amid frowning and closed windows. The children had run away, and the disgusted glare of the women remained in the square. Someone had certainly seen her talking and laughing with Setareh, a woman who had gotten pregnant by a stranger. She saw that they were watching her between the cracks behind closed windows. She was cold, and the whirlwind from the square was swirling around her legs, straining as if to lift her and carry her away, carry her where . . . where would it toss her?

She smiled faintly. She could say that Setareh had blocked her way, that her little boy was ill, that it was only hello, how are you; she could talk to her mother, and she could say . . . say what? What could she say?

She went on her way. The wind blew dried bits of dung along the ground. She hunched over, face-to-face with the wind. This cold had a nasty bite. The chill ran through her bones; it was different from the cold weather in Shiraz, where it drizzled continuously and you wanted to walk in the street, under the tall cypresses, where snowflakes fell softly on your face without getting you all wet, and the squares were all green, with tall water fountains and houses with big, windows . . . How far away that city was . . . how far.

The tap-tapping sound of a hand patting bread onto the walls of a kiln sent a pleasant warmth through her veins. She was in the village — the smell of fresh bread and a cow that mooed and a kiln around which women were gathering, waiting for a turn.

She saw the kiln from a distance, and the gathering of village women, and the old matron with her eternally black clothes, who was sitting over the kiln. She always wore black and she was always alone . . . the old virgin of the village . . . Mother used to say she devoted herself to the people, to the village. It went back many years to the time when tuberculosis had struck the village and a hungry black djinn had come from who knows where and was eating the flesh and blood of men. So the djinn would let the village alone, the old matron, who was fourteen years old in those days, sat before a water bowl. With an incantation that the matron before her had chanted, she saw and heard in the bowl of water that a fourteen-year-old girl must remain a virgin forever, so she did, and the black djinn turned white and harmless and stayed right there in the air of the village so he could prevent anyone from getting close to her.

A round wooden bowl full of bread sat beside the old matron. Everyone gave her their first loaf of baked bread. Maryam sped up. She saw wooden trays of dough beside women waiting their turn, and women who had seen her turned around one by one and watched her.

Before she reached the tall familiar bread kiln, she said: "Hello . . ."

The women kept their eyes on the old matron's face, some of them shifted in discomfort, and they said softly, under their breath: "Hello . . ."

The old matron, with sharp pursed lips and a look that pierced like a drill, stared into Maryam's eyes. Her tattooed hairless eyebrows were raised. The green star on her chin twitched as if talking to itself. Two red ringlets were affixed to her hard, bony temples. From underneath her black veil, her long thin hair, like red bloody snakes, stretched to the ground.

Maryam collected herself under the old matron's hard and heavy gaze. For a moment she remained confused, saw the old matron give a woman a threatening hand gesture, and heard her say: "What's wrong with you? Are you dumbstruck? Did you see the Virgin Mary or something?"

She saw the old matron's sneer, saw the woman who gave her a ball of dough. The old matron's wrinkled brown hands patted out the dough. The other women drew their veils over their faces and busied themselves with their work. From the corners of their eyes, they watched her leave.

She had gone a few steps when she heard the dry sound of the old matron's ululation, which ricocheted off her back like a whip. Cold as ice, horror ran through her soul, and she heard the women's small titters, as if they were laughing at Setareh.

Under the heavy stares of the women, Maryam retreated into an alley, an old familiar alley that seemed to have become even narrower and darker with the winter's cold. She leaned against a wall. She closed her eyes and opened them an instant later, terrified. She feared that the walls would come forward and crush her. She shook her head vehemently, and then, at the thought of the distant city with its tall cypress trees, a faint smile appeared on her face.

She continued and came to another alley. The doors to the houses were open, with elk and deer horns mounted over them, symbols to drive away any calamity or disaster. It would take eight more years to become a doctor, and then she would return to the village, and maybe she could patiently remove these talismans one by one from the houses . . . She would open a place and get help from the girls in the village . . . She had seen what the old matron had done with the woman next door. Five years ago, when the woman had gone into labor, the old matron had waved the branch of a date palm that she had lit in the brazier. She had waved it through the air in the room so that the djinn who threatens women in childbirth would let go of the woman's liver. She had seen the woman lose her voice in pain and beg, her body convulsing, that salt be poured on the fire again. She had seen the old matron, at the cry of the baby, cram a fistful of burning cow dung between the legs of the woman, and she had heard the cries of the woman.

From the bend in the alley, she saw their house, with antlers mounted over the door, which, as usual, was open. Her gaze slid down the door and she took a deep breath. It seemed as though the door had been freshly painted. Blue. She smiled, seeing a rooster perched on the low courtyard wall, and a chicken, pecking the ground next to the wall, lifted its head up for the rooster.

She went through the courtyard door. The whole place was unkempt and disorderly. Chicken droppings and dried-up dung were scattered everywhere. She saw her mother bent over the well drawing water. She was preoccupied. Her profile was thin and gaunt. Maryam walked quickly toward the well and said excitedly: "Hello . . . Mama."

Mother shook her head hard, as if to drive away a hallucination, but a moment later she turned back and straightened, joy lighting up her face. She dried her hands on the hem of her petticoat and suddenly paused in hesitation. Maryam ran toward her and saw the stinging bitterness in her face. Stunned and tired, she looked at her, not knowing what to do.

"How are you, Mama? Y-you're not feeling well?"

Maryam threw her arms around Mother's neck and kissed her.

Mother drew back slowly, imperceptibly, and asked hoarsely: "When did you get here?"

"Now, just now."

Mother took her bag. "It's a good thing you came . . . very good."

She seemed to be talking to herself. Maryam looked at her. Her hair had turned completely white; her thin, sad lips were pressed together. They went toward the room together.

"Mama, has something happened in the village?"

"No . . . why do you ask?"

Mother's voice was hoarse and rusty. She wouldn't look at Maryam. She was listening to the sounds outside. She seemed to be apprehensive. They reached the room. Mother put the bag in a corner, sat beside the brazier, and pushed back the ashes in it with some tongs. She seemed to be keeping busy so she wouldn't have to say or hear anything. The silence began to make Maryam anxious.

"Is there fighting in the village?"

Mother emptied a tin of charcoal into the brazier. She put a glowing ember on the charcoal and started fanning it.

"No, what fighting?"

She was evasive and reticent in her answers. Maryam wanted to say that the old matron had ululated, but she could not; sweat broke out on her brow. She was embarrassed. Mother pursed her lips and lit the charcoal in the brazier.

"How long will you be here, dear?"

"Two weeks."

"Good . . . very good."

Mother heaved a long sigh. She was looking down and stoking the fire with the tongs. Maryam stood up and went toward her. She put her arms around her neck and kissed her on the forehead.

"Are you sad, Mama?"

Mother forced a bitter smile. "No, thank God, nothing is wrong with me."

"Then what happened? Where did Akbar go?"

"Akbar . . . he has gone to the mill . . ."

Maryam took her mother's face in her hands and looked her straight in the eyes. "Mama, what is it?"

Mother's lips quivered; her eyes welled with tears and in between sobs she entreated: "Is it . . . is it really you?"

Maryam's hands went limp. She let go of her mother and said with surprise: "Of course it's me . . . who else could I be?"

Mother, who was now sobbing, grabbed her shoulders and entreated: "You mean, nothing . . . nothing's changed?"

"Well, what could have changed, dear?"

The gate creaked. Maryam saw the old matron, who had come into the yard. Behind her were the village women and the children, who had suddenly appeared. Mother stood helplessly, kissed Maryam and said: "It's nothing, it's nothing."

The old matron was standing in the door frame, with one hand on the door and one hand on her hip. She smirked. Mother was now standing up.

"She's pure . . . my daughter is as pure as the Quran."

"Well, now, we've got the thief and the stolen goods; we'll test it out."

Maryam was leaning against the wall. The room had grown dark. The village women, with heads of a thousand serpents, were peeping over the old matron's shoulder. Mother said with a sob: "It is a lie . . . it's a lie . . ."

The old matron stepped forward, entered the room, and said: "It doesn't lie, don't speak blasphemy . . . don't make your dead turn over in their graves."

Mother quietly swallowed her sobs. The old woman came closer and gestured at Maryam with her brown, thin hands. "Get up . . ."

Maryam looked with terror at her mother. Mother grabbed the old woman's skirt, pleading: "Right here in the room is better . . . out there is indecent; they'll see."

The old matron's smirk widened. "More indecent is that in that city of strangers she has disgraced everyone."

A thousand bulging black eyes watched Maryam, and in the midst of the hot breaths and the gaping mouths of the entire village, she heard her mother's voice:

"Wait till her brother comes . . . he has gone to Shiraz to pick her up . . . wait till he comes."

The black bulging eyes were getting close. A thousand hands were reaching for her, and Maryam saw the two brown snakes that coiled around her arms and other snakes that grabbed her feet and lifted her. Something like a chunk of stone was caught in her throat and was stifling her scream.

She shook her head vehemently. A hand grabbed her hair and pulled. She looked over the water cellar and saw that the children, big and small, were standing on the mud-brick walls. The air was full of noise, and noises were whistling past her head, wrapping around her neck, and she couldn't breathe.

"The djinn has appeared in the old matron's dream three times."

"I saw it, too. I saw that the djinn was turning black as before; then I heard it say, it is the fault of the girl who is away from here."

Her body burned, as if a thousand snakes were biting her, as though she were caught between thousands of Satan's stones, stones that were moving toward her, rolling over her, crushing her arms and legs and her whole body.

A hand laid her on the ground. Two old women grabbed her legs and pulled them forcefully toward themselves. Some women sat on her legs; her hands were pinned to the ground, and two hands were holding her head. Her legs were spread open. A woman was handing the old matron an egg. The old matron was standing in front of her. Maryam's eyes were burning, she could hear the voices:

"Not even a single tear."

"Her unfortunate father is shuddering in his grave."

The village was full of bulging eyes. The old matron was sitting and groping her legs with her hands. Some hands spread her legs apart. The matron's sleeves were pulled up. Her eyes were continuously opening and closing.

"Move over, dear, let me see what I'm doing."

"She's right, it's dark . . . move back."

The lump of stone in her throat had grown bigger. A brown snake was moving between her legs. She couldn't feel the weight of the Satan's stones on her arms and legs. The world had turned into the shape of a small egg, and her leg was trembling from the egg touching it. It seemed as though an insect was jumping up and down there. A raspy snort came out of her mouth. It was the sound of a chicken's gasp, one whose throat had been cut. She shook herself and a strange scream emerged from her throat: "Oh, God!"

The women pulled back. The old woman ordered: "Hold her tight." And again she pushed the egg. The women were watching quietly. She saw the old matron's long finger, which was like a snake, twisting under her skirt. The old matron cleaned her finger.

"Oil."

She felt the old matron's slippery, cold finger between her legs. She had become soaking wet with sweat. She was cold and shivering. When the old matron raised her finger, her face shone and her eyes sparkled. The women, with their eyes glued to her mouth, remained silent. The old matron patiently shook her hand toward the palm trees where the old djinn lived and said: "Thanks."

The sound of ululating resonated through the village. A woman emptied a sugar bowl on her head. Mother had fainted in the women's arms. Maryam was watching with glazed eyes. The old woman came forward with her oily hand and kissed Maryam, who lay motionless, and said:

"Doctor, you make your mother proud, you bring pride to your village."

Maryam could hear nothing but the sound of the wind that had been ricocheting between the Satan's stones.

— *Translated by M. R. Ghanoonparvar, Persis Karim, Atoosa Kourosh, Parichehr Moin, Dylan Oehler-Stricklin, Reza Shirazi, and Catherine Williamson*

Reza Farrokhfal

Born in 1949 in Esfahan, Reza Farrokhfal graduated from Shiraz (for-
merly Pahlavi) University and Concordia University in Montreal. He
began his career publishing stories in *Jong-e Esfahan,* a well-regarded
literary journal edited by Houshang Golshiri in the 1960s. Farrokhfal
has published numerous stories and articles in Iranian journals and
newspapers. His short story collection *Ah, Istanbul* was published in
1988 in Tehran. He has also translated novels by Graham Greene and
Alexander Solzhenitsyn into Persian.

In 1995, Farrokhfal moved to Montreal, where he continued
studying and writing on literary theory, criticism, and semiotics. He
currently teaches Persian literature at McGill University.

"Ah, Istanbul" was selected from the collection by the same name.
The story touches upon the complexity of love in difficult times.
F. Scott Fitzgerald held that it is dangerous to transplant one's dreams
from one period of life to another. Farrokhfal implicitly seconds that
idea and suggests that it is precarious, if not impossible, to transplant
the dreams of one era to another.

AH, ISTANBUL

Her eyes were gray. Having come up the three flights of stairs and the narrow corridor of the publishing company, walls stacked to the ceiling with boxes of books, her eyes must have turned this color. But I hadn't noticed her. I hadn't even heard her voice asking the office boy for the way to the manager's office. I was engrossed in my own work. The door of my office was half open. I was working on the translation of a tiresome sociology text. I would write some sentences, rub them out, then write them again. When I lifted my head for a moment, I saw a medium-height woman wearing dark clothes from head to toe — as is fashionable these days — passing by my office.

I took off my glasses and pressed the corners of my eyes with my fingers, to ease the pulsating flow of blood in my veins. From the early hours of the day, my eyes didn't seem to cooperate. It was the result of the previous night's sleeplessness. I glanced at my watch. Half an hour till noon, but the manager, the old man, still hadn't shown up. I lit a cigarette, rose, and walked to the window. The sun bothered my eyes, but it was no longer the lewd, gaze-stopping summer sunshine that scorched and cleared out our street full of bookshops for a whole season.

I'd heard the sound of the old man's door opening, and his laughter, and thought to myself that he must have another of his old friends visiting him, so I carried on working. The sociology text wasn't progressing. The office boy came in and said, "Agha is asking to see you." And the old man, from amid the purple haze of pipe smoke surrounding his face, had introduced me to the woman: "Our boss — or as they call them today, our editor," following up this comment with one of his long, protracted laughs, which could only emanate from a person of his generation. A yellow folder lay on his desk. Puffing on his pipe, he was telling the woman, "I should tell you that bringing out a book these days is like coming to grips with a wild beast. The beast will only surrender if one had lost a lot of blood oneself. Being a publisher myself . . ." This was his habitual catchphrase.

The woman had asked, "What about poetry? Do you also deal with poetry as part of your imprint?"

I murmured to myself, "Who does she think she is?" And the old man, as if attempting to answer a sad, ponderous question, sighed deeply and said, "No, no, just like translations of fiction or history books . . . publishing poetry these days has a lot of problems." The old man's pipe kept going out, and he would have to interrupt the flow of his speech to light up again. It had only been a week since he had quit cigarette smoking and picked up the pipe for fun. He accompanied the woman to the top of the stairs to see her out.

In those days, all kinds of people came to our publishing offices. They would ask directions from the bookshop on the ground floor and come right up. Sometimes Fazli, the fellow downstairs, would send up bothersome characters just to annoy us. He could have got rid of them right there in the bookshop. There was also the occasional distant, budding talent submitting manuscripts from the provinces by registered mail. The old man referred all of these to me so I could read them and give an opinion. He would lean back against his chair, point at me, and say: "No, no, don't be mistaken! I'm telling you this in my capacity as a publisher so you can spot the best talent exactly where you least expect it." He was lying. I knew that he had never yet published a single page without the recommendation and opinion of another friend or acquaintance. But he would puff up proudly and, staring out at a patch of pale sky behind the booksellers' street, framed by the dirty window, say, "In this trade there are times when you mustn't be afraid. You have to have guts and make a choice; in a nutshell, you have to score!"

Work on the sociology text still wasn't progressing. There were other manuscripts, too. That dignified, elegant man, Mr. Mehryari, who had been denied permission to travel outside the country, would occasionally turn up. At the ripe age of sixty-five, he had translated some poems from French into Persian. The old man, our publishing manager, said that he was very fluent in French and English. I was completely intoxicated by the man's expensive aftershave, but at a loss as to what to say to him about his translations.

In the evenings, before going home, I would look in on Fazli at the bookshop downstairs. Fazli always had some sunflower seeds, raisins, or something on him, and he would throw a handful on the counter and we would start chatting. When I finally got home, tired and beat, I would take a cold shower and close my eyes. I would tell myself that I was listening to a constant, endless drizzle of rain and the flow of water was washing away the remains of words clinging not just to my mind, but also to my skin. If I weren't going anywhere in the evening (where would I go to?) I would sit behind the desk again. I used to leave my unfinished work for this time of night. Around midnight, when I would look up from my work, my brain had stopped functioning. I would get up and stagger to bed, a book in hand, always remembering the English painter's quote: "It is through suffering for art that we come to find our respite in it once again." But my bleak and drowsy mind would corrupt these words, and I would deliriously blurt out to myself, "It's through suffering for art that we are exhausted and fall asleep once again."

The old man had said, "Well, I never! So she has been here all this time?" He was puffing gently on his pipe, still staring at the pale patch of sky over the booksellers' street. As if speaking to himself, he was saying, "They're all going. They're all leaving here." I wasn't particularly surprised by what he said. The old man went on, "She used to be a beautiful woman. She still is. I know her from way back, from when she was about twenty-three, twenty-four years old . . . she's the one who's translated this novel." He shoved the yellow folder on the desk toward me. "Before she leaves, she's coming back here to get an answer from us. I think it must be an interesting work." I had glanced at the pages in the folder. There were about two hundred, written in a tiny feminine hand. The book itself was there, too.

"She was a talented woman," said the old man. "At one time she used to paint. She even had a few exhibitions. I think she's written some poetry, too. But it's strange that this woman never took anything seriously in her life. In those days she had quite a fan club. I don't think you would have heard of her. You're too young."

Every day, about twelve-thirty, I would pop out of the office for lunch. If I didn't want to share Fazli's food, which he would bring each day in a small pot from home, I would go to Havagim's cafe. I used to know Havagim the Armenian from many years before. I would pass by the bookshops. At the first junction I would cross the street. Always, at that time of day, a waft of cold, fetid air from the open door of a cinema on my way would brush my face and stifle me. Turning into the side street, my glance would fall upon the lettering in white on the window of a launderette: "View an album of all the different plaids available." A few steps farther, on the opposite sidewalk, under an elm tree's canopy of leaves and branches, was Havagim's café. That day I had taken the yellow folder containing the translation, and the book itself, so I could take a look at them over lunch.

In the café I sat at the table by the window. I placed the folder carefully on the table beside me. The two former design students were also there. What with university holidays being indefinitely prolonged on a regular basis, they were fast approaching their thirties. In the early days of the revolution, they would come here with other students, male and female. They would order down-to-earth food and engage in political debates. But now these two were the only survivors of that group.

One of them, the one with the brown goatee, had finished his meal and was picking his teeth with a matchstick. He threw me a familiar glance. It was their habit to have philosophical discussions over their meal, and then when they had finished eating, to fix their gaze on me in silence. Once in a while when I felt up to it, I would return their gaze, but they couldn't stand it and would quickly look down. While I waited for Havagim to bring the food I lit a cigarette and opened the yellow folder, as if it contained a rare and precious manuscript. I read the page I fell on: "The ship was nearing the warm, clear waters of the Mediterranean; the clearest waters in the world." It was the opening sentence of a chapter. I read on: "He opened his eyes to the white cabin walls of the ship, but recalling the events of the night before, he rolled over and a delicious morning sleep overtook him." My hand went to my shirt pocket to bring out a pencil and strike out a dangling modifier, but I thought there would be plenty of time for such trivial details. As I washed down mouthfuls of food with sips of iced water, I looked over the original. I didn't recognize the writer. It struck me as being one of those pocket book series with brightly colored covers that they sell in hotel or airport shops. The woman had translated the title as *Double Dealing*. Its publication date was New York, 1980. I thought to myself that she'd therefore probably not bought the novel from one of the bookstalls here. For a long time now, the city's bookstalls were selling only the worst leftover foreign titles, ones that had appeared before 1979. I remembered one of the old man's aphorisms: "Half the translator's job is always what he chooses!" The old man didn't leave me in peace with his sayings even while I was eating.

I closed the book tentatively and lit up. I had finished eating. As I was contemplating the street scene before me in the afternoon sunshine, I fell to thinking about the woman: a woman who had never taken anything seriously in her life, and had now decided to undertake a translation. Strange that I couldn't remember her face. The only thing I remembered was that she had pale eyes. But were they blue or gray? It had been years — perhaps since my thirties — since I had been sidetracked by this sort of memory blank.

But despite all my curiosity I kept postponing reading the translation. Finally I took home the yellow folder and the book and spent a few late nights reading them in bed. My disbelief turned into despair after browsing through the book, and reading thirty, forty pages of the translation. It was a stiff, amateur rendering, even containing some gross errors. The main character of the novel was a middle-aged man, an expert in Byzantine art history who was traveling by ship from North America to Europe to continue his research. On board, a troupe of Hungarian artistes — among them a young girl — aroused his curiosity. Before meeting the girl, this professor of art history had had nothing to do but spend the days on deck or nights at the ship's bar getting drunk and recalling unhappy memories of his marriage (his wife had left him), his relations with his lovers, or his quarrels with university authorities. The best years of his life had seen him turn into a drinking, distrustful, cynical person who one would expect at any moment to end his life by throwing himself into the ocean's heaving waves or swallowing a dozen sleeping pills late one night. But coming to know the Hungarian girl, who was of Gypsy origin, led to a torrid love affair. The suspicions of the troupe of artistes (whose members included one or two secret agents) were aroused. A mysterious murder takes place on board. One of the male dancers, who had been the girl's closest friend, evidently commits suicide by slashing his wrists. The ship anchors in Greece, and the art history professor and the girl escape to Istanbul.

The events of the book in that historic city mesmerized me, and I confess I had trouble putting down the last pages of the translation. The main character had found the twin passions of his life — Byzantine art and the Hungarian girl — united in one place, and instead of returning to North America, chose to stay permanently in Istanbul. But this happiness was short-lived. One morning he wakes up in the hotel to find that the girl has left him. Had she been kidnapped by her country's secret agents, or had she used their love affair as a means of escaping from her country with the money and assistance of an American? All these questions remain unanswered, and the story's protagonist, heartbroken and more cynical than ever before, could only try to blot out everything from his memory by frequenting inns and libraries, and writing and rewriting his documents in that ancient harbor. The only memento left by the girl was a pair of green socks in one of the cupboard drawers. Had the girl deliberately forgotten the socks? Had she been in such haste to depart that she had left behind this pair of socks? (and this was the cruelest answer to the question), or then again, had the roughness of the secret agents coming for her blinded them? It was a depressing enigma.

The night I finally finished the book, my sight was blurred from the tiny feminine handwriting. What had this woman been thinking when she chose this book for translation, especially in this day and age? It was a novel with all the clichés and ingredients of a bestseller or even a blockbuster film: suspense, romance, sex, the cat-and-mouse games of secret agents of an Eastern bloc ally, and an American hero. But even if it was a masterpiece of its kind, there was still no question of publishing it. I turned off the light, and before sleep could weigh down my eyelids, I pictured the old publisher's face as I gave him my opinion. Trusting the memory of people of his generation was always a letdown. I laughed out loud in the solitude of the dark room.

I asked the office boy where the manager was. He had arrived early in the morning. I picked up my pack of cigarettes and headed off to deal with the translation before it was too late. Old Mr. Mehryari, with his translations of French verse which had been thrown at me, had been enough to waste hours and hours of my time. I knocked at the manager's door and entered his office. But Mr. Mehryari was there. The office boy hadn't told me that. I had interrupted the conversation with my entrance. The old man was almost certainly telling Mehryari about the difficulties of the publishing trade or the political situation. I pretended I was looking for matches. I shook Mr. Mehryari's hand with an apologetic smile on my face. The manager gave me a fresh box of matches. He was dragging on his pipe greedily with the air of a novice, and as I was leaving the room, I heard him say to Mr. Mehryari, "This is exactly the case of an object in an unexpected place," using one of those Arabic expressions he occasionally liked to throw pompously into the conversation.

I was just getting down to the sociology text when Mr. Mehryari came straight to my office from the manager's. He came and sat right in front of me, smelling of that intoxicating aftershave of his.

"So how is our project doing?" he asked.

He had carefully slicked back his light brown strands of hair. He had a firm, bony, tight-lipped face. He was wearing a brown tweed coat even though the weather hadn't turned cold yet. I took out the notebook with his translations from my desk drawer. He had clean-copied the poems in blue fountain pen. The manager would say, "Each time I see the elegant writing of this man I am truly saddened. We have to find a solution." And to silence me he had emphasized, "Nothing is perfect from the word go."

"I wanted to have the final say from you," said Mr. Mehryari, "What should I do?"

I hadn't expected to get to the final say so quickly.

"As I told you, I recommend you read contemporary works," I replied.

"I also told you that I'm not totally ignorant of the works of recent poets."

I was about to ask whose poems he had read, but I bit my lip. I was fairly sure he would give me some irrelevant answer.

Mr. Mehryari was enamored of travelogues, books on psychology, and thrillers, and read all of them in the original.

"I mean literature in general — poetry, novels . . . you know, the Persian language has acquired new capacities for poetic expression, lexicographic nuances, fresh words . . ."

Mr. Mehryari was silent, but I continued.

"If your translation had come out in Persian let's say thirty, forty years ago, it would have been a good translation in its own time . . ."

Mr. Mehryari didn't let me finish.

"So you think this translation is not suitable in its present form?"

"It needs more work. Maybe another publisher will accept it as it is, but it's a shame, it's really a shame."

Again Mr. Mehryari fell silent. He was tapping his ash into the ashtray. I noticed his gold Rolex watch; it had a matte finish with a reddish glint to it. His silence was beginning to irritate me. But finally he said, "Well, at the very least I can give this notebook as it is to my friends to read." He smiled and added, "Maybe I'll even give it as a gift to someone."

"That's not a bad idea," I had to say in response. He picked up his notebook and books from the desk. He placed them calmly in a large envelope with which I provided him. He said good-bye and left the room. What else could I have possibly done for him?

I got up and went to the window. There in front of me on the wall behind the opposite sidewalk were vivid, amateurishly sketched graffiti: faces underscored with slogans urging everyone to rise collectively like a band of brothers against the total invasion of the enemy. Each time my eyes fell on those words, I felt vulnerable. I didn't have the patience to fiddle with the sociology text. I started pacing around the room. You could still smell Mr. Mehryari's aftershave. I had rid myself of him, but felt like a person who had slit the throat of a rare animal from ear to ear. Mr. Mehryari was a fan of hunting, too.

The office boy showed up. "Agha is calling for you," he said.

As soon as I entered the manager's room, he said, "Well? How did you get on with Mehryari?"

I couldn't help myself and responded with one of his own pompously sarcastic comments. "You know the parable about the people who took refuge in the cave?" I said. The old man guffawed and said, "I do it, I do it . . ." He lit his pipe and told me with a serious look, "Before I forget, that lady friend of mine has invited us to her house tomorrow afternoon at five. I might get there a little late, but I would ask you please to be there punctually." Whenever he wanted to discuss something seriously with me, he would use the formal "you."

"You've read her translation, haven't you?" he asked.

"No, I haven't," I replied, "there are still a few chapters left," I lied to the old man.

That day I didn't manage to progress a single page on the sociology text. When I came out of the office I felt like talking to someone, so I thought of paying a visit to Fazli in the bookshop. Although it was still daylight, Fazli had put on all the lights inside. He gestured toward the shop's display window and said, "Look! Just like a wilderness!" He scattered a handful of raisins on the counter and brought over a steaming glass of hot tea from the back of the shop.

"The early evening used to be the beginning of our sales," he said.

His chubby face with the tall forehead gleamed under the light of the lamps. You could never tell he had spent a whole day, and many long years from morning till evening, behind that bookshop counter. His appearance hadn't changed one iota in the fifteen years I knew him. Only the short wavy hair over his forehead had fallen out. He had carefully and painstakingly arranged the printing samples next to himself on the counter. Fazli did the proofreading and pagination of the books. He had an unfailing eye when it came to proofreading.

"I'm the last to pull down the shutters in this street," he said.

"This shows what a conscientious bookseller you are," I said, taking a sip of tea.

"In the old times, when we shut down the shop the night was still young. Nowadays you feel terrified on the streets an hour from now."

"Why should a big guy like you feel terrified?"

"You mean you don't get terrified? I can't help it. At home I'm restless like a headless chicken. You've got to go out somewhere in the evening. Even if you don't go anywhere, there's got to be somewhere you know is open. That way at least when you're at home you feel at peace. That's the way I am, at any rate."

"I have so much work these days that at night I just want to go home and go straight to bed."

"No, I can't do that," he said. "I sit by the radio and listen to the news from the start of the evening. After that I fiddle around with the Arabic stations."

"Fazli, my friend, forget these things! Just lie down in your bed, close your eyes, and imagine for yourself all the places that are open . . ."

He was munching furiously on the raisins. "This sort of thing is past me. Man, it's past you, too!"

I laughed at what he had just said. Behind the brightly lighted windows of the bookshop, the ghosts of peering pedestrians hurried past in the dark. A couple of times I was tempted to lead the conversation around to that woman. Fazli personally knew the who's who of all the writers and artists. He was even acquainted with the forgotten corpses of the literati. But I could feel that the smallest reference was enough for this old dog of a bookseller to read my hand. When I left the shop, I thought of walking home on foot. Walking would do me good. Behind me I could hear Fazli's voice telling me loudly, "You've got to come over to us one night. My wife will cook you whatever your heart desires; I'll fix you up with anything else you need myself . . ."

That night I couldn't get to sleep. I kept leafing through any literary journals and quarterlies I had left. In the year right after the revolution, when I was really broke, I gave a few series of journals to Fazli to bind and sell at a good price. There was no mention of that woman or her poems. I knew there wouldn't be. The pages smelled of aging, rough paper. I picked up the yellow folder with the translation and went to bed. I thought of Fazli who, at that moment — an hour after midnight — had fallen asleep with his ear glued to the shortwave radio, listening to music played by an Arabic station.

For the last time I looked at some passages from the *Double Dealing* translation. It was the kind of novel that could engage even a fussy reader like me. But was I not mainly fascinated by the background to those events? And wasn't the reason for this fascination more to do with imposing my own imagination onto a trite romantic thriller? I remembered that even in the most exquisite piece of literature one can find a symbol or metaphor as old as literature itself. I turned the light off to sleep, but sleep wouldn't come. In a semiconscious state I could see the view of a harbor, at night, with the reflection of lights on water, and it suddenly occurred to me that out there, by the sea, no fate is sealed. I could see myself sitting behind my desk in the publishing office, wrestling for hours with that woman over a sentence. I couldn't silence her, and worse still, I felt that whatever I knew about writing a clear and proper phrase was so trivial, so useless! The woman had risen from her seat and was scrutinizing me with an air of ridicule. Her eyes were of no particular color.

About twenty minutes after five, I found myself pressing the buzzer on the building door. When I went up the stairs, on the third floor my hostess had come out to welcome me at the entrance to one of the apartment doors — number 12. I couldn't believe this was the same woman whose face I had forgotten. Her face was exceptionally familiar — as if I had seen her many times in the past. With a sincerity that felt a little unexpected, she greeted me and led me to the living room.

"I kept thinking you had lost the way."

I replied something about the directions happening to be quite clear, and sat myself gingerly on a sofa. I breathed a sigh of relief. She knew the manager would arrive later and she said, "I would have preferred to have you both over for dinner, but what with the mess here, just before my departure . . ."

I didn't let her finish and thanked her. While she had gone into the kitchen, I took the opportunity of looking around me. It was a small apartment with bare white walls and large windows, and all the air of a dwelling where the owners had suddenly lost interest and were about to leave: empty bookshelves and boxes, covered by a layer of invisible dust that had settled on every displaced object or knickknack, taking the shine off them. On the wall opposite me were the traces of two large paintings which were now sitting wrapped up behind the door. It looked as if our hostess had temporarily tidied up the furniture to receive us. She had placed a bunch of yellow chrysanthemums in a ceramic vase on a table. I thought to myself that this house and its objects would have been such a place of fantasy under different circumstances.

Our hostess was saying that the house and its entire contents, down to the kitchenware, had been rented out to a couple she knew. She had returned from the kitchen with two cups of coffee. She was saying that by doing this she had rid herself of the bother of wrangling with peddlers. But there was still more to do. She needed to put her personal bits and pieces in order or throw them out. There were books and drawings that she didn't have the heart to discard. She was going to take those with her. Lighting a cigarette she said, "I've always hated moving. Even the thought of all the things I've done in this time, or what I need to get done in the next few days, makes me ill. Just this one reason was enough to prevent me from thinking of leaving all these years. Even now I'm not sure . . . it feels as if everything is temporary. Even going somewhere else is temporary. But it looks as if there's no other solution." She put the pack of cigarettes on the table and sat opposite me.

"Well, you do the talking now. Tell me what you're doing," she said, putting the cigarette between her fingers to the corner of her mouth.

"I don't do anything special . . ." I replied, following up with a brief and compressed account of my work at the publishing house. She said the old man had spoken very highly of me. I immediately answered that the old man had a habit of exaggerating everything. She laughed.

"Yes, I know him well; I've known him for many years. But I don't think he means to exaggerate about you, not at all."

As she was talking, her glance would occasionally fall and rest upon one of the objects in the room. Was she involuntarily thinking of the things she needed to get done before leaving, or was it her habit to show off, with complete confidence, the exquisite silhouette of her face with that aquiline nose? Once when she turned around like that and looked at me, I could see clearly that her eyes were gray, but capable of reflecting a spectrum of aquamarine to cerulean with their limpid, expressive pupils. I said to myself that whatever had happened had been due to these very eyes. These were eyes with a life of their own. One could easily ignore the rest of her features. Even those few strands of gray hair that had escaped from the wave of her hair on the pale, small forehead. She had made no attempt to hide those few strands of gray hair. All I could do at that moment was to commit to memory an image of her face I was then seeing vividly and tangibly. Her face betrayed no particular age. My shaky hand stretched out toward the cup on the table and I took a last sip of coffee. It was cold and bitter. My hostess finally broke the silence.

"Did you read the novel?" And without waiting for my answer, she rose and crossed the room. She carefully wiped a record and put it on the stereo, returning to me with a smile. It was a string quartet, and I remembered that I hadn't listened to music in a long time.

"Yes, I've read it."

She lit another cigarette, offering me one too, and then said eagerly, "Well, I know my translation must have its problems, but what did you think of the novel itself?"

I had prepared some answers, but I said with deliberation, "I have read the whole text once from beginning to end, and some passages even a few times over . . . I'm not familiar with the writer."

She seemed to be agog with attention, sitting in front of me. I went on.

"Now that I think about it, I see that the visual descriptions of the places in the story, or should I say the setting of the story, had a lot of attraction for me." I had the sense of gathering momentum for a theoretical discussion, and for a minute it felt as if I was the young man of letters holding forth for a girl of his own age. But inevitably I carried on, "For instance, for me the description of the nights at sea, and the ship's bar with its odd customers, was very interesting. But this can be just a subjective thing. To tell the truth, for many years, ever since childhood, in fact, I've dreamed of sailing on a ship . . . quite apart from this, the city of Istanbul, the backdrop for an important part of the story's events —"

She interrupted me and said, "Ah yes, I felt exactly the same way the first time I read the book."

"This novel makes me think of a film, I can't remember what it's called, *Invincible, Immortal,* by Alain Robbe-Grillet . . . That film also took place in Istanbul. It was a wonderful film, in black and white."

She was all amazement and smiles as she said, "You saw that film, too?"

Coming up with the film was nothing short of a godsend. I could have spent the entire time until the arrival of the old man reminiscing about it and avoided giving my view on the book and her translation of it. "Years ago," I said, "seeing this film at a student film society, I realized what a beautiful city Istanbul is."

"I saw the film, too, in Paris. I've also seen Istanbul, and this time on my way I'm going to stop over for a few days."

She got up and went to the kitchen and came back to the living room once more with two cups of hot, fragrant coffee. "So you've seen that film, too, and liked it . . ." she said. "I will think of you in Istanbul."

I thanked her and said, "But I have to say I wouldn't know what I'd feel if I saw that film now. There are some films you shouldn't see twice. It's best to keep the memory of it intact."

Staring at a point in the room she said, "I agree with you completely. The same goes for certain places, and even certain people . . ."

"Yes, take Istanbul, for instance; what with our homeless compatriots there now it may not be such a pleasant place for sightseeing anymore. But a harbor is always a harbor, and the presence of a sea of freedom within a few paces is a comfort to the soul."

I had abandoned myself to the unpredictable logic of the conversation — come what may. It was getting dark. My hostess put the lights on and threw a purple shawl over her shoulders. She said, "Oh, I've been longing for a good chat for some time. These days all I hear is the nonsense of politics and the timing of when everything is going to blow up . . ."

The doorbell rang, and the manager walked in with a bouquet of roses. He was wearing his best suit. With a foretaste of his usual laughter, he explained to the hostess, "I'm not much of a man for ceremony. I was wandering the streets for quite some time before I finally made up my mind and bought these flowers. I couldn't think what I should be doing for you. I'm getting old, and the truth be told, I can't bear good-byes anymore. I thought I should actually try to forget all about you leaving."

Our hostess placed the flowers in a vase from the kitchen and put them on a small desk near the window. The manager said, "Looks as if you were deep in a discussion."

"Yes," said the woman, "this gentleman and I have realized that we have very similar tastes."

The manager threw me a blank look and sat down. When we shook hands, I realized he did so with caution. He seemed in top form. He took a sip of his coffee, lit up his pipe, and with a grunt of satisfaction, blew out the smoke. He said, "This gentleman managed to reduce one of my friends to despair just yesterday." Our hostess turned around and looked at me curiously. She smiled.

"Just imagine," said the old man, "A man of about my age thinks of doing a translation in these darned times. And one day he even gets up and comes to our office with a notebook full of symbolist, or, as these gentlemen would call it, metaphoric poetry . . ." The old man pointed at me, and then laughed long and hard. His eyes had a mischievous glint, and between his droopy lids his eyes were moist slits. He wasn't looking at me.

The old man leaned back in his seat and said, "This young man and I have been in deep discussion for quite some time over newfangled words which, between you and me, are often nothing but concocted and confusing." He sighed and went on, "Well, maybe I'm getting old and crusty, but I do believe in any case that our language has evolved a lot, and I do know this: translation of poetry is an impossibility!"

"That's a rule of thumb. There are exceptions to the rule," I said.

"Yes indeed," said the manager, "and to me, the task of the translator is to find those very exceptions." He was silent for a moment. He dragged noisily on the pipe, which had gone out. "But what was interesting for me was that this person had thought of translating verse at this particular time," he said, addressing the woman. "I gave the poems to this gentleman to read and give his view. And do you know what kind of view he gave? He came up to me and said, 'You there, have you heard about the parable of the people who took refuge in the cave?'" The old man gave out another one of his throaty laughs.

"I think this sort of direct confrontation with a work of art is actually a good thing," the hostess said, with such simplicity and confidence that my stomach lurched. The old man immediately took her up on it, saying, "I agree. That's quite right. This particular friend is of course a very educated, well-read individual — goes without saying; but he's not quite with the times. The important thing is for a person to be up to date. In any case, I agree with our Mr. Editor here. There was nothing we could do for that person. Those poems were unpublishable, and for me as a publisher . . ."

I could feel that the old man's professional boasting was about to begin. At a suitable moment, on the pretext of browsing through the books that had been piled on top of one another on the living room floor, I got up. The books were exactly what one would expect to find in a house like that: novels, poetry, a few old Sufi texts — some read, and some unread, and expensive art books. There were also a few indoor gardening guides, a short teach-yourself-yoga for the enhancement of body and spirit, with color illustrations. That night it was agreed that the manager would sell the art books and send the money, in any way that he saw fit, to the woman.

I began to watch the two of them. The hostess got up and put on another record — yet another string quartet. That was at my request. She told the old man in a loud voice, "Do you see what similar tastes we have?" And she stood for a few minutes in front of the roses. She bent her head, smelled them, and said, "I love the scent of roses. It's there and not quite there at the same time." I should have left the old man alone with his memories. When the woman next sat down beside him, the old man looked like a father having an intimate and confidential chat with his young daughter.

On the black desk there was only a woman's leather handbag, a key ring, and an ashtray full of cigarette butts. Without meaning to, I lowered my head so I could smell the old man's roses, too, and as I did so, my eyes fell on the drawings that had been mounted on the wall in small wooden frames. They were watercolors of landscapes. I heard my hostess say, "Don't look at those, they're very old. I haven't had the chance to remove them yet." There was also a group photograph. The hairstyles and fashions dated the picture to at least twenty years before. I recognized the woman's face from among the others. I thought to myself, what a total incarnation she was of all the intellectual beauty one imagines about oneself at the age of twenty-five: a young girl with high cheekbones and short hair, wearing a wide plaid shirt over a pair of jeans . . . and all of a sudden I yearned for my own innocent idealism of those early years. In another picture frame, one saw the black-and-white portrait of a man who, despite his masculine good looks, resembled a simple and forgotten sacrificial lamb.

In between the soft and melodious sound of violins I could hear snatches of the old man's conversation: ". . . despite all that, I'm not unhopeful." He was never unhopeful. People like him somehow lived a good hundred years happily and knowingly. He was saying, "It's exactly at a time like this that new faces arrive; new writers, translators, energetic publishers . . . What's wrong with it, let these young faces drive us out . . ." By the time I sat down again at the table, the old man didn't seem so hopeful after all. He was saying, "What can I say, it's more like a breathing contest — we're all holding our breath. Some people run out of breath before others. That's all it is. And you can't criticize anyone, either. But for a person like me, leaving here means starting life all over again, and it's too late for that."

"I would never have imagined myself that one day I would have to leave here for good," said the woman, "but here one feels lonelier by the day. My mother died last year. None of my brothers is here, and all my close friends have gone — even people you don't see from one year to the next; they're nothing more than a name in the phone book or on the neighbor's doorbell which you happen to see every day; and then one day finally you have to rub out the name from the phone book, or you see that the familiar name has disappeared from the doorbell . . . It's only a drop, but it's as if the drop flows to an ocean of loneliness." And after that, she got up and, heading for the kitchen, said, "But let's not talk about it anymore. Things are sad enough as they are."

She placed three cups of coffee on the table. They were the last cups of coffee we were having. I had finished my cigarettes. Just for a change, I'd borrowed the old man's pipe for a smoke. Our hostess said, "Now tell me, and I want you to tell it to me straight: how is the book I translated? Can it be published? Is it any good?" The old man had lowered his head. I knew that he was holding his breath. In answer to her question, I merely said, "It is excellent, Khanum, excellent!" The old man let out an obvious sigh of relief. His eyes were shining, and he fell to speaking again.

Our hostess saw us to the bottom of the stairs to say good-bye. In the light of the old man's beat-up Chevrolet reversing, I could see a lonely woman, standing at the end of a tree-lined street in front of the door of her building. A dog was barking from behind the wall of another house. The old man quickly drove out of the side street and turned onto a highway that wove past dark hills into the city center. He was dropping me off at home. He was humming some verse under his breath, and I could hear the occasional word. The cool autumnal night breeze brushed my face from the car's open window.

There are days when not only one's eyes, but also the mind doesn't seem to cooperate. The organs are drowsy and dispersed right from the start of the day. I sat behind my desk again. That yellow folder was still on the desk. I had sharpened my pencils earlier. I said to myself, "It can't be that the only way to collect my thoughts is on the back of a tough sociology text." But it was wasted effort. My cigarette had burned out and lay in ashes. I lit another one. I knew it was one too many. The night before, near dawn, I had remembered some words in my sleep that were juxtaposed flowing and balanced next to each other, taking the form of a stanza: "Eyes which blend in like a cricket to the color of its surroundings." What an empty, irrelevant comparison that was, in the light of day . . .

The office boy showed up and said, "Agha has called and said he won't be coming in till the afternoon."

At twelve-thirty, I went to Havagim's café, as always. I sat at my usual place by the window. Havagim, that cursed man, had also put some yellow chrysanthemums in a glass of water on the counter. The former design students had started their meal before me. Their faces looked dirtier and more unkempt by the day. One of them, the same one with the brown goatee, told his friend, "I tell you the truth, my friend, today I'm in a rare mood!" And his friend replied, "So you should, my man, that's the kind of mood that's called for." I could hardly swallow. The food was tasteless, and it felt like eating after a long illness. I sank into my chair in the autumnal afternoon sun, pouring into the café through the window. It was as if at any moment that woman could pass by the window and catch me off guard by myself while I was eating a mouthful of food (and what a nonsensical act that was!).

I strolled around the streets for an hour or so, and then went back to the office and sat at my desk. I convinced myself that sometimes working can be a form of amnesia. But the sociology text, with its long and winding sentences, had not progressed a single page. I had lost my confidence in the translator from the very first pages, and felt compelled to check every sentence against the original. From the commotion in the corridor I realized that the manager had arrived. He was ordering the office boy around as usual. Against habit, the old man shook my hand. He told the office boy to fetch some tea. "I'll be at death's door before he learns to do his work properly," he said as we went into his office.

Without further ado, I embarked on the subject of that woman's translation. The old man lit his pipe, exhaled with a cough, and asked, "Now what was the title of the book?"

"*Double Dealing.*"

He got up and went to the window. He was looking outside, as if he was following someone he recognized with his eyes. I took a sip from the glass of tea the boy had brought me, and I said with some hesitation, "I don't think we can publish it. It has passages that . . ."

"Well, cut those passages, modify them, reduce them."

"The problem isn't just that. The novel itself is just a commercial, romantic thriller."

"We'll archive it, then," said the old man, turning around.

Maybe he read the surprise and questioning in my face, which led him to approach me and, without meeting my gaze, carry on. "What matters is not just the one work. People's work, taken singly, may contain errors, may be less than perfect, but when people get involved, they learn to correct their mistakes on their own. What matters is the larger picture, and the continuity of it all. It wouldn't have been right to let our mutual friend down. It's only then that she's encouraged to think about carrying on with her work. Let her think we'll publish her translation."

"But . . ."

"But what?"

"But what if she comes back one day or writes us a letter, or asks about her book? What then?"

The old man stood above me and put a hand on my shoulder.

"I like that. I like your way of ultimately taking everything so seriously. But remember that in our trade, not everything we say has to be necessarily acted upon."

I realized there were still things I had to learn from that old dog.

I lifted my head from the sociology text. By then it was sunset. I left the office. I didn't feel like looking in on Fazli, but I didn't feel like going home, either. I jumped over the dried-up, putrid stream by the side of the street, and stepped onto the tarmac. When I looked back, I saw Fazli — not in a bookshop in the middle of town, but as if I had abandoned him at a stall with a single lit bulb, in the midst of a vast and dark wilderness. A dim red hue could be seen in the sunset sky, but the sidewalks, the odd dried-up tree, and the graffiti had sunk into a smog-filled darkness. Cars drove past me noisily and with bright headlights. I was standing there, unable to put one foot in front of the other. The woman was leaving at the break of dawn to go to the airport. She had a few days' stopover in Istanbul. Last night she had told me at the last moment that she would send me a postcard from there, to the bookshop address.

I would spend other days working on the sociology text, other noons at Havagim's eating lunch, other evenings chatting with Fazli, and sometimes I would walk home in the town's empty streets. I recalled reading somewhere that a fool is someone who tries to take the dreams of one part of his life to another. I told myself that an even greater fool is someone who tries to take the dreams of one era to another. I felt as if the old man's evil spirit, with his cruel words, had penetrated me over time. I walked on, and just as I was letting out my stifled breath, I found myself involuntarily thinking of the Arabic proverb: "Ah, *ey ba-id ul-ahd,* you breaker of promises . . ." and realized that these were indeed the old man's very own decaying and tired words.

— *Translated by Roxane Zand*

Reza Daneshvar

Reza Daneshvar was born in 1948 in Mashad, Iran. He studied Persian literature at both Mashad and Tehran universities before beginning a career teaching theater in Mashad. He went on to become the head of the theater program in Khorassan province and vice president of the School of Arts in Mashad. In 1982 he moved to Paris, and has been living and writing there ever since. From 2003 to 2005, he has been teaching in residence, under a grant from the International Cities of Asylum, at Cornell University, in Ithaca, New York. Daneshvar has written seven plays, published four novels — *Ashura Ashura, The Hut-Dwellers, Prayer of Death,* and *The Virtuous Sovereign,* the last of which was published as *Le Brave des Braves* in France — and two collections of short stories, *Hey Hey Jabali Ghom Ghom* and *Mahbubeh and Ahl.* His work reflects his immense knowledge of and fascination with the popular vernacular, proverbs, the folklore of Khorassan, and his masterful command of the Persian language.

"Mahbubeh and the Demon Ahl" is a haunting story that can be read on many different levels. Recounted as a folktale, it explores the anatomy of violence against women, the nature of repression, and the ways in which folkloric superstition explains, reflects, and supplements such violence and repression. Seminal events in the story take place parallel to major events in contemporary Iranian history: Mahbubeh is born during World War II, gets married on the eve of the coup d'état against Mossadegh, and her daughter's wedding takes place at the time of the revolution of 1979.

MAHBUBEH AND THE DEMON AHL

The story they told was that Mahbubeh's father's aunt, Hajar, was responsible for the family's uprooting in the year one thousand three hundred and eighteen of the Hijra.[1] A few months before Mahbubeh's birth in the city, the wind demon unleashed a savage storm from his sack, tearing up God's good earth, and exposing, bit by bit, for all to see, the remains of the aunt, gruesomely slain. Wailing and scandal filled the land.

Everyone now knew that the mysterious veiled woman who, under cover of night, in remote caves and abandoned shepherd's huts, had slept with any man who came to her on horseback, was none other than Hajar. The veiled woman never appeared in the same place twice, they said, and it took great luck to find her. What's more, she never gave herself to a man who came on foot; only riders interested her. To the chosen ones who reveled in the sweetness of her favors, she spoke not a word, though at the height of ecstasy she seemed to murmur, "My regal, nocturnal horseman!" into their ears.

The number of men who sought her passion and the heat of her whisper multiplied, desperate souls galloping through all the barren places around the village till dawn. Exhausted by their nightly quest, they would succumb to sleep in the morning and dream of delights yet to come. And so they began to neglect their tasks, stopped toiling in the fields, and the little village gradually crumbled into ruin.

One sleepless night, Hajar's husband — one of the few remaining able-bodied men in the village — quietly crept out of bed, leaving behind his apparently sleeping wife. He slipped into a neighbor's stable, where a saddled horse awaited him, and joined the riders of the night. Hours passed as he rode the land. The cold nagged at him to abandon his search and return home. But before his desire for the legendary

---

Special thanks to Deborah Tall for editing this story.
[1] The calendar of the Muslim era begins in 622 C.E., the year of Mohammad's departure from Mecca to Medina.

veiled woman abated, the scheming stars aligned in his favor. He found his way into the enchanted realm of her body and was soon immersed in the nectar of her ministrations. From that night on, the veiled lady was never seen again — that is, not until the night the demon loosed his winds.

Gales rose as the gossip mongers wagged their tongues, tying the disappearance of Hajar to the vanished lady of the caves. The fearsome wind carried such grime that even the gossipers' words, like the trees and houses, were coated in dust. Windows flew off their hinges and fires were snatched from hearths. Haylofts caught fire and dried-up trees burned for hours. Anything that dared stand in the way of the wind was battered down. Trapped in their huts, the villagers abandoned hope. Gardens vanished, walls collapsed, sands shifted, animals were buried, and finally the churning earth disgorged the remains of the missing woman. Only then, in the glaring sunlight that followed the storm, could they confirm that the veiled woman had, indeed, been Hajar.

Indignant, the village men blamed Hajar's husband, who, utterly humiliated, shouldered the blame and took it upon himself to journey to the city court so that he could receive his just punishment. But alas, the winds had so distorted the collective history and identity of the village that there seemed no remedy for the despair of the men and the torment of the women. The fields were devastated and the wells dried up. Dead animals slowly decomposed under the sun, and the fatty stench carried disease. Finally, weighed down by their memories and few belongings, the villagers departed for other places, became strangers in distant lands. But the men were forever after haunted by the infamy of Hajar, who was, after all, more or less a blood relation of them all, and the women were trapped by walls of suspicion the men built around them as a consequence of Hajar's betrayal.

A few months after their arrival in the city, Masumeh, who was mistakenly named Mahbubeh, was born.[2] Fearful of future disgrace, her father had secretly prayed for a boy child. Her birth, therefore, did not gladden him. But there was an added source of distress: a few weeks

---

[2] Masumeh is a girl's name meaning "innocent and pure." This was the title of Imam Reza's sister who is buried in Qom, Iran. Imam Reza was the eighth Shi'a Imam, or leader. Mahbubeh is a girl's name meaning "beloved."

before the delivery, the child had issued blood in the womb, and when the mother detected the blood, she was so horrified that she was driven to the brink of death. This strange development persuaded the parents to sacrifice an innocent lamb before the proper, designated time to welcome a baby.

Mahbubeh's uncle, her mother's brother, had already declared that the child was to be a boy and that he would grow up to be as fierce as a lion. But her father, in the grip of his forebodings, worried aloud, "Our family is blessed by the birth of boys, but our unfathomable fate brings us nothing but misfortune with girls. Just look at Hajar, the only female of our generation."

The uncle snapped back, "*My* family is blessed with an abundance of girls, and they all grow up to be chaste, noble, and faithful like the blessed Masumeh. And each time providence gives us a boy, he grows up manly and brave like his godly patron, Ali, whom he serves loyally, like a slave."[3]

Then the uncle made sure to inscribe Ali's name on the right side of his pregnant sister and the name of Masumeh on her left.

When Mahbubeh's mother went into labor late one night, her husband buried his feverish head under the blankets. But Mahbubeh's uncle rushed through the dark alleys of the city toward the mosque to pray for the health of the mother and child before the morning call to worship. Just before dawn, Mahbubeh was born. Despite her father's anxiety, and although she arrived just a few months after the storm, she was a creature of calm. She had long hair, lay quietly, and her eyes, wide open, seemed filled with astonishment.

Her mother's anxiety, however, only worsened because Hajar, too — as she had heard her say herself — was born just this way, looking like a woman, with long hair and wide open eyes. What's more, Hajar had added, a girl born with wide-open eyes like that is the property of Ahl, as she, Hajar, had been.[4] "Ahl took me away and now I am not Hajar anymore," Hajar had lamented. "My name is Mahbubeh

---

[3] Ali is the first Shi'a Imam, the Prophet Mohammad's son-in-law.
[4] According to Persian folklore, Ahl is an ogre who usually appears as a large man with a nose made of clay and yellow or red eyes. He steals and kills children as they are born, and eats the livers of women as they are giving birth. In folklore, Ahl was used to explain the death of a child or a mother during childbirth.

now. Hajar was the one who was taken by Ahl." (As fate would have it, a few days later, because the official in charge of issuing birth certificates was hard of hearing, Masumeh's name was in fact mistakenly registered as Mahbubeh.)

On the very night of Mahbubeh's birth, Ahl, wasting no time, staged his assault. Her uncle had not gone very far when he heard the birth cries rising from the house. The baby girl, gawking at the world like a startled, lost animal, had just been placed beside her mother on a bed of ashes, circled by bricks, when the mother began to turn green from some constriction in her throat and stared transfixed, as if drawing her last breath.

Mahbubeh's father, from within his refuge of blankets, plunged into delirious hallucinations from which he was never to fully recover. But, as luck would have it, Mahbubeh's uncle, midway to the mosque, had bumped into Ahl.

Years later, an older cousin, Mahbubeh's playmate, and a perennial source of both pain and pleasure, told her about her uncle's strange encounter with Ahl.

On his way to the mosque, in the dim light before dawn, the uncle had arrived at a stream, created by the storm that now divided the city. There, at that juncture, he had seen the silhouette of a man, bent over the water, who seemed to be waiting for the uncle to cross the stream. Thinking the man was about to bathe, the uncle covered his head with his cape and sped on, but he was stopped in his tracks by the screech of a newborn. And before it was too late, he turned on his heels and pounced on the man, not giving him a chance to touch the water with whatever it was he held in his hand. He quickly grabbed at the man's face and tore off his nose. Warm and wet, like a chunk of moist clay, the nose writhed in his palm. The whole frame of this strange creature now glowed a phosphorescent red, and yellow sparks flew from his eyes. If it were not for the prayers the uncle mumbled in the secret of his heart, he'd never have been able to shield himself from the venom flung at him. But heroically, he managed to roar, "In the name of the Holy one, the all powerful, you are to put back the liver of the mother where you found it and restore the child, unharmed, to her mother."

This, the cousin concluded, was how Mahbubeh's life had been spared and her mother rescued from the claws of death. "But who knows," he added menacingly, "if Ahl did not tamper with your identity and change it in some way. It is quite possible that my *real* cousin, whose name was Masumeh, is not you at all."

When Mahbubeh's uncle had returned home that morning of her birth, he heard joyful ululation all over the house. He sat in a corner and uttered not a word. He was busy stringing a necklace out of the lump of clay in his hand, waiting for the women to finish their business with the baby. They were washing her in salt water so that, when she grew up, she might have a firm body and a pretty face. They placed crushed candy between her legs so that her womanhood might smell good and taste sweet, and they swaddled her in white. Finally they put her in the arms of her uncle, who placed the newly made necklace around her neck, whispered prayers in her ear, and wrote her name inside the cover of the Quran. He advised the women to dry the umbilical cord before tossing it into the river, so that the baby girl might become a woman of great forbearance and few words, and eventually, when she came of age, marry not just anybody but a man who is upright in the sight of God.

A few days later, the uncle completely vanished, and for years his family nourished the hope that they might still hear from him, receive a letter from some far-off country. It was only Mahbubeh's cousin who, with his curious brand of meanness, whispered in her ear, "Wherever he is, even if he is in Russia, the demons must have gotten him by now."

Mahbubeh's mother insisted she always wear the clay necklace in remembrance of her uncle. But the cousin used this as a pretext to torment her. He was relentless, cunningly cruel. At playtime he dispensed misery to his playmates, and like the king of snakes, breathed dread into Mahbubeh's dreams. He exacted obedience, and any hint of rebellion, no matter how small, was punished by his fat fists. His poisonous tongue alone could leave his opponents lifeless.

"You see this girl?" he would say, pointing to Mahbubeh. "An ogre named Ahl has taken possession of her. If you take away the necklace her uncle made for her from Ahl's nose, she'll drop dead in a split second."

One day, fed up with her cousin, Mahbubeh walked into a dark closet to welcome death with open arms. She tore off the necklace and from the bottom of her heart she called out for Ahl. On this same day, her cousin — weary of pretending to be a pirate at sea, bored by bloody battles, kingly exploits, and chasing scorpions through the cracks between bricks — was entertaining himself by relishing the pitiful cries of a tar-smeared cat. It was in the darkness of the closet that Mahbubeh suddenly realized the truth — that Ahl was none other than her cousin.

The next morning, Mahbubeh and her cousin were taken to a religious school and registered as students. Mahbubeh's father, holding their hands, helped them down a seemingly endless stairway to a dingy little room where Mollabadji, a toothless, green-skinned, white-haired hag with red eyelids and breasts that drooped to her knees, presided over a bunch of wrinkled children. The students were listlessly mumbling the litany that was their lesson.

"*A* is for animal, *B* is for beast . . ."

Mahbubeh's father, who after the eventful birth of his daughter had placed all his hopes in the life hereafter, listened to the mournful chants, his eyes filling with tears as he recalled the sad fate of the orphaned children of martyrs in the pages of the sacred writings. He sat beside the children and rested his aching head on his aching knees, joining the funereal incantations until the crone commanded silence. And within that stillness, which was like the damp bottom of a deep pit, she asked, "What do you want, sir?"

"I want to place these two children under your command. I'll offer you their flesh but keep their bones. Give them a taste of your rod. This girl here is a dumb donkey, always silent. This boy here is a mad mule."

The crone replied, "Rest assured, man of God, I know how to beat them into shape."

As soon as Mahbubeh's father had left, the rod of discipline descended crushingly on her poor cousin's head. As he let loose a piercing cry, Mahbubeh's heart filled with pity for the little Ahl. And, then and there, she realized that the old, green, white-haired crone, whose breasts came down to her knees, was actually Ahl. All the pain and suffering that her cousin had heaped upon her immediately vanished from her memory.

The following day, the cousin stubbornly refused to go back to the religious school. His father was not as devoted to a religious education as her own father was, and so the boy was sent to a regular secular school instead. From then on, the cousins saw little of each other, until one cold night, while sitting near the pleasant heat of the hearth, a strange affection in the air drew them closer. But this moment of pleasure was marred by dread.

Mahbubeh's cousin and his family were guests at her home that Friday night. She had just finished studying and memorizing some thirty pages of the Quran for which the old crone was rewarded with a kerchief full of candy and a crisp hundred-toman bill. Her mother was soaking three kilos of rice in water to prepare the meal.

Friday nights in general were happy times: cooking rice, sitting around and talking, even if they did not have guests to entertain. On Friday nights she hardly ever heard the usual "I-said-you-said" bickering between her parents. She could hear her mother's discreet giggling and her father's more or less cheerful disquisition on the purity of imams and martyrs.

On that particular Friday evening there was a heavy snowfall. The guests would need to stay overnight, and so the pleasant hours lingered on. After dinner, the father, boastful of a daughter who could read the Quran, decided to indulge in a bit of innocent fortune-telling.[5] So he opened the Quran to a random page — the *sura* on women, it turned out — and handed it to Mahbubeh.[6] Like a seasoned reader, she did full justice to all the nuances and ups and downs of vocalizations. Head high, her father used the occasion to brag to his brother-in-law who, like other modern folk, had sent his son to a secular state school where faith was undermined and boys became worldly dandies, believers in ungodly science. Slyly, he placed the Quran in the hands of the cousin and asked him to read a verse or two for the edification of the group.

The boy, stammering and stumbling, clumsily made his way through a line or two before his father's fist came crashing down on his head. The reading was stopped in disgrace. The boy hung his head and sulked for the rest of the evening, until he eventually fell asleep. Mahbubeh, who had suffered much degradation under the green-skinned crone for years, was able to empathize. Her heart bled for the young

---

[5] Persian speakers have to learn how to read the Quran, which is in Arabic.
[6] *Sura* means chapter.

Ahl, and her compassion left her sleepless. She moved closer to her cousin and, as when they were little, she snuggled against him and whispered in his ear, "Are you sleeping? Listen, I've seen Ahl."

She had been in the women's bathhouse, she told him, with its labyrinthine rooms leading one into another. There was more steam than usual, and it was darker than usual, too. The women were mostly silent, but curiously, quite a few of them offered to wash and scrub her clean. She turned them all down. She found the heat so unbearable that she felt faint and fell asleep. It was then she saw Ahl.

In her dream she was married to him. Her mother-in-law belonged to a tribe of ogres. Mahbubeh recognized that such was her lot — to be married to Ahl. Ahl told his mother, look, I've brought you a maid, and he ordered Mahbubeh to treat his mother with utmost deference. Mahbubeh obeyed, greeting her politely. The mother-in-law immediately shoved a broom into Mahbubeh's hand, handed her a bucket with a hole in it, and set down before her a huge tray, heaping with mung beans, lentils, and rice. The whole pile was infested with mouse droppings and sand pebbles. Then the mother-in-law got all dolled up and left for another ogre's wedding. She should sweep the house, the mother-in-law ordered Mahbubeh. She should also water the garden using water from the courtyard pool, clean the rice, separating the good from the bad, cook dinner, and put henna on her hands and feet in readiness for the bridegroom. If the courtyard is not swept clean, the house will fill up with snakes and scorpions, she said. If the trees are not watered, her womb will only be able to deliver dried-up babies. If the food is not cooked and ready, her husband will chew on her liver instead.

The courtyard was small, but no matter how much she swept, there seemed no end to the dirt. The bucket was useless, and there was blood and pus sloshing about the pool. The cleaning of the heap of rice was a chore for forty women. She sat by the tray and wept, waiting for her husband Ahl to return and kill her.

Suddenly, one of the women who had offered Mahbubeh a rubdown tore off the towel she was wrapped in and glared obscenely at her nakedness. Mahbubeh awoke and quickly covered herself. The woman laughed. "What a lovely bride you'll make. Not a single flaw or blemish on your body." Mahbubeh looked at her hands and feet and saw that they were hennaed. She felt feverish. She sprang up and quickly gathered her bundle of belongings and put her clay necklace back on. But the fever stayed in her body, and each time the memory of the dream of her marriage to Ahl flashed through her mind, she told her cousin, she felt the fires of hell roaring inside her.

Sweet God, how cool were the hands of her sympathetic cousin. The snowstorm was gently penetrating everything, sifting through the ceiling, through the comforter, and settling under her loose cotton dress. It was the sky-blue dress with little white flowers that for years had lain folded at the bottom of her mother's trunk. Long ago, her mother had received it from Hajar as a gift, and she had just bestowed it on Mahbubeh as a reward for learning to read the Quran.

"Hajar! Hajar! O martyrs in heaven!"

It was the father returning from his nightly visit to a favorite martyr's shrine in his dreams. He had been particularly grateful at that Glorious Threshold of Purity for his daughter — a weak vessel, so meek and mild — who could flawlessly read the Quran. He had secretly whispered in his heart that, after all, the daughter of the prophet was a female, too, as were so many others in the holy hierarchy. They were all mothers and sisters to the great men of faith. That night, during the little pilgrimage in his dream, he had put his infinite gratitude into words. And it had seemed to him that the holy imams, although invisible, had smiled in approval, and their eyes, also invisible, had glinted with satisfaction. Then, with embarrassment for having doubted his daughter's potential, he had rushed back home. It was there that the stench of iniquity met his nostrils. Dashing though the interminable corridors of sleep, he woke up, jumped out of bed, and rushed into the other room. There, writhing under the quilt, he found an evil spirit like a dragon struggling to free itself as if from the slime at the bottom of a swamp.

"O heavens above, this must be the ghost of Hajar the whore!"

Shrieking madly, he tore asunder the sleepers' curtain, and the violent rain of his fists fell on the young couple. He pulled a chunk of hair that dripped with blood from his daughter's head and reduced her to a seeming heap of bones thrown into a corner of the room. Her cousin, lips gashed, eyes swollen, cheeks scratched and bleeding, was flung to another corner. Poor young man, he couldn't conceive how a joyous moment had abruptly turned into a nightmare.

When the brother-in-law heard about the outrage from the frothing mouth of the father, he beat the young man some more, until the aunt stepped between them and put an end to the gruesome display of brutality.

"Stop this at once! You're behaving like raving lunatics! They have slept next to each other since childhood. Why dump the filth of your thoughts on them?" She held the young ones in her protective arms and took them to her house. Thus, that night, in this manner, were Mahbubeh and her cousin introduced to love and its forbidden dimensions.

During the two weeks that Mahbubeh stayed at her aunt's, in spite of the pain and frightful memories of that night, she and her cousin continued to savor the delicious gifts and anxieties of love in all the nooks and crannies of the house. But their secret lovemaking, which inspired their bodies and enlightened their souls, never went beyond mere kissing, fondling, and awed glances.

Their beaten bodies still recalled the pain they had suffered, and their wounds bled at times. Mahbubeh's uncle cast disgusted glances at them, meant to humiliate. The absence of her mother made Mahbubeh choke on tears. But in spite of all this, her days were filled with caressing sunshine, and at night, listening to the songs of her body, she experienced a slow blossoming that filled her with happiness. She felt a pure contentment with herself as a woman. All this was owed, she thought, to her cousin, who diligently made fresh discoveries of all the things her girlish body could offer, eager to open new doors. But, when it came to opening all the doors, an ancient instinct prevented her from straying too far from the path of moderation. As in the fairy tale "The Imprisoned Princess and the Demon" the unraveling of each knot led to another hidden entanglement that held its promise for yet another tomorrow.

Until, on one of those tomorrows, her mother came and took her away, and what she had steadfastly kept protected from the sweet attentions of the cousin was handed over to the manipulations of an obscene old sorceress.

*   *   *

During her two-week absence, Mahbubeh's father had found her a pro-
spective husband. He had also instructed the mother to make sure that
their daughter was still, indeed, a virgin, lest they lose all respect among
their neighbors and relatives. The mother took Mahbubeh to an old
woman considered an expert in matters regarding virginity. After many
humiliating manipulations and tests, their minds were put to rest.

The suitor was the neighborhood grocer. He was her father's part-
ner in religious observances. Each time she was sent to his store to buy
something, his yellow crust–laden eyes repulsed her. He would ingrati-
atingly toss a packet of fruit roll, some dried figs, or a fresh pomegran-
ate into her grocery bag. The moment she was out of his sight, she
would unburden herself of these unwanted gifts. In her eyes, the grocer
was Ahl incarnate. His breath smelled of ill-digested liver. Each time his
fingers, like tongues of flame, reached for her chador, she would cringe.

She had no doubt her parents were trying to marry her to Ahl.
Just as in her dream, she made up her mind to die. She would sit patiently, she decided, by the tray of rice and wait for Ahl to come and
tear her liver apart. The sweet melodies of her body were now completely silenced. The memory of those joyous nights with her cousin
sank into oblivion, never to be re-ignited, even when he came to visit
her in secret.

The wedding was to happen two months hence, after the solemn
months of Moharam and Safar.[7] During the first half of Moharam, her
father spent his nights at the mosque in ritual mourning and lamenta-
tion, while her mother was occupied with domestic chores. Mahbubeh's cousin would come to keep her company. They'd sit silently on
the stairs leading to the roof, listening to the sounds of wailing rising
from every mosque in the city, and he'd hug his knees sorrowfully. On
one occasion, when he made a move to resurrect their bygone pleas-
ures, she ran away, terrified. The poking fingers of the old witch,
searching for the evidence of her virginity, had instilled in her a lasting
dread. For Mahbubeh, that was the day the idea of love had come to
an end.

---

[7] The first and second months in the Muslim calendar, Moharam and Safar, commemorate the
days of fighting against the Ummayyid leader Yazid, and the martyrdom of the grandson of the
Prophet, Imam Hossein, in Karbala in 680 C.E. The deaths of the Prophet Mohammad, the second Imam Hassan, and the eighth Imam Reza are also commemorated in the month of Safar.

One night her cousin had a piece of news for her — possibly hopeful news. It was about Elijah, the immortal, wandering green-cloaked prophet, who comes to the aid of those whose prayerful requests come from the very bottom of their hearts. For the next forty days, he instructed, Mahbubeh was to sweep the threshold of their house before each sunrise and bless the name of the Most High. It wouldn't hurt to add some of the prayers she had learned at religious school. But her intentions should remain secret. For forty days she was to commit no sin, no matter how small, and on the fortieth day the green prophet would appear.

No one knew in what form the prophet would reveal himself. Perhaps he'd come as a human being, perhaps not. He might come in the guise of an acquaintance, or of a total stranger. She should not be deceived by appearances. The more he insists that he's not the green prophet, the cousin explained, the more confident she should be that he is. Cling to his garment and do not let go. That's the way he is: one should never let go of him. And right then and there, state your request. Talk to him about your pain, and until your request is granted do not let go of him. He shall save you from Ahl and all this nonsense about marrying the grocer. And then we'll wait until I've finished school. When I'm an engineer, I'll come and make you my wife. Don't forget to ask for all this from the green prophet. Starting tomorrow I won't come to visit you. It's true we're not doing anything bad, but it's risky for us to get intimate. You should never sin — never. Say your prayers on time. Each time you sweep, do your ablutions. I'm going. You won't see me until the end of the forty days.

During the forty days in which Mahbubeh sprinkled water and swept the alley, he remained true to his promise. But when the fortieth day had come and gone, the cousin didn't show up. In the days that followed he never came. It was the green prophet who kept him away. The same green prophet to whose garment Mahbubeh had clung.

The green prophet wore greasy blue overalls and had a long string of yellow worry beads that he twirled around his finger. He sported a huge mustache and spoke like a thug. In the beginning, he pretended not to know what the fuss was all about. He said, "Let go of me, girl. Who the hell is the green prophet you're talking about?"

She couldn't find anywhere to grab onto his workman's clothes, so she clung to his string of worry beads until the string broke and the beads scattered everywhere. Embarrassed, Mahbubeh ran after them, and as she was busy gathering up the beads, her chador slipped off her head. It was only then that the green prophet agreed to listen to the story that came pouring out of her heart. Before she had time to pull herself together and cover her head with the chador, he had caught a glimpse of her necklace and laughed.

"Now that you've broken my beads, give me your necklace to make up for it," he teased.

Mahbubeh hesitated, then told him, "These aren't ordinary beads. This necklace is a souvenir from my mother's brother."

"If that's the case, then good-bye."

"O green prophet, don't go. Here, you can have the necklace."

This is how the green prophet's worry beads came to be replaced by her clay necklace. One day, years later, she would see that necklace twisting and turning wildly on his prayer rug.

Mahbubeh and the green prophet sat on the stoop and talked all night. She poured out her heart, and the green prophet kept asking questions. Each time she answered one, he came up with another. By sunrise he had come to know everything he needed to know about her. He knew all about Ahl, about Hajar, the wind, and the ruined village. He knew about her uncle's disappearance, the story behind the necklace, the cousin who wanted to become an engineer, the grocer around the corner, even the scary dream she had had in the baths, and the dreadful secret of the ugly crone's fingers. The sun had come up, and pedestrians had begun to go about their business. The green prophet stood up, shook the dust off of his pants, and banged on the door of her house. Her father, who was about to step out, opened the door, and his face quickened with rage. The green prophet shoved him aside, pushed his way into the house, and announced, "I'm the green prophet. I'm asking for your daughter's hand."

One by one the days, like drops of water, dripped on the calm surface of Mahbubeh's mind and made a slight noise. Her head felt as if encased in the steamy pool of the bathhouse, her world blanketed by a thick mist of bafflement. The wedding day was drawing near. The green prophet turned out to be a thug by the name of Asghar "Ten-Wheels," a truck driver. Right from the beginning, from the moment he shoved her father aside, he had everyone on a short leash. The neighborhood grocer, under suspicious circumstances, was assaulted and stabbed. He closed up shop and went on a pilgrimage. Word was sent to the cousin that if he dared show his face he'd end up with a broken leg or be chopped into tiny bits the size of his earlobe. Many a night the cousin would come anyway and keep watch, throw pebbles at her window, climb the wall all the way to the roof, and on many an occasion, he'd even call out her name. But the windows were shut, the door to the roof was locked, the lightbulb outside the house was dead, the alleyway pitch black, and his voice got lost in the fog-infested regions of Mahbubeh's mind. When he finally threw caution to the wind and banged on the front door, they had all gone to the baths to prepare the bride for the wedding. Mahbubeh didn't see her cousin again for twenty-five years, not until the day her own daughter, Masumeh, was married. He told her then that Ahl and his ilk were everywhere. They are from another planet, he said, just like the rest of us.

On her wedding night it was windy. At sunset, a large corona circled the sun, and a murder of loud, cawing crows flew close to the earth. The tattered clouds were burned away in a last burst of sunlight, and then the wind began to howl. It rattled the glass in windowpanes and uprooted antennas from rooftops. Lampposts broke. Electric wires snapped, and all the lights went out. They had no choice but to borrow kerosene lamps from the neighbors. They gathered all the dusty oil-burning lamps they could find stashed away until a sickly yellowish light filled the bridal chambers.

From far away, the wind carried the anxious howls of beasts and drowned out the music of tambourines. Having lost their enthusiasm, the women banged listlessly on their instruments in their quarters. In the men's quarters, they listened to mournful religious sermons. In the basement, the bridegroom and his buddies drank vodka, and when the wind seemed bent on destroying the world, they came out of the house singing their drunken songs. Even when they seemed to have disappeared into the wind, one could still hear them singing, "Hajar is getting married today, look how she's being carried away. Dum-de-dum-de-dum."

That night, in the whorehouses all over town, the riffraff got drunk, lost their tempers, and brandished knives. By the time the bridegroom stumbled into the bridal chamber, the kerosene lamp was sputtering.

He hung his ripped jacket on a nail, took off his bloodstained shirt, and came to Mahbubeh's bed. When her stifled cries turned to weeping, the bridegroom's jacket fell on the lamp and caught fire. According to the solar calendar, this was the year one thousand three hundred and thirty-two of the Hijra, and Mahbubeh was fourteen years old.

For a few months the young couple stayed in her father's house. They put fresh paint on the walls of the fire-blackened room, and the broken lamppost in the street was repaired. The grocer quietly came back and reopened his store for business. The father, though he could not abide the drunken episodes of his son-in-law, said nothing, and the mother kept to herself. Because the son-in-law was a truck driver, he spent most of his time on the road anyway. When he did come home, he was either dead tired or dead drunk and out of his wits. He never parted with Mahbubeh's necklace and was often seen twirling it around his finger, but he would occasionally bring her gifts from his travels: bracelets, gold earrings. When he was in a good mood, he'd tease her about mistaking him for the green prophet and for revealing her innermost secrets to him. She thought he was Ahl himself, and said that he'd been lying in ambush for years, watching her every move. Joking, he would growl and act like a monster, and end up hurting her delicate rib cage. His breath always smelled of vodka and garlic. His lovemaking had nothing in common with her cousin's affectionate touch. Even after many years, he remained a stranger, a blackguard she could never hope to love. The pale memories of her cousin faded further.

The husband could be generous, and he helped her father, who because of his excessive preoccupation with religious matters was sinking into financial ruin. The father gradually softened toward his son-in-law and was grateful that things had turned out so well for his daughter. He still hoped that the son-in-law would one day reform and stop drinking, his only obvious shortcoming. Mahbubeh's mother, meanwhile, nagged her to start having children. But Mahbubeh was still waiting fearfully for the moment when her husband would drag her off to his mother, who, as in the dream, would treat her like a maid.

The true ferocity of her husband's soul had not yet been revealed — until one day a group of minstrels passed by the house.

A group of children and idle men followed the minstrels. Neighborhood women were out watching. The minstrels played their instruments with all the passion they could muster. A young peasant with a thick mustache sang a popular song and the children echoed its refrain. It was during the refrain that Mahbubeh, who still had henna on her hands and feet, opened her window. The children were singing:

> The bride puts henna on her hands.
> If henna is hard to find, she puts on her bracelet of gold.

The singer had heard the sound of the window opening, so he looked up smiling and sang:

> Out the window you look, smiling, gazing at me from behind your
> chador longingly, still gazing, your chador trembling,
> There's nothing like your kiss in the whole wide world.

Then the choir of children gathered under the window and accompanied the singer at the top of their lungs. It was the sly grocer who spilled the beans, informing the husband, Asghar "Ten-Wheels," of the goings-on, reciting the words of the song as if they were facts. The husband, just back from a trip, saw blood. The image of Hajar the whore popped into his mind, and when he reached home, he went berserk. He tore a gold chain from around his wife's neck and clawed at her flesh. He undid his belt and began whipping Mahbubeh for what seemed like thirty years. From then on, whenever he happened to be in one of his dark moods, he wanted to know who the singer was, how did he know that she still had henna on her hands and feet? Where and when had she met and probably kissed him? And when he was dead drunk he was seen to weep.

From then on, in his imagination, all the women he'd pick up on the road were, like Mahbubeh, women whose husbands were on the road, Hajars who'd wear their chadors but go off with truck drivers.

The father, who had also heard the story from the grocer, said nothing. But he seethed silently as he heard the muffled, tormented shrieks of Mahbubeh day after day. Finally, one morning he declared to his household that they must immediately move. He'd received a message from on high in a dream that the house was no longer suitable for the living. It should be dedicated to the dead, become a Muslim graveyard. In a fit of madness, he kicked his wife and family out of the house, and as the first candidate for the graveyard, lay down, stretched out his legs, and died.

The son-in-law took out a loan on his truck and came up with a down payment for a new house. Finally Ahl was able to move his wife into his own home.

Mahbubeh discovered that she had no mother-in-law, but her husband soon invited an old woman to live with them as her companion — and to spy on her when he was away. The old woman turned out to be the same one who had stripped Mahbubeh of her towel in the bathhouse and admired her flawless body. From the first day, a spirit of dark fear descended upon the house. When Mahbubeh complained to her husband that she was scared of the old crone, he barked at her that maybe she was keeping secrets from him, maybe she was missing her beloved cousin, or the minstrel with his thick mustache; maybe she didn't want a witness around when she strayed from the straight and narrow path in his absence. He so utterly silenced her with these jealous tirades that even when the old woman's hulk of a son, who was a sergeant in the army, started visiting while the husband was conveniently away, Mahbubeh was afraid to say a word. The sergeant had obscenely bulging eyes, and he never took them off her window.

Mahbubeh's days were spent sweeping the courtyard, cooking, sewing, and imagining things. Although she wanted to avoid the old crone, out of sheer proximity she sometimes found herself chatting with her.

During one of these talks, the old woman told her that if she were curious, she could teach her how to perform sorcery. Mahbubeh responded sarcastically that she was more interested in learning how to undo sorcery.

"They're one and the same," the old woman declared. "By your conquest of things you undo them. And that's sorcery."

"What is conquest?" Mahbubeh asked.

"First you drain the life out of it, then you take its place," the crone replied.

"How does one drain the life out?"

"It depends how strongly it resists death."

The conversation ended abruptly when Mahbubeh's mother appeared in the doorway, and the topic was never brought up again. But this brief exchange contained the seeds of sorcery within it. It lodged itself in a niche in Mahbubeh's soul, and like an arrow shot expertly, it went on flying forever.

Mahbubeh's mother had other children to take care of, so she didn't have time to visit very often. Her aunt was no longer on speaking terms with them, and so Mahbubeh had no news of her cousin. Her imagination was, in any case, now preoccupied by the two-month-old fetus in her belly. One day, as she was weaving something for her future baby, the door to her room was flung open and the sergeant sauntered in. He said that he had come to visit his mother, but she appeared to be out. He was wondering if he could wait for her in Mahbubeh's room.

Mahbubeh had no idea how to respond. She hastily pulled her chador over her head. Since the man had remained standing, she said, "Why don't you sit down?" But she immediately regretted her misplaced graciousness and searched for an excuse to leave the room. She was about to do so when he blocked her way.

Twenty-five years later, when she heard that a beefy sergeant had been hacked to pieces, she hoped that it was him.

That night, when the old woman returned home she went straight to Mahbubeh's dark room. She turned on the light, but when she saw the crazed look on Mahbubeh's face and her clothes in tatters, she ran away terrified. The following day the sergeant was back, this time accompanied by his mother. Mahbubeh was still as the old woman had found her the night before. The sergeant ordered her to "snap out of it" and "stop playacting." Then he slapped her until the flood gate of tears broke open. Mahbubeh cried until exhaustion overtook her. The crone and her son left the house, never to be seen again.

When Mahbubeh opened her eyes it was still dark outside, and the light was on inside the room. She saw a woman sitting in the middle of the floor, peering into a mirror she had taken off the shelf, applying kohl to her eyes. "Who are you?" Mahbubeh asked.

The woman had a pleasant laugh. "Who do you think I should be? I'm your aunt, Hajar."

"You're supposed to be dead. Your husband cut you to pieces."

Hajar shrugged. "Such is the way of the world. So what are you going to do about it? Are you going to just sit and wait until they cut you to pieces, too?"

Mahbubeh was about to say, "I don't do the things the likes of you do," but she bit her tongue and remained silent.

Hajar said, "When your good-for-nothing husband comes home, tell him what the sergeant did to you. Let him eat his heart out."

"But what will he do to me if I tell him?"

"He'll chop you to pieces. Tell me, do you like the way I've done my eyes?"

"I can't see. My eyes are burning. I'm tired." She fell back asleep.

When she awoke in the morning, she put the mirror back on the shelf, gathered up her makeup from the floor, and told herself, "I'll tell him. May he burn in hell." Calmly, she put on several layers of makeup.

But her husband was brought home that day wrapped up in a bloody blanket, his bones all broken. His truck had gone over a cliff, and he had gone flying into the mouth of death.

It took two or three years until he came back to the land of the living and was able to return to work. During those years, they were forced to sell almost everything they owned, down to the nails in the walls, in order to eat. Mahbubeh didn't want to lose the house, too, so she went knocking on doors to plead for help. Finally, after the birth of her daughter Masumeh, her uncle found her a job in a canning factory.

Mahbubeh's firstborn was delivered free of charge in a hospital for the poor. She was so preoccupied, and the hospital so crowded, that she forgot that every girl born in their family was in danger of becoming Ahl's property. It so happened that an escaped criminal had been shot and was undergoing surgery. The hospital was emptied of regular visitors and policemen were all over the place.

Sara was the name she had chosen for her baby, but her husband, who had never forgotten the stories she related to him on the day she mistook him for the green prophet, preferred to call the baby Masumeh — and that was that.

*   *   *

The factory was on the other side of town, and it took her an hour on the bus to get there, so she had to leave the house early in the morning. There was much loud honking, and great plumes of dust were kicked up from the road. Even before she arrived at work, Mahoobeh felt drained and sickened.

The bus was usually packed, and often she had to stand the whole way, hanging from a pipe, sweating profusely, milk flowing uncontrollably from her breasts. One day she came down with a cold and developed a fever. In spite of her illness, she continued going to work until the cold turned chronic and her lungs lost some of their function forever.

One day a man sat next to her on the bus; his mere presence made her insides churn with revulsion. She gasped for air as the world seemed to spin around her, and she got off the bus a stop before her destination. But the man got off the bus, too, and started following her.

"Will you come with me?"

"No," Mahbubeh cried.

"Why not?"

"I'm married."

"So what? I'm married, too. As many times as the number of hairs on your head."

"Let me be, sir."

The man laughed. "How can I let you be, sweet morsel? You were mine from the moment you were born."

Mahbubeh furtively glanced at him. The man had no nose. A dirty dishrag had been stuffed in the middle of his face. She was too sick to feel scared. "What do you want, sir? For God's sake, let me be."

"How can I let you be? You women enslave us."

"I'm not scared of you. Go!"

"You know you're coming with me. I'll wear you out."

The conversation she had had about sorcery many moons ago with the old woman ricocheted in her mind like a bullet. She roared, "Get lost, monster!" And in her heart she prayed: "In the fearsome name of the Almighty, All Powerful One."

At night she told her husband, "I saw Ahl today."

"Wretched woman, Ahl is here right beside you. You're looking at him."

"No, you're not Ahl. You're just a sick man."

"So talk to me. Tell me what happened?"

But she had sunk into sleep, and the husband, bored and depressed, had little interest in her story. When her mother came into their room later that night with the news that her cousin had been arrested, she didn't even wake up. Her husband grumbled, "He probably asked for it." And when Mahbubeh did wake up, she couldn't remember what she had heard while half asleep, so whatever her bitter husband said, she simply nodded in agreement. "You're right, a wise man never meddles in the affairs of the state." Then she rushed out to catch the bus.

Little Masumeh and her father learned to walk at the same time. The father limped, and the toddler took tiny steps as Mahbubeh watched, smiling wearily, like a mother to them both. In spite of everything, the past few years had been good to her. The child was growing, her husband was able to stand on both feet, and a second child was on the way.

Slowly Masumeh walked on her own. The husband bought a truck on installment from his company and was on the road again. The second child arrived. Mahbubeh returned to her duties in the kitchen, the yard, the little pool, and the patch of garden. The years accumulated. A third child arrived. The husband was drinking heavily and had forgotten all about the cousin and the minstrel with the mustache. He didn't even pay much attention to Mahbubeh anymore. His interests were mostly outside the house.

Motherhood was the sole preoccupation of her day-to-day existence. No matter how much she swept their little yard, it never seemed clean. No sooner had she served a meal then she'd have to start preparing the next one. No matter how often the water in the pool was changed, it turned green with moss in no time. The tray with its mound of rice was always waiting for her to separate the grains from the dirt and droppings. Her husband was either off in the wilderness somewhere or home drunk. To add insult to injury, he had begun to snore. On the nights he was home, Mahbubeh could not sleep. And when she did sleep, she was beset by raw, distressing dreams. She felt like an empty, rusty, old chalice. Sometimes, during her chores, she'd dream with her eyes wide open, talking to the beans or lentils as if they were the days of her life, asking, "Who am I?"

She was thirty now, and the years were rushing past. Once in a blue moon her husband would wrap his legs around her, and as on earlier occasions, tell her that it was time to crank up the machine and make another chicken. Even on her eldest daughter's wedding day, she was pregnant. When she was pregnant, she felt as if the baby were slowly killing her, taking her place. Often, she'd remember the words of the old woman and the savage night when her son, the sergeant, had assaulted her. The memory of it made her feel as if her very bones were on fire.

It was during Masumeh's wedding that she heard about the upheaval that turned the world upside down.

On Masumeh's wedding day, the men were assigned to a neighboring house and the women were entertained at their own house. Mahbubeh's eyes were tearing up because of the smoke from the cooking fires in the yard.

Her mother cried out, "Open your eyes and see who's here!"

It was her aunt who hugged her and began to cry. Twenty-five years had gone by since the day her aunt had opened her shielding arms to her and taken her into her home.

"Your cousin wants to see you," her mother said.

The aunt added, "He was freed from prison just yesterday. He heard Masumeh was getting married, and so he has come."

Wiping her stinging eyes, Mahbubeh said, "He's most welcome."

Her mother went to call her cousin, and Mahbubeh rushed upstairs to put on her chador. She was coming down the stairs when she saw him, gray with age, standing in the swirl of smoke. His distracted look made her recognize him at once. When he was not busy doing something, he had always looked distracted.

She was about to greet him and, as was traditional, welcome him, but her tongue tricked her. "Cousin, where have you been all these years?"

"Dealing with Ahl. That's all." Her question and his answer made them both burst out laughing. She recalled their last meeting.

"That green prophet you sent me was an odd one. Instead of rescuing me from Ahl, he himself turned out to be an Ahl of sorts himself."

Her cousin replied, "Ahl is everywhere. He's from another planet. Just like us."

With the corner of her chador she touched her smoke-stung eyes and said, "I know. He conquers our life and soul and then takes our place."

They walked out to sit by the pool, where tea was being served from a samovar and sherbets were being made. Awkwardly, in sentences broken by pauses, they related abbreviated versions of the lives they had been living the past twenty-five years until Mahbubeh suddenly asked, "Don't you think it's time you married?"

"Not until the revolution has achieved its aim," he vowed.

Then, with the same enthusiasm he had had when he wanted to become an engineer and marry Mahbubeh, he told her that the world was in turmoil, that the king and the army, who were the earthly representatives of Ahl, were about to be killed once and for all.

"You say such strange things, Cousin." Mahbubeh sighed. "If you want to know the truth, Ahl is everywhere on earth. Once he was on the bus with me. He even followed me."

He had so much to tell her, and Mahbubeh was all ears, but somebody called her and reluctantly, the mother of the bride rose.

"You haven't changed, Cousin. You're still like the little boy who'd get into sword fights with other little boys."

The most sorrowful smile in the world appeared on his lips as he said good-bye. "By the way, did you know that Hajar's husband was also released with us?"

Since the night of her wedding — that windy night her husband had come to bed dead drunk and the house had caught on fire — this was the first time she yearned to make love.

Her husband, like most nights, was tired and restless. His face was locked in a frown; he was in no mood for anything. But Mahbubeh was dreamy. The festive spirit of the wedding had taken hold of her. It seemed that seeing her cousin had broken the wall that for all these years had held her back from her husband. For the first time she wanted him — her rider through many a wilderness. She put her hand behind his head and caressed his coarse hair.

"Are you sleeping?"

"I'm tired."

"I saw my cousin today."

"Congratulations."

"Poor thing. He's gotten so old. They gave him hell in prison."

As on other occasions when she had mentioned her cousin, she expected her husband to say that her cousin had gotten what he deserved. And the moment he opened his mouth, she planned to cover it with kisses. But this time he said nothing. She held his shoulder and gently pulled on it. He told her to save her story till the morning. She pulled on him again and, irritated, he asked if there was something wrong with her. With lips turning to lead, she said, "I want . . . I want you. Hold me in your arms."

The husband roared, "You should be ashamed of yourself. It's your daughter's wedding night. At your age, it's downright vulgar to be horny."

"I'm not yet forty."

"Your breath reeks of old age."

After a brief silence that chilled her to the bone, she heard him begin to snore. She wanted to die. She shook him again. By now he was in a dark and dangerous mood, wondering why she wouldn't let him sleep, the bitch. Mahbubeh said she had something important to tell him. And then, in the gloom, as yellow flames gathered in his eyes like little streams of poison, slowly, solemnly, she told him about the terrible deeds of the army sergeant, as if narrating a fairy tale.

The husband slowly rose from bed and vanished like a bubble into the night. For the first time in her adult life, she completely undressed and slept as peacefully as a child.

A few days later, she heard that a retired army sergeant, a giant of a man, had been hacked to pieces, and she hoped that the victim was none other than her sergeant. That was the year of the great upheaval, when the world turned upside down. According to the solar calendar, it was the year one thousand three hundred and fifty-seven of the Hijra.[8]

Six months later the husband was back, bearded and disheveled, wearing dusty green fatigues. It was a warm afternoon toward the end of

---

[8] The year 1357 is the equivalent of 1979, the year of the Revolution.

summer, the last days of her pregnancy. The children were at school, and her youngest daughter was by the pool playing with water. The husband casually said hello, ignoring her shock and unease. He went straight to the pool and did his ablutions in preparation for prayer. When he went upstairs to their room, he called her. Mahbubeh dragged her heaviness up the stairs. He was in the midst of praying, so she waited for him to finish. He looked up and announced, "The noon prayer is done. Later I shall recite the evening prayer. You know that the evening prayer contains four verses?"

His eyes were yellow. Really yellow. The scab on his cheek was redder than before. It was the first time she had ever seen him pray. Her heart sank.

He pulled out a long slim knife that was tied to his ankle, raised it above his head, brought it down, and half buried it in the floor by the prayer rug. The knife caught the sunlight and flashed an ominous, bluish glint.

"You know — or don't you — that the evening prayer has four verses?"

Mahbubeh said that she knew. The husband explained that today he felt like reciting it with only three verses.[9]

"You understand?"

Mahbubeh said that she didn't. It's simple, he said, he wanted to say the evening prayer in three verses. Did Mahbubeh understand now? She said she understood. After the third verse, which ends with the prayer of salutation, he added, if she or one of the children were still in the house, he'd cut them to pieces with his knife.

"The children are at school."

Wherever the hell they were, he didn't want to see them ever again. He swore by the glory of the Almighty Vengeful God that when he was done with the prayer of salutation, he'd kill her and the children unless they all left the house forever. Mahbubeh was about to ask where were they supposed to go, when he rose and began the evening prayer. During the second verse his eyes turned solid white. When he prostrated himself, she saw her clay necklace on the prayer rug writhing like a snake. Mahbubeh realized that Ahl had captured her husband's soul

---

[9] Muslim law permits shortening the evening prayer into three verses when there is an urgent matter at hand. Here the husband is emphasizing the urgency of his ultimatum.

and taken his place. During the last moments of the prayer, she pulled the dagger out of the floor and plunged it into his left shoulder blade, a soft spot that seemed to have been created for that very purpose. Then, like the riders of years gone by, those who rode with longing for her aunt, Hajar, wandering all the lonely places of the world, she straddled Ahl and twisted the knife in the wound.

The first day of autumn seemed to have arrived with a gale. It was so sudden that when her children returned from school and started crying behind the locked door, the wind was blowing too loudly for her to hear them.

She fetched four garbage bags and got down to the hard work of undoing the spell. Only once, through the howling wind, did she hear the voice of her children calling her name, and she told them, "Mahbubeh is gone. Hajar is here."

— Translated by Ashurbanipal Babilla

Goli Taraghi

Goli Taraghi was born in Tehran in 1939. She studied philosophy and literature at Drake University in the United States, and upon her return to Iran taught at Tehran University. She began her writing career with a collection of short stories, *I Am Che Guevara Too,* in 1969. Her first novel, *Winter Sleep,* was published in 1973 and has been translated into English and French.

Taraghi probes the inner emotional world of her characters through a stream-of-consciousness narrative technique. She is an expert storyteller with an ironic sense of humor. Her story "The Great Lady of My Soul" received the Contre-Ciel Award in France. Her most recent books are *Scattered Memories, In Another Place,* and *Two Worlds.* Two of her recent collections, *The House of Shemiran* and *The Three Maids,* have been published by Actes Sud in France. This is the first time that her novella *In Another Place* appears in translation. Taraghi lives in Tehran and Paris.

IN ANOTHER PLACE

The quiet and untroubled life of Amir-Ali was turned upside down one night for some unknown reason, which may be attributed to a mysterious disease — a bout of successive yawns and vomiting — or to the onslaught of some psychological disorder (even though Amir-Ali possessed a fully sound mind). The date, and even the exact hour, of this occurrence can be determined: Friday, October 9, 1998, eleven minutes after midnight.

His diaries, letters, and miscellaneous writings are in my safe-keeping. The reason for this intimacy and trust is simple. Amir-Ali and I grew up together and were always with each other. Those who knew us from afar thought we were brothers or close relatives. There was in-deed some resemblance, an acquired one. Our mannerisms, the way we walked and laughed, and especially the way we talked were very simi-lar. I was the one who unconsciously imitated him. Ever since the be-ginning of our friendship — that of two young classmates — Amir-Ali was someone important to me, someone special, different from all the others.

Life had made a gentle and rational being of him, a civilized man, an obedient husband, vice president of a prestigious company, capable of all the necessary wheeling and dealings and the customary negotia-tions. Yet I, who had known him from way back, knew that another Amir-Ali lurked behind that presentable and sane facade, imprisoned in the silent depths of his being, waiting to escape. I have had no news of him for years, but I am sure wherever he is (and God knows where that is) — at the end of the world, at the North Pole, on a turbulent ocean, in some obscure jungle, or in a small village hereabouts, near or far — he is well and happy and will one day turn up.

What I mean by "happy" is a certain type of happiness that per-tains to Amir-Ali's mentality and his world. It is not our type of hap-piness, yours and mine. I mean you and I and all the rest of us conservative and farsighted people, the domesticated and docile lot. I have laid out his writings, his letters, and his notes, and I am trying to sort out my memories of him: the childhood days, the summers he spent with me and my family in the country, his sayings, his wishes, his strange fantasies, his love of celestial happenings and cosmic mysteries (the little astronomer), and his secret war against his father, his teachers, and all those who wanted to mold him into a model son or student, the day he left Iran to continue his education abroad, the day he returned, the night of his wedding, the last time I saw him. I am putting all these moments together in an attempt to reconstruct his life. I want to know him, to know the real Amir-Ali. By examining him, his relationship with others, his hit-and-run tactics, his concealed anger, his obstinate silences, the mask he wore for the world and the way he deceived himself and others, and by taking apart the nuts and bolts of his personality and his past, I want to discover something new about him — and, if you will, the truth about myself. There is much for me to learn. The "whys" are many.

I will start with that particular evening, from that party and the emergence of that mysterious being, yes, that invisible shadow that is so hard to describe, the second Amir-Ali.

It is as though we are watching a movie, sequence by sequence: Amir-Ali is asleep; he goes to bed early and is a sound sleeper. He hardly ever dreams and rarely has a nightmare. When he closes his eyes, a white and translucent veil descends upon his thoughts and memories, like heavy snow silently blanketing the city, the snow of oblivion. He is among that rare group of men who do not snore. He does not get thirsty in the middle of the night and he does not go to the bathroom at the crack of dawn. He feels lazy in the morning and likes to snooze. Or lie half awake with his head under the sheet and think of things he is fond of: imaginary expeditions in empty deserts, snow-covered steppes in arctic regions, cosmic happenings and the off chance of discovering life in a distant galaxy, in another form, in a better place. But where? He doesn't know. Perhaps right here, in this very city, in his ancestral land, beyond the pale of industry, somewhere in harmony with his thoughts and beliefs, in proximity to things he loves and in tune with his psychic ebbs and flows and his internal pulsations, somewhere near to him, to his true self.

But Amir-Ali cannot allow himself this luxury. He knows he must be at his desk by eight o'clock. And this "must" is written on his brain in red capital letters. If not, he may forget. And he will forget. At the behest of his wife, he works out before breakfast, and with her resolve he watches his weight and his figure. He is a handsome man and looks at least twenty years younger than he really is. Women flutter around him, and his wife (Malak-Azar) has her little jealousies, but her mind is at ease. She knows that this man is hers, like her children, her identity card, her house, and all her belongings and antiques, and that without her he is incapable of asserting himself. And this is more or less what everyone believes. Everyone except me.

Malak-Azar is sleeping next to him like a bouquet of flowers — delicate, beautiful, and fragrant. She breathes gently and smiles even as she sleeps. She is probably dreaming of her husband and her children, and she is happy. Sometimes, as she lies half awake and half asleep, she reaches out and touches Amir-Ali's shoulder or the side of his neck with her fingertips, as though she wants to reassure herself of his presence beside her. During the night she often opens her eyes and stares at her husband. She snuggles up to him and in a tiny voice whispers sweet little nothings in his ear. Sometimes she wakes him up to hear his voice, to make sure that he is well, that he is happy, that he is satisfied with their conjugal life, and that he loves her as much as he did when they first met and fell in love.

Amir-Ali is a sound sleeper. He wakes up, rolls over, mutters something incomprehensible, caresses his wife's bare shoulder, and falls asleep again. And yet he doesn't like to be awakened and talked to in the middle of the night. He could say, "Leave me alone, darling, let me sleep. Can't it wait till morning?" But he doesn't. Perhaps he is too kind or isn't in the mood for it. He knows that opening his mouth and uttering something like "Don't bother me, dear. I want to sleep," is too dangerous. His words could be interpreted in a thousand and one ways. It wouldn't be worth the trouble.

Malak-Azar loves this man more than the entire world. This is what she says — to everyone, to me, even to strangers — and she enjoys this confession. Her pleasure is accompanied by anxiety and apprehension, by a muted stress hidden behind her triumphant smile and the apparent composure of her voice. She is bent on convincing me that she loves Amir-Ali more than ever. I don't mind. No contest. But she will not give up. She must plunge her invisible dagger deep into my heart and with feminine cruelty reopen the scars of my old wounds.

(She is right. I understand. It is an old story, which is of no concern to others, and there is no place for it in this story.) She avoids looking at my face, because she is frightened of detecting the smallest flicker of doubt in my eyes. She knows that I can see through the multiple layers of her countenance and that I am well acquainted with all the different faces hidden behind her many masks, like the progression of an oil painting from a faint penciled sketch to the final layers of paint, apparently complete, but never quite finished.

Amir-Ali is also the name of one of Malak-Azar's maternal uncles, who died many years ago. No one talks about him or mentions his name. His photographs have been removed from the walls, and a collective effort has been made to dim all memory of him. His name is a reminder of a painful loss and saddens the family. It would be best to call Amir-Ali by some other name. Malak-Azar is enamored with ancient Persia. She would love to call her husband by some noble name going back to Achaemenid or Parthian times, but Amir-Ali is not familiar with the names of antiquity. He likes his own name and considers it a part of his body, his soul, and his destiny — just like the date of his birth. Like the color of his skin or even his height. He is accustomed to his name and knows that without it he will be someone else. He doesn't even like Amir and Ali to be separated and that he be called by one or the other. When writing his name, he joins the two parts with a hyphen (Amir-Ali), and this connecting line attaches his name to him like some life-sustaining umbilical cord.

Malak-Azar thinks her husband's innocent face and timid eyes resemble those of a gazelle (*ahu* in Persian) and calls him Malak-Ahu. Thus she bestows half of her own name to him, the better half of it, in fact, making him an integral part of her own ancestry. She would, if it were possible and if she had the nerve, give him the whole of her name. They would, the two of them, be shaped within the mold of a single name and become inseparable.

Amir-Ali laughs at his wife's words; he has submitted his will to hers. His life and destiny are in her hands and he shows no initiative of his own. Others believe that Amir-Ali's absolute submission to his wife emanates from his fervent love for her. But I, who know him like the back of my hand, know that his birth coincided with the appearance of a comet in the sky, and that he is in fact an elusive and unattainable creature. He does not belong to anyone. No one. He has a secret world of his own that he does not reveal to anyone. I was able to peer into this inner world because we were childhood friends and grew up together. I am aware that he does not have the will to oppose his wife's wishes. He gives in easily because he wants to be left alone. For instance, his job was chosen for him by Malak-Azar. Sitting behind a desk at a commercial company must be deadly and boring for a man like Amir-Ali. But he puts up with it because he has become lazy and indifferent and prefers his decisions to be made for him. He is unable to take a big step and change his life. Why? I don't really know. All I can make out of his letters and diary is that Ami-Ali has different selves: one for public show, an infantile one devoted entirely to his mother, and a secret self whose clandestine existence is hidden in the depth of his inner life. He puts a mask on his face and his apparent happiness is a big lie. He detests his name being changed. Whenever his wife calls him Malak-Ahu, the image of a captured gazelle, shaking with fright in anticipation of being slaughtered and roasted over fire, appears before his eyes and his heart sinks. He could protest, disagree, say no. But his lips stay sealed and his delusive smile deceives all.

Malak-Azar is a sensible and farsighted woman. She has a good sense for the right measure and limit of things. She thinks before she speaks and she is always calm and collected. She appears cold and conservative and cannot laugh wholeheartedly, nor does she know how to make others laugh. She restrains herself and does not dare give in to her heart's desires. Or to what her body needs — such simple needs as stretching a leg that feels numb for lack of movement, or relaxing and leaning back in a chair, or closing her eyes when she is too sleepy or tired. Her body and her mind are restrained by two thousand rules, two thousand considerations, precautions, and doubts. Two thousand scruples and fears. She cannot even tell her husband that she loves him madly. In her cautious mind "madly" and "madness" are taboo words that should be rejected. An inherited pride ties her hands and feet and restricts her movements. She knows that her husband is made of different stuff and he has to be constantly controlled. In her hands Amir-Ahu has become a sensible and docile man who appears to be satisfied with his life. I watch him from a distance. I am waiting. As always. Perhaps there will be a miracle. Perhaps something will happen. But what?

I don't know. Or I don't want to discuss it, not yet. Where were we? Oh yes, we were observing the husband and wife sleeping next to each other. For the first time, Amir-Ali tosses and turns freely in the king-size bed. He is restless. He is thirsty. He feels hot and the soles of his feet burn, as if he has a fever. A pesky mosquito flies persistently around his face and then goes away. Half asleep, Amir-Ali waits for the mosquito's return and its vicious attack. There is no sign of the insect and he sighs with relief. He pushes the sheet away from his face and at that very moment the mosquito's horrible buzz explodes in his ear and he is bitten on the forehead and neck. Amir-Ali is so angry that he wants to hurl something to the floor and smash it, like the enormous and ornate chandelier hanging from the ceiling with all its crystals and prisms and umpteen pendants, or that expensive porcelain bowl sitting on the bedside table. He hates this ancient bowl that reeks of old age and bygone days. There is one similar to it at his grandmother's home, and it reminds him of death and mourning.

Amir-Ali has a simple and sensitive nature. He loves all types of flowers and houseplants, things that are alive and grow. He loves the open air and the sky and wide-open horizons. He loves to sleep on the rooftop or in the garden. He hates overcrowded rooms with their low ceilings. He wishes he could remove all the antiques — all those expensive jars and bowls and Qajar period paintings and unearthed pre-historic objects — from the tables and walls and replace them with flowers and plants. He wishes he could draw aside the curtains, place his bed next to the window, and fall asleep gazing at the moon and the stars.

But Malak-Azar is, well, a princess. She was brought up with silk rugs and velvet curtains, and she is afraid of empty spaces and austere rooms. The intimidating portrait hanging from the bedroom wall — the one facing the bed — is that of Malak-Azar's great-grandfather, who looks down at her all through the night with his glaring and piercing eyes. Malak-Azar feels safe in the midst of the old chinaware, which is a part of her ancestral heritage. The continued presence of these centuries-old objects is comforting to her. She maintains a tender relationship with them and considers them her own property. Her very own.

In the middle of that night, Amir-Ali has forgotten the flowers and plants; his only concern is to fight the damned mosquito. He slaps himself hard on the forehead and the neck. He feels something slimy and blood-soaked under his fingers and a big smile spreads over his face. He stretches. He yawns and presses his face to the cool edge of the pillow. Sleep hovers behind his thoughts and in between his eyelids. One half of his brain has been switched off, but his body is alert and anxious. His hands are awake and fail to find their natural position. His eyes are closed, but he can see the chandelier overhead and can feel the weight of all those shades and bulbs and glass pendants on his chest. He thinks of the sky beyond that thick plaster ceiling, of open spaces, of wide-open horizons, and of the possibility of life in another form. In another place.

Malak-Azar rolls over. The tip of her icy toes touches her husband's leg and makes him shiver. The neighborhood cats shriek and begin to fight, and a she-cat calls out to her mate, caterwauling painfully. Amir-Ali sits up. His heart is pounding. He cannot breathe. He thinks he has eaten something that didn't agree with him and that the strange tenseness of his body is due to overeating and fatigue. That evening they had had a dinner party and Amir-Ali had started yawning from early in the evening. One yawn had followed another until the guests were called in to dinner. His yawns were something unusual, wide and endless, originating deep in his gut and causing him to arch his back and stretch his limbs while his eyes teared profusely. These yawns, like those of a monster, were hardly expected from a polite and civilized person such as he, and not one but ten in quick succession while the guests were talking. They were watching him from the corner of their eyes, and Amir-Ali, embarrassed, was covering his mouth with his hand, trying hard to keep it closed. If he were left alone, he would have laid his head down on the table and fallen asleep. But how could the host justify dozing off right in front of his guests?

Amir-Ali could sense his wife's anxiety and her reproachful gaze from afar and struggled to control himself. Once or twice he forced himself to laugh — an awkward and lifeless laughter — and at one point he made an irrelevant remark in the middle of some serious discussion. In spite of his every effort to look sober and fully alert, his eyelids would unwittingly drop. He stared at people (meaning "I am awake, I am with you") and he nodded in agreement to whatever was being said. He was in a strange state. It seemed as though the objects around him, the plates on the table, the barbecued chicken on the serving platters, the chandelier's glass pendants, were all multiplying, and he felt a curious angst in his heart. He felt like someone who has drunk a bad wine or taken the wrong medication. He closed his eyes and dozed off for a second. His head fell forward on his chest and his body curved to one side. He was about to fall off his chair when he suddenly woke up and stared about him with vacant eyes. "My God!" exclaimed a lady, and someone laughed. Malak-Azar's reproachful look shot toward Amir-Ali like a poisoned arrow, flying in between crystal glasses and over the heads of the assembled company, hitting him in the chest and piercing his heart. This was the first time that her well-mannered and refined husband was behaving irrationally and contrary to the rules of etiquette. To cover up the incident, the guests attacked the barbecued chickens, and someone embarked on narrating lengthy and inane jokes that everyone had heard a hundred times. The storyteller, holding his sides, laughed loudly at his own jokes, while the others forced themselves to smile.

The doorbell rang. A young woman rushed in, agitated and distressed, shouting and complaining loudly as she made her entrance. She threw her head scarf and long overcoat to the side and began blaming her spineless and incompetent husband for anything and everything that was wrong with the world. It turned out that the lady had been stopped right in front of her home, as she was about to get into her car, for failing to observe the proper Islamic dress code — a common occurrence. She rings their own doorbell several times, but no one answers. Her husband, who was busy cleaning a crate of grapes to make wine, refuses to open the door. The lady resorts to her neighbors. The neighbor to the right opens the door a crack and gestures with his eyes that he has company and that his guest is busy smoking opium and he hastily closes the door. The neighbor to the left (God knows what he was up to) pretends he has not heard the doorbell. Luckily an acquaintance arrives at the scene and talks to the revolutionary guards. He hands over his own ID card and the title to his car as bond, and the lady's case is deferred to a later date.

The male guests sided with the wise and farsighted husband. "Anyone else would have done the same thing," they said. This further angered the lady, and she became infuriated. "I would have opened the door," she retorted. "Even if it meant my own arrest. This revolution has forced a lot of people to show their true colors, especially you yellow-bellied chicken-hearted men."

The yellow-bellied chicken-hearted men laughed, winked at one another, and went on eating. The women seized the opportunity to attack their husbands. And this led to a host of accusations and complaints.

The wives argued, "We are the ones who work." (They were right. One of them sewed children's wear; another baked pastries, translated books, and wrote film reviews; and the third gave private English lessons and offered a bridal hair and makeup service.) "We are the ones who run the household and bear the responsibility of raising our children. You honorable gentlemen chickened out from the very first day. You suffered from a thousand psychological disorders and sought solace in the golden pipe."

The men smiled without defending themselves and nodded at one another as a gesture of union and sympathy.

Amir-Ali used this opportunity to leave the room. He went to the bathroom and held his face under a stream of cold water. He unbuttoned his collar and took several deep breaths. He felt better, opened the door, and peeped out. There was no one around. He sneaked out without making a sound. He went out into the courtyard and stood behind a tree. The heavy lethargy of a few minutes ago that had numbed his body like an anesthetic lifted from his brain, giving place to a gentle and sweet hum. A leaf dropped on his head, slid down his face, and fell off the tip of his nose and onto his shoe. A humid breeze touched his face, and a pleasant aroma reached his nostrils from the neighboring garden.

It was a bright night, and the seven stars of the Big Dipper dazzled his eyes. As a child, he used to sleep outdoors, on the rooftop, and he would count the stars until, in a trancelike euphoria of lightness, he imagined that his body was floating in space.

The first gift I gave him was on his fourteenth birthday. It was a small telescope, which became a permanent fixture at his window for many years to come. Despite his tender years, he was already something of a philosopher. He was head and shoulders above other children his age and a thousand miles ahead of them in intelligence and knowledge. He had the look of an adult, capable of thinking things out. His head was always buried in books, history books — the history of ancient Egypt, the history of early civilizations, the history of the origins of the universe, and the emergence of human life.

He was a year my junior. Only one year, and yet he behaved as though we, the older boys of our street and soccer champions of the neighborhood, were incapable of understanding his important pronouncements, and were not endowed with much brain power. He did not put on airs. That was Amir-Ali — reticent and reclusive — and that was the way we had accepted him. He was kind and handsome and minded his own business. He was engrossed in his own world and in this world he traveled to the farthest reaches of the earth. He had pinned a world map to the wall of his room. He knew the names of all the cities, ports, and even small islands in the midst of distant oceans. With a red pencil he had drawn circles around certain cities, ports, and islands.

We would close our eyes, and Amir-Ali was our travel guide. He was the one who would decide which route we should take. From Tehran we would drive to Turkey. We would imagine the dusty roads, the mountains, the roadside teahouses, the minarets. Greece was across the border, and Amir-Ali knew all its tourist spots, all its temples and historical sites. He would say, "Look there, look carefully." And I would run, stumbling behind him without really seeing anything, merely getting tired and sleepy. I preferred staying where I was, in my own country, where people spoke my own language. Amir-Ali would travel alone all over Europe by rail or on foot. He would hitchhike or bum a ride on trucks until he got to the Côte d'Azure in southern France. There he would board a ship for North America. His imaginary adventures continued, taking him to South America and then to Africa. He did not bother with me. He knew I was a wary and cowardly traveling companion. He would not let me go.

From behind the windows, a concoction of sounds could be heard: loud peals of laughter, the clatter of silverware, the sound of a door repeatedly being opened and shut, and a sentence that sounded as if it would go on forever. Amir-Ali could not bear the idea of returning to the drawing room and rejoining that crowd. He was sure the moment he set foot back in the room he would start yawning and feeling drowsy again. But he had to go back. He knew that Malak-Azar was impatiently waiting for him and that she found his behavior unacceptable.

He waited a while longer, then walked around the courtyard, collected his scattered thoughts, went back inside, and forced himself to smile at the guests — with his lips tightly pressed together. He pretended to be interested in the topic being discussed and nodded in agreement or shook his head in disagreement (meaning, "I have heard all your arguments, I have been here with you"). The guests realized that Amir-Ali was not feeling well and refused to engage in conversation with him. They quickly accepted his contradictory remarks and agreed with him on every point.

Let us return to where we first began. Malak-Azar is sleeping, and her sweet restful slumber pains her husband. Amir-Ali tosses and turns. He feels terrible and doesn't know how to interpret this bout of illness. Never before had he experienced such nausea and anxiety. Insomnia also is a novel experience that terrifies him; especially when his wife is sound asleep and unaware of his condition. He wants to open the window. He needs fresh air, and he loves to sleep in a room bathed in strong light. But Malak-Azar wakes up with the slightest noise or the first ray of light, despite the soft wax she puts in her ears and the black scarf she uses as a blindfold. Amir-Ali's petulance grows by the minute. A small wound gnaws at him from within. The heat, the mosquito, and that evening's overeating are all mere pretexts. He knows in his heart that the reason he feels ill and nauseated is the letter he wrote the previous morning — in spite of himself and after being coerced — to an influential person in the government. It was a letter full of false flattery, containing a pack of lies, proposing in veiled terms a bribe, and expressing his obedience. The company's state of affairs is not brilliant, and he knows it is necessary to write such letters.

Even worse was his hypocritical participation in Friday's congregational prayers. Malak-Azar's brothers had insisted that he make an appearance in such a gathering. It was irrelevant that he did not know the Quranic verses by heart. It would be enough for him to get up and down on his knees in sync with the rest of the worshippers. This was what so and so and such and such did.

Malak-Azar's brothers wore black, fingered their prayer beads, and went up and down on their knees. Their movements were synchronized with the others. It was evident that they had good practice. They looked angrily at Amir-Ali and, with their glaring looks, asked what the hell he thought he was doing. Why was he standing motionless as though in a daze? Who was he staring at? Why wasn't he paying attention? Bend down, you idiot. Kneel. Say your prayers. Move your lips. What are you doing? Why are you frozen in that pose of prostration with your head stuck to the prayer stone? Get up. What the hell are you doing? Are you asleep? Face the crowd! Why do you have your back to them? People are looking at you. They have noticed, you fool. Move.

Looking deathly pale and perspiring profusely, Amir-Ali was squirming and fighting his body. His actions were not deliberate. He simply could not force his limbs to move in time with the others. His back, his legs, his head did not respond to his will. It was as though his limbs were tied to invisible strings that were being maneuvered by an invisible puppeteer. Had he gone mad?

At the end of the prayers, his angry brothers-in-law cornered Amir-Ali and subjected him to a barrage of questions. Have you gone mad? Why did you behave that way? Did you want to get yourself arrested and dragged off to jail? Did you want to put your own life and our reputation at risk? Amir-Ali was dazed and exhausted, and his head was spinning. He did not know how to defend himself. A heavy cloud shrouded his mind, and he could not remember what had happened. From the moment he had entered the crowd of worshippers to the time he left, Amir-Ali felt that everything — all the words, sounds, movements, and genuflections — was part of a timeless and surreal dream, far from the reality of that morning. He was in a strange state of mind (Amir-Ali's notes at this point are very confused. It is clear that he cannot explain himself). The only thing he could remember and kept repeating was: "I couldn't help it." And this is the explanation he offered Malak-Azar. But I am sure that the painful significance of this apparently simple statement, which nobody took seriously at the time, marked the beginning of later episodes.

The worst thing to do is to think in the dark. Amir-Ali breathes gently. He lies still. He is sure he will fall asleep in a few seconds. Malak-Azar's hand is resting on his shoulder, but unlike other times it feels cold and obtrusive. The sounds of the previous evening — all those people talking and laughing and their glasses clinking and clanking — are fresh in his memory. God, how he hates these boring parties, always the same people, the same talk of politics, the same dishes, the same stale anecdotes — like an old gramophone needle stuck at the end of a record, making its final absurd sound.

Unlike her husband, Malak-Azar loves parties. She cannot bear the idea of being alone at home. The frightening weight of the minutes and the tangible presence of time torment her. When she thinks of the future, her heart aches. Old age terrifies her more than death. She likes to wear heavy makeup, to hide her real face. She likes others to look at her and admire her eternal beauty and what little is left of her youth. Their flattering lies give her encouragement. The reality of her existence depends on the admiring looks of others.

Once again Amir-Ali hears the persistent drone of the mosquito and seethes with anger. Where is it? His hand is ready to strike. With his eyes closed, he listens for the blood-sucking insect in the dark. He has pulled the sheet up over his face and is about to fall asleep when he feels a sharp burning sensation in the heel of his foot. His feet have been exposed and the enemy has attacked him in that sensitive spot. It is nothing important, just the bite of a miserable mosquito. But trivial incidents are sometimes the beginning of major events. And Amir-Ali, in that darkness, in that chaotic situation and mental confusion, feels that an invisible enemy has assaulted him from behind.

The itch in his foot soon becomes a burning sensation that spreads under his skin. He sits up. He is bathed in sweat. A ray of white light penetrating the heavy velvet drapes illuminates the sheets and Malak-Azar's face. He looks at his wife, and his heart sinks. He does not like her gaping mouth. She does not look like her usual self, the way she always does when she is awake. Another face, a much older one, has replaced her face, and this new impression is unfamiliar to him. Everyone looks different in their sleep, in darkness or in white moonlight. It's simple and natural. But that night, all the world's simplest incidents seemed absurd and unnatural to Amir-Ali. Pangs of anxiety pass through his heart, and he feels inexplicably distraught. In the wake of his anxiety and confusion, something strange happens.

Suddenly his right arm begins to rise, all by itself and seemingly under the command of someone other than himself, until it stands erect above his head like a dead branch. What is the meaning of this? He does not understand. He is confused. He tries to return the arm to its original position. No use. The arm seems to no longer be a part of his body. The hand is clenched into a tight fist, and a throbbing vein has appeared on one side of the wrist. Once again he uses all his strength to force the arm back to his side, but again he fails. Then as he watches helplessly and in utter amazement, he sees this dubious arm, this foreign body, make a strange move. The arm stretches up even higher, moves back, pauses, turns, and then, against Amir-Ali's will and free of all control, it descends like a heap of rubble on his wife's fragile and beloved head.

Malak-Azar is jolted awake; she leaps out of bed with a loud scream. She switches on the bedside lamp and calls her husband. Amir-Ali is even more frightened than she. He is panic-stricken and cannot understand what has happened. Dazed, he looks at his wife. He has lost his power of speech, and his body temperature has suddenly dropped. Malak-Azar has had a terrible fright and feels weak, her eyesight has dimmed. She thinks perhaps a piece of wet plaster from the ceiling fell on her head, or perhaps an earthquake shook the house and a book fell off the bookshelf. Or maybe a wild cat pounced on her head. Or perhaps her own hand somehow struck her face as she slept. She imagines a thousand and one incredible explanations, and her heart continues to pound.

She catches sight of Amir-Ali. She is horrified and becomes even more frightened. Malak-Ahu's face has turned deathly pale, his mouth is gaping, and his eyes are about to burst from their sockets. Her questions turn to anguish for her husband. She holds his hand (the same damned hand) and shakes it. She calls his name. She notices that her innocent gazelle cannot speak and that his hand is as cold as that of a corpse. He cannot answer her questions.

"Oh God, he has had a stroke," she tells herself. And she gently lays his head back on the pillow. She feels his forehead. Takes his pulse. Listens to his heart.

"He has suffered a stroke. He is dead," she thinks, and trembles like a leaf. She is about to call a physician, who is an acquaintance, when Amir-Ali — stuttering — regains his speech. He reaches out and takes the receiver from her hand. He mutters something incomprehensible under his breath and tries to explain, but only manages a confused and incoherent jumble of words. He racks his brain for a convincing lie. His confusion is no less than his wife's. He is too terrified to think. He cannot believe it. He must explain. He must calm her down and prevent her from making a racket. He wants to cover up the incident. At least for the time being.

Hesitantly, he begins a sentence, then gives up. He is frightened of himself. What if his limbs begin to move on their own or his face becomes distorted? He touches his teeth and thinks for a moment that his two upper incisors have grown into fangs, like Count Dracula. He looks at his wife's white neck and covers his face with his hands. He must look at himself. He must make sure. Perhaps he is dreaming. He may have a fever. He may be delirious. He gets up and runs to the mirror on the wall. He fumbles for his glasses. Malak-Azar cannot understand what he is up to. She is confused and screams. It is an old habit of hers. When she is at the end of her rope and feels that all the doors are closed on her, she screams. Amir-Ali looks intently in the mirror. His face has undergone no particular change. His teeth are where they should be, in their normal size and shape. He calms down.

Malak-Azar's scream jolts him. He goes back and takes her trembling hands in his and kisses them. All the while his brain is churning like a machine. He is searching for a plausible explanation. He must make up a story and cover up the whole thing. They must while the hours away and allow the night to pass. In the morning, he might find a way out. In broad daylight, things can be viewed more rationally. For now, he must calm his wife. At last he explains with utmost embarrassment that as he was about to kill a mosquito, a pesky one that had bitten him all over his body — he shows Malak-Azar the bites on his hands, neck, face, and the heel of his foot — he, idiot that he is, at the height of sleepiness and fatigue, mistook her beautiful and lovely head for his own. And now he doesn't know how to apologize to her nor what to tell her. In short, he doesn't know what the hell to do.

Half awake, half asleep, Malak-Azar looks at him and fails to grasp what he is saying. She has had such a fright that she cannot think. She feels dizzy. Amir-Ali is utterly ashamed and confused. For a moment, he thinks he should tell her the truth. But he does not have the courage to confess. The whole thing is utterly incredible. Even for him. Malak-Azar rubs her temples and forehead. She is in pain, and her vision is still dim. She takes two pills from the bottle of tranquilizers she always keeps handy. She presses her head to Amir-Ali's trembling shoulder and waits for the palpitation of her heart to subside. She is a sensible woman. She never acts hastily and does not start a quarrel over nothing. There is no reason why she should not accept her husband's explanation. She looks at him from the corner of her eyes and feels sorry for her terrified gazelle. She notices his sad face and his pleading look, that of a boy who has been bad. Malak-Azar forgets her own pain.

"Oh, God, how helpless he looks. What will he do without me?" she asks herself. And she caresses his neck with the affection of a forgiving mother. "He has taken my head for his own," she tells herself, and to her this mistake has an amorous connotation. This man is so utterly hers that he does not seem to have an existence of his own and thinks that he and she are in reality one and the same. "He has taken my head for his own," she repeats to herself and laughs silently. To her this sentence bears a romantic significance. It may even be said, a mystical meaning. The concept of losing one's self in another being: it is with this sweet and alluring thought that Malak-Azar closes her eyes and goes to sleep, that silent and peaceful sleep reserved only for happy women.

Amir-Ali was happy that the horrifying episode of that night had ended well, and temporarily forgot the incident. With good will and smiles — more forced than genuine — Malak-Azar too had attributed the incident to her husband's natural lassitude and romantic absent-mindedness and had tried not to think of the symptomatic conduct (his yawns and his dozing off at dinner) that had preceded it. These things happened. There were people who did strange things in their sleep. They sleepwalked on top of narrow walls. They even committed crimes.

The one who could not forget the events of that night was Amir-Ali himself. He would recall those suspenseful moments and shudder. Malak-Azar trusted her husband and her mind was at ease. But not completely. She watched him like a hawk. She would not allow him to be alone even for one moment to think, to think vain and harmful thoughts, thoughts that were beyond the limits. Domesticating Amir-Ali had not been easy. It had taken a long time for him to understand that he was the son-in-law of a respectable family and that this was a status he could not take for granted. It had its own rules and regulations, like a foreign language with its own rules of grammar and idioms. He could not just put some words together haphazardly and make up meaningless sentences. With this new language, one needed to have new ideas, new feelings, a new outlook, a new voice, new dreams, and new aspirations. You could not simply enter an unknown territory and take the seat of honor. To enter this world, you were required to observe a special etiquette, follow certain customs, and engage in a thousand types of give and take.

My pessimism was not unjustified. I did not believe that Amir-Ali could manage this. God knows how he had struggled with himself and how tolerant he had been to put up with the vice presidency of the Yarn and Spool Imports Company. Others considered him a lucky man. In the uncertain circumstances of the revolution, many had lost their lives and others their livelihood, but he, thanks to a successful marriage, had acquired an affluent life and a respectable social status. He should thank his lucky stars, appreciate his windfall, and stop complaining. And not being an idiot, he seemed to be doing all three. If he had not met Malak-Azar, God only knows on top of which mountain or in the middle of which desert he would now find himself, counting stars and journeying through galaxies.

A month or two went by peacefully. It appeared that the worst was over and that life had returned to its normal routine. But that invisible being, that obtrusive shadow, was waiting in the wings for the right moment to make its appearance.

Amir-Ali and his mother-in-law were born on the same day of the same month, but twenty years apart. Malak-Azar attributed this coincidence to Nature's wisdom and regarded it as a sign of the enduring union of the two families. Every year she celebrated the happy occasion and invited all her family and friends. Deep in his heart, Amir-Ali was unhappy for having been born on the same day and the same hour of the same month as his mother-in-law. But he pretended to be happy and proud. The mother-in-law was not fond of her son-in-law, either, and deep in her heart mistrusted him. But she too did not reveal her mistrust and faked her love for him. They both knew that they were deceiving each other and realized that deceit was the only course of action.

The mother-in-law's seventy-fifth birthday and the son-in-law's fifty-fifth was a more important occasion than any of the previous years' celebrations and called for something extra. Malak-Azar decided to give it the full treatment and to pull out all the stops. Even though a large and noisy party could attract too much attention in the neighborhood and alert the brothers at the nearby Revolutionary Committee, she went ahead with her plans. This was the first time she was throwing caution to the wind. From her point of view, Malak-Ahu's birthday was an important event, equal to the discovery of America.

Amir-Ali had intended to say, "Please, I beg you. For God's sake, forget about this birthday party." He had wanted to say, "Forget about this boring and repetitive affair." But he had stopped himself. Malak-Azar was extremely sensitive and was easily offended. Keeping her anger to herself, she would not even protest. She would simply force a cold smile, retreat into herself and become a stranger, cold as ice. She would avenge herself, and her vengeance was quiet and steady as Chinese water torture. She would keep silent. She would knot her plucked eyebrows into a frown. She would answer all of Amir-Ali's questions with utmost courtesy and would consent, with utter generosity, to all his words and actions. Each "my dear" with which she started or ended a sentence would sound worse than a hundred reprimands to Amir-Ali, causing him much pain. She wore a different mask for each situation, and it was impossible to discover what went on in her head behind those masks and what her true feelings were. One could not even tell whether she was happy or miserable.

Let us return to the birthday party. Uncle General, or Uncle G for short, was Malak-Azar's oldest paternal uncle. He was a retired military officer who lived alone, had lost most of his friends in the early days of the revolution, and now, to pass his time and forget his sorrows, had nothing better to do than to socialize. He loved parties, weddings, pastimes, and gambling. He attended every memorial service, every celebration of a new birth, and every circumcision.

He was afraid of being left out by the others — the younger happy-go-lucky generation. Early each morning he called up all his acquaintances to remind them, with much ado, of his continued presence in this world. If he heard of a party to which he had not been invited, he would become sick with grief. He would think a thousand suspicious thoughts and would attribute the whole matter to a major conspiracy.

That evening he had shown up really early, when the hosts were not yet expecting any guests. Malak-Azar had just showered and was in her dressing gown. She swore under her breath at her silly and pestering uncle and rushed to get ready. She knotted her husband's necktie for him. Objected to the plain shirt he had chosen. Asked him to change it and told him which pair of trousers to wear with which jacket.

The next guests to arrive were the company's other shareholders and their wives. Uncle G adored beautiful women and would in advance prepare a routine of savory anecdotes and scientific speeches to pour into their delicate ears. The retired general liked to portray himself as a worldly man, knowledgeable of the latest scientific developments. His information came from European magazines and foreign radio broadcasts to which he added his own embellishments and then presented the mix to the assembled friends. That evening he had decided to talk about the origin of the universe.

No one was in the mood for a discussion of planets and stars. The hot topic was the trial of the mayor of Tehran and the fate of the city's construction companies. Uncle G was trying hard to redirect the discussion to the heavens and the stars, but each time he opened his mouth someone would interrupt him and his sentence would be left unfinished. When dinner was served, the conversation turned to other subjects. Those who had recently traveled to Europe talked of the latest news in the world of film. A male guest attacked the American cinema and defended the third world cinema. The ladies protested.

There was a moment of silence and Uncle G seized the opportunity to ask, "Has anyone seen the film on the origin of the universe?" No one had.

"Then let me tell you all about it," he said, and Uncle G was about to begin when the lights went out. There was a power outage. It was the best time to bring in the birthday cake. They all agreed and drank to the health of the hosts. The cook came with the news that the water had also been cut off. Someone told a story about burglars who had broken into their neighbor's house and had decapitated two women and a man. Uncle G, who quivered each time he heard bad news, said, "Please, no talk of such things." And in a chorus of small ahs and ohs the ladies agreed.

"The world outside is an ocean of darkness," Malak-Azar said. "But in the midst of this black sea here we sit — thank God — on an island of brightness, heedless of what goes on around us. We are still ourselves."

A gentleman said, "We think we are ourselves. We — you, I, and all these dear friends — we are out of the loop. Totally out. We count for nothing. Nothing!" And he minced this last word between his teeth and spat it out with venom.

Amir-Ali moved his left leg, which was feeling numb, and sat up straight. Two minutes later he felt that familiar sensation of pins and needles in the sole of his left foot. It felt funny. His foot had swollen and was pressing hard against the sides of his shoe. Worried, he moved his chair slightly back and put some distance between himself and the edge of the dining table.

"Let us imagine," said Uncle G, "that we are at the start of creation. Total darkness reigns everywhere."

Amir-Ali's left foot was now hovering above the floor. It had lifted up and was swaying left and right. It was shaking and refused to obey its terrified master. In its black leather shoe, the tip of the foot was like the barrel of a concealed pistol looking for a victim. Horrified, Amir-Ali looked at his arms. His rogue arm was not moving from its position. He felt relieved, but at the same time he was very much worried about his foot. The heel itched and felt ticklish. Piercing pain shot through the tip of his big toe, and he felt a weakness in the pit of his stomach. Hard as he tried, he could not force the foot down. It was no use. That sly mastermind, that hidden alter ego, had taken control, and it was not clear what it intended to do.

Malak-Azar, seated at the other end of the table, was a safe distance away from her husband's foot. But two other people, his esteemed mother-in-law and Uncle G, were sitting at either side of him and their legs were not too far away. Confused and shaky, gripped by a vague fear and alerted by an instinctive warning, Amir-Ali guessed that something unpleasant was about to happen and decided to get up and make his escape before it was too late. He gripped the arms of his chair with his free and obedient hands and almost got up, but he remained half-stooped. One foot — the left one — was riveted to the floor and did not move. Hard as he tried, he could not move the foot. Malak-Azar was watching him in the dark and Amir-Ali could feel her eyes on him. The lights came back on. The birthday cake was brought in and Beethoven's Ninth Symphony was prepared to be played. Amir-Ali's left foot was as restless as a wild boar and clawed at the carpet.

"The birth of man and that of the cosmos should be celebrated together," said Uncle G, and Malak-Azar placed the first slice of cake in his plate.

At this point, Amir-Ali's left foot decided to do something strange. It recoiled, paused for a moment, and then with full force struck the retired general's ankle. Uncle G dropped the loaded dessert spoon which was on its way to his mouth and groaned in pain. The mother-in-law jumped out of her seat, Malak-Azar half rose from her chair, and the guests began to talk confusedly. Chaos followed. Uncle G was rubbing his leg and groaning. Amir-Ali was in a sweat. What was he going to say? How was he going to explain this dreadful incident? How was he going to exonerate himself? There was only one course of action open to him: To escape.

Uncle G bent down and looked under the table. Someone had kicked him in the ankle. Who was it and why had they kicked him? Under the table, mother-in-law's small feet caught his eye and brought back memories of old love. He rolled up his trousers and massaged his ankle. It had been at the receiving end of a hard kick. At his age, his bones must be brittle and there was the risk of a fracture. They brought him a glass of water, and Malak-Azar saw her husband hurrying out of the drawing room and her heart sank. Uncle G was staring at Malak-Azar's mother with astonished eyes. Clearly he thought the kick had come from her. And the reason for it went back many years to a lovers' quarrel. And now, on the eve of the lady's seventy-fifth birthday, this old and unhealed wound (so Uncle G thought) seemed to have reopened and that unconscious kick hinted at a secret love and masked a painful and delicious significance.

Moaning and groaning all the while, the wounded general was staring at Malak-Azar's mother with languorous and grateful eyes, which seemed to tell her that the kick had been sweeter than any caress. He even whispered, loud enough for the lady to hear, a line from the poet Hafez: "Old as I am, embrace me tightly one night . . ." But he could not remember the rest of the poem. He sighed. He laughed, a laughter mixed with sorrow and regret. Someone placed a hand on his shoulder and this unexpected gesture of kindness moved him to tears. He pressed his face to that manly hand and began to sob loudly.

Uncle G's laughter, followed by his loud sobbing, led the guests to believe that the good general was in a grave state of mind, what with the revolution and the war and some of his comrades falling prey to the firing squads. And that languorous look and his poetic murmurings were clearly an indication that he had become momentarily insane, and it was easy to conclude that the story about having been kicked under the table was nothing more than an emotional cry for attention and affection. A gentleman, who knew something of Uncle G's past and had been privy to some of his secrets, smiled knowingly, and a young lady mumbled under her breath, with much sorrow and regret, mind you, that old people became childlike, and she shook her head sadly.

Uncle G was helped up from his chair and taken to the drawing room limping — for the benefit of the guests, most of them thought — and there he was eased into an armchair. He sighed with satisfaction. Then, turning and looking at Malak-Azar's mother amorously, he blew her a small kiss with his fingertips and closed his tearful eyes. Malak-Azar went running to her husband and informed him that her foolish uncle had totally lost his senses and was acting bizarre. He laughed. He winked at her mother. He blew kisses at her and whispered love poems to her. It now appeared that the story of his being kicked in the ankle was a mere fantasy, invented by her poor uncle to attract attention and sympathy. All through the evening he had wanted to talk, to show off his knowledge, but no one had taken him seriously. The poor wretch! But one point remained a mystery. If he had not been kicked, then how come his ankle was swollen and red? Malak-Azar was not an idiot. She had seen with her own eyes that Uncle G's ankle was inflamed and badly bruised.

Amir-Ali broke out in a sweat and his face flushed, and this did not escape his curious wife. He said, "I don't know. Why, yes. You are right. Poor Uncle G!" And he shook his head and laughed pointlessly, gaping. He scratched the back of his head and hastily pointed to the hairline cracks on the wall. "It is high time we repainted the house," he said.

Malak-Azar was too clever to be outwitted so easily. If she decided to hush up the incident, she had good reason to. She did not want her guests to find out anything about the incident (which she herself did not quite understand). She did not want to pester Uncle G or her husband with too many questions that evening, but she made up her mind to get to the bottom of it all later, in good time.

Trembling and pale, Amir-Ali returned to the drawing room and tried to explain his absence by a few lame excuses. He took a cigarette.

Held it in his hand. Stuck it between his lips. Looked for matches, then gave up the idea and threw the cigarette down on a table. His out-of-control leg was now quiet, but his heart was pounding and a strange confused feeling was swirling in his body. He knew that Malak-Azar would not leave him alone and that she would pursue the matter more persistently than any smart sleuth. Perhaps the best thing to do was to make a clean breast of it and ask her for help. He would confess that his body had gone mad and that an invisible creature, an evil spirit, had taken possession of it. But no, no one would believe him. They would say he had gone crazy and there would be a scandal. The best thing to do was to wait, and for the time being, to cover up the incident.

Uncle G's happy ankle ached with a sweet and passionate pain. His home was at the end of the street. Amir-Ali volunteered to accompany him home, and Malak-Azar looked at him quizzically, her eyes full of suspicion and doubt. She wanted to say no, but she checked herself. She wanted to say, "I will come along, too," but she held her tongue. As yet, she was not sure of anything. The best thing to do was to wait and, as always, be sensible and patient.

Uncle G was clinging to Amir-Ali's arm and limping along, muttering quietly to himself. He was in heaven, feeling tipsy and jolly without having touched a drink. He wanted to tell Amir-Ali of his old love, which had been fanned back to life, but he could not bring himself to do it. He made some vague references to Leyli and Majnoon, the legendary lovers, and to Romeo and Juliet, and he sighed. Once or twice he stopped, rubbed his injured ankle, groaning and laughing at the same time.

The night watchman blew his whistle and Uncle G snapped out of his ecstasy. He shook Amir-Ali's hand and entered his house, happy and content.

The night watchman greeted Amir-Ali. He stood there expecting a tip. Amir-Ali told him he had left his wallet at home and the watchman's broad smile vanished. "I am your obedient servant," he said, but the flattering edge of a few moments ago was gone from his voice.

The lights were out and black mourning banners drooped from the rooftops of a few houses. Outside his home, it was another world. No one knew of his or his mother-in-law's birthday, and no one was celebrating his entry into the world. A man on a nearby rooftop was busy concealing a satellite dish. When he saw Amir-Ali he stepped back and disappeared into the darkness. A patrol car drove by. It slowed down. The revolutionary guards sized him up. They did not say anything and went on their way. A man was pacing the sidewalk in front of his house. He asked Amir-Ali for the exact time. It was two in the morning. The man was clearly worried. He needed to talk to someone.

"Are you also waiting for your children? I have a son and a daughter and every night I pace the street until the wee hours of the morning waiting for them to come home from a party. I can't lock them up in the house, can I? I am afraid they will get arrested and whipped. God is punishing us for our stupidity and ingratitude. We had a better life. Didn't we? And we say nothing. Not a word. We are dead. A crowd of shadows in hell."

How could he answer this man? He, too, was a shadow man, a pale reflection of a forgotten self, dressed up as a healthy, wealthy creature, clean-shaven, wearing a double-breasted jacket matching his white trousers. And that night's elaborate banquet flashed in front of his eyes, with its food-laden tables, shining silverware, crystal glasses, old china, precious antiques, fine carpets and kilims, European-style paintings, and velvet drapes, and he felt the burden of all those objects weighing him down. He was terribly exhausted, but he didn't want to go home. There was also no place for him in those dark, half-paved lanes in that big boisterous city, in the midst of those brick towers, in that world of formality, contradictions, and conflicts. He only puttered around on the sidelines. Nothing depended on him and there was no one to congratulate him for his existence or to offer condolences for his demise.

That night, and those that followed, the husband and wife went to bed in silence, lay with their backs to each other, and neither slept a wink. They both thought of the same incident, and that "incident" was something terribly confusing — like a shadow on water — elusive and unattainable. They did not know where to start or what to say. For the time being, they preferred not to speak about it at all. But both, in their loneliness, reviewed what had happened, moving from one night to the next, from here to there, from what he had said to what she had said, only to reach a dead end. Malak-Azar cast her eyes to the distant past. She started from the day they had first met and moved forward, pausing on small differences, on potential misunderstandings, on forgotten quarrels and reconciliations, making shortcuts, going back, opening the dossier on some incident, analyzing it, speculating, only to reach a wrong conclusion that led nowhere.

Fearing an interrogation and a confession (to what sin?), Amir-Ali used every excuse to stay away from his wife. He knew that what had happened that evening had nothing to do with her. He did not understand it and he did not want to think about it. He was sure that any explanation he offered, to himself or to his wife, would be premature and unfounded. Time eventually unveiled the secrets of unexpected happenings, things that at first appeared mysterious and hard to fathom, and Amir-Ali preferred to wait and allow things to take their course, and the reason for the incident to be eventually revealed to him.

Malak-Azar, in contrast, was angry and restless and could not understand his stubborn withdrawal and his strange behavior. Silence had built an invisible wall between them, and their conversations and smiles had become phony and artificial. They both feared that something terrible was going to happen and neither wanted to face the bitter reality. With concealed embarrassment, they kept their distance. Neither one had the courage to express their confused thoughts and unknown fears. They did not want to believe that something uncommon had entered into their ordinary and uneventful life. They did not talk about it, and this "refusal to talk" was like a wound that moved through their bodies and souls, causing them pain. Each expected the other to step forward and explain, and the other would not, out of excessive pride or caution.

Malak-Azar expected her husband to open up his heart to her like a sensible boy, to talk about his problems and ask her, as always, for guidance and help. But to her astonishment she saw that Amir-Ali, with the persistence of a stubborn child, was doing his utmost to blur the subject and avoid telling her what was going on in his heart. The thought of Amir-Ali keeping something secret from her was killing her. How was it possible? Were they not, the two of them, like one soul in two bodies? Amir-Ali's silence was unforgivable. And unfathomable. She felt humiliated. She felt that by covering up his ailment, Amir-Ali was insulting her. This man was hers inside and out and had no right to hide anything from her. And this was something he had never done until that day. Never.

Insomnia was Amir-Ali's latest unusual affliction. As soon as he closed his eyes, his brain would set to work and a series of confused images would appear behind his closed eyes. He had become conscious of his body and constantly watched his arms and legs. His hands, which until recently had served him like a faithful nanny, combing his hair, carrying food to his mouth, buttoning his shirt, washing his body, and tying his shoelaces, the hand that wrote, caressed, and was ready to serve him obediently, had become, for some unknown reason, a nefarious enemy that obeyed someone else, some unknown and invisible being, and God only knew what lay in store for him. Anything could happen. What if he, without wanting to and unconsciously, took Malak-Azar's delicate throat in his hands and strangled her? What if he picked up the metal vase on the table and smashed it on her head? Or took a kitchen knife, slashed her body, and cut off her head? The agony, the sorrow, and the shame of such acts were bad enough, but worse yet was the explanation: How on earth was he going to explain his actions? Would he say, "My limbs are out of my control, and my brain is receiving orders from someone else?" No one would believe him. His being found guilty was a foregone conclusion and his fate was clear: execution or the lunatic asylum. He would most probably be executed, hung from the construction crane in front of their house.

All night long he would struggle with these horrifying fantasies and flutter under the sheets, rolling from side to side, sleepless, troubled. There was no doubt that these things would not happen. It was impossible. He had a sensitive and delicate soul and a big, kind heart. But after that night's incident, he had lost confidence in his sensitive soul and his kind heart. At night, he tucked his hands under him and woke up abruptly with the slightest movement of his body. One night, two nights, two weeks, two months, how long could he allow this to go on? The most sensible thing to do was to put distance between himself and Malak-Azar, for a short time, mind you, and sleep in a separate room. In the boys' room, or in the spare bedroom. It made no difference. Anywhere.

Malak-Azar listened to her husband's strange proposal and thought she had not heard or understood him properly. She laughed. She touched him affectionately on the cheek and fastened one of his shirt buttons that was undone. It was a clean, freshly ironed shirt, and the soft blue of the fabric went well with his complexion. She chose her husband's shirts, and his shoes. Embarrassed, Amir-Ali's head was down and his eyes were glued to the floor. He just kept repeating his brief explanation — with much stammering, coughing, and half-finished sentences — that this, for reasons which he could not reveal for the time being, was in the best interest of both of them. And he could not say more, because there was nothing more to say.

Both of them? Which two did he mean? Were they going to be two separate entities now, a separate you and I?

Amir-Ali could not explain himself. He repeated what he had already said and uttered those final words — "the best interest of both of them" — in a manner that left no room for argument. Malak-Azar died and came back to life. She felt dizzy, and a thousand conflicting thoughts rushed through her head. Each of them in a separate room? One of them upstairs and the other downstairs? For twenty years they had slept together like Siamese twins, joined so tightly that separating them would not be an easy task. It required surgery and it was going to be painful, for both of them; though less so for Amir-Ali. This would not be possible without one of them losing his or her life. It was just unthinkable. News of it would spread. What would people say? A rumor would circulate that they had had a fight, that their relationship had soured. Other rumors would follow with gross exaggerations. Their life story would become a subject for gossip and scandal would follow. Never. It was just not possible. She would not agree.

Amir-Ali was fighting with himself. He thought his wife was right, and a combination of grief and shame settled on his heart. Malak-Azar argued that this kind of separation — sleeping in separate bedrooms — was the beginning of true separation. And she listed so-and-so and so-and-so — couples who had mutually consented to sleep in separate rooms and had ended up divorced and miserable. The third couple she mentioned was a poor example. The man was very happy with his present situation and the woman had found herself a new husband, someone younger than herself, who did not snore and slept snugly by her side.

Amir-Ali laughed sincerely at his wife's unfounded speculations. He held Malak-Azar in his arms and pressed her to his chest. He nearly succumbed to her wishes and almost told her: "Very well. I accept," when his eyes fell on a pair of scissors on the table and his heart sank.

It was the same thoughts all over again, the same delirium, the same fears. "What if I pick up the scissors and . . ." No, no. He had to get away from her. There was no alternative. He had to sit down alone and collect his thoughts and find the cause of this affliction, this confusion, these sudden attacks of madness, a madness that nestled in his body, in his bones, in the chemistry of his blood.

Without waiting for the argument to continue and, without waiting for anything else to be said, he pushed Malak-Azar aside and picked up his pajamas and slippers. He took refuge in the guest bedroom, which was large and comfortable, well lighted, with thin lace curtains and devoid of objects and antiques and paintings and mirrors and chandeliers.

The first night was difficult for both of them. After a long period of tossing and turning and feeling guilty and lonesome, Amir-Ali finally fell asleep. He liked the room's cool air and the empty space gave him a sense of tranquillity. This was the only room in the house where a plant, a living one, had been placed next to the window. (Malak-Azar was allergic to plants and all the flowers in the vases were artificial.) The bed was large and he could easily stretch out his arms and legs. On the second night, he turned on the bedside lamp and read in bed. He drew the drapes aside, flung open the wooden shutters and slept under a bright moonlight, and contrary to his usual habit, stayed in bed until late morning.

Malak-Azar struggled with herself. She would push away the sheet and turn her pillow over and over again. She would feel hot, then cold. She thought she was hungry and craved something sweet. She would go to the fridge and eat several spoonfuls of honey or strawberry jam. She always ate too much and felt nauseated afterward. She would take the bottle of water from the fridge and drink two or three glassfuls, one after another. Her belly would swell up and she would have a stomachache. Then she would return to the bedroom, take refuge in a corner of the bed, pull the sheet up over her head, and try to sleep. But she could not. She would toss and turn until dawn.

One night, she got up and climbed the stairs barefoot. Her heart was pounding. She held her breath and stopped behind Amir-Ali's door. She put her hand on the doorknob and stood there motionless. She wanted to open the door with one movement of her wrist, go in, slip under the sheet and snuggle up to him, so close that he would feel compelled to confess to his mistake. It was a good idea, and yet she could not bring herself to turn the doorknob. Her pride would not let her. They were not speaking to each other. She could not belittle herself. She expected Amir-Ali to come back, humiliated and sorry, caress her, kiss her hands and feet, and beg her pardon. Perhaps he was waiting for her, in need of love and attention. Men were like that. They would make an apparent fuss, but in truth they were like lost children in need of a mother.

Encouraged by this reasoning, she drew a deep breath and turned the doorknob with all her might. The door was locked. No, it couldn't be. She tried again and again. Her body felt hot all over, as if she had been stabbed a thousand times. By what right had he shut her out? By whose permission and why? She didn't know what to do. To knock, shout, or break the door down? She was beside herself. Every atom of her love had turned into anger. She banged on the door with her fists and feet. He opened the door, sleepy, yawning, and ill-tempered. Malak-Azar was not used to his frowning and angry face. Her anger gave way to shame and regret. She was confused and at a loss for words. She took a step back, ran back downstairs, went into her room, closed the door, and lay on the bed, staring at the ceiling, awake. She did not know how to console herself.

She was hurt and humiliated and did not know what was going on. If they had had a fight, one of those fights over nothing that is so common between husbands and wives, if they had had a serious disagreement, fine, it would be understandable. They could discuss it. One of them could retreat from his or her position. They could reach a settlement. Or go on with their quarrel. All these were possible, if only Amir-Ali would offer a clear and logical reason for his actions. But he wouldn't. He was as slippery as an eel. He played the fool. He talked nonsense. He put on an act. He mumbled. He would kill you with his stupidity, but he wouldn't talk.

Everything passed in darkness, in the painful ambiguity of conjecture and uncertainty, in vague words and dubious behavior. His words echoed in her ears — the confounded creature! "It is in the best interest of both of us!" What do you mean by that? Explain. Why are you silent? We have shared the same bed for twenty years. Now, all of a sudden, it is in our best interest to sleep apart? Why? And then that absurd behavior. If you have gone mad, okay, I understand. We will go to a neurologist. To an ear, nose, and throat specialist. To a gastroenteritis specialist. To . . . oh, I don't know. We will go away. We will go abroad and visit the children. We will do something. There is no ailment for which there is no cure.

Malak-Azar's private monologue went on and on. She was troubled by the distance that Amir-Ali had put between them. She was addicted to this man's presence, addicted to the scent of his skin, to the gentle rhythm of his breathing, to his cautious and deliberate movements in bed, to the rustling of the newspaper he read before sleeping, and to the slurping sound he made as he drank water when he woke up. She pictured him sleeping soundly (which was not far from the truth), and it made her more restless. She hid her head under the pillow and groaned. She felt like smashing something. She wanted to claw at Malak-Ahu's face and torment him. She wanted to make him jealous and miserable, to rob him of his sleep.

She told herself that the best weapon was indifference, to act as if nothing had happened. Good morning, dear! Did you sleep well? Fine. What a lovely day! Warm and sunny! What a lovely smell of freshly toasted bread! She told herself, You could even whistle or hum to express your happiness. You could stretch your limbs contentedly. You could lie back in an easy chair and laugh for no good reason at all. You could dress up, carefully put on your makeup, wave good-bye, and leave the house. You could come back late at night and offer no explanation about where you had been. You could say I have already had my dinner but not reveal where or with whom. You could even pretend that you have had a good night's sleep, better than ever before, and express your appreciation of your husband's decision. And if all this didn't work or proved too difficult and painful, if all these games failed to make Amir-Ali jealous and didn't stir him into action, if he had become deaf and dumb and blind and it was not clear what in the hell was wrong with him, then you could take the porcelain bowl from the bedside table and smash it right on his head.

Amir-Ali came to the breakfast table, still sleepy and absentminded and totally unaware of his wife's deliberations and plans. He looked at her from the corner of his eyes and sighed with relief. He had expected to find her sad and frowning, but here she was, vibrant and smiling, smartly dressed and made up and in good humor. He thanked his lucky stars for not having gotten involved in an ugly scene of accusations and counter-accusations, and his conscience was relieved. He had a hearty breakfast and failed to notice the burning anger that seethed behind his wife's seemingly joyful eyes.

The nights that followed were the same. Malak-Azar would struggle with herself. She would get up and walk about, smoke a cigarette, sit up in bed, and stare at the melancholy shadows around her. At last she could not take it anymore. How long could she go on with this game? She realized that she could no longer smile and put on a brave face. She had to go away for a few days.

She packed her bags and went on a short trip with her mother and Uncle G (wanting to say, Dear Hubby, I can do without you, I'm quite happy on my own), and she had a terrible time, much worse than she had expected. She could not forget Amir-Ali, not even for one moment. She walked, talked, slept, went here and there, did this and that, and still Amir-Ali was on her mind and pangs of pain pierced her heart. Pretending to be happy was much more painful than putting up with misery. She had planned to be away for a week, but she could not bear it and returned home earlier. Amir-Ali was not at home. She told herself he had gone to visit his mother. She dialed her number, the old maid answered the phone, and Malak-Azar started inquiring, quite casually and calmly, about her mother-in-law's health, and then asked the old maid to pass the receiver to her husband. She was told that the lady of the house was not feeling well and that the master was not there.

Never mind! He must be visiting one of his friends. He would turn up sooner or later. He was not dead, after all. Half an hour passed, it was now eight o'clock, the usual time for the master of the house to come home. But he didn't. He did not arrive at nine o'clock, either. A series of blurred images passed before Malak-Azar's eyes, like a confused delirium, and her body began to ache with worry.

Where can he be?

She heard a car stop and she jumped up. "Here he is," she told herself, and her heart began to beat faster. No, it was not Amir-Ali. It was the neighbor's car. She felt cheated, disappointed. She seethed with anger. She swore at her own weakness. She did not want to be a captive to fear and anxiety, a captive to jealousy, a captive to everything and to nobody. She shrugged. She picked up a magazine and began to leaf through it. She felt nausea rising from the pit of her stomach. She was lying to herself, she was fed up with this game.

She called me. She asked how I was. She beat around the bush. She cast several barbed remarks my way — some of her old and bitter ones — and she chuckled. Then she finally came to the point and asked if Amir-Ali was at my place.

She knew he was not. She was just sharing her anxiety with me. Her bouts of rage and sorrow, and her loud outbursts were mine. She did not need to put on a mask for me and pretend. She was herself. She hung up.

Where in the hell was he? Where? These questions, worries, and inner struggles were new in Malak-Azar's life. She had believed that her life was in perfect order and that the regimen that governed it was firmly anchored. Such unpleasant incidents always happened somewhere else, to someone else. Death always visited the house next door. Now, suddenly and unexpectedly, something had shifted, was out of place. The ground under her feet was rocking, and a rogue nut had jumped the track, moving out of the rational sequence of causes. She did not know what had gone wrong, or what had been wrong in the first place.

Then came the sound of someone unlocking the front door. Malak-Azar was all ears. It was the cook. Once again she looked at the clock on the wall. Time stood still. The hands on the dial were frozen. She put her hand on the telephone receiver and waited. "Ring, go on, ring, please ring," she muttered. And the phone rang. She could not believe it. She did not have the courage to lift the receiver. She calmed herself. She wanted to sound cold and indifferent. For a second she thought she should not answer the phone, punish Malak-Ahu and let him know that she too had social engagements of her own and did not stay at home. On the sixth ring she picked up the receiver. Her heart was pounding.

It was Uncle G. "Hello, my beautiful darling doll. Hello . . ."

Malak-Azar screamed and hung up. She felt like grabbing Uncle G by the throat and squeezing hard. The phone rang again. Again it was Uncle G. He wanted to know what had happened.

"Leave me alone," she yelled, and slammed the receiver back on the phone so hard that it fell off the table and broke in two. God only knows what would have happened next if right at that moment she had not heard Amir-Ali's cough from the end of the hallway. It took

Malak-Azar a few seconds to regain her composure. She felt heat returning to her body but her arms and legs were weak.

"I was certain he would come back," she told herself. "Where can he find a better and cozier place?" She wanted to shout and reprimand him, but she checked herself. For a moment she thought she should kiss his face and show her happiness at his return. She even took a step forward, but she froze before reaching him. She looked down and masked her emotions. No, why should she belittle herself? She would be patient. She would wait as long as it took for Amir-Ali to capitulate. Eventually he would get tired and he would go down on his hands and knees in front of her.

Weeks passed in the same manner until Malak-Azar could not go on with this buffoonery. She could no longer deceive herself and bury her head in the sand. Reality, however bitter, was better than this sham. She wanted to find out everything right then and there. She wanted to hear the truth from her husband's own lips. What was going on in this man's head? What was the truth of it all? She caught Amir-Ali in his room before he could leave the house. She closed the door and forced him to sit down. She put her hands on his shoulders to hold him there and sat down in front of him.

Amir-Ali looked at his watch. He said he had an appointment. An important one. It had to do with the company business. Let us leave it for this evening, he said, when we can talk things over at leisure. And he got up to leave.

But Malak-Azar was determined. She grabbed his jacket with both hands and made him sit down again.

"On the evening of the birthday party," she said, "when the lights went out, what really happened? Who kicked Uncle G's ankle?" Had it really been her mother, the venerable lady? If so, why had he run out of the room, his face ashen? Why?

Like a snared gazelle, Amir-Ali made a desperate struggle to free himself and remained silent.

"Why?"

Silence.

Malak-Azar noticed him looking around, waiting for a chance to evade the subject and to escape. She moved her chair closer to his, pressed her knees against his shaky legs, put her hand under his chin, and forced his timid face up toward hers. She seemed to be encouraging a naughty boy to open up. Her voice was gentle and without any trace of threat or reproach.

"What is it, my love?" she asked. "Speak to me. I am your wife. Do you remember?"

Apparently he did not remember, and suddenly in a firm and confident voice which was not expected of him, blurted out that everyone has a secret and is entitled to keeping a corner of his life private.

He had put his foot in his mouth. What did he mean by "private"? Which part and which corner of his life? Had Malak-Ahu another self independent of his wife's? It was a tactless statement that had come out involuntarily. He himself didn't understand how his tongue had turned and how these words had taken shape.

Malak-Azar, who had not expected this reply, said: "I am a stranger in your eyes, am I? Don't you trust me? Don't you?"

Amir-Ali could not trust his tongue and his voice. He realized that he had no control over what he said, and he was afraid that words would tumble out of his mouth contrary to his intentions. He picked up the water bottle from the bedside table and, unlike his old well-mannered self, began to drink right from the bottle. Malak-Azar objected to his rude behavior. The water was cool, and he raised the bottle to his mouth again and — gulp, gulp, gulp — drank to the last drop. He felt calmer. Malak-Azar was irate, but she held her tongue. This was not the right time for reproach. This man was like a child, obstinate and stubborn. He had to be tricked. She began praising him. Men love being praised. Even a hard nut like Amir-Ali could be cracked with a slick tongue. She softened her voice (perhaps too soft) and laughed. A bitter sorrow lined her laughter, and falsehood fluttered in her overly gentle voice.

She held Amir-Ali's hand (the same unkind hand that had come down on her head) and caressed it. She lowered her head and kissed his fingertips. She sensed little feeling in this muted hand and felt offended. She could tolerate everything as long as her pride was intact, and yet she swallowed her anger.

"Amir-Ali, we were once so close, you and I," she said. "We didn't hide anything from each other. We were like one soul in two bodies. Have you forgotten? There is nothing in the world that I haven't done for you." (She wanted to say, you owe everything you own in life to me, but she checked herself.) "You must speak. You must tell the truth. Why did you move to a separate bedroom? Why are you shying away from me? Why?"

She had raised her voice involuntarily and her last "why" rang with menace. Amir-Ali took off his jacket. He had run out of cigarettes. He crumpled the empty packet and threw it down on the table. He picked up the matchbox and began to twirl it between his fingers. He struck a match. Blew it out and put the burned matchstick back in the box. He struck another one and held it lit until it burned his fingertips. Malak-Azar hated people who put burned matchsticks back in the box. This was exactly what Uncle G did and it made her angry. She took the matchbox from him and removed the burned matchsticks. She realized he was not feeling well. A throbbing blue vein had appeared on the side of his forehead. Why was he so distraught? She did not know this man. This was not her beloved gazelle. He had become a stranger bent on deceiving her. It was obvious. And why did she love him so desperately?

The first thought that would occur to her was that he belonged to her, that he was in love with her, that he could not survive without her. Perhaps choosing Amir-Ali had been the only hasty decision of her life. Had she really fallen in love with him or had it been out of spite for me? Whatever it was, she would not submit to defeat and admit that she had made a mistake. Never! She would continue on the course she had chosen to the end. She would do anything and everything to prove that she had been right. She had made up her mind to make out of Amir-Ali a creature after her own heart, and she had succeeded. A success that had lasted all of two decades. It was no joke. She had managed to stay high and dry in spite of all the adversities, the revolution, the war. Her house had been confiscated and the doors of the Yarn and Spool Company had been padlocked twice. For four years she had gone from one citizens' committee to the next and from one district attorney's office to a higher one, until she had finally succeeded in getting her house back, in reviving her semi-bankrupt company, and in reinstating Amir-Ali as its vice president. And now that she wanted to sit back, stretch her legs, and peacefully celebrate her success and her husband's birthday, Amir-Ali was disrupting the orderly pattern of their life. He would quibble and rebel for no reason. Maybe he was scared of getting old? Maybe he feared death? She had heard that men suddenly act up when they approach sixty. And instead of continuing with their growth and transcendence, they suddenly panic and become avaricious. If this was the case, then Amir-Ali's deteriorating health was temporary and it would pass. She only had to bite her fingernails and be patient. For Malak-Azar, the greatest humiliation was accepting sorrow and sickness. She would never accept defeat. She would go on fighting.

It had taken her a long time to corner Amir-Ali and she was not going to let him go. She wanted an answer, a clear and candid one.

"What is the meaning of all this," she asked with persistence. "Answer me. Have you gone mad? Are you sick?"

The word *sick* came to Amir-Ali's rescue. "Yes, you're right. You should know that, yes, I am sick. Are you satisfied? I am sick, mentally sick. And very dangerous. I can kill. I am capable of anything. I have no control over my actions. Do you hear me? Do you understand?"

If left to himself, he would go on and on for hours. An unprecedented anger had been released from the depths of his soul, a sweeping rage directed toward an invisible person who represented all the rest and had no recognizable face, an anger directed at everything at hand, at the newspaper on the table, at the distorted lines of objects, at all the vexing noise that came from the outside, at all the blaring lies, at himself and Malak-Azar, and at the boring ugliness that swirled in the air like gray dust.

Malak-Azar was watching him, bewildered and terrified. She had never seen him so worked up and confused. She was not used to his panting and the beads of perspiration covering his upper lip. She thought he was play-acting, trying to fool her, wanting to silence her. What a lousy actor he was! A mental patient, my foot! Dangerous! No, the truth lay somewhere else. It was what he was hiding from her and did not dare express. For a few moments they remained silent. Then they both started to talk at once, cutting each other short. Neither one understood what was said or heard. Like a pair of drowsy and confused souls, they stood there, staring at each other. Something had been broken. They could not believe it. Accepting it was painful. Amir-Ali turned his head away, and Malak-Azar — involuntarily and for the first time in their married life — shouted at her husband, and her voice reverberated throughout the house. The cook heard the shout and dropped his spatula. And the cat sitting on the windowsill was startled and ran away.

The Yarn and Spool Imports Company was in bad shape. The shareholders were up in arms against one another, and the municipality refused to pay the money it owed the company. In spite of his reluctance, Amir-Ali was compelled to go to the office and call for a board meeting. Malak-Azar's brother, who was the chairman, blamed all of the company's woes on Amir-Ali's ineptitude and accused the company's veteran accountant of embezzlement. The old accountant defended himself and became so emotional that he nearly had a heart attack. The other shareholders intervened and helped the old man, who was having difficulty breathing and had ripped his shirt open, out of the room. Amir-Ali told the board members that he would ask for a meeting with the mayor or his deputy and would solve the company's problems single-handedly.

Three days later, a high-ranking official of the municipality received Amir-Ali in his office. Two other people were also present. Whenever Amir-Ali was to meet with government officials, he would let his beard grow into a stubble and he would wear an old suit. He had also memorized a few lines from the Quran and would come up with an Arabic quotation whenever necessary.

The high-ranking official began to speak, and Amir-Ali for his part praised the gentleman's intelligence, humaneness, and piety. The other two people also spoke for about an hour. Amir-Ali nodded in agreement from time to time. Everything was going well when suddenly Amir-Ali's stomach began to growl. It seemed as though two thousand frogs were croaking in his intestines, and their sound was being broadcast from a set of invisible speakers. His guts were about to explode. The high-ranking official was flabbergasted and involuntarily moved away from Amir-Ali, and the other two stared at him with alarm. The rumblings subsided and there was a moment of silence. A semblance of order returned to the meeting. But the high-ranking official had hardly opened his mouth when Amir-Ali's stomach growling gave way to long hiccups — hiccups so unnatural and powerful that everyone in the room, himself included, was startled. Amir-Ali was struggling with himself and panting hard. He felt a great nausea churning in his stomach and thought he might throw up on the dossiers on the table at any moment. Something like a wild beast, like a horrifying monster, was in his belly and it was struggling to break loose and leap out. The faces that were turned to him were angry and frowning. Their voices echoed in his ears and their irate looks pierced his body. He put his signature to a letter. He was still holding the pen when suddenly, unexpectedly, his body emitted a dreadful noise that jolted everyone. The high-ranking official got up in anger and his minions picked up their dossiers and started for the door. They were still on the doorstep when Amir-Ali threw up on the papers in front of him.

He returned home utterly broken and exhausted. He went straight to his room, locked the door, and lay down on his bed. His bowels were no longer growling and churning. It was as if nothing had happened, as if they had not been on the verge of explosion a mere sixty minutes ago. But his body was no longer that old lovable organism that he so cherished. Every part of it, every limb, was at war with him and had risen against him. His brain was being unfaithful to him, it had joined forces with an evil power, and God only knew what kind of a plot it was hatching against him.

Malak-Azar was not at home, and Amir-Ali breathed a sigh of relief. He did not have to explain anything to anyone, nor did he have to pretend that he was well and happy. No one understood his ailment. Once or twice he had thought of seeing a psychiatrist, but he had soon given up the idea. He did not believe in psychology or psychiatry. He had no time or patience for such things. His cure did not lie in tranquilizers and sleeping pills. He knew that the root of his ailment — if it qualified as such — lay somewhere in his past. It was an old virus that had nestled in his heart and soul. His body had not run amok without a cause. And it was not jostling him for no reason. He had to find out. But how far back did he have to go?

Amir-Ali's childhood memories are fragmented and vague. In his mind he has preserved certain days, incidents, and a few handpicked segments of the past (those that are agreeable to him), and he has consigned to oblivion certain other and older fragments. His memory is full of black holes, full of lapses in time and silences. He needs help remembering his past. I have known him since our childhood days. We were friends and classmates. I can still picture him. He was tall and handsome, reclusive and reticent. He was not one for playing soccer or running races or ganging up with the neighborhood boys. His greatest pastime was flying colorful kites and going to the movies. It would take him a long time to detach himself from the plot and events of a film he had seen. He loved seafaring movies, the story of some lonely captain and his sailors, casting anchor at every port and calling no place home. He traveled with these films and their adventures, and one could tell from his absent gaze that he was in another world.

Then there was his kite flying. He had involved me in this game, and yet I had no passion for running around. We both lived in Shemiran, in the northern suburbs of Tehran. At the time, Elahieh and Amanieh hills were still bare and undeveloped. Amir-Ali's kite had three colored tails trailing behind it, and it would fly high and almost reach the clouds. It would fly so high that it would become a blurred dot in the sky. My kite, on the contrary, would hardly leave the ground, and after only a few minutes would get tangled up in the only lamppost or tree on the hilltop. I can never forget Amir-Ali's loud and excited laughter or his wondrous gaze. Whenever he was about to send his kite aloft, he would grow silent, turn his attention inward, hold his breath, and gaze at the sky without batting an eyelash. His actions seemed funny to me, but I would keep silent. Now that I think back, I realize something that I could not grasp as a child. I picture his face, happy and mesmerized. I now understand that a sensation much deeper than childish pleasure rippled in his eyes, and that he was absorbed in something far beyond his immediate surroundings. If I called out to him, he would not answer. If I tapped on his foot, he would not respond. His eyes were fixed on his kite, and no one and nothing else existed for him. He was flying with his kite, sailing the wide expanse of the sky among the cosmic islands.

One day his kite did not come back. As it flew high in the sky, it swung this way and that. It allowed itself to drop and, as it was falling, it suddenly soared again. It played cat and mouse with Amir-Ali. It had its own playfulness. Then slowly it began to rise higher and higher until it reached a cloud and hid behind it. It played peek-a-boo for a moment and then, with the persistence of an intoxicated bird, shot up so fast that the end of the string tore away from Amir-Ali's fingers. We had lost the kite. We sat down, waiting for it to return. Nothing happened. It had disappeared. It was on a joy ride in another place, in another time. Somewhere far beyond our view and our reach. I was certain that Amir-Ali would wait for his kite on the hilltop until nightfall. But no, he did not wait.

"One day it will come back by itself," he said. And he ran all the way down the hill. He had opened his arms wide and his sleeves flapped in the wind as he ran. He gripped a tree branch and swung from it.

"God only knows where my kite is," he said, laughing. Then he relaxed his grip and fell to the ground on his back. He closed his eyes and slept. It was as if he had fainted. He did not move. He was playing dead, a death that was temporary and pleasurable.

I carefully go over Amir-Ali's diaries. His references to his mother are like a half-solved crossword puzzle. I have to find the relevant letters and fill in the blanks. And still I get nowhere. There is always a word that remains incomplete. And I can't find the missing letter. The image of his mother remains hidden, like a sacred icon, behind a veil of vague words and cautious references. Whenever he writes about her, his handwriting changes and his prose is different. It is as though he is afraid or cannot overcome his embarrassment. He withdraws his pen and hesitates. He writes a sentence, then crosses it out. It is clear that he is fighting with himself. He wants to say something, divulge a secret, but he cannot. I remember his mother. I mean his mother when she was young. She was thin and fragile, and beautiful in a subtle way. A beauty that went unnoticed at first glance. She was neither beautiful nor ugly. She was not conspicuous. It was only after a second or third glance that her clear, bright eyes and her sweet smile revealed themselves. From then on, whenever you looked at her, she was beautiful. I know that he had a deep affection for his mother, a quiet, unobtrusive, and yet bothersome love. In the midst of whatever we were doing and wherever we were, he would suddenly worry about her. He would say he had to go. He must. His excuses were all lame. He would say he had an appointment with the dentist, or that his father was waiting for him. All lies. The other boys would complain, but I was the only one who knew the real reason for his leaving us. He was afraid that his mother might feel lonely and grieve. He did not trust her serene, happy appearance. He knew that she put up a facade and did everything to keep him from finding out how much she suffered. Outwardly she seemed to have everything and to be happy with her life. But behind her facade of pride and confidence, there was a childlike woman with the sorrowful simplicity of an innocent young girl who wandered about in the large luxurious rooms of the house, who wept under the bedsheets where no one could see her, who waited day and night for her husband to return, and who did not dare approach him when he did.

As a young boy of four or five, Amir-Ali slept in his mother's bedroom. He knew and understood even then that, in spite of her gentle smile and kind hands, his mother was utterly miserable and wept quietly under the sheets, with her face buried in the pillow so that no one would see. The only thing Amir-Ali could do with his small hands was to smash things. These crying fits were a nocturnal exercise. In the morning, his mother turned a new leaf and put on a different face. She applied rouge to her lips and cheeks, but the effect was temporary. Ten minutes later the artificial redness had been wiped from her pale cheeks and dark lips, only to be replaced by a ubiquitous gray, the color of swallowed words and furtive grief. The only enduring redness in that tired and sapless face was that of her eyes and eyelids.

Why did she pretend to be happy? Was she ashamed? Was she afraid? Perhaps this was the way grown-ups behaved. They had two faces, one for the day and one for the night. Amir-Ali did not like two-faced people, and his small brain could not grasp the meaning of duality and contradiction. He would become confused and frightened, and everything seemed unreal to him, like one shadow on top of another. He would stand in front of the mirror and look at himself. He saw that he was no different from the night before and the day preceding it, and he would feel reassured. He had promised himself to have only one face when he grew up, his real face, just as he was.

His father had four, six, ten faces. Cardboard faces. And none of them was for his mother. When it came to her, he was faceless. Just an empty circle with two pointed ears, like a flat caricature drawn by a child. When it came to the maid, he had two pairs of eyes with a big watery mouth and moving lips. At times this face would grow long and narrow, with a pronounced frown and sparks flying from its eyes. This was his ugliest face — mean, jealous, and dangerous. It was with this face that he had drawn a gun on his elder son. Amir-Ali's brother was crawling on all fours, trying to get up on his feet, wanting to get away, when he would be kicked from behind and fall down again. The gun barrel circled his face and neck. His mouth was gaping with fright and he could barely utter a sound. His father watched him in this helpless and frightened state and gnashed his teeth in pleasure. The bone of contention was the neighbor's comely wife. His mother was watching the fight from behind the window, and her sad and happy faces had merged, like a pair of ink drawings on wet paper. Amir-Ali was standing next to her, trembling. He couldn't understand why his mother did nothing. Why wasn't she screaming? Why had she placed her hand in front of her mouth and closed her eyes? Amir-Ali wanted to scream for help. He wanted to save his brother by calling out to the neighbors or the servants. He wanted to pick up a vase and, from behind, smash it over his father's head. But his mother would not let him. She was pressing his head to her skirt to stop him from watching the scene. He had already seen too much. Boys of his age were not allowed to witness such scenes, and she had placed her finger on his lips to indicate that he should keep quiet.

It was several months later that his father ordered his cot to be taken out of his mother's bedroom and placed in his older brother's room. The first night was very hard on him, and he cried for a long time. The following nights — for a whole week — he couldn't sleep, but then gradually, out of necessity, he got used to the new situation. He accepted the fact that he had grown up, and he realized that growing up meant putting up with the loneliness that accompanied it. His brother smoked before sleeping — five or six cigarettes, one after another — and he would fall asleep with his glasses still on the tip of his nose, his reading lamp left on, wearing his day clothes, and with his teeth unbrushed. One of those nights, Amir-Ali was still awake while his brother talked in his sleep. The moon sat in the middle of the sky like a wakeful and transparent eye, privy to all the world's secrets. The lights in the house had been switched off. Amir-Ali pushed the sheet aside. Waited a moment. Briefly looked at his brother. Stepped down from his bed and slowly tiptoed toward the door. He was barefoot and he stepped on something sharp. "Ouch," he said under his breath, but swallowed the rest of his groan. As he fumbled, he upset the glass of water sitting at the foot of his bed. The glass fell on its side and rolled toward his brother's bed. It came to a stop when it hit a chair. Nobody woke up. He continued to tiptoe toward the door, which made a cracking sound and then opened with a deafening creak.

It was an exceptionally bright night. A tall man with his back to him stood in the middle of the courtyard, by the pool, near the flower bed. He was not moving. Amir-Ali's heart skipped a beat and his mouth felt dry. He wanted to run away, but his feet, heavy and cold, were glued to the ground. He wanted to scream, but he had lost his voice. The man stood at some distance from him, looking like a dark silhouette, a surreal being. The figure brought his hand out from under his long coat and looked at his watch in the moonlight. A white-robed phantom emerged from behind the trees. It came forward, extracted a hand from under the robe, pointed to someone, and stopped. The silhouette turned and looked cautiously at the windows. Amir-Ali recognized his father's profile. What was he doing there at that hour of night? The woman in white disappeared behind the trees, and his father followed her, slowly and quietly. A moment later, a light went on at the end of the courtyard. It was the young maid's room, the one who stared at his brother and whispered in his father's ear.

His young heart was filled with rage and disgust. He decided not to say anything to his mother, and this was the first painful decision of his life. He kept silent and learned to weep under the sheets in the middle of the night, just like his mother, just like the grown-ups with their cardboard masks. He lowered his head, pressed his lips together, and a big silence settled in his small body. As he grew up, his way of life, even his physical appearance, his smile, his voice, the penetrating look of his eyes, all changed. He stopped dreaming, and the void inside of him turned into a type of lethargy and silent passivity. People attributed his indifference, which bordered on resignation, to his practical wisdom and whispered to each other that he was a sharp, calculating operator.

On those days I saw Malak-Azar almost every day. She was hurt and desperate. She clung to me (just like in the romantic days of our youth) and, putting her pride aside, poured out her feelings and confessed her thoughts. She had put two and two together and concluded that Amir-Ali had fallen out of love with her. A husband who runs away from his wife and sleeps in a separate bedroom (making sure the door is locked from the inside), and strikes his wife on the head (she was now sure it was Amir-Ali's doing), and who deliberately and premeditatedly vomits on the municipality's dossiers with the intention of bringing about the ruin of his wife's company, does not love her. Not only that, he is sure to be in love with some other woman.

But who? For a moment, the vague image of a young, beautiful woman flashed before her eyes. This was the first time she had considered such a possibility, and that invisible "other woman" suddenly assumed a presence more tangible than all the existing realities, more real than the glass of water on the table, than the breeze caressing her cheeks, than the shoes on her feet, more real than she herself. In all like-lihood, the others already knew, but had kept it from her. Uncle G was a nosy blabbermouth and often put his foot in his mouth. Malak-Azar reasoned that her nosy uncle must have wanted to tell a story about Amir-Ali. He had intended, out of malice, to hint at Amir-Ali's relationship with a certain lady, and Amir-Ali had shut him up by kicking him under the table. Yes, that must have been it. Plain and simple. There had been no other reason.

A new window opened on Malak-Azar's fantasies, and a black curtain was lifted from before her eyes. She accepted without a moment's hesitation what her feminine logic dictated. So that was it. Another woman! Her first feeling was one of fear. The fear of finding herself abandoned and unprotected in a dark maze, all alone. She felt that she had lost her grip, and that the ground was shaking under her feet. It was a feeling similar to death, like watching her own funeral. She felt a chill come over her, and her stomach churned. She grabbed at her long hair and yanked. Her scalp hurt and she felt pain. The feeling was real, that of a living organism, that of a discontent and inflamed being. The chill of death gave way to a hot flush and an unbridled anger ran under her skin. The valves of her heart were opening and closing with fever-ish frenzy and, with each passing second, love was being replaced in her heart by hate. At that moment, she was capable of setting the house on fire, killing herself and Amir-Ali. She had not believed one word of what he had said about his mental illness. She told herself that all his theatrics were part of a grand scheme, orchestrated for a reason, for a precise and calculated reason. Amir-Ali was a cheat and a liar and un-faithful, like all other men, like so-and-so and so-and-so, and she, Malak-Azar the gullible, had been fooled by his innocent appearance. What a mistake! Not even once had she tried to find out what he was up to, and only now she understood why he came home late on certain evenings and why he quickly hung up the phone whenever she appeared.

Where did he go and with whom did he associate? All his words and deeds now seemed suspicious to her. Even his face looked ugly and monstrous. There was no doubt that another woman, a young one, was involved. The word *young* echoed in her brain like an ear-splitting blast, and a moment later a blind jealousy, more biting than the sharp pain of a thousand tender wounds, nestled in her body and soul. The prospect of having to compete with a younger woman was daunting. A blurred image of the other woman, her unbeatable rival, appeared before her eyes and clawed at her heart. She wanted to know everything: when they had first met and where. Her name, her age, her address, her phone number, and, most important, her looks. Was she tall, taller than she? Was she slim or plump, blond or brunette? She was determined to find out. Her ignorance of these facts was driving her crazy. A hundred times a day, she would ask herself "Who?" and she felt jealous of the imaginary women.

From the moment she had met Amir-Ali, her instincts had warned her that this would happen sooner or later, and at the back of her mind she had always worried about it. She had tamed Amir-Ali as much as she could by giving him a life of ease — without any financial worries — by sweet talk and languorous caresses, and by a thousand and one amorous ruses. But she knew that part of this man's being remained untamed and unconquerable, and this dark and unknown corner frightened her. Her imagination would run ahead of the logic of events. She wanted to catch Amir-Ali red-handed, in the act, as he was lying next to his mistress. She wanted to open the door to the room (which room?), and gaze into his frightened eyes. And then? Nothing. In Malak-Azar's confused mind, time would end and the world would come to a stop. She could not visualize what would happen next. She would go back and start all over again. She would change the scenario. She would alter the scene, the time and the place of his betrayal. She would get to the point when she was about to open the door. Their own bedroom? A room in a hotel? Never mind. Her imaginary camera would show a door, a closed door. She would turn the knob. The door would slowly turn on its hinges. It would open. The camera would track forward. It would move past the window. It would move up the side of the bed and focus on the faces of Amir-Ali and his mistress, caught in close-up. Here her imagination would fail. The film would jam in the camera and the viewfinder would only show a frozen frame. And then there would be darkness. Total silence. A black screen. The end.

There was no end to these scenarios. Unrelated fantasies and destructive nightmares had driven the plain reality of everyday life out of

Malak-Azar's mind. She felt disoriented. In her mind, the east and the west had changed places. She was unable to find herself, she could not see herself, she could not come to grips with being in a specific time and place. And yet life went on and her everyday routine — getting up, saying a cheerful "good morning," getting dressed, working out, chatting with this and that person on the phone, seeing to the household expenses, going to parties — continued. Objects changed their place. An old porcelain bowl, the tall crystal lampshade, and the cut-glass vase were moved from one room to another. Drapes were drawn aside. A crumpled newspaper was tossed into the wastebasket. Windows were opened and closed, and all this was done by a stranger, by an absent Malak-Azar, who had become a pale shadow of her old self, of the successful and triumphant woman who would go from one bright room to the next, and who firmly believed in her enduring happiness. Now, without warning, unprepared and surprised, she had stumbled, as though an invisible hand had suddenly pushed her from behind. She had slipped, lost her balance, and fallen into life's unexplored ruins, down the abyss of blind urges and primitive dark instincts.

Days passed at a slow and monotonous pace, devoid of all smell and color. Life was a photocopy of events past, a mechanical reproduction of things that had lost their original form. Amir-Ali felt it was impossible to carry on and decided to write a long letter to his wife to explain everything — from that first night to their latest disagreement. He sat down to write. His first attempt turned out too short and he tore the letter up. The second and third attempts were too long. The fourth and fifth drafts were incoherent and confused. He ran out of paper. He called the cook and asked for some paper. When the cook entered the room, he sniffed and said, "Master, there's a funny smell in this room," and asked permission to open the window. Amir-Ali had also noticed an unpleasant odor coming from under the bed and the chairs. He thought that perhaps there was a dead mouse somewhere and looked for it everywhere, but found nothing. The stench was coming from his own body, the smell of putrid flesh. He took a bath and washed himself thoroughly from head to toe. He soaped himself. He rubbed his body with a coarse loofah. He stood under a hot shower until his skin began to burn. He smelled himself and felt nauseated by the smell. Some part of his body was rotting. He stood before the mirror and carefully looked, one by one, at his teeth. He thought that perhaps an abscess had opened in some hidden part of his body, perhaps between his toes or in his armpit. He examined himself from head to toe. He was intact. No scratches. No wounds. No abscess. And yet there was a stench emanating from his pores. What would happen if Malak-Azar saw him in this condition? What if this foul smell, the smell of rotting flesh, reached his sons? All doors were closed to him; the world was up in arms against him and he did not have it in him to fight destiny.

The only course of action was to go away. He packed his suitcase, picked up his checkbook and all the cash he had in the house. He wrote a two-sentence letter to his wife explaining that he was ill, that he was going away for a few days, and that one day he would explain everything to her. For now, the only thing he could do was to leave and put a distance between himself and his loved ones.

Amir-Ali set off with no particular destination in mind. His car was large and comfortable, and he was enjoying driving out on the open road. He had not been on the road for a long time. He felt free, and freedom was a novel experience to him. The foul odor of his body had subsided and he could breathe more easily. He pressed on the gas pedal and drove on, not knowing where he would end up. He drove past Karaj. He drove past Hamadan. Then he stopped at a small roadside restaurant and had lunch. He felt drowsy. He lay down in the shade of some trees, stared at the afternoon sky, and watched the patient passage of clouds, catnapping contentedly and lightheartedly. His eyelids drooped, then lifted again, and his body, serene and reposed, felt void of all temptations. Playful happy-go-lucky birds chirped noisily on the branches, and prudent and wise ants were scurrying to and fro on the ground. He spent the night at a wayside inn. He got up several times to look out at the crescent moon and the twinkling stars, and he slept with his eyes full of memories of cosmic rays and mysteries of the universe. He started off again at the crack of dawn. There lay ahead of him, as far as the eye could see, bare and barren land, and then suddenly in the midst of that parched emptiness, a row of green poplars stood together like neat schoolboys. Farther on, in the heart of the desert, a small oasis came into view like some rare occurrence.

A hitchhiker signaled him to stop. The man was going to Kermanshah. Kermanshah sounded like a good place to visit. Amir-Ali didn't know that part of the country. He didn't know any part of the country. He had been brought up in Tehran and he had stayed there. His travels abroad had been only on business, for making purchases or obtaining licenses for the Yarn and Spool Company.

Outside the city, the hitchhiker got off at the bend of a dirt road and went on his way. The sun was setting. The end of the horizon was linked to a world of color, and a mass of orange light was descending from the sky. Driving on that dirt road was not easy. Once or twice his wheels sank into the soft and muddy soil and the car stalled, then labored forward a few yards and got stuck again. It was growing dark. Amir-Ali got out, took off his jacket, spread it on the ground, and lay down on it. The earth was silent, and the nearby mountains were still. The vastness of the desert gradually seeped into his body, carrying him forward like a light-headed kite.

He thought of Malak-Azar. Her chiming voice tinkled softly in his ear, and the memory of her perfumed body tickled the back of his throat. Some fragments of this woman still lingered in him, and her absent presence hung from the edges of his thoughts like a cobweb spun by an old spider. When he was away from Malak-Azar, he missed her, he missed an imaginary Malak-Azar, who had the hypnotic voice of a mermaid and a comforting embrace as vast as an eternal plain. Deep in his heart he longed for this absent woman who was nowhere.

He traveled for two months. The repugnant smell of his body had disappeared and his rebellious limbs were at peace. He called home once, but before he had a chance to speak Malak-Azar had slammed down the receiver. The second time he called he was told that the lady of the house was not home.

"It's still too early to go back," he told himself. "The time is not ripe for me to return. My wife is still angry. I must wait a bit longer. Be sure of myself."

He spent another month traveling, going from one village to another, from one satellite town to the next, from one teahouse to another, driving aimlessly, drowsy and half intoxicated, oblivious of time, unaware of particular people and places, mindless of the Yarn and Spool Company and of duplicate and triplicate accounts. During the day, he drove on the edges of vast deserts, and at night he lay down and gazed at the sky and open vistas. And yet, he was still tied to the past, and obviously the sane thing to do was to contact his family and put an end to their worries and uncertainties. His mother was still alive, even though her life was hanging by no more than a thread, as unreliable as a soap bubble in the air. He had to see her before she died.

The door to his house was locked, and the lock had been changed. Hard as he rang, no one answered. He realized that he could not go to his office looking completely unkempt. Uncle G's house was around the corner. He went there and the old man was shocked to see him. He took a step backward and gaped. His mother-in-law was there, too. She was peeking from behind the upstairs bedroom window and quickly withdrew her head. Amir-Ali inquired about his wife, and Uncle G kept staring at him in astonishment.

"Where have you been all this time?" he asked.

Amir-Ali was in no mood to explain. He repeated his question. Uncle G sighed. He placed his hand on Amir-Ali's shoulder and cleared his throat. He was preparing for a long lecture. He extended his right arm forward (evidently he had rehearsed this pose in front of the mirror), stretched his neck, and with the voice of a retired actor, devoid of any resonance or excitement, explained that Malak-Azar had gone abroad. And that she had put the house up for sale, and that the key had been given to so-and-so (meaning me).

Amir-Ali was neither surprised nor distressed. He seemed to have expected this all along. He bid a hasty good-bye. He shook his head and was about to leave when Uncle G called him back. He had another piece of news for him. Bad news.

With a voice that had again taken on a dramatic tone, he said, "I am sorry. I don't know how to put it. It is not easy."

Amir-Ali's heart sank. Uncle G was mumbling. He wanted to prolong Amir-Ali's misery as much as possible. He took a handkerchief from his pocket and blew his nose, once, twice, all for theatrical effect. He coughed. Amir-Ali's eyes were glued to Uncle G's mouth. At last he could take it no longer.

"My mother?" he asked, and he turned deathly pale.

The doorbell rang. The mother-in-law's head reappeared behind the lace curtain, and a moment later was gone again.

"Please allow me to open the door," Uncle G said.

Amir-Ali followed him to the door. He felt like kicking Uncle G in the ankle again.

"Please. What has happened?" he asked.

Uncle G had reached the door. "You have been missing for three months," he said. "And during all this time you failed to contact your wife or your children or your mother. What did you expect?"

Malak-Azar's brother and I arrived on the scene together. When Amir-Ali saw me, he heaved a sigh of relief and stepped away from Uncle G. He knew that I knew everything. I went straight to the point. I gave him the key to the house and told him that it had been placed in my trust and now I had to return it. Then I told him calmly and coolly (I knew how much he detested excitement) that his mother was in the hospital, that it was hopeless, and she could pass away at any moment.

My car was parked right outside the house. I offered to drive him to the hospital. He accepted and ran out ahead of me. I had called the hospital before coming here. The nurse who answered the telephone had made me understand that the patient was on her deathbed. I was not sure that Amir-Ali would get there in time. The hospital was in the city center and traffic was heavy. The cars were being stopped and the spaces under their seats and inside their trunks were being searched. Amir-Ali was struggling with himself and his hands were shaking.

"When was the last time you spoke with her?" he asked.

For a moment, I thought he was talking of Malak-Azar, and my heart sank. I looked at him. He meant his mother. His thoughts were with her. There was an accident at the intersection. Someone had been run over. People were shouting. Two men were beating each other up. We had to make a U-turn and choose another route. Amir-Ali repeated his question.

"Two days ago," I replied.

"How was she?" he asked. "Please tell me. Tell me how she was."

I couldn't drive and speak at the same time. We were in front of a school. Children were running around. It was chaos. A truck was unloading bricks at the end of the street. The road was blocked. Amir-Ali was going out of his mind. He was sweating. He got out. "I'll get there faster if I walk," he said. He got out of the car and started to run. I let him go. There was nothing I could do. I wanted to tell him of Malak-Azar and give him her message. But I couldn't.

The hospital was crowded. There were lines everywhere, in front of the elevator, in front of the pharmacy, in front of the restrooms. There was a disorderly line in front of the information booth. His mother's name was not to be found on the patient list. The information clerk said perhaps the patient had been released.

A voice whispered deep inside Amir-Ali that he had arrived too late, that it was all over. Perhaps she had been admitted under another name. He gave her maiden name.

"When was she admitted?" the clerk asked. Amir-Ali did not know. He shook his head.

"You need to know the exact date of admission," the man said. "A hundred patients come and go every day. Many of them die. Let us hope your patient is in good health and has been released."

It took another ten minutes for the information clerk to find her name. Room 502, fifth floor. The elevator went up only to the third floor and then went back to the second floor and stayed there. Amir-Ali climbed the stairs two at a time and finally reached the fifth floor. A number of visitors were sitting quietly in the waiting area. Their heads were down and their eyes were mostly wet with tears. A framed photograph of a nurse hung from the opposite wall. She had a sweet face and held her finger to her lips. The door to a room opened and a doctor, followed by a few nurses, emerged. A young boy and girl got up from among the visitors. Their eyes were glued to the doctor's mouth. They followed him. After a few steps the girl stopped, leaned against the wall, and buried her face in her hands. A nurse was passing by with a tray of medications. Amir-Ali stopped her. He told her he was looking for his mother and mentioned her name. The nurse pointed with her head in the direction of the room across the hall.

Then she was still alive. Never mind that an IV was connected to a vein in her arm and a tube inserted in her nose and that she looked like a plucked chicken, and that her face was drained of all color, and that the line on the heart monitor was almost flat. She was still alive. She was waiting for him. She was not going to leave without saying good-bye.

Dazed and trembling, Amir-Ali stood in the doorway. He could not bring himself to walk in. He would have liked to put this frail creature into a bag and take her far away. A nurse entered the room. She looked at the patient, took his mother's pulse, tidied the sheets, and shook her head. Amir-Ali felt that something inside him was shifting, that he was about to collapse, and that the particles of his body were scattered in the air like the ashes of a cremated corpse. He held on to the wall and slid forward. Did his mother remember him? Perhaps she was looking at him with her soul, with a third eye, with a mind that was outside her body. His mother's white hands rested on the sheets, lined with spidery blue veins. Her fingertips quivered. He sat on the edge of the bed, put his hand under her chin, and turned her face toward him. Two translucent circles shone deep inside her eyes, two windows to another life. She nodded her head and smiled. It was as though the old lady sitting on the brink of death had been waiting for this last encounter with her beloved child.

Amir-Ali caressed her white hair and closed her eyes. A major chapter of his life had come to an end. He felt that he no longer belonged to anything or anyone and that all the sunny shores and the clear and bright skies and all the green fields and vast deserts were waiting for him.

Malak-Azar had moved most of the valuables — the carpets, the antique *objets d'art,* and everything else that had belonged to her — out of the house. Only the drapes and the beds, stripped of their mattresses and sheets, remained. The cabinet doors were left open, their interiors emptied out. The drawers had been pulled open and left in that state, in complete disarray. The floors were covered with old newspapers, torn papers, and photographs — Amir-Ali's photographs. His clothes — pressed trousers, clean white shirts, double-breasted jackets, neckties, imported scarves — all lay in a pile at the foot of the wall, like corpses on a battlefield. Each pair of striped gray trousers, each pair of leather gloves, each silk handkerchief, and each pair of polished leather shoes hinted at some old memory. His father, with his avaricious body and his lustful gaze that betrayed carnal desires, his mother, with her aristocratic silence and hidden grief, his wife, with her delicate body and her cardboard masks, and Uncle G, with his pitiful dread of old age and death, were all there, milling about, mementos of a lost life.

Malak-Azar had left him a note on the kitchen table, cold and concise. There was no greeting, no "Dear So-and-so," nothing. It just told him in very few words that she had no intention of coming back and that she did not want to see him again. <u>Ever</u>. And this last word she had underlined twice for emphasis. (She had also sent me a short letter. With a temporary address and a secret telephone number that I was not to pass on to anyone else.)

Amir-Ali lay down on the empty bed in the master bedroom and stared at the low ceiling and the antique chandelier, which weighed down on him with its massive bulk. Scenes from his life passed piecemeal before his eyes, like a hodgepodge film shot with a cast of strangers. Perhaps it had all been a dream. Perhaps he himself was an obscure character in someone else's dream, a stranger. The walls, the doors and windows, even the smell of that house, were unfamiliar to him. Malak-Azar still wandered in the rooms like a faint ghost and kept an eye on him from the far side of another world. He got up. Packed his things. Took some money and dollar bills that he had hidden away at the back of a closet (instinctive farsightedness) and stuck them in his pocket. He put the half-dead plant of the guest bedroom under his arm and he was on his way.

One night at a wayside teahouse, he looked at himself in the mirror and was startled. A sixty-year-old man was looking back at him. Until then he had fought the onslaught of age. He had looked twenty years younger than his real age, and he had hidden, by hook or crook, those twenty years somewhere behind his face. He had watched his figure and his good looks like a hawk. He would not touch fatty foods or sweets, and the clothes that Malak-Azar carefully picked out for him presented him as a youngish man of good taste. Now he had become someone else: a middle-aged man with a small double chin and sunburned cheeks, with a deeply furrowed forehead and crow's feet around his eyes, with a graying stubble and white hair showing up here and there on his head and in his eyebrows. He had bought a pair of roomy and comfortable Kurdish trousers at the bazaar in Sanandaj. He did not mind letting out his paunch and did not fear the judgment and inquisitive looks of others.

Amir-Ali stared at the image in the mirror with growing astonishment. He realized that he knew this face, with that familiar look and that wry smile, and that he had seen it somewhere before. He went closer to the mirror to take a better look. He had imagined a different reflection of himself, and this being in the mirror was quite someone else. He and that other person stood facing each other like two strangers, and Amir-Ali realized that this new person, with his different looks, was no other than his second personality, he who commanded his limbs and made his bowels rumble, that invisible being who followed him like a shadow and who was at war with him. But perhaps this shadow, this alter ego, was not at war with him after all. He had been a friend, forgotten and banished, and thus wounded and in a rage. They had now made up and had no other option than friendship. Amir-Ali did not dislike this easygoing, unkempt self, with his sunburned complexion, his earthly and rustic air. The image in the mirror was looking at him with inviting eyes. He had come a long way and seemed to be tired, as if wanting to sit down and stretch out his legs. After so many years of absence, he wanted at last to settle down in his rightful place. The two approached each other until they merged. And only a memory remained of the man who was once the head of the Yarn and Spool Company.

Amir-Ali is in his car, driving on mountainous roads. He has no destination in mind. He enjoys this aimless driving, this trip toward unknown and unexplored deserts. He is glad that no one knows him and that he is not imprisoned in a mold. His body is tranquil and his limbs are at peace with him. He has rolled down the driver's side window and the autumn sun shines on his bare arm and his face. He feels he can drive on forever.

He spends the night at a small roadside village and looks at the blue ocean above his head. A gaunt cat comes and sits beside him. His right hand reaches out and pets the cat on the head. His hand is full of kindness. His eyes look deep into the sky, at the bright crescent moon and the galaxies dispersed in the universe. He thinks of somewhere beyond the farthest celestial bodies, of a world parallel with another, and of a past that is renewed and of a time that is yet to come. And for a moment he envisions his childhood kite as it soars above the clouds, and he sees himself amidst all those galaxies, transformed into a little speck, floating in space. His body aches with ecstasy and an indescribable pleasure creeps into every cell of his body. For a moment he thinks that he has disintegrated, been pulverized and absorbed into the Milky Way. His kite is flying along with him, its colorful tail gently swaying this way and that. Perhaps he is dreaming. In whatever state he is, asleep or awake, he is happy, the innocent joy of a speck floating in space. It is not easy to understand and it may sound like nonsense. But nonsense or not, this is how Amir-Ali feels and it cannot be expressed in any other way.

*   *   *

Let us observe him: He has been awakened by the crow of a rooster. It is not yet sunrise. He is at a roadside teahouse, sleeping on a wooden couch under a satin quilt, and he feels cold. He hugs his knees, and a cool breeze brushes over his face. The smell of freshly baked bread is in the air. He is hungry. He opens his eyes a crack and stares at the fragments of his dream flying away. The air has warmed up to a pleasant temperature. He can smell the aromas of his childhood summers, the scent of the wet mud and straw mixture of the orchard walls and the whiff of the sticky resin oozing out of the pine trees. No one is staring at him, no one is judging him. He can roll over, he can shout. He can speak and pour out the unspoken words that have remained imprisoned in his chest. He can choose, protest, decide, or do nothing. No one can tell him that he has to stand up for something or against someone, or to be the Iranian ambassador to the Court of St. James or the president of the Yarn and Spool Imports Company. He can lie down under the trees and listen to the crickets if he feels like it. He can realize his old dream and become an astronomer or he can water his plot of cucumbers and plough his land. He can transform himself into any shape and metamorphose. He can die, and opting for death is a choice he can make.

Uncle G had read somewhere that all the occurrences in the world are somehow connected. He had wanted to pontificate on that, but he had not been given the chance. But for once in his life he had been right, and those who were busy eating dinner around the table that night did not realize how a series of thin threads hung from each word, each random encounter, each minor incident, and how these threads were interwoven like the colored fabrics of a cosmic carpet. If that pesky mosquito had not bitten Amir-Ali's foot on that eventful night, in all likelihood nothing would have happened, and the destiny of Amir-Ali and Malak-Azar and her mother and Uncle G and the Yarn and Spool Imports Company would not have changed course. The same can be said for my destiny.

— *Translated by Karim Emami and Sara Khalili*

Behnam Dayani

Behnam Dayani has published one volume of short stories, entitled *Hitchcock and Agha Baji and Other Stories,* in 1994.

Like Hitchcock's *Psycho,* "Hitchcock and Agha Baji" is a story about the tyranny of the past over the present. It first appeared in *Short Stories from Iran and the World,* edited by Safdar Taqizedeh and Asghar Elahi (Tehran: Safdar Taqizedeh, 1993).

HITCHCOCK AND AGHA BAJI

On that sunny autumn Thursday afternoon, between the hours of two and seven, three unusual incidents took place. From three to five, my friends and I went to Mahtab Cinema to see Hitchcock's *Psycho*. At six-thirty, Agha Baji came to our house to visit my grandmother. Fifteen seconds later, the tile floor in the bathroom collapsed and I almost fell through into the stone pit below. Apparently, these three simple incidents have nothing to do with one another. But behind this simplicity, there lie numerous complexities.

It's afternoon. We have two periods of grammar and literature. We're sitting in the classroom. The atmosphere is filled with conspiracy and intrigue. We're about to rebel against our teacher. But the remarkable part is that the instigator of our supposed rebellion is actually our principal. By making us do this, he wants to pull the rug out from under Mr. Chabok's feet. Mr. Chabok, our language teacher, must be on a temporary contract, which is why it's possible to fire him so easily. He is a university student with a hefty build. He has a bony face and a protruding jaw. He always grinds his teeth.

He is an irritable teacher, but sometimes he can be very informal and friendly. Granted that we're eighteen years old, and we're in twelfth grade, but the day he smoked in the classroom, we all flipped. The weird part is that he was asking the kids for matches. They say he says fishy things. I really don't get that impression. Though he once did say something that wasn't half bad. When we were talking about the Queen of England and her husband, he said that in the end, only two kings will be left in the entire world — the king in the deck of cards and the King or Queen of England.

Tahmures Yazdani was the first person to bring up this business of fishy talk. One day, after Mr. Chabok left the classroom, he gathered all the kids around, his eyes gleaming with excitement, and said, "Did you see the back of his coat collar?"

We all stared back at him like zombies.

He smiled indulgently as if addressing a bunch of idiots. "He's got the sign of the Third National Front pinned to the back of his coat collar!"[1]

The truth is, we hadn't seen anything. Even if we had, we wouldn't have understood it. Tahmures has a big head and talks big. He says his dad is in the ministry of foreign affairs. He always concludes his essays with the famous concept of "Positive Nationalism." Even if the topic of the essay is, "Write a Letter to Your Father and Explain Why You Have Failed." Once, a few of the kids and I asked him some questions about Mr. Chabok and his fishy discussions. But he only raised his eyebrows and said, "He is a traitor."

So we are sitting in the classroom and whispering among ourselves. We don't know why Mr. Chabok hasn't showed up yet. Either he has smelled a rat himself, or else someone's told him about the setup. The truth is that we are all ashamed to pull this spineless, nasty trick on Mr. Chabok. The head boy keeps insisting that the principal is in the loop and encourages this move. But none of us really believe that yet. Tahmures, whose irritating schemes have fallen on deaf ears until now, leaves the classroom in frustration and returns, short of breath, with the principal himself. The principal looks at us angrily and says, "So why are you all still sitting down?! Get up and leave!"

Slumping with shame, we reluctantly pick up our books and leave the school. Some people go home. Some stand around at the intersection and light up cigarettes. Alexander, Abbas, and I go to Mahtab Cinema. The movie is *Psycho,* starring Anthony Perkins, Janet Leigh, Vera Miles, and John Gavin. All three of us are *Movie Star* magazine readers, and I am a Hitchcock fan. I have memorized the list of frames in which Hitchcock has appeared in his movies far better than the extended formula of ethane and methane. I have seen almost all the Hitchcock films that have been shown in Iran. Once, Abbas cautiously compared Hitchcock to the director Samuel Khachikian. With great disdain, I advised him to quit making such futile analogies. *Vertigo* is the best

---

[1] This story takes place in the mid-1960s, during the reign of Mohammad Reza Shah Pahlavi. Much of the political subtext and the allusion to the Third National Front (a faction of the nationalist opposition to the Shah) refers to the atmosphere of political persecution and fear that accompanied the royal dictatorship. "Fishy talk" is subversive or implicit political talk, an indication of opposition to the Shah's regime. Secret police informers existed among the students and in the school administration.

film I have ever seen in my life, and the best director is obviously Hitchcock.

Mahtab Cinema is almost deserted. Only three or four of the best rows are filled. After some desperate negotiation, we obtain permission from the usher and sit in the front. Supposedly Hitchcock has requested the theater doors to be shut as the film begins, but they are not. At the beginning of the film, there is a minute of silence and darkness. One or two people crack jokes and several others whistle. But the three of us are already in a world of our own. As if we are in a different orbit.

The film takes our breath away, from the beginning when it focuses on a window in a building, to the very end, when Anthony Perkins is sitting in the sheriff's office with a blanket around his shoulders, not whisking away the fly on his hand. The shower scene — well, that's special, of course, but the most excruciating scene is when Vera Miles goes down the basement stairs alone, to see what's happening down there. All three of us are clutching the arms of our seats. We're hunched over, and are pulling ourselves back in our chairs. As if we don't want to go down with her. But Vera Miles doesn't pay any attention to us. She goes down the stairs, one by one. In the basement, she sees a woman from the back, who is sitting on a chair. She calls out to her. The woman doesn't answer. She touches her shoulder. The chair turns around. The music screams. Just like when the edge of a sharp razor is scratched across glass. Vera Miles's hand hits the hanging ceiling lamp from sheer fear. The shaking light twists and distorts everything, blurring all lines and boundaries. Sitting on the chair is the skeleton of an old woman. Gray hair tied back, with a straight part in the middle. Some remnant of dry and wrinkled skin, black eye sockets, and a void mouth.

It's been about an hour since I got home. I don't even remember how I came out of the cinema or how I got back. I put the book *Physics and Mechanics* in front of me, and I am trying to read tomorrow's lesson. The words keep moving out of focus, and the old woman's face replaces them. I try to fade out that image by shaking my head a few times. I stand; I see the neighbor's windows. The windows go out of focus, the old woman's face takes their place. I walk a few steps and stare at the flowers on the carpet. The flowers go out of focus, and the old woman's face appears in their place. I go to the refrigerator to eat something; the lightbulb blinks, and the old woman's face replaces all the containers of food. Trembling, I stand above the heater and fix my eyes on the blue flames. The flames dance around, and the old woman's face appears among them. I try to make myself busy. I move from spot to spot aimlessly, like a lunatic. Unfortunately, no one is home, otherwise I could talk. I switch on the radio and turn it up high. The strumming of the *tar* and the *kamanche* fill the room and I calm down a bit.[2] I am about to pick up *Physics and Mechanics* when someone knocks on the door.

The door of the house is wooden. It has a bronze, crescent-shaped knocker. As far as I remember, no one ever uses the knocker nowadays. Everyone rings the doorbell. I don't know why I am suddenly overwhelmed with fear. I come to the top of the stairs and listen carefully. A few seconds later, the rat-a-tat of the knocker comes again. The strikes are irregular — short, short, long. As if the striker's hand is weak, without energy. I come down the stairs and turn on the hallway lights. The lightbulb is only forty watts. For years, it has been a safe haven for the flies to sit on and do their business. A halo of dirty yellow light falls on the surroundings. I stand behind the door, and ask, "Who is it?"

No one answers. I open the door. I expect to see a person, but there is no one there. The door frame, black and empty like a hollow grave, appears before me. Suddenly, my heart beats faster. The hairs on my body stand on end, and my insides churn. I take a couple steps back, and ask out loud, "Is anyone there?"

A head slowly enters the black frame from the left side. Gray hair with a straight part in the middle. Wrinkled skin, deep-set eyes, a pointed nose, a toothless mouth, a few strands of long, black hair on the chin, all of this framed by a white scarf and covered by a black veil. My common sense recognizes this face, and says: "This is Agha Baji."

But something else inside me erratically says: "This is the old woman from *Psycho*."

Just like Anthony Perkins, who clasps his hand on his mouth when he sees the body of Janet Leigh, I cover my mouth with my hand, so that my life doesn't jump out of my body from fear. I stumble a few

---

[2] Persian string instruments.

steps back and hit the sink. Suddenly I lose my balance and I feel like one of my legs is sinking. I let out a loud yell, and grab the edge of the sink along with the drainpipe. I look down, and I see that one of my legs has sunk into a black hole about the area of one tile, and my other leg is stuck at the edge of the adjacent tile, which is about to collapse and fall down. With a speed unexpected of someone of her age, Agha Baji enters the house and approaches me. Just then, the adjacent tile and a few others collapse. Now, the entire lower half of my body is in the hole, and the upper half is hanging on to the sink. Agha Baji realizes what is going on, and stops. Whimpering, I plead for her help. She takes her veil, ties one end of it to the wooden handle of the water pump, and throws the other end toward me. The water pump is a hefty cast-iron contraption. In the old days, they used it to pump water from the underground water reservoir in the cellar to the water tank on the roof. With the help of the veil, I pull myself up and collapse in the hallway. Agha Baji doesn't get too close to me. She's a sharp old woman and must have understood that I have been frightened by her.

She goes to the foot of the staircase and calls out to my grandmother. She calls out "hey" several times. She still calls my grandmother "brother's wife," even though it's already been about fifty years since her brother died. When she is convinced that no one is at home, she sits on the bottom stair. She takes out a pair of metal-rimmed glasses from a pouch in her head scarf. Once she adjusts her glasses behind her head with an elastic band, she looks at me with careful concern. Even though she has rescued me, she's still the old woman from *Psycho*.

An acrid odor has permeated the whole area. Something between alcohol and vinegar. I guess that the odor is coming from the hole that I was suspended in. It's so pungent that it makes me dizzy. Exasperated, Agha Baji looks around several times. She's probably thinking of a solution for my condition. She takes out two pink objects shaped like horseshoes from another pouch in her head scarf and puts them in her mouth. Her face assumes shape, like a flat tire that's suddenly raised up on a jack. The pink objects are her false teeth. She can't talk or eat without them. At this moment, my grandmother comes huffing and puffing into the house, carrying a bundle in her arms. Her face is red, and steam is rising up from her. She was probably at the public bath. Before I pass out, I glance at Agha Baji, who has now assumed a human face and is no longer the old woman in *Psycho*.

*   *   *

Half an hour passes. I am upstairs and I feel a little better. My grandmother believes that I passed out from shock. She is sitting beside me
and wants to force me to eat a piece of rock salt. She says God took pity
on me that I didn't fall into the pit. I put the salt in my mouth and confirm her point. By now, she has put the neighbor's father and mother and
their fathers' fathers and all their ancestors in the grinder, and ground
them up, making minced meat out of them with all her insults and
curses. She has decided to go to the police station first thing in the
morning to complain. The next-door neighbor is Armenian. I still
don't get why she wants to complain to the police. She explains that the
neighbor is using his cellar reservoir as one gigantic wine cask and is
making wine in it. The wall of the well, which is the boundary between
our house and their decrepit cellar water reservoir, has crumbled, and
that's why the tiles collapsed. Now I understand where the sour smell
of alcohol and vinegar came from. My grandmother slaps the back of
her hand and bites her lip in shocked disapproval. She is wondering
what the hell she would have done if I had actually fallen into the pit.
I have a feeling that what she is saying doesn't make sense. What does
the collapse of our well have to do with the fact that the neighbor is
making wine in his cellar? I try to dissuade her from going to the police. If she starts getting into the pure-impure discussion with wine and
whatnot, there will be no stopping her. But Agha Baji settles the issue
with two statements. First, she suggests that we pour a sack of lime in
the well to clean up the wine. As for the neighbor, she believes that each
person will answer for his own deeds in the next world. Besides, she
adds, hell needs street sweepers, too![3]

My grandmother lets it go at that and sets up the tea things. Then
they sit beside each other and begin to — as they call it — mingle. I
don't really know Agha Baji that well. I only see her a few times each
year. Within the family, they say that she brings bad luck. Some also
think she can bring the evil eye if she's rubbed the wrong way. Her
name is Gol Baji Khanum, but everyone calls her Agha Baji.

After I read a few pages of *Physics and Mechanics,* grandmother calls
me. She puts a cup of freshly brewed tea in front of me, and beckons to

---

[3] Refers to a crude street poem, a derogatory comment about Christian Armenians whose role
in the afterlife is supposed be to sweep the streets of hell.

Agha Baji. Agha Baji is sitting across from me, staring at me. Maybe she is offended that seeing her frightened me so much. She says: "I've never seen Jonah and the whale, nor have I built the dam of Alexander, but even if the tribe of Gog and Magog had encircled me, I wouldn't be this shaken with fear."[4]

Then she turns to my grandmother and complains: "As soon as your grandson set his eyes on me, he almost died of fright!"

My grandmother throws a reproachful glance toward me, and tells her in a consoling voice, "He didn't mean to be disrespectful — you must forgive him, Agha Baji. He's a bit prone to delusions."

I say, "It . . . it's because I saw a film today."

Grandmother waves her hand dismissively at what I say and replies, "Talking about film and cimnema again?"

No matter how hard I've tried, I haven't been able to get her to learn how to say "cinema" correctly. I explain that the film was very suspenseful and frightening. Both their ears prick up. In a few sentences, I explain the gist of the story to them. My grandmother laughs and says, "Baji dear, are your ears big enough to absorb that tall tale?"

But Agha Baji's manner is suddenly transformed. Her look makes me feel unsettled. I have a feeling that she wants to draw something out of my insides. Without getting off the floor, she slides her legs over to me like a grasshopper and sits beside me. She asks me to tell her the whole story. I tell her the story, not from A to Z, but a good summary. Stunned, she fixes her stare on my mouth without blinking. When the story is finished, my grandmother gives us each another cup of tea. The room is uncannily silent. Agha Baji seems to have withdrawn into herself and her stare is fixed on the flower pattern in the carpet. I don't dare say anything else. I'm afraid that she will turn into the old woman in *Psycho* again. To break the silence, my grandmother coughs and asks with a laugh, "So who was the operator of the film?"

She has learned from me that every film has a director. But she confuses this word, too, like "cimnema," and always says "operator" instead of director. Before I answer her, I glance at Agha Baji, and her lips are quivering. She weeps silently. Puzzled, I look at my grandmother in search of an explanation. She gesticulates with her eyes and brow, urg-

---

[4] Examples of fantastic tales from Persian folklore, the Alexander legend, and the Quran.

ing me to leave the room. I get up and go back to my *Physics and Mechanics.*

One hour has passed. It's dinnertime. My grandmother wants to keep Agha Baji for dinner. I hear them arguing about it from upstairs. Finally, Agha Baji comes downstairs, remarking that she wants to cook halvah to take to the cemetery tomorrow to visit the dead.[5] When we are saying good-bye, I try to console her about the unpleasant incident that occurred at the moment of her arrival. I whip out some fancy phrases that I've learned from grown-ups: "You have honored us with your presence." "Your visit is precious to us, more precious than our eyes." "You blessed us, your servants." "Please privilege us again."

Agha Baji waits until my gibberish is finished. Then she says, "Will you take Agha Baji to observe this show sometime?"

I don't understand what she means. I get nervous. I worry that I am about to offend her at the time of her departure, too. But what she actually means is the simplest among all the different scenarios I could conjure. She wants me to take her to see the film *Psycho.* That's why I can't believe it. To avoid committing a gaffe, I give her a neutral answer, I say, "Please, whatever you say."

She nods her head, and disappears in the dark.

When I tell my grandmother about it, she isn't really surprised. She says, "Don't judge Agha Baji the way she is now that she's like a marshmallow. Once upon a time, the earth used to tremble beneath her feet!" I get curious, and inquire about her more. After dinner, she tells me Agha Baji's life story.

At night, as I lie down in my bed, the old woman from *Psycho* is about to pop into my mind again. I think of Agha Baji to distract myself. Her life is more like a film than reality.

When she is fifteen, the governor of Karbala asks for her hand in marriage.[6] (I later discover that this happened at the time when Iraq was still part of the Ottoman Empire.) No one knows where the Turkish Pasha who was governing Karbala had heard tales of her beauty —

---

[5] The pasty sweet halvah, made from flour and saffron, is offered in commemoration of the dead.
[6] Karbala is a holy city for Shi'ites.

of long tresses of hair like embroidered flowers in a tapestry, down to the curve of her waist. Her brow as smooth as marble. Eyes, brown as the eyes of a gazelle. Thick, bow-shaped eyebrows. Nose like a chick-pea. Lips parting in a smile like the shell of a pistachio, and the dimple in her chin — an abyss for lovers to plunge into. Hard as I try, I can't make Agha Baji's current face correspond to such features. Most awkward of all is her current chin, full of grooves and wrinkles with long hairs growing on it; nothing whatsoever to do with a pretty dimple.

The Turkish pasha had offered many gifts in return for her hand, one of which was a fully grown white horse, the size of a pony, with horseshoes made of gold. Miss Baji took the wedding vows with the groom in absentia. Riding among twelve camels transporting her dowry, accompanied by soldiers wearing fezzes, she set off for the border. (It's the threshold of the First World War. The end of the Qajar dynasty in Iran and the Ottoman pashas in Turkey is near, and there is turmoil everywhere.) On the way, the news reached them that the hapless old pasha had left this world. The fifteen-year-old Miss Baji was left alone with a number of lusty befezzed Arab soldiers, the gifts of the unfortunate deceased governor, and twelve dowry-laden camels. That night, she sewed all the Persian and Ottoman gold coins into the lining of her dress, and early in the morning she fled back to her father's home, riding her golden-shod horse.

Ten years later Miss Baji became a bride again. This time, her husband was the leader of one of the tribes of Lorestan.[7] He was a sun-burned nomad, about six feet tall, whose brutality and greed inspire my grandmother to say that he would "devour the donkey along with its load, and the corpse along with the grave." His name was Ja'far Gholi, but he was called "Jeff." (Was this a memento from British friends, or a personal choice? No one knows. This was the Pahlavi era — the time of the forced settlement of tribes and nomads. The plan was to make the nomads pay through their noses for all the havoc they had wreaked in the last hundred years. Forcing them to drink the poisonous Qajar coffee wasn't fashionable anymore. They were now speaking about injections of air in the veins, and injections of water in the knee.)[8]

---

[7] A mountainous province in northwestern Iran, mainly inhabited by nomads and semi-nomads.

[8] "Qajar coffee," made with poison, was used on occasion by Qajar kings and their allies to kill their adversaries. Torture and assassination methods evolved to more sophisticated techniques

Jeff was a one-armed man. When his right arm took a bullet in battle, he cut it off himself, from under the shoulder, with a Cossack sword. He was a bitter man with a broken spirit, who confronted all life's disenchantments in two ways: smoking opium and tormenting his wife. And in both these habits, he had a fastidious and distinctive taste.

On the night of the wedding, he established who was boss. He returned the young bride with her white dress and uncovered hair to her father's house. She was holding an unstained handkerchief in one hand, and a mouse lamp in another.[9] (According to my grandmother's definition, a mouse lamp is something that looks like a teapot with a wick coming out of its spout. The wick soaks up and burns the oil inside it.) Before the sun was up, Miss Baji had been turned into "Mouse Lamp" Baji. Her father had a heart attack from the shock, and in his sickbed accepted the demands and conditions of his mendacious, greedy son-in-law. He paid his daughter's inheritance in full, in advance, along with six kilos of superior saffron from the Ghaenat region. The sun has just reached the wall when "Mouse Lamp" Baji changed into "Saffron Baji," and this is how they began their married life together.

Jeff had a heavy hand (as he should have . . . since he only had one hand, his body wasn't well balanced), and he responded to every mishap with a jab in the mouth, a slap, smack, or strike. My grandmother says a man who is an opium addict has only two ways of preventing his wife from going on the prowl.[10] Either he must father so many children that she won't have time to scratch her head, never mind be tempted to do anything else, or in the midst of the warm and tingly feeling of the opium high, when the pipe is ready and he is feeling good, he must use the pretext of the wife's earache to give her a puff, so that the next day, the wife can make up the excuse of a toothache for another puff, and so on and so forth, until the day comes when they both sit on opposite sides of the opium stove and scratch their noses, and talk rubbish in their husky opium-addict voices. However, Mrs. Baji did not show talent for either of these two scenarios. She gave birth to seven children, six of whom died, and opium, alas, did not suit her constitution. But as she had come to her husband's home in a

during the Pahlavi dynasty (1925–1979), such as injections of air into the veins and water into the knees.

[9] The unstained handkerchief is allegedly proof that the bride was not a virgin.

[10] Opium addicts have diminished sexual desire and prowess.

white dress, she could only leave in a white shroud. So she suffered and stayed.

On moonlit nights, she tied her baby to her back and headed out with Jeff to Sofeh Mountain. It was a rocky ledge towering over *takht-e poulad,* which is Esfahan's cemetery. Watched over by her husband, she rubbed the opium in the radiance of the full moon. In those times, they would rub opium either in the vicinity of fire, or under the sun. But Jeff the opium addict believed that opium rubbed in the radiance of the full moon induces a high that is out of this world. The full moons come and go. Moons become new and old. Crescents develop into full moons, full moons into crescents . . . Until one night, Jeff cut the trip short and died right up there under the moonlight. In the morning, the assembly of mourners realized something strange. Jeff's healthy hand — the same hand he used for slapping his wife — had been cut off from the wrist.

Questions, investigations, and inquiries led nowhere. The family and relatives made some lukewarm protests, and the body was finally put to rest. Moreover, what did it matter if a one-armed man lost the other when he died, especially if he had never done anything good with it?

Mrs. Baji was left with a few pots and pans, a couple of worthless kilims, a ten-year-old daughter, and the need to keep up appearances in spite of her dire state.

A few weeks later, Mrs. Baji sold the furniture and the house, and disappeared with her daughter. Five or six years passed by. There was news that she had a charming little house and lived in Tehran. She was probably clever enough to have secretly saved a few of the gold Ottoman coins in the lining of her dress. Her daughter grew up. She managed to give her a respectable wedding and a worthy dowry to take with her. The girl became pregnant, but died during childbirth. To avoid her grandchild being brought up by a stepmother, Mrs. Baji came to an agreement with her son-in-law. She took in the baby, tended him for years, and brought him up. Now that she has been old for a long time, she is respectfully called Agha Baji.

I still can't fall asleep. Hard as I try, I can't understand why Agha Baji wants to see *Psycho.* Maybe it's just an old woman's whim and will be forgotten tomorrow. I am not frightened of the old woman in *Psycho* anymore. I calmly replay the basement scene in my mind and go to sleep.

A few nights later, when I get home, I see that Agha Baji's grandson is there. She has named him Siavosh.[11] (Which ordeal has he successfully triumphed over? Which fire has he overcome? Maybe the story of Siavosh invokes the tale of her own tribulation.) Siavosh is a medical student and an intern in a hospital. He's a quiet, heavy young man with straight hair and has a way of speaking that sounds more like humming. After the initial rubbing of his hands together in silence, he curiously asks about the film that I have promised to take his grandmother to see. I get nervous again. The truth is that I am embarrassed to take Agha Baji to the movies. Maybe because my friends show off and say that they've been to the movies with their "girlfriends" and here I am ending up having to go with Agha Baji. He starts laughing when I tell him about what happened that day with the film *Psycho* and the ordeal that followed with the bathroom floor. He says, "You started it, you have to finish it! Really, it's all your own doing!"

He reaches into his pocket and gives me 20 tomans. I want to pass the buck to Siavosh and make him take her, but I feel too shy to do it. He's probably very busy, otherwise he would have thought of it himself. My grandmother eggs me on. I console myself with the thought that this is a good deed, although I doubt that any angel is going to keep track of it up there in heaven. Siavosh has a cup of tea, and we make the arrangements for the next day. He thanks me shyly and leaves.

The next morning, I go to my appointment. It's the first trimester and my classes are not that serious. Agha Baji is ready and sitting there waiting for me. She is wearing her party dress, a silver-colored veil with little white polka dots, and black plastic boots up to her calf, fastened with a zipper instead of laces. We take a taxi, and get off at Shah Square. I am still embarrassed. But I realize that no one is taking any notice of us. So we don't seem unusual. I take her arm and bit by bit we head down the street.

When we get to the cinema she perks up, as if she was sleepwalking until now and has suddenly woken up. She looks at everything very

---

[11] Siavosh, son of Kay Kavous, is a prince whose life and tragic death has a prominent place in Ferdowsi's epic poem, the Shahnameh. Siavosh was made to go through fire to prove his innocence against the allegations of his stepmother, Soudabeh.

carefully. She is watching my every move. As if she is collecting memories. Or uncovering a secret or cracking a code. I buy tickets and we enter the cinema. She stands in the middle of the lobby and stares around as if in a stupor. To get her out of this state, I motion to the refreshment stand and ask if she would like something to eat. She shakes her head. I carelessly ask, would she like to go to the restroom? I immediately regret it. I guess that was an offensive question. Besides, going up and down the stairs to get to the bathrooms at Mahtab Cinema knocks my breath out, never mind Agha Baji's.

Fortunately, the cinema is not crowded and everyone is doing their own thing. Agha Baji is startled by the sound of three or four chimes a few minutes before we sit down. They open the theater doors. She throws me a questioning glance. I hold her arm and guide her inside the theater. We ask the man at the door if we can sit up front. He gives us both an inquisitive look, but says there's no problem. As we enter, Agha Baji stiffens. Standing there with an open mouth, she stares at all the empty seats. A few other chimes bring her back to motion. We go ahead and sit seven rows from the screen. I steal a look at her. She is sitting cross-legged on the chair, adjusting her veil. The lights go off, and for about a minute, everything is covered by darkness and silence. Moments later, the glare of the usher's flashlight falls on us. He probably thinks we are up to something and wants to catch us at it. As Agha Baji turns her face toward the light, the usher switches off the light right away. Relieved, I lean back and wait for the beginning of the film. I am sure that I am not going to be scared of the ending. Agha Baji is by my side.

For the entire duration of the film, she does not utter a sound. Not a cough or a sneeze, or a yawn, or a sigh, a groan, a movement. Nothing. Hunched over, she's staring at the screen like a statue. When the shower scene is finished, I look at her. She is still motionless. I suspect that she has fallen asleep. I bend forward a little to see how she is. She turns toward me, frowning. Embarrassed, I lean back and become immersed in the film again. I had decided to watch her in the basement sequence, but I got so nailed by the film that I forgot. Toward the end, the part where they take Anthony Perkins to the sheriff's office, I cautiously throw her a glance. The only difference is that she is now grabbing the chair in front of her with both hands.

The lights go on. I take a deep breath and get up. I put my hand on her shoulder and call her name. She moves her head a few times, as if she is talking to herself. I politely explain that the movie is finished and we must leave. She pulls herself toward the front of the chair a little. She puts her feet down and gets up. On the whole, she looks tired and drained, but her eyes are shining. As we exit the cinema from the side street, she covers her face with her hand so that the bright light doesn't bother her. Then she looks this way and that a few times, as if she has forgotten where we are. It's one of those days when the sun is shining and everything seems brimming with life. A cool, pleasant breeze is blowing. Boys and girls from the Hadaf schools pass us by. The sparrows chirp and twitter as they frolic among the branches of the trees. I am suddenly overcome with a feeling of immense joy. I put my arm around her shoulder and elatedly ask, "So, Agha Baji, did you like the movie?"

She gives a faint smile and nods.

I ask, "Did you figure out the story?"

It takes her a few moments to answer, "Yes . . . but I haven't figured out the way of the world yet."

It's cramming time before the final exams. Early mornings, I walk back and forth in a side street behind the Swiss embassy on Pasteur Street. I curse at the books and I curse myself. Whenever my grandmother sees me, she angrily says, "You're going to get stomach cramps and the runs! You're going to get a cough! Look at him! He's thin as a rake! Eat something! Sleep a little! You're going to get sick!"

I can't deal with this kind of talk now. My lips move all the time like people mumbling magical incantations, or like old men with false teeth. I am reviewing all my subjects. Physics, Chemistry, Algebra, Animal Biology, Plant Biology, Evolution, English . . . oh . . . oh! What was the formula for the friction of bodies on a flat surface? . . . Damn the effect of hydrochloric acid on methane . . . How to draw an ellipse on coordinate axes? . . . What kind of protein can be found in the hemocyanin of invertebrates? . . . What does suberification in plants mean? . . . Archaean, Alconican, Cambrian, Silurian, Devonian, are the Precambrian and first eras in geology . . . Hamlet, whose father is dead, is the chief character in the play. . . . Everything is jumbled up in my mind.

One morning at seven-thirty I see Siavosh in Pasteur Square. I am in no mood to say hello, but we run directly into each other, so there's no way I can get out of it. Several times, back and forth, we ask how are you, and several times, back and forth, we thank each other.

I suddenly remember Agha Baji. I feel close enough to my fellow cinema-enthusiast to ask after her. In a gloomy tone, he murmurs that she is the hospital. What is her illness? He just says, "Old age."

That night, when my grandmother hears about this, she makes me promise to go and visit her at the hospital. She herself has a bad leg and can't take one step forward. I moan and groan a little, but I accept.

The next afternoon, she has wrapped up a bundle of gifts in a cloth for me to take for Agha Baji. I lift the cloth layers and take a look inside. There's a bag full of sugarplums, a few pieces of rock candy with a dizzying fragrance of saffron, a set of fine blue prayer beads, and a travel-size water pipe with its crystal water jar and a bag of tobacco. I didn't know Agha Baji smoked a water pipe.

"She had quit, but now it doesn't matter anymore," Grandmother says.

The room in the hospital has two beds. The bed closer to the door is empty. Agha Baji is lying on the bed next to the window, looking at the sky. Siavosh is sitting on the only chair in the room, reading a newspaper. I enter and say hello. I've been smart enough to buy three white carnations. Both of them are surprised and delighted to see me. Siavosh walks around the room nervously. He finally finds a glass and puts the flowers in it. I put the bundle on Agha Baji's lap and give her my grandmother's greetings. She opens the bundle with interest. She takes out the gifts one by one with appreciation. When she gets to the water pipe, she beams with happiness. Siavosh casts a look of displeasure in my direction and warns his grandmother against smoking the water pipe. He's about to throw the bag of tobacco in the wastebasket under the bed. But he doesn't. He probably thinks I would be offended. He explains that smoking a water pipe would be dangerous for Agha Baji. He spices up his explanations with a few medical terms to drive the point across. Then he concentrates on serving me refreshments. I thank him and say that I have to go. He insists that I sit down, stay a few minutes and eat something. Then he glances at his watch and says that he is late for his class. He gives a few major and minor recommendations to his grandmother. He shakes hands with me and leaves. There are a few moments of silence. I glance at Agha Baji. She points to the water pipe with her eyebrows. She winks encouragingly toward me and invites me to take part in the forbidden act. Happy to collaborate, I get up and remind her of everything Siavosh said. Nonchalantly, she shakes her head and says, "You have to be your own doctor."

I fill the jar of the water pipe halfway and give it to her. I adjust its wooden body on top of the crystal water jar. She wets the mouthpiece of the pipe with her mouth and sets it in the hole. She takes a puff and gets the bubbling action going. It seems that there is too much water in the jar. She blows into it and about half a cup of water spills out from the pipe to the ground. She puffs again, and this time the water is exactly right. Under her supervision, I take a handful of tobacco. I wet it under the sink in the room several times, and then I squeeze the tobacco so that it absorbs the water well. Then I arrange it on top of the water pipe. Suddenly both of us realize that we have forgotten the most important thing: charcoal. Where could one get charcoal? Upset by this obvious oversight, she looks around a few times. Then she thinks of something, and asks, "Aren't there any coffeehouses around here?"

I take the head of the water pipe and leave the hospital. She had guessed right. In the side street next to the hospital, a few people are sitting under the shade of a weeping willow drinking tea in front of a coffeehouse. I enter and ask for hot coal. The coffeehouse waiter delicately places a few pieces of hot coal on the pipe head. I want to pay him, but he does not accept any money. On the way back, I keep blowing on the coals to keep them burning. I enter and give the pipe head to Agha Baji. She puts the pipe on her knees and sits up straight. She swallows her saliva, and puffs out her chest. She puts the mouthpiece on the side of her lips and begins to puff. I am standing directly in front of her, watching her, engrossed. When the smoke begins to come out of the pipe, her lids get very heavy. She closes her eyes and bends to the left and right like a pendulum. She hums a song under her breath that I can't understand. It's probably in the Lori dialect. Although I can't make out the words, it sounds sad.

Suddenly the door opens and a short, fat nurse rolls into the room. With her eyes popping, she stares at Agha Baji and says, "I beg your pardon? We might as well have called Samia Jamal for the party, too!"[12]

---

[12] Probably a famous singer or dancer of the time.

With a touch of indifference and a trace of mockery, Agha Baji stares straight back at the nurse. Then she openly breaks out into song:

If you had told me you would visit me by my sickbed,
I would not have foregone the pleasure of illness, for this world or the next. . . .

The nurse narrows her eyes and rolls her head several times. Then with contrived anger she grabs the water pipe from Agha Baji's hands and says, "When water flows upward, the frog sings an *abu-ata* song."[13]

She empties the pipe head into the garbage bin under the bed and pours the water from the jar. When she's done with that, she wheels in a carriage from behind the door into the room, fills up a syringe with a red medicine and distilled water. For the first time, she glances at me. I go to the window and look outside. Not too far away, a flock of pigeons is flying around. One of them, pure white, is flying higher than anyone else. I had meant to be looking away until the nurse was done with the injection, but I become completely engrossed in the pigeons and lose track of time. Alone or in groups the pigeons sit on the roof of a two-story house on the opposite side of the street, except for the white one, which is still in relentless flight. I feel compelled to pursue it with my gaze until it sits down. As if the pigeon knows this, it keeps on lowering its altitude but then goes up again. I tell myself that if the pigeon sits after I have counted up to three hundred, then Agha Baji will get well and go home. I start counting. But in the middle, I forget whether I had said that Agha Baji will go home safely if the pigeon sits *before* I count to three hundred or *after* I count to three hundred. Now I don't know whether I should count slow or fast. I am afraid that Agha Baji's life may be hanging on my counting. Suddenly I panic and my heart begins to beat fast. I regret this deal that I made with myself. I worry about the pigeon. The closer I get to three hundred, the more I worry. I close my eyes and stop counting. I imagine Agha Baji in her youth. I haven't seen it but . . . long tresses of hair, like embroidered flowers in a tapestry, down to the curve of her waist. Her brow, smooth as marble. Eyes, brown as the eyes of a gazelle. Thick bow-shaped eyebrows. Nose like a chickpea. Lips, parting in a smile like the shell of a pistachio, and

---

[13] *Abu-ata* is one of the *dastgahs* or scale systems of Persian classical music. This proverb essentially means that really strange things happen during unusual times.

the dimple in her chin — an abyss for lovers to plunge into . . . I open my eyes. Having done a few spectacular somersaults as a finale to his flight, the pigeon finally sits among the other pigeons and is lost from sight. I turn around and encounter Agha Baji's tired and teary eyes. I smile, and to break the silence, say, "Agha Baji, do you remember we went to the cinema together?"

She narrows her eyes and shakes her head as she remembers. She asks, "Why do you think the son kept his ma's skeleton?"

I hadn't thought about *Psycho* from this angle. I wanted to explain that every film has a distractive gizmo. The mother's skeleton is the distractive gizmo of *Psycho*. But I figure that this explanation is too long and complicated. For this reason, I use Hitchcock's own term and say, "Agha Baji, the mother's skeleton is the MacGuffin."[14]

I instantly regret having said it. Showing off my knowledge of cinema to Agha Baji, of all people. Filled with shame, I look at her. Her face, furrowed from the sheer incomprehension of what I had said, suddenly opens up. With a bitter smile, she nods her head knowingly. She looks at the sky from the window and says, "Yes. You are absolutely right . . . the last nail in my coffin . . . the final touchstone!"

I now see that the matter has become even more complicated. When I said MacGuffin, Agha Baji heard "my coffin." I let the matter go at this point, but I am deep in thought about what Agha Baji's own MacGuffin could possibly be.

Agha Baji does not survive the hospital. A month and half later, when my grandmother returns from the burial service, she is in a foul mood from the heat and rage. I put a pitcher of ice water and a fan next to her and leave the house to get out of her way. When I return at night, I see from her red eyes that she's had a good cry. Dinner consists of leftovers. We sit in silence on the floor around a tablecloth. I take my time and eat little mouthfuls so that she'll begin talking. She finally lets out a long sigh, and says, "What is a human being? Sighs and blood . . . God rest her soul — no one respected her will — either when she was alive, or when she died. I hope at least they'll respect her will in the next world."

---

[14] Hitchcock's MacGuffin referred to some object that was significant to the characters but not of great interest to the story — for example, the secret formula in *The 39 Steps* and *Torn Curtain,* and uranium in wine bottles in *Notorious*.

I look at her with curiosity. She recounts that according to Agha Baji's will they were supposed to bury a box beside her, but the grave diggers refuse to comply. The matter was referred to the higher authorities. They too opposed it, claiming that it was against regulations. Finally, they put all their heads together, and the matter was resolved by buying another grave site next to Agha Baji's and burying the box there. Astonished, I ask, "Box? What box?"

She says that it was a metallic box, somewhat larger than a box of candy; it had a lock, and was sealed on three sides. But what was in the box? She thinks for a few moments and says, "God only knows."

I feel my hair standing on end. I get up and begin pacing this way and that. I say, "MacGuffin, MacGuffin was in the box!"

As if she has heard an insult, she screws up her face and says, "*What* was in there?"

I say, "The touchstone . . . Jeff's hand . . . don't you remember?"

She freezes. Without blinking, she moves her eyes from side to side. She is probably rummaging about in her memory for details of the past. She looks like she suspects something. But then she shakes her head back and forth several times. As if she is erasing something unpleasant from the tablet of her mind. She waves her hand toward me dismissively and says, "Oh go on, go and get your head examined! This is all a lot of hot air . . ."

She can't accept what I said, or maybe, she just doesn't want to.

That night in bed, I decide to go visit Siavosh the next day. But then I change my mind. What would I tell him? Give him the good news? And anyway, how do I know that my speculation is correct? There could have been anything in the box. Anything, including Jeff's hand. By the way, "Why *did* the boy keep his mother's skeleton?" I don't know, but I think that in a world this big and among the three billion people who live in it, only Agha Baji, and possibly Hitchcock, could have known the answer.

— *Translated by Nahid Mozaffari*

Farkhondeh Aghai

Farkhondeh Aghai was born in 1956 in Tehran. She earned a master's degree in sociology at Tehran University. Her first collection of stories, *Green Hills,* was published in 1987. Her second collection, *A Little Secret,* was published in 1993, and won the Gardun Literary Prize for that year. Her later publications include two other short story collections, *One Woman, One Love* and *Clay Cats,* and a novel entitled *The Lost Gender.* Aghai often writes about women in contemporary Iran, depicting their inner psychological turmoil as well as the ways in which they have learned to cope with or resist social and gender injustices.

A Little Secret is from her collection of stories by the same name, published in 1993. It takes place in the women's ward of a hospital in Tehran during the Iran-Iraq War (1980–1988). Vaji, like many other women, has spent her entire life nurturing and worrying about other people. In her poignant story, she gradually comes to grips with her own affliction and reality by witnessing the tragic unfolding of the life of a young, gravely injured soldier convalescing in the same ward.

A LITTLE SECRET

Vaji pulled the blanket up over her chest. She pursed her lips and braced herself. The pain was getting worse. A pain that started in her legs and moved up to climax in her belly. She clutched her stomach. A cold sweat drenched her body. A shudder ran through her spine. She heaved a tired and heavy sigh. Her mouth was dry, it tasted bad. With great effort she picked up the glass of water and took a sip. The cold water touched her lips and made its way down her parched throat. She fell back on the pillow. The pain was gone. Comfortable, calm. There was no sign of the agony that had her twisting only a moment ago. She closed her eyes and heard the calm and constant voice of a young man whispering lovingly.

"If you don't come tomorrow I'll be really hurt. For God's sake, please come. I miss you. It's so easy to get here. You go to the station and take the bus to Hasan-Abad. You get off in the big circle and it's a two-minute walk. Everyone knows where it is; people will show you if you ask. Then you come to the fourth floor. The women's ward. Well, don't tell them. Pretend you're going to school. Fine, don't come alone. Come with one of your friends. Why don't you just come with A'zam? Where is she? Give her the phone; let me talk to her. What's there to be shy about? We're going to be family. I have something to tell her. Something. Don't get upset. I just want to thank her for getting my letters to you. She's been great. The guy who falls in love with her is going to be really lucky. Not everyone is like you. I've been here for two months. You haven't even come to say hello. I'll wait for you tomorrow. Come on, you're making excuses again . . ."

The man's voice seemed to go on forever. Vaji knew that as long as she listened she would hear him. She got up, closed the door, and went back to bed. She pulled the blanket up over her head and went to sleep. For the past two months the mornings at the hospital had started very early. The night nurse, with tired and bloodshot eyes, would shake the thermometer in the air and put it in the patient's mouth and walk away. Another nurse would show up with a notebook.

"Any bowel movement?"

She would make a note, take the thermometer, read it, make another note, and leave. The next nurse would come carrying bedpans. She would check the numbers on the beds and hand them out to some of the patients and leave. Another nurse would follow with a basket full of syringes. She would look at her notebook and walk up to a bed.

"Roll up your sleeve."

She would tie the plastic strap tight around the arm and say as she prepared the syringe, "How many days have you been in bed here? How many kids do you have? Girls bring good luck. I have two. When was your operation? Okay, that's it."

She would put the syringe, now filled with blood, back in her basket and leave. The head nurse would arrive pushing a cart full of bottles of pills. For each patient she would count one, two, three pills, put them in a paper cup, and place it on the counter.

"Well, take them. It's better if you take them while I'm here. I've heard you don't take your pills. Are you trying to save some money?"

Another nurse would bring the injections, and then it was the janitor's turn to sweep the floor and mop it with a piece of burlap. An orderly followed him with sponges and detergents to clean the bathroom, and then a woman with a wet rag dusted the dresser and the window ledge. She would throw away the wilted flowers, rinse her rag, and with her departure, "Mr. Mohammad" would put the breakfast tray on the counter. The head nurse would report on the beds in a loud voice and turn them over to the morning shift and leave. And then everything was like the day before, with people constantly coming and going, noon and night.

Vaji picked up her teacup and walked out of the room. Her roommate was combing her hair. Vaji knew that if she waited another minute the room would reek of the pungent and repulsive smell of toothpaste. Work was well under way in the ward, but the patients who still had the energy to walk had not yet left their beds. In the hallway Vaji sat down on the couch by the window. Hasan Azarmi, the patient in the room next door, was the first to finish his breakfast and was walking over with his cane to sit next to her. They had seen each other every day for quite a while. Azarmi said hello under his breath and sat next to her, facing the elevator. He lit a cigarette and ran his hand over his bandaged eye. He did this every few minutes. It was as though he wanted to make sure it was still there. Vaji didn't have the patience for

Azarmi. With that cigarette that never left the corner of his mouth and the smoke that made her nauseous. As always, she opened the window and sat with her back to him. By the time Azarmi lit his second cigarette Vaji got up and walked back to her room. The doctors would be there at nine.

"How do you feel today?"

"I'm better, but last night I was in terrible pain and had a fever again."

"The nurse didn't give you a shot for your pain?"

"I didn't want any. But Doctor, you said I would get better after the operation."

"Definitely. The pain you have now is because of the operation and the stitches. Today at noon we're having a meeting to discuss your case. We'll decide on your treatment and medication."

"Is it dangerous?"

"No. It's just a small tumor the size of an egg. If it becomes necessary, we'll talk more about it later."

The doctor walked over to Vaji's roommate, who had kidney trouble. Under the sheets Vaji pressed on her stomach. She thought the tumor was larger than an egg. Perhaps the size of a round and solid ball that had hardened.

Her roommate was sitting next to the window. "The doctor said I'm released."

"Good for you."

"Don't worry, you'll be released soon."

"Yeah."

And with her thin yellow hands she counted: five, six, seven. She was the seventh person who had roomed with her and was now leaving, and still her situation was unclear.

"I'm going to the room at the end of the hall. Everyone's there. Aren't you coming?"

"I'll come later."

The woman left. Vaji thought, "Mrs. Amini was my first roommate, and now the seventh one is leaving. Mrs. Amini had cancer. It was her breast. Her left breast. She was a nurse. How could she have not realized? She was in the hospital for two months." Vaji had just been admitted. And Amini had died a week later. Vaji thought, "Mine isn't cancer. It's been two months and I'm still in good shape. Only the occasional chill, fever and pain. That's not unusual after an operation. Everyone has it."

And she touched the egg in her stomach. No, it was bigger. The doctor had made a mistake. In fact, they had taken two-pound tumors out of some patients' stomachs. The doctor had said, "It's a small cyst. A one-hour operation." And they had opened up her stomach but the cyst was still there.

"There's nothing wrong with me. I know."

She listened. She could hear Azarmi's quiet voice through all the noise and confusion.

"But sweetheart, why didn't you come? I had my eyes on the door all day. Someday I'll make up for all these days. You'll see. I've been waiting since this morning. I had put out fruits and pastries, thinking Miss Ashraf would be here any minute. In another minute. In another minute. In another two minutes . . . You're really cruel. I smoked a whole pack. Don't worry about my cigarettes. I get them somehow. I dreamt of you all night. I was sure you'd come. Of course you couldn't come in the morning. By six-thirty I went downstairs and told the guards. They're nice guys. I told them if you come on your way from school to bring you over to me. All you have to do is give them my name. Why? The doctor came. He said in two days he'll open up my left eye. Don't worry about it. One eye is better than none. I shouldn't have called you. But frankly I didn't have the heart. I thought maybe you came but couldn't find me. Obviously you didn't care at all . . ."

Two nurses started laughing.

"She stood him up again."

"Next time find a better fiancée."

The head nurse started yelling, "Mr. Azarmi, Mr. Azarmi. Please be a bit more considerate. Dr. Sedaqat has been waiting for a free phone line for an hour."

"All right, sister.[1] All right. Okay, fine. I'll call back tonight. For now, good luck."

The nurse asked, "She didn't come today, either?"

"No. But she's definitely coming tomorrow. I'll talk her into it."

---

[1] After the revolution, it became customary to address women as "sister" and men as "brother" to relay the sense that all Muslims are brothers and sisters.

They're lucky not to have a telephone at home and that her daughter isn't interested in this sort of thing, Vaji thought. She didn't like Azarmi's pushiness.

Slowly her body became hot. The pain was quietly crawling up her legs, heading for her stomach. Vaji curled up. She knew that in another minute she would be in agony. With all her might she pulled herself up and rang the buzzer. She passed out before the nurse could inject the painkiller.

When Vaji opened her dark and swollen eyes, a cool breeze from the window was stroking her body. In the dim light coming from the hallway she saw that the other bed was empty. From the corner of the door she could see the large circular nurses' station. One of the nurses, still holding her knitting needles, was napping. Two chairs were pulled together, and another nurse was sleeping on them. Vaji got up. She felt a dull pain in her stomach. She picked up her veil and wrapped it around her. From the corner of her eye, a nurse was discreetly watching her slow and heavy walk. There was no one there, not even Hasan Azarmi. The telephone, black and silent, was hanging on the wall. Vaji wondered how long she had slept. Was it noon or afternoon? She couldn't remember. She thought her husband and daughter, Farrokh, must have come while she was asleep. She sat by the window. Maybe they hadn't come. If they had, she would definitely have awakened. She got up, went back to her room, and turned on the light. A bag of fruits was sitting on her bedside table. So they had come when she was asleep. Was it her husband, Mokhtar, or Farrokh? Or both? What had they done with Reza? Cute little two-year-old Reza. Farrokh had said, "Don't worry, Mom. I'll take care of him."

But what can a young girl do? She counted. Fifteen, sixteen, seventeen, eighteen. She was eighteen years old now. Her young and cheerful eyes shone in her moonlike face framed by the veil. The black veil suited her. It brought out her fair skin and round face. "Mom, don't worry. Reza has gotten used to it. Sometimes he doesn't even remember."

So life went on without her. Peacefully. Everything was in its rightful place. She shuddered. The little worry inside her was growing larger. Her heart ached. Mrs. Amini, too, had been bedridden for two months. Then she had died. But she was a nurse. How could she not have realized that she had cancer? Every afternoon she would walk in the hallway. With her arms crossed she would gently caress her left breast. Unconsciously. She was no different from the patients being released the next day. Just a bit thinner, a bit paler. And one morning Mrs. Amini was gone. Without saying anything to Vaji. When she died everyone said, "She had cancer." Vaji thought, "Mine isn't cancer. If it was, I would know. It's not." In the beginning, the pain would come once a week and then she would have no more pain until the next week. Then why now, after the operation, was she in pain every night? And it didn't even leave her in peace during the day. The next morning the doctor was at her bedside.

"It's all your imagination and fear. The day before yesterday your case was discussed at the meeting. Everyone's opinion was favorable. We first diagnosed that the tumor is in the uterus and that we would remove it by a simple operation. But during the operation we realized that a benign tumor was in the area of your stomach and intestines. Of course, we took biopsies and as a result we couldn't give you a definite answer until today. But from now on you should put your mind at ease. The committee decided not to perform another operation. Over the next few months we will treat you with chemotherapy and medication as an outpatient."

"When can I go home?"

"Whenever you want. But in my opinion it would be better for you to stay here. You will be under more supervision."

She could hear Azarmi's voice: "I adore this great mother-in-law. Good for her. It's good you asked her permission to come. You can't believe how great I felt yesterday. After you left, all I did was think of you. To be honest, I didn't think you'd come. The guys from the neighborhood came over yesterday morning. Your brother was there, too. No, there's nothing to be afraid of. You should've been there. They brought tons of fruit and nuts and cigarettes. By the way, Ashraf, why did you get so thin? What are you worried about? Really? Believe me, walking with a cane is a lot of fun. Come over again tomorrow. Please. Well, if you have to study, come the day after. Come so that I can see you more. Next time you have to come to my room. What's there to be embarrassed of? Aren't we engaged? But it's not good in the yard. Yeah, I saw the two women. Really? Are you serious? Was it really your mother?

Why didn't you say something? I saw her staring, but she had completely covered her face. I didn't recognize her. You should have introduced her. There was so much fruit and pastries upstairs, and you left without eating anything. Your mother is really kind. After you, I love her. You don't mind, do you? I told my mother and my family to only come on Fridays so it will be easier for you to come over. See how thoughtful I am? I'll wait for you tomorrow. Okay. The day after. This time you have to come to my room. I'll be hurt if you don't. Stay by the phone. I'll call again after these people are done with their calls. Good luck."

Vaji thought the man would never stop talking. She wished the phone wasn't right outside her room. The constant ringing, talking, pleasantries, compliments. What else is there to talk about with a patient other than their health? Vaji thought that if she had been Ashraf's mother she wouldn't have come, and she wouldn't have let her daughter come, either. Then she leaned forward to watch Azarmi leave with his cane, dragging his leg behind him.

So Ashraf had come. Right when she was sleeping. I would have seen her if I had been awake. Farrokh had come, too, but I was unconscious. Azarmi is right to have hope, but what about me?

Vaji could hear Nahid at the end of the hallway. She knew that by now she was crouched on her bed, shaking her dark skinny hands, and with her thick Dezful accent she was screaming.[2]

"Don't get me wrong, but you hear this is the capital and it means people from everywhere else in the country should be homeless and destitute. Their young should stand in front of bullets so the high and mighty can live their easy comfortable lives. So they can strut down the street and show off. No way! We toppled that throne. And we'll deal with this menace, too—so well that even you'll say well done. You have no conscience. Day and night they drop bombs on our heads and we don't make a peep. Then you come here to the capital, and it's as though there's no war at all. Once in a blue moon they sound the siren just for the heck of it, and these miserable creatures run and hide in a hole. You people have no shame! I pray you'll all be barren and childless. Leave me alone. You're breaking my arm. Bastards. Am I lying?"

And her voice would die off in her throat as she struggled. In a

---

[2] Dezful is a town in southwestern Iran, near the border with Iraq. The city, under constant missile attack, was devastated during the Iran-Iraq War.

few minutes, in the silence of the hospital, a woman with large broad hands would noisily collect the pitchers from the counters in each room and she would dip her red bowl into the small slippery ice cubes and pour them into the pitchers. And now a woman whose nose had been bandaged was looking at Vaji:

"You've had an operation?"

"Yes."

"Is it tough?"

"No. It's only tough after you regain consciousness."

The telephone rang, and Vaji stopped paying attention to her roommate. A second later, the nurses were all running around in a frenzy. Vaji could see them come and go from the narrow opening of the door. But she only realized why when the sound of the military march rose from the speakers. She walked out of her room. The patients were all standing in the hallway watching. They were taking the stretchers down on the elevator and bringing folding beds and dusty mattresses out of storage. Two people were setting up the beds and another one was wiping them down. The speakers were broadcasting the military march and the latest news from the war front. Two janitors and an assistant nurse were going room to room, and the head nurse, Mrs. Naseri, was shouting orders. Hers was the only constant voice that could be heard every day, from seven in the morning until two in the afternoon.

"Pull this bed forward. Push that one back. Now bring in that folding bed and put it between the two.

"Okay lady, I know you're sick. But please help us out a bit. There's a war going on, and it's out of my hands. Quickly. Yes. Take your things to the other room."

Vaji thought this was the best time to change her room. She took her clothes out of the dresser. Naseri's voice rose again. "No, Mrs. Vassel, you stay in this room. We can keep an eye on you here. Mr. Habib, help them take out that dresser and make room for the bed.

"Mr. Azarmi, what are you doing getting in the way? You better go make a phone call and stay out of the way.

"Okay, that's fine. So far we've made room for all the women in this section of the ward. The other half of the ward will be for the brothers."

The ambulance sirens from the street and the sound from the loudspeakers drowned out Naseri's voice. Within the hour one more bed was added to the rooms with two beds, and the rooms with three beds were transformed into rooms with five beds. A long row of folding beds stood along the hallway walls and young men — once in a while an older man — lay on each. An hour still remained before the regular visiting hours, but the rooms were already packed with crowds of people crying and weeping at the patients' bedsides. In the hallway, someone was rubbing the shoulders of a woman who had passed out. The tables were piled with bouquets of flowers and boxes of pastries. Vaji thought, "How did they find out so quickly?" There were still patients coming out of the operating room. It was past two o'clock, but Naseri's voice could still be heard. The air conditioners and fans were working full force. The windows were open. Still, hot, and suffocating air filled the rooms.

Mokhtar had come alone; later Vaji's mother came. She stood next to Vaji's bed. There were people from Dezful visiting Nahid, who was now Vaji's roommate. A few others stood around the bandaged face. Vaji had trouble breathing.

"Let's go out to the yard," Vaji said.

"Isn't it bad for you?"

"No. It's actually very good for me."

Ignoring the pain that pressured her stomach, Vaji put on her chador and made her way to the yard through the mob. Mokhtar was calm, but every time his eyes met Vaji's his upper lip quivered.

"Farrokh didn't come?"

"No. She had to study."

"The doctor said there's no need to operate."

"He told me, too."

"When did he speak with you?"

"Yesterday. You were sleeping when we came. The doctor stayed to speak with me. How many times did I tell you to go see a doctor? You didn't. You waited till things got worse."

"There you go again. There's nothing wrong with me. I'm just weak. I want to come home."

"Why?"

"What do you mean?"

"Nothing. I just mean, are you uncomfortable here? Don't they take good care of you?"

"I miss Reza. They bring in more war casualties every day. They need beds. There's nothing wrong with me, I'm just taking up someone else's bed."

"Stay a couple of weeks and rest. At home Reza is naughty and he'll get on your nerves."

"I want to come just for him."

"Actually, it's better if he doesn't see you. He's gotten used to it. If you come home and then have to go back to the hospital he'll be upset again."

Vaji looked at her mother who, though silent, was listening intently. "Mother, say something."

Mother looked at Vaji. Her eyes were brimming with tears. In a choked yet calm voice she said, "It's better if you don't come. Stay another week and rest."

An hour later, when Vaji returned to her room, the janitor was sweeping the floor. Nahid was looking at her burned legs, talking to herself.

"I'll leave when my legs get well. Anywhere is better than here. I hate it here. I hated it from the start. Once in a blue moon I'd come to visit my relatives. I don't want to come to Tehran anymore."

Vaji took off her veil and lay down on the bed. She knew that one word from her would get Nahid started again. Nahid stared at the woman whose eyes peeked through a bandaged face. Her dark, olive-skinned face turned crimson. She slapped her knees.

"God doesn't love me. He stuck me here with this bitch again. There was no cure for me in Dezful. Dear God, don't make me needy of this person and that. You know, present company excluded, most of these Tehran uptown snobs are godless. I hope their houses come down on their heads. They have no religion; they don't believe in God. Oh God, could these planes come and bomb *this* place one day? What's the matter; why are you all standing here again? Am I lying? Every time there's a siren these delicate ladies jump into their husband's arms. Aren't we women, too? A dozen times my kid has gotten so scared from the sound of the planes and the bombs that he peed in the middle of our meal. You don't even wear proper head scarves. It's beneath you. Our kids are being martyred by the dozens. Our beautiful young people go to the front and never come back. You snub your nose. Bitches. Let go of me. Let go of my arms. It hurts. You can't find a single honorable man anymore. Leave it to me to teach them all a lesson. The country is being washed away and these godless uptown snobs are fast asleep."

The patients are all gathered at the door, and the nurse has injected the sedative but it still hasn't taken effect. The woman's voice resonates in the ward:

"Strangle me. Kill me. Just like the others. Her shirt is open down to her navel and she throws a lace scarf over her head. I'll rip her apart myself. Shameless. God, God, save me. What was my sin? Why did you do this to me? Everyone dies from mortars. Miserable me, I get burned by boiling water. I have no luck."

And now the head nurse is standing over Nahid. The woman cries and beats herself on the head. The head nurse says, "What? What's the matter, lady? Why are you screaming? Did you give her the sedative, Nurse? Fine. Go to sleep. You'll be released in two days. Every damn day you make a scene. Your nerves are bad. Well, so are everyone else's. Nurse, stay with her. If she starts screaming again let me know."

The head nurse had barely made it out of the room when Nahid roared, "She's one of them."

"What did you say?"

"I said it's no one's fault. It's all because of the water. Anyone who drinks the water here goes crazy."

"You're at it again? Quiet."

The patients had not yet dispersed. Vaji, despite her pain, left the room. She didn't want to be there. Next door, by the window, Azarmi was sitting up in bed eating pistachios. A young man with his shoulder all bandaged up was lying on his back and moaning. Next to him, a middle-aged man lay in bed with his eyes closed and a woman, apparently his wife, and a few young girls and boys stood around him.

His left arm was in a cast, and there were weights hanging from his legs at the bottom of the bed. In his right hand the man was quietly clenching a stem of narcissus and once in a while he would raise it to his nose and smell it. The janitor had come to kick the visitors out, and now Azarmi, with a cane in one hand and a chair in the other, was off to sit next to the telephone. He is going to start talking any minute now, Vaji thought. And she walked to the window at the other end of the hallway. The woman standing next to her was looking out at the street, blowing kisses. A four- or five-year-old boy was perched on his father's shoulders, laughing. So why didn't Mokhtar bring Reza to see her, to wave to her?

"Sister. Sister . . ."

An old Arab man with an IV in his arm was sprawled on a folding bed. He could barely speak Persian.

"My arm. My arm hurts, sister. The needle in my arm hurts."

The old man's right arm was all swollen where the IV had been inserted. Vaji turned to call the nurse.

"Not that I don't want to see you. But if you can't, I won't insist. I really miss you. Sometimes I want to come and get you myself. I'm tired of this. No. They're really nice kids, especially the sisters, they really take care of us, but you know, it's not just a day or two. Especially in the women's ward. The doctor says it will take a long time for my eye to heal. I'm in no hurry, but I'm worried about you. Nothing. Just like that. I feel bad you didn't do well on your test. It's all my fault. But I'll make it up to you. Forget it. When I get out of here I'll study with you every day. You'll definitely pass. No, I still remember the lessons. If I take one look, I'll remember. Still I'm lucky to hear your voice. I have a roommate from Bostan. He got shot in the shoulder. His love is still in his village. There's an old guy, too. He's a wreck. There's always a herd of people around him. Not that I'm jealous, but I'd be really happy if you came. You don't have to study any more now. I know you failed the test, but we'll make up for it."

"Cut it short, brother. You're driving us crazy."

One of the young boys lying in the hallway had had enough.

Azarmi was still talking, and the janitor was bringing the trays of food and Nahid was snoring and the bandaged face was looking at herself in the mirror. The pain in her legs had quietly started. Vaji knew that it would creep higher and higher and it would squat on her stomach. She pressed the emergency button.

"Nurse, please, sedatives."

"Why?"

"The pain has started."

By the time the nurse pulled the syringe out of Vaji's flesh, Nahid from Dezful, the bandaged face, the tray of food, Azarmi's voice, the black telephone on the wall, the constant ringing, the swollen hand, the narcissus, the moans of the young man, had all faded away. Vaji had clenched her fists and was pressing hard on the large egg inside which did not resemble an egg at all. Silence filled the hospital. With her eyes closed, Vaji could hear only the sound of water dripping at regular intervals from the faucet, and then she didn't hear that, either.

And Mokhtar, serene and happy, was carrying Reza on his shoulders, and Reza was blowing kisses to his mother and waving to come into her arms. Vaji was far away, so far away that despite all her eagerness she could not reach out to take him into her arms. Farrokh, wearing her modest black veil, had come to take Reza from Mokhtar's shoulders, to cradle him like a mother. And to cover him with her black veil, and underneath it Reza was struggling and Farrokh was taking him away, and Mokhtar, without uttering a word, was watching her. And now Reza was no longer there. Farrokh wasn't there, and Mokhtar's shadow had faded and the sound of the water dripping from the faucet had replaced it. Vaji opened her eyes. Nahid had pulled the sheet over up her head and the bandaged face no longer had those hazel eyes with which to look at Vaji.

Her dry and bitter mouth bothered her. Vaji got up, pain was swirling around in her back. She put on her head scarf and walked out into the hallway. The beds were all arranged in rows down the hallway. All the lights, except for one, had been turned off. Next door, the middle-aged man had stuffed the wilted narcissus in his nostrils and was sleeping. In the hallway a young man was smoking in bed. He heard Vaji's footsteps and turned his face to the wall. The smoke from his cigarette bounced off the wall and faded away. They had amputated both his legs. The sheet at the foot of the bed was flat, as though he had never had legs. The other young men were all fast asleep. Under their beds, duffel bags were thrown here and there next to bags of fruits, pastries, and canned food. The old Arab, holding on to his IV stand, was standing at the window watching the city sleep. Vaji, despite her grogginess, still wanted to walk. Outside her room, she stopped thinking of Reza, Farrokh, and Mokhtar. The coughing, the vomiting, the chills and the fevers, the one vomiting blood, the cigarette being lit, the groans of pain, the buzzer that woke the nurse up with a start, were all there. But still there was silence that lasted until the night shift transferred everything, neat and tidy, to the day shift. And the nurses would come again with tired and bloodshot eyes carrying thermometers, bedpans, vials of blood, bottles of pills, and syringes; and then the janitors would follow with their brooms, sponges, and wet rags, and the wilted flowers would be thrown away. Then the toilets would be flushed, faces washed, once in while here and there a comb would be put to use and a toothbrush would clean someone's teeth, then there was the breakfast tray and after that the voice of the head nurse reporting on the beds, and now Mrs. Naseri's voice filled the ward and the doctors came one by one to visit their patients and then the ward's doctor who would examine the rest. Vaji stood at the window in her room. The bandaged face had been taken to the operating room and Nahid had gone off with her flask to drink tea in her old room.

"Mrs. Vajiheh Vassel, bed number twenty-two."

Vaji shuddered at the sound of the words. She turned around. A beautiful young woman dressed in white, holding a folder, with a smile on her lips and light hazel eyes, was waiting for an answer. Vaji, who had never seen the woman before, went toward her bed. She was bent over as she walked, it seemed to lessen her pain.

"That's me."

The woman's smile vanished. "I'm the social worker. I wanted to speak with you, if it's okay."

And now the woman was pulling a chair up to Vaji's bed.

"What is your husband's ID card number?"

"Two-zero-eight-one."

The woman looked at her folder and read: "Place of employment, Rey. Place of residence, Shahr-e-Rey. And you are thirty-five. You have two children. Daughter seventeen, son two. A fifteen-year age difference is a lot, isn't it?"

"I couldn't have children. I went through treatment until God gave me Reza."

"Who is he with now?"

"He's with my daughter, Farrokh. When Farrokh is in school my mother keeps him."

"You've been here for two months. The hospital in Rey referred you, a Dr. Farsi. Well, excuse me for asking, but do you have any problems or issues with your daughter?"

"No."

"Look, Mrs. Vassel, I'm a social worker. I visit most of the patients here. My intention isn't to pry into anyone's private affairs. But to the extent possible, I have to solve the problems that I can handle. I mean, I want to, and my job requires it. How? Well, for example, if you are a patient here and there is no one to take care of your child, we will introduce him to a child-care center or other things of this nature. So you have no problems with your daughter. Do you want to use a child-care center?"

"No. My mother is there."

"And about your husband, his job, salary, his behavior. Does he really treat you and the children well?"

"Yes. He just won't bring Reza."

The woman, made a note with her delicate white hands,

"I'll speak with your husband. Now, about the hospital. For example, your roommates, nurses, doctors, is the food good? Do you have any complaints?"

"People leave me alone."

"You mean they ignore you?"

"No. I mean I don't care. There's always food and everyone is always around. They don't bother me."

"So you have no complaints about these things. If you have any questions or concerns I'm all ears."

The woman did not expect Vaji to say anything. But perhaps just to have said something, Vaji replied, "This Mr. Azarmi talks too much. He's always on the phone."

The woman looked at her file.

"He talks a lot. He thinks of nothing else."

"Put yourself in his shoes. Twenty years old, in love with a schoolgirl. His left leg is paralyzed, his left eye is blind, and soon he will lose sight in his right eye as well. With a body full of shrapnel that cannot be removed. You only see his laughter and his appearance."

"He says his eye will heal."

"I spoke with him. He is just beginning to find out about the extent of his medical condition. In any case, I will ask the head nurse to change your room so you won't be bothered by his phone calls anymore."

"No, no. It's fine here. If I want to change rooms then . . ."

"As you wish. Do you have any other questions?"

"About my illness. When can I go home?"

"The doctor says you have a small cyst in your stomach and intestines that will gradually go away with medication. But you shouldn't be in a hurry, you have to be patient. Your attending doctor believes your recovery is certain. The only problem is that it will be slow and gradual. You have to bear with it until you are one hundred percent well."

"That's what the doctor said."

"Yes, there is nothing more to it. Do you have any other problems?"

"No. Thank you very much."

"If you need me, dial extension 280 or come over to my office on the first floor, room 109."

Vaji followed the woman with her eyes and saw her waiting in front of the elevator. So she doesn't visit all the patients. She only sees some. Yesterday it was Mr. Azarmi, and today Vaji.

She tried to get up but couldn't. With every movement, the subtle pain in her stomach soared and dug deep into her bones. The phone rang and the voice of a woman echoed in the hallway.

"Bed number six, telephone.

"Bed number six, telephone."

Two men dressed in green wheeled in the woman with the bandaged face. One of them climbed up on the patient's bed and stood there, and the other one, strong and bulky, stared at Vaji.

"Sister, turn your face away."

Vaji turned to the wall. She had already seen how two men lift a patient up and throw her on the bed with full force. She still remembered the pain. When she opened her eyes she had for a moment seen the man's round fat face with that green cap standing over her and pushing her bed back and forth. They had just lifted her up like a piece of sacrificial meat and thrown her onto the bed, so that the man waiting there could grab the corner of the sheet and pull it to the middle of the bed and then, with one leap, jump down so that the nurse would bring a gown to cover her up. The bandaged face was wearing a gown, but the nurse came anyway to tidy her up, pull the sheet over her, hook up the IV and hang the urine bag to the bottom of the bed, and then she was done. The operation was over and now Nahid was standing over the patient and watching her.

"Indecency is all over her face. All these people from Tehran ever think about is their getup and their appearance. Oh, look how big my nose is. Oh, how ugly I look with this nose. What if I have it fixed?!"

Vaji muttered indifferently, "She had an accident."

"It's an excuse. It's just an excuse. Why do you believe it? I know these people from Tehran. The accident is an excuse."

Vaji closed her eyes. She didn't have any patience for Nahid's comments. Nahid left the room without another word. Azarmi was talking again:

"You go every day? In this heat? Don't get too tired. No. Who am I to disapprove? Actually, you were right to register for the make-up classes. No, I swear it's not because of me. Whether you get out of the house or not, I know you won't be coming to see me, I'm sure of it. Yes, well, your family and friends could think you failed because of me. Your classmates could say her love went to war, came back lame, and she has failed her exams. I'm not kidding. Then they'll start picking on you by singing the wedding song . . . and add: Watch out for the groom's lame leg! Hey, don't cry. I was just kidding. Ashraf, I swear I'm so down that I want the world to disappear. Come over so I can see you. Don't even come to my room if you don't want to. It's okay in the yard. What? Really? Congratulations. What did your sister have? Twins? That's great. How many kids do you want . . . ?"

This man will never run out of breath, Vaji thought. But oddly enough, Azarmi's voice didn't bother her anymore. She saw that there, outside her room, life went on. From the corner of the door she could see the hallway. The old Arab, holding his IV stand, walked slowly down the hall. His gown was completely open in the back and with his right hand the old man had bunched the two sides together and held them tight in his fist. Slowly, he pushed the IV stand forward and walked. From behind, you could see his dark and wrinkled thighs. He would go as far as the elevator. And then he would slowly pull the IV stand and walk back. Now he was wearing a white Arab headdress. He saw Vaji from the hallway. He nodded, she smiled, and he set off again. The wheelchairs came and went. A man with a missing leg, a missing arm, or a missing eye. Pain filled Vaji's stomach. She closed her eyes. With all her strength she clenched her stomach. Cold sweat drenched her body. She tried to think of Reza, of Farrokh and of Mokhtar, but pain did not release her until the moment of unconsciousness. When she opened her eyes Farrokh was standing at her bedside.

"Mom, do you feel better?"

"Yes, my girl."

"When are you coming home?"

"Real soon. Did you do well on your exam?"

And Farrokh laughed, with that peaceful smile and those perfectly straight teeth framed in that black veil that drew one's eyes to her face. And her smile began to fade until it was no longer there, and now Farrokh was far away and the pain no longer crawled up Vaji's legs, it was constant, there inside that large egg that did not resemble an egg at all.

Every few hours, the pain would start again, no longer from the legs but from the stomach, and it would climb all the way to the head, and from the other end it would stretch down as far as the knees. Then the body was feverish and the pain would climax. And then it would shrink, and inside the egg it would flutter, while heavy beads of sweat would cool on the skin and the moment would arrive when Vaji would let herself go limp on the sweat-drenched mattress.

In the morning Nahid came to Vaji's bedside with her duffel bag. She kissed her, said good-bye, and left. Vaji looked around, and the bandaged face was no longer there, either. She too was gone. Without farewells. Yesterday or the day before? She couldn't remember. How many is it so far? Six, seven, eight, nine. The ninth person had left, too. Mrs. Amini was the first one — she had cancer. She was a nurse, how come she had not figured it out? Carefree, she would stroll along the hallway. She would put her hand on her left breast and squeeze. She had a secret there, which she kept all to herself. She had shared a room with Vaji for a week. She had not even guessed what was really wrong with her. She had said that her heart ached and then one morning she was gone. They said she had cancer. One word: cancer. And every day, every hour, every minute, she had kept her hand pressed on that secret to make sure it wouldn't pop out. And now the ninth person had left. Vaji thought that one day it would be her turn to get up and kiss her roommates and to say, "I have been released. Good-bye. I don't have cancer. I know. If I did, I would know it. I'm not that clueless." Mrs. Amini had told Vaji that she was a nurse. How could she not have realized she had cancer? Why couldn't she have taken that secret and thrown it away? And every day she would press her hand on her left breast and caress it as though it were her child. As though it were her husband and she must spend night and day with him, caressing him. Vaji thought it is more intimate than a husband, than a child, than anything. It is one's self, that secret that you have to cover, to caress. And there is no place to leave it so that it won't come back, because it will, and it will come and sit there on your left breast. And when you raise your arm to pull it out by its roots, you unconsciously caress it again. As though it's your child, as though it's your husband; no, even more intimate than them, as though it's your own self.

"What is wrong with you?"

Vaji looked at the large belly of the woman sitting on the bed where the bandaged face used to be. She had lost count of the patients who came and went. The woman was sweetening her tea.

"There's nothing wrong with me. I mean I know what's wrong with me, I just can't explain it."

The woman did not understand.

"A small cyst. It will go away with medication."

"I'm seven months pregnant. The doctor says the baby has died in my belly. I don't believe it. It's impossible for something to die inside someone without them realizing it. They're operating on me tomorrow. Are operations tough?"

"Not too tough."

"Do you want some tea?"

"No."

And when the woman was silent, there was Azarmi's calm and familiar voice:

"Why not? Every time I look in the mirror I'm ashamed. You didn't do anything wrong. You're right not to come. Those days, when I was healthy and on my two own feet, you barely answered me when I said hello. Now? Well, it's obvious. Lame and carrying a cane. I guess tomorrow, when I lose this other eye, too, you'll have to take me around by the hand. I'm not talking nonsense. The doctor said so himself. If I go abroad, with lots of expenses and many procedures, they may be able to save this eye, or they may not. For the love of God, don't cry. I don't have the heart to tell you all this, but I owe it to you. Look, I didn't go there for fun. I went for God and for the Prophet. I know this is a test. But why should you suffer? No, I swear I'm not kidding. I am begging you, please don't cry. Listen, one day I fell in love with you, and now I kiss your angelic face and say, you go your way and I'll go mine. No more you and me. Just pretend I was blown to pieces right there. Finished. If you want your letters back, send your mother to pick them up, otherwise I'll burn them myself. Don't cry. You'll cry for a day, a week, a month, and then you'll forget. But if I'm there in front of you every day, I won't be able to stand it myself. It's no big deal. God is testing me. The more I think, the more I know that our paths are separate. I swear if you torture yourself I'll never forgive you. Don't sob like this. Don't break my heart. Don't make me feel worse than I do already. Forget it. Good luck. Good-bye."

And he broke into sobs. Vaji arched her entire body forward, hoping to see Azarmi leave, but she didn't. Two nurses sat quietly at the table with their backs to him. And now it was the pain again that gripped Vaji's stomach and it would soon fill her entire body. She closed her eyes and bit her lips. For a second she opened her eyes. Her roommate was ringing the emergency buzzer. Vaji pressed her fist to her stomach; she knew that painkillers would not work, and she passed out. When she opened her eyes Farrokh's hand was on her forehead.

"Mom, I love you. How are you? Can you hear me?"

Vaji smiled. She smiled at that face, at those bright eyes in their black frame. Mokhtar was standing to the side.

Vaji whispered, "How many more days do I have to stay here?"

Mokhtar's upper lip quivered. His face paled. Quietly he said, "Bear with it for another day or two and we'll go home."

Vaji had wanted to say, "Come here," but her breath would not cooperate. And Mokhtar came without having heard her. By the movement of the woman's lips he knew he had to come close to hear what she had to say.

"Mr. Azarmi, do you remember him? Next door. Go see him."

And Mokhtar was about to go when Vaji's lips moved again and she whispered:

"Take Farrokh. Take Farrokh with you. He's a good boy, don't leave him alone."

— *Translated by Sara Khalili*

Asghar Abdollahi

Asghar Abdollahi was born in the southern city of Abadan in 1955. After graduating with a degree in theater from Tehran University, he began a productive career in literature and film. He writes novels, short stories, and screenplays, and directs films.

His first novel, *The Sun in the Darkness of War* is about victims of the Iran-Iraq War (1980–1988). He has published two collections of short stories, *The Wicker Shelter* and *Beyond the Fog*. His stories touch upon life in southern Iran and the persistence of the human spirit through the horrors of war.

The story that appears here, *A Room Full of Dust,* takes place in a large southern city, at the height of the Iran-Iraq War. It won the 1999 Gardun Literary Prize.

A ROOM FULL OF DUST

CHAPTER 1

Elfi's little room was bathed in semi-darkness: the walls and the furniture, the clothes hanging on the wooden coat rack, even the lampshade, everything was yellow, brown, or red. The candle burned with a still flame. Not a breath of air penetrated the room.

"What is that sound, Adna?"

Adna was looking through the window. The street wound along the metal wall around the oil refinery. On the right side were the deserted gardens of the oil company employee housing. A caretaker stood alone under the red brick doorway of the administration building, rubbing his hands together and shifting his feet.

"Is my voice so weak you can't hear me?"

"It's raining outside."

Adna turned and looked at Elfi's bed. His old head stuck out from under the blanket. His eyes stared at the gray ceiling.

"There's probably no rabbi left in town. Do you think, Adna, there's someone left in the synagogue if I . . ."

Adna smoothed the back of her long skirt with her hands as she sat down on the Polish chair near the window.

"That gesture, Adna! You look like a sixteen-year-old girl."

"What gesture?"

"Straightening the back of your skirt."

"You never stopped being a professional voyeur, Elfi! I used to watch you in the store when you showed magazines and books to your customers. I could see your wandering eyes. You haven't changed, Elfi! Not one bit."

"Was I a bad husband, Adna? I admit I wasn't a very good bookseller. But as a husband? You're still in love with me, aren't you? I knew you were watching me from behind your cash register. I would rush the ladies' orders. I always sent them to you. You have always loved me, haven't you, Adna?"

"Well, yes. I even dyed my hair black to please you, without ever asking you about the woman with the black hair. I waited in vain for you to say something."

"You should have asked me earlier. Now I have forgotten. No matter, Adna. Your hair has gone white."

"There's no more hair dye in the market. Even the black market vendors have gone away. The taxis too. There is no one left."

Adna got up and went to the window again. The raindrops thrummed against the fogged windowpane. With the back of her hand, she wiped some of the moisture off. In the middle of the street a man wearing a navy blue cape was bending down and pumping air into his bicycle's rear tire. The guard standing near the brick building said something inaudible. The man pointed to the air pump, raised his arms, and waved them. Then he turned around and glanced toward the store entrance. Someone was calling him.

Adna said, "I believe Idris has opened the store."

The man dragged his bicycle up to Adna's window. Now the guard had also removed his bicycle from the wall. He put it on his back and crossed the street, walking toward Elfi's bookstore.

"Idris is here. He had told me he wasn't coming back," said Adna. "Do you see him?"

"I don't see him. But the guard is taking his bicycle with a flat tire to the store. Only Idris would take care of flat tires in the pouring rain."

"He told us he wasn't coming back because he wanted us to believe he had a place to run to, away from the war. It was only a bluff. I was sure of it. He hasn't changed. In '53 when I hired him he was only fifteen years old. I told him I was Jewish. 'I am Hebraic,' I told him. 'So?' he answered. 'We are buddies.' He touched his white collar with the tip of his fingers, and winked at me. I thought he was a communist. A week later, I walked in on him in the storage room performing the Muslim prayer."

Adna noticed the man with the cape hunched over his handlebars, pedaling away. It was raining harder now, and the brick buildings and the bushes near the gardens appeared like red and green spots. Suddenly a jolt shook the room. The window shook and Adna stumbled backward, barely missing Elfi's bed. Elfi held on tightly to Adna's wrist.

"Don't be afraid. It is far away."

His hand was cold. Adna was shaking and looking at the window, her mouth wide open.

"Sit down, Adna. Here, near me."

Adna sat, her eyes riveted toward the window and the blackish smoke that was darkening the world.

"You are trembling, Adna. Go down to Idris."

"No, no!"

Adna emptied the air from her lungs several times in a row. She leaned down to get a better view of the smoke that was covering the window.

"Is everything all right? Madam Adna, Mr. Elfi. . . ?"

Adna waited for Idris to enter the room but he just kept knocking on the door.

"Madam Adna?"

Elfi squeezed Adna's wrist.

"Tell him to come in. Otherwise, he'll stay there knocking till tomorrow."

"Come in, Idris!"

The door opened and Idris appeared. Holding the air pump in his hand, he gaped at the elderly husband and wife.

"Sounded like the boom of Stalin's organ.[1] It feels like the shells landed straight into a reservoir of ammonia. I felt the jolt. I was putting air into the guard's tire. I thought I had overinflated it."

"You were right in coming to see us," said Elfi.

Idris couldn't hear Elfi's frail voice.

"Huh? What are you saying?" He took a couple of steps forward.

"I am saying you were right to stay . . . I don't have much time left to live, Idris."

Idris's lips moved, but he didn't say anything. He looked at Adna, and shifted his shoulders uncomfortably. Adna was pale, exhausted. She was hunched up, like when she was cold. The shrill sirens of ambulances and fire trucks echoed in the street. Adna stared at Elfi's long, yellow, skinny fingers. Then she looked at his eyes, which continued to stare at the gray ceiling.

"Elfi . . . Elfi . . . Idris!" she screamed.

---

[1] A series of cannons or missiles discharged simultaneously; called "Stalin's organ" because they were used by the Soviet Army during World War II. Saddam Hussein's army used these in attacking Iran during the Iran-Iraq War (1980–1988).

Idris threw the pump down, walked around the bed, and knelt down next to old Elfi. He looked at his eyes. Elfi's mouth was open. Idris put his head closer and leaned his right ear on his chest.

"Where is the cemetery for the Jews, Idris?" said Elfi.

With his ear still glued to Elfi's chest, Idris tried in vain to listen for a heartbeat.

"It isn't far, Mister," Idris said.

"I never went there. I don't even know how Jews get buried. What about you, Adna?" Elfi asked.

The room shook again. Adna slipped off the bed. If Elfi hadn't held on to her, she would have run away. Idris shut his eyes and didn't stir. The shells landed one after the other, but the ambulance sirens covered the whistling boom of Stalin's organ. Idris counted, "Five . . . six . . . seven . . . eight . . ." The shells continued to fall.

"Are you crazy? You sons of bitches!" screamed Idris. "Listen to this racket!"

There was silence. Even the sounds of the ambulance and fire truck sirens had died down. The window was dark. The rain beat against the panes without being visible. It was coming down harder and harder.

"Is someone knocking at the door, Adna?"

"No, no. It's the rain on the windowpanes."

"God be blessed! He is sending us at least the rain . . . keeping the sun from me, I who have read the *New York Times* every day . . . You see, Adna, I had my reasons for asking you to dye your hair. You accepted it because you loved me, didn't you, Adna? And I said to this blond Englishwoman — probably the wife of one of the engineers in the company — that I did not carry *Life*. Or the *Financial Times*. I lied to her so she wouldn't come back. I couldn't really stop her, after all. One cannot chase customers away, Adna. If I have stayed here, I had my own good reasons. I kept telling myself that God was everywhere. So why travel thousands of kilometers to find a God who is everywhere. Also, at the time, I used to play the violin; I had promised myself that one day I would reproduce the song of the ringdove, which can only be heard in this area. Well, I failed, but I did have my reasons."

Adna stared at Idris. She had bitten her lips so much there wasn't a trace of lipstick left on them.

"In your opinion, Idris, does the synagogue still have a rabbi who could come and see us?" asked Adna.

"I'll go over right now," answered Idris.

"Here, even the ringdove's foreboding song was different. Anyway, not possible with a violin bow. Probably easier with the finger. Vibrating the strings three times with the index finger. Five-second silence. Two more times. Silence. Three times . . . "

"Go ahead, Idris!" said Adna.

Idris glanced toward the dark windows, then opened the door and left. The room shook again. Objects fell here and there. Adna gave a little shriek, then became silent. Idris opened the door. A corner of the ceiling had collapsed and gray particles of plaster floated in the air. Idris could hear Elfi's murmur.

"The magazines are filled with portraits of Frank Sinatra. I had thought to myself that this fellow could one day become president of the United States without even trying that hard. Shimon used to say that I was right. According to him, Sinatra's fans numbered more than the total population of Jews . . ."

"Go ahead, Idris! Let's not waste any time," said Adna.

Idris could see neither the husband nor the wife. The cloud of dust was blocking his view. He hesitated a little, then left.

Adna said, "Keep your mouth closed, Elfi. The room is full of dust."

"I am trying to remember the name of the damned mailman who used to leave the packages of magazines and books in front of the door. He had been told, 'Have you ever seen a Jew give a tip?' He threw the packages in the front every time, and walked away. He even did it once when it was raining. Willy's copy of *Absalom, Absalom!* was in that package, and ended up getting completely wet. Well, one day, I grabbed him by the collar. 'Hey, man, don't you know there is someone in here?' I asked him. 'You were playing the violin in the back room,' he answered. 'One can hear you croak all the way out here.' Then he added, 'What do you Jews want to do with the Holy Land? To lie down there and read the *New York Times,* yes?' That day, just like now, I tried hard to find something to quote from the Torah, but I wasn't able to."

The window collapsed. Glass shards fell into the room. Adna was on her knees, rubbing her face against Elfi's hand, praying as she trembled. Smoke filled the room. Adna could no longer hear what Elfi was murmuring.

"I was seeking the promise of fragrant horizons here, in this land of the Orient, in this world of mystery and intrigue, this country where the dust is filled with the scent of coral and fish scales. Where if you strike the strings of the violin three times . . . then maybe you can mimic the song of the ringdove."

Idris went down the stairs. He opened the door to the storage room. The guard was still in the store, looking at the black smoke flooding the street.

"I must go. I'll be back to pump air into your tire," said Idris.

"Give me the pump. I'll do it myself," said the guard.

"Will you wait till I come back?"

"Oh, yes, this is my district."

"If the shooting starts again, take shelter in the storage room."

The guard pulled off his cap and wiped his forehead. He looked at the greasy palm of his hand. He was about to say something, but a dry cough prevented him. He began to cough, unable to stop. He held his stomach and leaned forward. Idris, his hand on the handlebar, waited for the cough to come to an end. The guard inhaled deeply. His eyes were tearing. He was out of breath.

"What smoke! I almost choked to death. But, what smoke!"

"All right then, I'm going. There's some Pepsi in the fridge. It will cool off your throat. I'll be right back."

Idris was running, holding the handlebars of his bicycle as he ran. He was running through the black smoke. He jumped onto the seat and began to pedal. He pedaled blindly. He couldn't see a thing, but he knew the street well, it didn't matter. He kept his mouth and eyes shut. Leaning over the handlebars, he pedaled like a professional cyclist. When he heard the ambulance bellow, he half opened his eyes and took a breath. The smell of the ammonia and the sticky fumes were starting to numb him. The ambulance siren rang so near Idris couldn't tell whether it was coming from behind him or driving straight into him. The ambulance was getting closer. Idris didn't know if he was driving in the middle of the road or on the side of it. He slipped down from the seat onto the middle bar in order to set his foot on the pavement. He dragged his right foot. He stretched his leg to see how far he was from the curb. The ambulance was approaching. He began to yell and scream for the ambulance driver to hear him.

"Hey, ho! Watch out! I'm here! The bicycle!"

The ambulance was driving straight toward Idris. It went past him, blowing him aside. The ambulance disappeared. Idris closed his mouth and eyes again. He accelerated. Everything was still black. The street remained invisible. He heard the tires of the ambulance slide on the greasy, slippery asphalt and then a terrible sound. The siren continued to bellow, although the ambulance stood still. It had hit the refinery's metal wall.

Near the intersection with the pier, Idris emerged from the smoke. He opened his eyes. He saw the road. He looked back. He could see nothing but smoke. In a little street near the Export Bureau, he got off his bicycle and moved the containers of tar littering the road. He got back on his bicycle and pedaled on. Three young *bassiji* were sitting on sandbags in a soldiers' shelter, looking out at the horizon.[2] They were waiting for the sound of Stalin's organ. One of them got up when he spotted Idris.

"Where are you going, buddy?"

"Synagogue. Synagogue."

Idris pointed to the road with his finger and pedaled faster. He drove past two old brick buildings, built in the Dutch style. He passed by a series of gardens with burned hedges and then turned right.

He left his bicycle leaning against the gate with spearlike bars. He stuck his hands through the bars and tried to undo the latch, but the gate was locked.

"Mr. Attendant! . . . Mr. Rabbi!" he screamed.

Once more he stuck his hand through the bars and fiddled with the latch. It wouldn't give. He stepped back a few paces. The barred windows of the synagogue's Tudor-style building were closed. He grabbed a stone and threw it. The stone fell against the brick edge of the window without making a sound. Idris bent down to pick a bigger one. He aimed it at the window, lifted his arm with skill, bent his right leg, and threw

---

[2] *Bassiji* are a revolutionary volunteer militia.

the stone. The light fixture above the door broke. Idris looked dumb-founded at the dangling electric wire. Not a soul around.

"Is there anyone in the synagogue? Hey, Rabbi!" he yelled.

Again he bent down, looking for a stone, but couldn't find one that would be harmless to what was left of the light fixture. The gutter was filled with sludge. In it, he found half a china cup. He approached the gate again; this time, without jerking his body, he threw it against the window. The projectile broke the neon light on the side of the wooden door. Idris shielded his eyes with his hand.

An old man, small, corpulent, and bald, wearing a long and un-tidy beard, carefully opened the door halfway and then stepped out.

"Would you like something else to break?"

"But I yelled and yelled and no —"

"When no one answers, it means there's no one in. What do you want?"

"Are you the rabbi?"

"No."

"I need a rabbi to take with me to —"

"There is no rabbi."

"What do you mean, there's no rabbi?"

"How can it be?! How can it be? No more rabbi, that's all."

"But Mr. Elfi is dying. There's got to be a rabbi."

The old man burst out laughing. He began to hop from one leg to the other, slapping his thighs with his chubby little hands. Idris watched, bewildered, as the old man danced.

"Is that something to laugh at?"

The old man had tears in his eyes. He straightened up, catching his breath, and nodded his head.

"Oh, yes. In fact, it's very funny. I am thrilled that Our Friend has finally knocked on Elfi's door, and that his eminence Mr. Elfi has fi-nally remembered he is Jewish, and that a synagogue actually exists!"

The old man articulated each word with such growing anger that when he was done the veins were popping in his neck. Then he gave Idris a hostile glare. He clenched his fist so tightly it seemed he could have punched Idris were it not for the gate protecting him.

Idris said, "I need a rabbi for . . ."

The old man let out such a loud scream that Idris jumped back a step.

"There is no rabbi anymore, I am telling you. Do you understand Persian or don't you?"

Idris made a gesture of impatience. The old man turned his back to leave, but stopped.

"We're in the middle of a war; otherwise I would have made you pay for the damages you caused. Saboteur!"

"What should I do now?"

"Go to Iblis!"[3]

"Who is that?" asked Idris.

The old man stopped again, and with a bewildered look stared at Idris.

"Who?!"

"The one you just mentioned."

"I mentioned someone?"

"Well, you said . . . I don't know . . . you said . . ."

The old man opened his mouth to say something but changed his mind. He turned and walked toward the door. He inspected the damaged neon fixture, shook his head, entered the synagogue, and slammed the door shut. The knocker vibrated on its metallic axis, ringing in Idris's ears. He felt ill at ease.

A voice yelled out, "Down! On the ground!"

Fighter planes were flying very low. Idris couldn't see who had yelled. By the time he saw the planes, the terrible rumbling had made him deaf. He started to run toward the right. Then he stopped. He turned around and dashed forward. He floated in the air for an instant, just time enough to protect his face. He landed in the gutter, which was filled with sludge. Idris didn't understand what was happening, neither where he was, nor whether the fighter planes were still around or had left, or what happened next.

Elfi was saying, "My soul has struggled for seventy years on this peninsula of sadness. Today I am tormenting you with these cold hands and . . ."

Adna began to cough. The room was filled with smoke and the ammonia fumes were irritating her throat.

"If it is true that one does come back in another life, next time I will be a safety pin or a little mauve spot on a Chagall painting. When

---

[3] Another name for Satan (*Shaytan*).

I am dead, look at things well. Touch them . . . You have cold hands, Adna. Why aren't you wearing any perfume today? Maybe my agony has lasted too long? Is that the chirping of sparrows?"

Only the sirens of ambulances and the shouts of firemen could be heard. They had invaded the street. They were running, dragging hoses on the asphalt and calling one another.

Adna heard a knock at the door. She tried to free her hand from Elfi's fingers, but they were gripping tight and not letting go.

"Enter, Idris!" said Adna turning toward the door.

Idris appeared on the doorstep. Adna gave a shriek and wanted to take refuge under the bed. If Elfi hadn't been holding her hand she would have run away, but she remained staring at Idris.

"Madam, I threw myself into a gutter filled with mud."

"Why are the sparrows singing although it is nighttime? said Elfi.

"The rabbi wasn't there?" asked Adna.

"No, madam, he wasn't there," answered Idris.

Adna signaled for Idris to come forward. Idris approached. He was nothing more than a pair of eyes. He was black from head to toe, covered in mud.

"Go wash yourself and come back quickly," whispered Adna.

Idris went out. Adna looked at the candle. It had remained the same size since she had lit it. It continued burning without dripping or shrinking. Even the breeze that now entered the room didn't make it flicker. A candle that should have lasted less than an hour remained intact.

Elfi was speaking as he stared at the ceiling. Adna watched Elfi's mouth move slowly and endlessly.

Adna said, "That's enough, Elfi! That's enough, stop talking!"

Elfi said, "I won't forget the world as long as the rabbi hasn't closed my eyes. I will remember the ringdove on the violin strings. I will strike the strings three times, then wait five seconds in silence to hear it ring in the ears of the world. Then two more times; I will drink a glass of water to soothe the lump in my throat. And I will add that, yes, indeed, I was only ten years old when I realized that I would die one day. Amazing, isn't it? . . . Is someone knocking, Adna?"

"The rabbi! He is here."

Adna loosened Elfi's fingers from around her wrist, and freed herself. Elfi's hand remained clenched as though he were trying to grasp the air. Adna stood up and dashed out. She rushed down the stairs, sobbing.

Elfi grabbed the hand of the man that now approached. He held it tightly. Adna's sobs could be heard from downstairs in the storage room.

"Talk to me about the sky! I have always believed the sky wasn't empty. Now I have the right to ask where my place will be. I sold thousands of copies of the *New York Times* and I read thousands of obituaries. I expect them to write two lines about me. Couldn't you intervene? Do you find me ridiculous?"

Adna returned to the room. She stood by the door. She was crying, looking at the red candle on the bedside table: it remained still and undiminished by even a millimeter. It burned without a drip. Its flame was still.

"The tide was low. The land of this peninsula was born out of sediments from the sea. Pieces of coral, of fish scales, of shark teeth turned into powder. But there will be a high tide . . . Where does this noise come from? Why is this noise in my veins?"

Adna was crying silently, staring at the candle. She moved closer to the bed, waved her hand in front of Elfi's eyes. Elfi continued to speak without even blinking. She signaled Idris to close his eyelids. Idris did. Elfi became silent.

Idris couldn't free himself from Elfi's fingers. He leaned over, put his ear to his heart, and nodded his head.

"He is released. Mister is dead, Madam."

Adna said, "Carry him downstairs, Idris."

Idris tried to open Elfi's grip from his wrist but couldn't. He leaned over him and invoked Imam Ali. With his right arm he picked Elfi up and placed him on his shoulder. With his foot, he pushed wider the half-opened door. He turned to look at Adna, then began to descend the stairs.

Adna bent down. She blew out the candle. It didn't go out. She blew again. The little yellow flame continued to burn. Adna took a few steps back, stopped by the door, and looked at the candle. Her eyes were shining. She closed the door behind her and descended the stairs in darkness.

Because of the wind, it began to rain in the room . . .

— *Translated by Leyla Ebtehadj*

Ghazaleh Alizadeh

Ghazaleh Alizadeh was born in 1948 in Mashad. She began publishing her stories in literary magazines in 1967 and published a collection of stories and a novel in the 1970s. Her most acclaimed work, however, appeared after the 1979 revolution in the form of two novels and one collection of stories: *Two Views* (1984), *House of the Idrissis* (1992), and *The Intersection* (1994).

This excerpt consists of the third and fourth chapters of Alizadeh's novella *The Trial,* published in the collection *The Intersection.* It is set in the autumn and winter following the U.S. and British–backed coup in August 1953 that overthrew Dr. Mohammad Mossadegh's government and restored the Shah to power. The main character, Colonel Mo'ezz, lives with his wife, Farideh, and their daughter, Sussan, in a house in Tehran where he also tends a small poultry coop. In this excerpt, Colonel Mo'ezz, not the brightest of men, is summoned to act as a judge in the military trials of nationalists and communists following the coup. Alizadeh portrays the atmosphere of the time and the characters of the military officers with great perception and wit.

Excerpt from
THE TRIAL

CHAPTER 3

In the afternoon, the colonel was taking a nap. The telephone rang. He opened his eyes and rolled over to his side. He got up grumbling. He thought that it was probably one of Farideh's relatives, someone from the tribes of maternal and paternal aunts and their offspring, or one of her carefree sisters, or the "palace-dwelling" cousins. Wearily, he picked up the receiver. A masculine voice said, "Colonel Mo'ezz?"

"Colonel Mo'ezz speaking. Can I help you?"

"This is General Qarib, Deputy of the Logistics Division."

The colonel stood up at attention. The hairs sticking out of his nasal cavities began to move up and down along with his quickened breath. "General, Your Excellency, you grace me! I am your devoted servant!" To reduce the shaking in his voice he threw in a cliché: "From which side did the sun rise today?"[1] He laughed and began to cough. He had learned these clichés from Farideh, and for this reason his manner of speaking sometimes had a feminine quality.

The general answered, "Colonel Mo'ezz, come to the Military Tribunal Headquarters tomorrow. Today, on a holiday, I am struggling under the weight of files instead of going to the Gardens of Abeali. These traitors had managed to penetrate everywhere. They send them to us after the interrogation process. The files are as thick as the *masnavi* with seventy tons of paper.[2] We're stuck in it up to our eyeballs. Come to our aid, O compassionate friend, in times of trouble!"[3] In a Turkish accent, he added, "Long Live the Dead! Death to the Living!"

They both roared with laughter. In the same accent, Colonel Mo'ezz answered, "Long live clocks!"

Qarib began to cough. "Son of a gun! You seem to be in top form.

---

[1] Meaning that since the general never calls him, today must be a different kind of day.

[2] A *masnavi* is a very long poem.

[3] "O compassionate friend," from *Shahrivar of 20*, refers to the month of Shahrivar of the year 1320, or the Allied invasion of Iran in August 1941, implying they shared some experiences together in the military.

Wait until you work with us for a month — we'll squeeze you dry. Tomorrow at seven o'clock sharp . . ."

"At your service, General."

The colonel was in a daze when he hung up. He sat on the edge of the bed and began to rock the stool with his toes. He rubbed his chin, and muttered repeatedly, "So finally, it's my turn." General Qarib is a benevolent man, he thought. Last year, Mo'ezz had argued with him over a few sacks of rice in the logistics division. He truly regretted it now, and slapped the back of his hand in remorse. But as he wasn't one to occupy his mind with anything for long, he consoled himself that such incidents are forgotten easily. He took *The Spirit of the Laws* from the half-empty bookshelf that Farideh had decorated with a doll. It was a present from his wife's uncle. He lay down on the bed, and flipped through it. He wasn't the reading type. He always fell asleep after the first or second page. His lids became heavy; he saw himself at the agricultural fair. Hundreds of chickens and roosters were walking in a long line. It was snowing.

An unknown voice said, "Come this way . . . a rare breed!" The crowd thickened. A man with a beret, his nose red and dripping, was bumping into people. In a huge cage, chickens the size of horses strutted about, puffing out their chests, each chest adorned with a row of medals and stars. A door creaked. The colonel woke up with a start. Then he smiled.

CHAPTER 4

On Saturday morning, Colonel Mo'ezz was awakened by the call of the rooster. He washed his face and shaved in the dim early morning light. He took his military uniform from the wardrobe, brushed it, and put it on, checking himself in the mirror on the dressing table. Boxes of Coty makeup powder, Crêpe de Chîne perfume, and cold cream were reflected in the mirror. Farideh turned over and pulled the checkered blanket up to her chin. It was getting cold.

The colonel tiptoed out of the house and shut the door gently. He got into a taxi and got off in front of the Military Tribunal Headquarters. A crowd had gathered behind the railings. Near the gate, some people were talking among themselves, their eyes sunken from lack of sleep. They had spread newspapers on the sidewalk. Old women sat quietly, looking like migrating birds left behind the flock.

The crowd made way for him. Hatred sparkled in their eyes. The colonel shrugged. He did not think of this wretched bunch as human beings. He walked through the garden, entered the huge building, and asked for the direction to Brigadier General Qarib's office. Along the semi-dark corridor, he anxiously opened the fifth door on his left. He went in, stretched his neck, kicked his heels together, and presented the military salute.

Brigadier General Qarib half stood up. He had a thin, hooked nose, a pointed chin, and protruding cheekbones. His tiny eyes were shining underneath thick eyebrows. He slapped the colonel on his broad shoulders. "Punctual as ever," he said, turning to the officers in the room, with a smile on his bluish lips, flashing his loose yellow teeth. "We served together in the logistics division. Throughout the six years, I don't recall the colonel having been even five minutes late." He flicked his nose on both sides, as if he were putting it back into place. "A soldier's discipline is his religion." He offered the colonel a chair near his own desk. The colonel sat down. The brigadier general stretched his neck toward him and whispered, "We're short of judges."

The door was opened and a corporal came in, cheeks flushed, panting, and speaking a mixture of Turkish and Persian. "A prisoner's wife has thrown herself under the justice minister's car."

"Stupid sluts!" snapped the brigadier general, tapping his forehead. "They're so useless they can't keep their husbands at home. Now that the slobs have landed in trouble, these cows want to take it out on the government. You have no idea," he said, turning to the colonel, "what a scene they make first thing in the morning."

"What can you do?" said the colonel, shaking his head thoughtfully. "That's the fair sex for you."

"What fair sex are you talking about?" retorted General Qarib. "They're the cantankerous sex . . . By the way, how's your good wife? We've recently become related to each other. My cousin has married one of your wife's relatives."

"It's an honor," said the colonel, bowing his head.

A young captain, red-faced, with a stocky and solid build, brought the general a voluminous file. The general took the file and leafed through it. The captain, smiling, kicked his heels, thrust out his chest, and stood at attention. His whole body was motionless, except for his mustache, which went up and down every now and again. The officer had gone red in the face trying to stop laughing. Colonel Mo'ezz frowned.

"You and five senior officers," the brigadier told the colonel, having raised his head from the file, "must go to Bench Six." He then paused, looked at his watch, and brushed his hair with his hand before adding, "You have half an hour before the trial begins."

An officer with glasses opened the door. They entered a corridor. The group set off. The dust-covered corridor was periodically illuminated by the light shining through narrow skylights. The thick soles of military boots slammed hard on the floor covering, and the noise echoed under the roof. As the group walked along, the administrative staff would make way for them, gazing at them inquisitively.

"How glorious," the colonel thought. Once again he was glad he had decided to join the army. In his mind, he formed a theory: "People are two types, weak and strong. There's nothing in between." Thrusting out his chest, he thought this was something he should tell his wife about. "The powerful are the crème de la crème of nature."

A waiter was carrying tea, his back bent, his face sallow. The colonel gave him a hateful look and developed his theory further. "People like him have no place in the realm of human beings. They have no brains." He nearly spat on the floor. "What is such a creature's life worth?" Turning back, he looked at the tall, shapely officers. They were healthy-looking, handsome, and elegant. "These are the type of men to build this country. Even chickens are different from each other. The Dutch chickens are fat and juicy." The colonel's train of thought took him to the sight of chickens grilled on charcoal. A fat officer was walking in front of him, his plump, round buttocks swaying rhythmically behind the slit in his military jacket.

They entered the courtroom. The court recorder, the accused, and the members of the public rose. The colonel stroked his thin moustache. The officers walked toward the rostrum. They sat behind podium-like tables. Colonel Mo'ezz surveyed the crowd. The photographers' flashing lights bothered him. He thought that now his image was entering the realm of history. He lowered his head and doodled on a piece of notepaper marked with the Imperial Crown. He drew his favorite image: the henna-colored rooster of Sabzevar.[4]

The prosecutor was a diminutive, thin man, quick-footed and passionate. He went behind the podium. He called the names of the six accused and read out the indictment. The skin under his chin was loose and trembled; his Adam's apple was sticking out and moving up and down. Colonel Mo'ezz doodled again, this time a turkey. The color of the prosecutor's face would change. He slammed his fist on the table. He walked along the rostrum and walked back. His cheeks looked as if they were on fire. His earlobes had gone red. He undid his top shirt button. His jacket felt too heavy. Protocol permitting, he would even have taken it off. His body was so powerful and dynamic, even the military trousers were getting in his way. Every time the prosecutor shouted or jumped around, Colonel Mo'ezz worried that the man's gold-plated buttons would snap off and shoot up toward the ceiling. A novel idea crossed the colonel's mind: "Prosecutors should wear flowing robes, similar to those worn by Arab men, because they need more space to be able to jump around and dramatize the offense." He had heard that to heed the call of nature, the Arab man only needed to sit down and lift his robe. He frowned and, imagining a foul smell, pushed his nostrils together.

Words such as "criminal," "perfidious," and "congenital traitor" echoed in his ears. He was not into politics. All he knew was that when Iran had won its case against Britain in 1952 at the International Court of Justice in The Hague, he had felt proud for several hours, had waved his fists in the air, and had shouted at the top of his voice in the courtyard of his house, "We really smashed them!" Farideh had shed a few tears of happiness.

Now the tables had been turned, and the former prime minister was in prison. It was a complicated game, defying his intellect. He didn't give it too much thought, figuring there must be some expedience in that.

He was tired of the noise. He would shift his weight from one buttock to another. Wind had built up in his stomach and was twisting

---

[4] A city in northeastern Iran.

in his intestines. He had a shooting pain in his backbone. The old hernia was raising its head again. It was a legacy of his time in the Russian prison.[5] The six accused took turns defending themselves. What they said weighed heavily on the brain, talking of injustice and the deprived classes. "Too much reading drives you mad," he thought. "Really, what was the use of these men's knowledge and understanding? Now they have to take all of it to the grave." He recalled falling asleep as soon as he began reading a book.

He gently tapped the tip of his pen on the table. He was grateful for having a healthy mind. He turned toward the window. A big fly was buzzing behind the glass pane. His eyelids were feeling heavy. The sweet taste of sleep was circling around his head. He rubbed his eyes. In his hands, he firmly pressed the flab around his stomach. "The court is not a reading room," he reproached himself. "The judge should not sleep while the accused are defending themselves." He half rose, shuffled his feet, and tried to summon up frightening thoughts to fight off the temptation to fall asleep. He imagined himself in the shoes of the accused. Picturing the execution scene in his mind, he felt a shooting pain go up his backbone.

The accused criminals would rise, heads shaven, their faces covered in stubble a few days old; they spoke of victory, emancipation, and the bright future. "What future?" he wondered. "Going to the graveyard?" He filled his cheeks with air. On the right-hand side of the note paper, he drew a lovebird in a cage. "All these atrocities are caused by books," he mumbled to himself. "They use deceptive phrases to shove evil ideas down people's throats."

The court was adjourned for a recess. They all went to have to tea. In the officers' common room he saw a familiar face: Captain Siavosh, from the Second Bureau.[6] He was tall, healthy, with a good complexion, smart and quick, the type that Farideh would call "fully formed." His jaw was adorned by thick black sideburns. His small mouth was as red as a radish. He walked briskly toward the colonel, held the colonel's big hand in his long, delicate hands, and smiled. The smell of an expensive aftershave wafted from his face into the colonel's nostrils.

---

[5] Another reference to the Allied invasion of Iran in 1941.
[6] Military intelligence.

"Well, well, well! This trial has brought all the old friends together!" the captain said, before letting go of the colonel's hand. "Can't you see the dawn of victory?" he said, winking at the sloping shaft of light under which a cobweb was glinting. "All the traitors have been exposed. Wait another six months," he said, raising his right arm, "and all those involved in this sedition will be eliminated. All the clamor will die down. Security is a great gift. What do you think?"

The colonel sipped some tea, and his empty stomach gurgled. "It's really interesting," he said, sheepishly shaking his head. "The general is personally very decisive," the captain went on, stretching his neck forward. "The people lower down are not. He was here on Thursday. Didn't you have the pleasure of meeting him?"

The colonel did not answer. He did not want Captain Siavosh to know that he was a newcomer. The young man spoke of everything, until the conversation reached the colonel's favorite subject. "I don't know why you don't raise turkeys instead of chickens," he said, snapping his fingers and raising his eyebrows. "I said this at a party and everybody agreed. Listen! The age of chickens is over. This is the age of the turkey."

"What about the eggs?" the colonel whispered.

"Eggs?" said the captain, smirking. "Nothing will happen to the eggs. They'll stay where they are. By the way," he said, suddenly remembering something, "why don't you come to Behkish's on Friday? It's just a cozy get-together. You can bring along your good lady. One doesn't live a thousand years. You know, I am a hardworking man and don't sleep more than four hours every night. The great American thinker, Dale Carnegie, says 'hard work is the secret of one's success, but a man also needs rest and relaxation.'" He gave the colonel another wink, picked up his cup of tea, and moved on.

An hour later, Colonel Mo'ezz saw the captain and the prosecutor talking in a low voice as they climbed down the steps.

It was nearly dusk when the colonel returned home, tired. He got out of the jeep at the crossroads. Dazed and confused, he looked at the graffiti on the walls. The wall between the shoemaker's and the launderer's shops was covered by the image of a checkered blanket. A clenched fist had torn through the blanket, sticking out like a mace. The colonel thought about the deep meaning of the graffiti: "Thanks to their uprising on August 19, the brave Iranian people have torn apart the rule of the blanket."[7] The thought of the metal bed and Dr. Mossadegh's torn blanket made him laugh.

The colonel took a deep breath. The wind was blowing, and a drizzle was wetting his face. He walked fast, into the Fakhrieh Mosque Alley. The windows were lighting up, one after another. The smell of food was streaming out from under the kitchen doors. A woman wrapped in a shawl was walking on the left-hand side of the alley. The colonel recognized his neighbor Dr. Ganji's wife, small and stooped, walking briskly. The colonel waved. The old woman did not notice him. Oblivious to her surroundings, she was deep in thought.

The man reached his house. He stood in front of the door. He put his hand on the doorknob. The chickens could be heard cackling in the cage. The house gave out the smell of lamb, potato, and tomato stew. He took a deep breath.

— *Translated by Hossein Shahidi and Nahid Mozaffari*

---

[7] The ailing Dr. Mossadegh held some of his meetings, including those with foreign officials, sitting on a metallic, military-style bed, sometimes wrapped in a checkered blanket.

Seyyed Ebrahim Nabavi

Seyyed Ebrahim Nabavi was born on November 13, 1958, in Astarabad. Educated at Shiraz University, he began working as a journalist in Tehran and Esfahan, first as a film critic, then a political analyst, and finally a satirist. After the election of Mohammad Khatami as president in 1997, Nabavi became a prominent writer in various journals calling for reform. As conservative forces cracked down on the reformist press, Nabavi was imprisoned twice, in 1998 and 2000, because, as he puts it, "my satire was too satirical, or perhaps it made people laugh a little and think too much." Along with several other journalists, he was recipient of the Hellman-Hammett Award in 1999.

Nabavi, who currently lives in Brussels, is a prolific writer of books, documentaries, screenplays, and articles. His novel, *Safe House,* is based on his and several other writers' prison experiences. He also wrote his own prison memoir, *Salon 6.* "First Love" first appeared in a collection called *Tehrangeles* in 2001.

FIRST LOVE

I'd decided to fall in love with someone a few months ago. It wasn't really my fault. Every time I passed by Mr. Mohammadi's bookstore, it was as if the devil himself grabbed my hand and dragged me into the store — straight over to the novels section, where he'd take out one of the books and hand it to me. I'd then be forced to leaf through it and eventually buy it. And I don't know why, but every time I'd read a book, I'd end up wanting to fall in love.

When I finally decided to do it, I looked for the prettiest girl in the neighborhood — you know, a girl close by, someone easy to fall in love with, someone that I didn't have to take a taxi to, someone who didn't live in a strange neighborhood where I'd have to run into kids who didn't know me, kids who'd ask, "What are you doing here?" And then beat the daylights out of me when I couldn't answer! Sima was our neighbor; I didn't have to face any headaches falling in love with her and that is exactly why I did.

You'll definitely ask what difference it makes to tell you when I was born; or how many sisters or brothers I have; or when I went to school; or that my father was a chemistry teacher; or that we lived in Tehran; or that when my father was transferred to Kerman and decided to live there we rented a two-story house in one of the old sections of the city that cost 150 tomans a month; or that after my father became the school's principal we moved to one of the public houses near the Paramount Cinema, where our house was only five houses down from Sima's; or that there were no neighborhood girls other than Sima who were my age; or that this is probably why I fell in love with her. I mean, *why* I wanted to fall in love with her. Are you satisfied now? You've made me say too much — do all writers have to explain their life histories like this?

But what about this Sima; this lady I fell in love with, or wanted to fall in love with? Three years before I fell in love with her, Sima was

---

The famous twelfth-century love poem "Leyli and Majnun," by Hakim Nezami Ganjavi, is in Persian literature akin to *Romeo and Juliet* in expressing the intensity and tragedy of love. The Persian title of this story is based on that poem.

a snot-nosed, whiny complainer who always used to stand in her doorway and peer out from behind the door, eyeing what was going on in the street. It was as if she stood in the doorway so if someone wanted to grab her, she could quickly shut the door and jump inside. What do you think Sima was doing standing in the door like that? Her sole purpose was to stand there stiff as a rod and stare at her little brother, Ali, who was always wandering around in the street. And God help us, if the day came that one of the kids got into a fight with Ali. That's when Sima would start raising a stink, crying and yelling for help. And God knows how much I hate crybaby girls. Honestly, I really didn't like that about her. But even more, it really scared me. So, whenever I wanted to give Ali a good beating, I'd drag him to another street and then I'd really let him have it.

Of course, I didn't just dislike Sima's crying and yelling. Her miserable face, covered with pimples, really turned my stomach. Her clothes also made me sick. She wore these cotton pajama pants and over them a red skirt. She looked like a clown. God knows I don't hate anything more than twelve-year-old girls who wear pajama pants under their red skirts. And she wore a pair of high heels — where she found them I don't know — I think she hoped it would make her look tall. And every few days, just because she was so ugly, I'd make it my business to give her brother a good beating!

But during those first few days when I started to fall in love with Sima, I stopped beating up Ali. After all, I needed a way of proving my love for her. So to make a long story short, in the early morning hours of that very day that I decided to fall in love with her, I put on a pair of white bell-bottom pants and borrowed my sister's brown and white plaid shirt (after promising her my life in return for the favor). First thing in the morning, I stuck my head under the faucet and washed my hair with cold water and a lot of shampoo. Of course, you shouldn't wash your hair with cold water because it drips down the back of your neck and makes the hair on your neck stand on end. But love knows no boundaries. Anyway, whatever it took, I washed my hair and dried it with my older brother's hair dryer. I looked like a million dollars! And then I shaved the few whiskers I had with an old blade that I had been saving for a few months for such a momentous occasion.

My mother took one look at me and shook her head from side to side. She wanted to say she was very upset but I ignored her. My mother then said a very bad word in Turkish to me — it meant I looked like a monkey. My mother and father spoke Turkish in the house. We (the children), didn't speak it but we were accustomed to hearing it. When I heard what my mother said, I was really offended. Obviously, I must have really looked good. My mother knew it, too. But she wanted to tease me. I didn't say a word to her because I knew in her heart of hearts she was admiring her handsome boy! I felt sorry for her that she couldn't just hug me and say, "May I be sacrificed for my pretty boy, he's as beautiful as the moon!" Just to be sure though, I went back into the bathroom and checked the mirror to make sure I didn't really look like a monkey. I made some faces. I stuck out my tongue. I stuck my fingers in my ears and crossed my eyes and tried to make some monkey faces. Maybe my mother wasn't all that far off!

I quickly came back to reality. I didn't want to ruin my first day of love so I went into the living room, where my older brother hid his bottle of 707 cologne behind the couch. I took about a half-glass of cologne and splashed it all over my head, neck, hands, and shirt so I'd smell really good. Of course, I knew tonight I was going to get it from my brother, but there was no turning back. For this love, I could stand any torment; a whipping from my brother was nothing. In any case, I took off and left the house. Actually no, now I remember, first I went to the kitchen to see my mother. After all, I figured, it doesn't bode well to fight with one's mother on your first day of love. I kissed her hair and bid her farewell. But my mother didn't answer; she just shook her head back and forth as if to say I was really stupid.

By the way, I forgot to mention that ever since I decided to fall in love with Sima, she started to change. She was no longer an ugly, sickly, lanky, twelve-year-old girl, her face covered with a million pimples. It was as if she grew up all at once. She got tall and her face was totally clear. She actually looked good — like a piece of the moon that an artist had painted on. So here I was, dressed in my new white outfit, going to see Sima's brother. For a few days now, he and I had been getting along well. I went to his house, where out front, under the shade of a tree, we began to play a game of chess. The whole time I kept my eyes on Sima. Then, twice in a row, Sima's brother used the Napoleon tactic on me.[1] In just twenty minutes, Ali — whom I had taught how

---

[1] A four-move tactic in chess that results in a checkmate for the opponent.

to play chess only a month before — actually managed to checkmate me — the best chess player in the neighborhood. I didn't even see the chess pieces. Damn this thing called love!

It took only twenty minutes for me to totally fall in love with Sima. I don't think anyone can fall in love this quickly. By the way, I never told you that my grade average was always higher than eighteen.[2] Of course, that day, Sima was wearing a pretty red skirt and had tied her hair in a ponytail and this probably made me fall in love even faster. But in any case, twenty minutes for someone to fall in love was not a lot of time, especially at nine o'clock in the morning. People are not even completely awake at that hour. Just imagine that Majnun saw Leyli yawning at nine in the morning. You tell me, how can anyone fall in love with someone who's yawning?! Or with someone who hasn't washed her face yet? On the other hand, falling in love at night is wonderful. The sky is full of stars, and the lights are on in the park and those of the cinema shine from far away. Actually, at night it feels different, as if someone pushes you toward love. But as I said, Sima looked really pretty and it didn't take any effort to fall in love with her even at that hour in the morning.

Anyway, that day I really indulged Ali. And he kept castling me — and I kept gazing at Sima. Sima's shoes were pink and they had little bows on the side. Everything about Sima was beautiful that day. Once again I heard Ali say, "Checkmate." At the same time, Sima came out of the house and stood above us. My heart was beating. I was really, really in love. She came and stood right by me and said to Ali, "Didn't you say he was a chess champion?" And then she pointed her finger at me. Honestly, I was really offended. She called me "he" as if I didn't have a name. I should have done something right then and there at the beginning of this love affair. But I didn't do a thing. I was in love in a bad way. And then Ali put away the chess pieces and left. Sima shut the door — as if she was mad at me. She must have realized I was in love with her. It was terrible. My mind was on fire and the sun was grilling my brain. It was now noon and not a great time for matters of love. I was also hungry, but if I went home it would be all over. I had a thought. I ran home and got the soccer ball and threw it in Sima's yard. Then I nonchalantly knocked on her door. Sima opened it.

---

[2] The Iranian grading system is from 0 to 20, 20 being the highest grade one can get.

I said, "Hello. Are you feeling well?"

She said, "Ali is sleeping."

I said, "A ball belonging to my person has fallen in your esteemed yard."

Sima gave me a weird look — as if I was crazy. She didn't say a thing; she just slammed the door shut tight. A few minutes went by and I was just about to knock again when Sima's mother opened the door and threw the ball (now torn up) at my chest. In her hand was a kitchen knife. To tell you the truth, I got frightened. I went home and didn't eat lunch. Instead, I just thought. My heart was on fire. I should have taken revenge like a man. But it was too hot outside to take revenge like a man.

Love and hunger had gotten mixed up and made me feel very bad. I went to sleep until five in the afternoon and then headed out again. Ali stood near the door to the house. And Sima was talking to her cousin. I blew up. I ran over to Sima's cousin and punched him hard in the nose and then ran home. The cousin ran after me. I shut the door and sat down on the ground behind it. Now Sima would realize she was dealing with a real man. Suddenly as I was sitting there behind the door, I heard the sound of breaking glass. Sima's cousin had thrown a rock through our window and broken it. Before my mother realized what had happened, I ran out the door. Ali and Sima and her cousing were running toward their house. I picked up a rock and threw it at her cousin. I was careful not to hit Sima. I was still in love with her. Sima's cousin's shoe had fallen off before he ran into the house. I picked it up, and since I had already sacrificed a window and a soccer ball for this love of mine, I decided to throw it with all my might into their house. When I heard the sound of breaking glass, my heart was relieved. But this didn't end matters.

The next day, I got a beating from my brother for the pinch of his cologne that I had used, and I got another beating from my father for the broken window of our house. And then my mother, in front of Sima's mother, pulled my ear and smacked me in the head. How painful that moment was for me. In the following days, Ali tore off our doorbell, and I retaliated by slashing Ali's father's car tire. Then Sima's cousin threw gasoline on the pine tree in front of our house and set fire to it. Since I was going to make sure I got the last word, one night when Ali, Sima, and her mother and father had gone to visit their aunt,

I jumped over the back wall to their house and, my heart burning with both love and hate, nailed holes through all of Ali's mother's pots and pans. This calamity led to Ali's mother and father coming to our house and my father paying Ali's father (who was his friend) for all the damages. From then on, our families saw a lot of each other, but I was forbidden from ever entering their house. And for the remaining year we stayed in that neighborhood, Sima never spoke to me again. But I loved her until the end, when I finally heard that she had married her cousin.

— *Translated by Leyli Shayegan*

Shahriyar Mandanipur

Shahriyar Mandanipur was born in 1957 in Shiraz. He received his master's degree in political science and is currently the editor of the literary magazine *Asr-e Panjshanbeh*. Mandanipur has published five collections of short stories, including *The Eighth Day of Earth, East of the Violet, Midday Noon,* and *The Mummy and Honey.* His latest collection, *Ultramarine Blue,* consists of eleven stories that relate in one way or another to the events of September 11, 2001. He has also written a two-volume novel entitled *Love and Distress.* He is generally considered to be one of the most successful and promising writers of contemporary Iran; his creative use of symbols, experimentation with language, time, and space, and awareness of sequence and identity have made his work difficult but fascinating to critics and readers alike.

This haunting story, "Shatter the Stone Tooth," replete with symbols, comes from his collection *The Mummy and Honey.*

SHATTER THE STONE TOOTH

He writes of the untimely heat in Guraab, of its sun that seems to shine a blinding purple, of a cavern with forty-four stairs and an image carved on its wall, and he writes of a dog who "transfers his fantasies of smell and sound to his companion." All of which I do not understand. He writes that he has a hut at the far end of the village, where at nights he writes on the walls; he didn't say what. Probably those verses that men hum under their breath or write somewhere when they feel lonely. He writes that he doesn't intend to come to town for the weekends anymore, that the days in Guraab are the end of time and it is best that he wait there. Then he writes a lot about the mud huts that are connected to each other by underground tunnels, and of villagers with trachoma, and of "gusts of dust that get into your throat and make you retch," and he writes, would you believe that dust can rot . . . I don't believe this is his letter. His earlier letters were not like this; they were real letters. Even his handwriting used to enchant. They were filled with words that men in love string together and that every woman loves to read or hear, even though just after they are read or heard they seem banal. But now look . . . lately . . . I will read so you can see what I mean:

"When they all take it upon themselves to kill a living thing but it doesn't die and even goes so far as to trust them again, I realize that all the things I have ever said to you were simply a mirage, the fantasies of a dog with seven lives who knows the secret to the engraved image on the wall and his fifth life is about to end."

In the days when he used to come to town, it was autumn and winter. We would go for a stroll on a deserted street. Perhaps you did this sort of thing, too, when you were engaged. Not much of it stays in one's memory, not the words that were spoken, not the jokes, perhaps only the image of feet treading in unison and the memory of a tree-lined dead-end street which does not look like a dead end. And one more memory; the smell of wintersweet flowers floating from behind the walls of a house on a rainy day. In those days, if I asked him to talk about the place where he was stationed, he would say, let's not talk about it. Maybe he just didn't want to change the subject, and then he would carefully look around to see if we were alone, and he would take my hand or he would . . . And he used to write nothing about Guraab. Perhaps he thought that if I knew where he was stuck and how he was suffering, I would be distressed. But he was becoming so unsettled I could sense there was something wrong.

Then, after two months of not having sent any news of himself, a letter arrived in May. The one that is mostly about Guraab. He writes that there are some words that cannot be carved on the wall or spoken to anyone; they can only be written in a letter, so that while writing one can picture their effect on the reader's face. At the end he writes two or three lines about that dog, and good-bye. With no "I hope to see you soon" or "I kiss your eyes" or even "say hello to this or that person." Do you know what he used to write in the early days? "My soul mate . . ." and other words that I cannot repeat. I would write back, you careless boy, what if they open your letter at the post office, what then . . . what would they think? It was obvious that he was painfully lonely, but whatever it was, his thoughts were occupied with me and the time when his military service would end. Now you tell me what this means:

"I climb down the stairs of the cavern at noon, I take a lantern with me, it is hell outside. A greasy sweat seeps out of my pores, I thirst for water, but I throw up the minute I drink. The men of Guraab, a few here and there, are sitting in the shadow of their huts smoking water pipes; they whisper to each other and keep a watchful eye on the road. They're not concerned with me, and I am comfortable down here where the vapors of the earth bloat and swell. I sit in the middle of the circular wall and listen. I hear sounds. Besides the steady sound of water trickling, there are voices that still linger from a thousand years ago or even before. Someone screamed, someone lit a fire, the condemned ones laughed, and another uttered incantations."

What anxiety his May letter caused me and, worse, the letters that followed. I wrote to him that it is better if you don't talk about Guraab. No matter how cursed the place, you are there, you represent the Development Corps, you are there to help them.[1] Think of how important your work is from a humanitarian point of view. I couldn't string

---

[1] Skilled and literate conscripts are sent to remote villages to promote development and to aid villagers with health, education, and modern agricultural techniques.

together complicated words the way he could. In any case, I meant I admire you for your service. Then, as though he developed a grudge against me, too, he started sending these letters, some only a day apart. Like this one, only three lines long; it's obvious he wrote it in a hurry. And what does it say? That they are lying in ambush waiting to capture him and to strangle him with a rope, but they still don't know where he is hiding. He writes that he alone knows of this hiding place and, of course, he won't tell them. Four times he has repeated that: he won't tell them, won't tell them . . .

No. How could I go? There are times when I don't even dare walk alone in the streets of our own town. I dreamed that a few men are chasing me, in the middle of the day, and nobody else pays any attention. I run through the crowds screaming. The men catch up with me . . . Would my father go with me? Could I go alone? I wanted to, what he must have thought of me . . . Besides, I was scared. I am still scared of Guraab. If the people there are anything like the way he describes them, they would have strung me up me in the middle of the village square. What? Where did he write it . . . Read! Right here: "Forty or fifty huts made of sun-dried bricks in the middle of a sunken plain and on three sides of the plain, high mountains of sulfurous sandstone and slabs of slippery rock.[2] No trees and no water. When soil decays, it sucks up the water and it seems as though it has never ever rained. The decay is spreading. It will scale up the pass and infest the surrounding plains and overrun everything." Well, isn't this scary? He writes:

"There is another village on this plain, it's called Gur-Gedaa, and guys from there come around here to steal. Dark skin, with even darker, dazed eyes. I'm scared, I'm scared of the look in their eyes. They shun me, too, like all the rest. Only this dog runs to me when he sees me. He comes and sniffs at my ankles. It's as though he smells a scent that I'm incapable of smelling myself. Even more appalling is the wheat crop. It has already turned yellow and it's pathetically scanty and short. I tell these godforsaken people, why do you fool yourself into thinking that you will have a good harvest this year? Their contentment and thankfulness makes me even more nervous."

He has told some guy named Farvardin, why are you so resigned?

---

[2] The Persian text refers to "mountains of Zarneekh." Zarneekh is a mineral compound of arsenic and sulfur, streaks of which run through the mountain.

If you go to town and work as a laborer, you will have a better life. There's water there for you to wash yourself. You'll have some money to check out the town in the evenings, you'll see colors, you will go to the movies, you will see things that you have never even dreamed of. If you go uptown, you'll see beauty and well-being all concentrated in one place, and you will finally realize that Sabz-Ali's sister isn't such a great catch after all.

He writes: "No one here has ever seen the sea. They haven't even seen a river. Once in a while they see a flood and they climb up to the top of the hill where the crevice leading to the cavern has slit open. When the water subsides they go back and rebuild their huts, a couple fewer each time. Just yesterday someone sold his daughter. They plucked her eyebrows and made her up and sent her to an Arab on the other side of the Gulf. Maybe she won't even make it to the other side. The kid had her heart set on getting some candy. Her father, Sadegh, needed the money to take his wife to town to give birth. The woman is past her eleventh month and she still hasn't given birth. The child is alive in her belly, but it will neither die nor come out. They say they can hear it cry. I went to the cavern to avoid hearing it. The dog had taken refuge there, too. He was sitting there listening. I am amazed at what this animal finds to eat around here. There isn't enough to feed the humans. I share my own food with him. Sometime he disappears for a few days. Maybe he goes to Gur-Gedaa . . ."

From what he writes, it's obvious that it was a large dog. An animal that doesn't choke to death when they throw ropes around his neck and pull from both sides must be quite a beast. He wrote: "It is white with black spots and is constantly panting from the heat. If spring isn't over yet and it's already this hot, the summer must be hell. I take off my clothes and try to fall asleep in the darkness of the cavern." At the end of this letter, he asks me, in the middle of the night when it is quiet everywhere, to go and turn on a water faucet so that water drips from it, and he wants me to listen to the drip, drip sound in the dark. He writes that this sound bears a secret and for those who discover it, all places in the world will become identical. Don't say it . . . no . . . you, of all people, don't say it . . . everyone tells me what's the use . . . don't tell me that either. Let me cry and get it out of my system. And don't tell me that I am still young and that I should be thinking of my future and my happiness. I don't want to. I wrote him this, that without you I won't exist, either. Think of me, too. I don't even want a wedding. Just come back, let's get married, have kids, and then go wherever you want, chasing after whatever dream you have. I wrote that I am still full of life . . . I put all caution aside this time, I thought maybe his feelings for me will be rekindled. I wrote your life and hope is still here . . .

No, he didn't come. He writes he now realizes that the existence of the chiseled image in the cavern is not without significance. A stone man is standing there. He writes that he is cleaning off the rest of the carving, then maybe he will understand what it means, with the help of his companion, that dog . . . When he was here I never saw him avoid people. He was simple and quiet, but he certainly wasn't shy with me. He was spirited and exciting, I was sure that once he fell into the routine of life, he would really make something of his life. His mind-set was such that any woman knew that once he started to work, if his heart was content, he would provide a decent life for his wife. And then this same man becomes such a recluse that he writes he can no longer stand the light; the sun shines to blind him.

He writes: "The poor villagers, despite all their ignorance, sometimes play me for a fool in their own way, and I get it. I tell them, you poor slobs, leave, go somewhere else, migrate to the seaside, you have never seen a rice paddy, you don't know what it smells like . . ." They all laughed at him. I am sure they laughed at him when he said such things. They had put him on the spot and asked, who are you, what do you do, why don't you know anything? It seems they blamed him for a couple of their palm trees drying up. "Farvardin was yelling at me, wanting to know why the well has dried up. I don't know, I don't know why none of the wells reach water. They keep on killing their hens one by one. It is a bad omen if hens cluck at dawn and some of the hens have started clucking. Rostam says, what do you think . . . what is wrong with the hens? Why don't they want to sit on their eggs? . . . Now what do you think we should plant in this soil? I don't know. Bibi Golabatun says, then what did you come here for? I tell her I don't know. She says our own men understand soil, seed, and rain better than you do. These men have planted this land for generations. And they'll be here to the very last day, not you. I don't know what to say. I came here to finish the remainder of my service and then go home."

He actually led a few of them by the hand into the cavern to show them the image. It took him a month to clean away the centuries-old dirt and to reveal part of it. A wheat field — or something similar — was carved into the stone. The man's hand is not empty. He has drawn a dagger out . . . I think he lost all hope and confidence in his work when he didn't manage to save the palm trees. He writes: "The sparse wheat grows here only out of a thousand-year-old habit, it is only a mirage of the fertility of centuries ago; once it becomes aware that it's a mirage, it stops growing." He writes: "Rostam dragged me over to his plot of land to boast about his harvest this year. I told him it's no good. He broke off a stalk and counted the seeds, thirteen of them. He said it's full. I said it's as little as alms for a beggar. He walked into the wheat, held his arms open wide and hollered, do you even know how I've struggled here, you who come from the city? I said that whether I know or not, this soil is dead, it no longer breathes and it can't be cured with fertilizers. He was insulted. He leaped toward me. I turned my back to him and headed for the village and he stood there clenching the thirteen seeds in his fist and yelling. Bibi Golabatun says I bring a curse to Guraab because the dog walks in my shadow. I tell her you are your own curse. If that dog peeks in through the door of your homes and stares at you, it means nothing. I tell her, every single one of you needs treatment at the hospital. Trachoma, parasites, smallpox, boils, and infections are festering in you. They cannot imagine a life without disease. But they avoid me because the dog has licked my ankle. The cavern . . . the cavern . . ."

I wrote, Why do you bother with these people? Don't confront them. Let them be. I wrote, It's me who should help you build your life, it's me who will bear you a child who will have no illnesses. He answered: "In your opinion, you, who live in the city and who if I am no longer around will hook up with someone else, in your opinion, why has that man buried his dagger in an animal's head, here, on the stone. There is an expression on this man's face that I don't understand, I can't stop looking at him. The expression has deepened as the stone has aged and peeled. His clenched teeth, the stone scar on his cheek . . . " I wrote, For the love of whoever you care for, don't go to that cavern, you'll get sick. From his response, I know he sneered at me when he read my letter . . . are you listening?

"Here the weather is free from all seasons and in this place, all the dreams in the world settle like sediment. I close my eyes and I see them. Would you believe that a person's sense of smell can fantasize? It can, but just as we free our visual dreams by closing our eyes, we need to free as well our fantasies of smell and hearing. The dog and I sit facing the lines on the stone wall and then it begins to happen. The scent of a stream, a whiff of the honeybee's saliva, the fragrance of lean meat, the blood of a sweet vein, the smell of thunder, the odor of an earthquake, the scent of a female . . ."

This must be his next letter, if I'm not mistaken — I didn't keep the envelopes. Starting with this one, even I have trouble reading his handwriting: "I told them, if you peek into my room again at night, in the middle of the night, I will go to the police and tell them all about the opium poppies you grow. Leave me alone. They had left me in peace for a while. But now they're picking on the dog. This animal is not that important to me. He is like all the other dogs on the road who get hit by cars, their cadavers squashed by trucks. His left thigh has a sore and he constantly licks it, but that's not important. Maybe one of the dogs from the village bit him, but just because he bites off the scabs, it doesn't mean he is rabid. If he is not like other dogs, it doesn't mean he is rabid. Sabz-Ali confronted me: he is, he is rabid. He said let's not tempt the devil, this year we've had no calamities. The animal was sitting farther away, panting. Well I feel hot and I pant too in this weather. Even stones pant here, so does the air. Rostam said this dog is a stranger, he is not from Guraab or Gur-Gedaa. Our dogs are thin and agile. This one is like the tame city dogs. There's no place for a strange dog in this village. It seems that the day and the time had come; I couldn't see that a few people had gathered around me, I only saw Rostam, who stood there, his neck stretched out. I felt like tearing that protruding vein on his neck out with my teeth or with a fork. No matter how many times they kicked me in my side I didn't let him go. They were pulling my hair from behind and I was smashing Rostam's head against a rock and my hands were bloody and they separated us. I said leave the animal alone, I will kill him myself. I even got the poison for them to smear it on the goat's guts. The animal ate it. I threw it to him myself. He devoured the entire intestine and disappeared. It is now three days that I sit in the cavern alone. There is no more to say."

How does a man suddenly become like this? No, I never want to lay eyes on him again. He can go to wherever the hell he belongs. But why did he waste three years of my life? I want to see him just to ask him this. What a difference between the things he said at the beginning and the things he says now. What do I care if the dog didn't die from the poison, that he went back to him, still panting. He writes: "The dog knows that I fed him the poison, and he's come back to let me know this." This has to mean something . . . What? — do you understand it? I don't want to know and I don't want to know what the animal on the stone carving — the one that resembles no other animal and yet bears a trait from all of them — actually is or what it signifies. What does two thousand years ago have to do with me, or the return of the dog . . . ? The villagers saw the dog return. The dog managed to escape from their clutches and went to hide in the cavern. Maybe he hid the dog there himself. I wouldn't put it past the person who wrote these letters. He writes: "I will not let them be until I find out which of us is genuine. Which one of us is real. Hot bread and cheese, milking an animal, shimmering robes in a rhythmic dance, a gurgling spring, a flute at sunset, have all been shed from my fantasies like the filth on my body that peels under my finger tips and falls off. Here everything whirls around in a wind tunnel and turns into dust. The black shadows of the days, the blackness of the nights . . . They gnaw on dry bread, they steal if they can, like dogs they hide their meager trifles from each other in a hundred little holes, they beat their wives at night and tell each other about it . . .

"These same people swarmed my cavern. I hadn't told them about it. I said I wouldn't tell. No one knew. I don't know how they found out. They dragged the poor animal outside with a rope. He wasn't howling. He was subdued. The rope squeezed his neck but he did nothing. They pulled him up from the branch of a dead tree that sits in the middle of the village. The children threw stones at him, they could have killed him then and there, but they wanted to torment me. They looked at me while they beat him with a stick and laughed when he thrashed about . . . Now that I write, the night has come and the dog is still hanging there. He is snorting. I am petrified of going out. He's probably calling me. He wants to stare at me with those sad eyes, like he usually does, but I want to go to the image on the wall. I have discovered something. The animal is not attacking that man — the way he is perched up on his hind legs, he doesn't resemble an animal about to attack. He's the same height as the man and has rested his paws on the man's shoulders; then why? . . . What do you think the shadow of a hung dog looks like on a moonlit night? Try to see it in your sleep. Although I know you won't be able to hear the sounds."

I am sure there was a lot of pain in his heart for him to take it out on me like this. It's not my fault if I didn't understand what he was talking about and didn't know how to respond. And this is his last letter. It wasn't written in sequence. There is no stamp on the envelope, it came with that package that had someone else's handwriting on it. It's the handwriting of a beginner. Maybe the handwriting of someone he has taught to read and write, perhaps he has spoken of me to him, said things that made the person bring this package and leave it at our door one early morning. Early morning! That is also how the letter begins. "Early in the morning when I woke up, it was quiet everywhere. I had fallen asleep at midnight with the sound of the dog's snorts echoing in my ear. When I opened my eyes I thought he must have choked to death by now and I looked out the window. The rope was still there, swaying in the wind, but there was no dog hanging from it. He had cut through the noose with his teeth. I laughed. I went over to the tree and laughed and when Sabz-Ali came I showed him the rope and laughed some more. One by one they came. They were terrified and this made me laugh even harder and it seemed as though they were scared of me, too. Fearful of the rabid dog, they sent their wives and children home and armed with shovels and clubs they started searching high and low . . . I'm going to look for that dog . . ."

He writes: "It's nighttime, no one dares leave his hut. On this hot and humid night, everyone has scurried into a hole. From afar, the dog's wails circle Guraab, the wail of a wounded larynx that is still in the tight squeeze of the rope. My stomach is churning and I must sleep, but I am not sleepy and the minute I shut my eyes it's as though my nose and ears also close up, and then they come: the smells, scenes, sounds, the sound of a dog's paws running over rocky ground, the sound of a metal chisel carving stone, the roar of fire, the groan of a woman whose husband has bent her over like a dog, the sound of all the dreams in the world. I want to sleep but my head won't let me . . ." There's more. Despite his dreadful state he has written more: "He woke me up with a start. It was him. I heard his paws on the window and the rasp of his constricted throat. I went to the window but he was gone. I saw his shadow going down the alleyway. This was the second night he had come to Guraab. Perhaps he was hungry. He stopped behind the door of a hut and rubbed his snout on the door. As though he wanted to chew on the rotting wood. Somewhere a woman screamed. Everyone put out their lanterns quickly. Now they know that it is safer in the dark. There was the sound of a shot and then the dog's howl. In the morning there were only a few drops of blood in front of the door of Farvardin's hut, nothing else. Farvardin says he aimed at the back of the dog's head with his loaded gun, point blank. But I'm sure he hasn't died. He will come again tonight. Even Farvadin stands in the middle of the road and yells, I will kill him a thousand times, if he comes back a thousand times, I will kill him . . . Still he will come . . . Why won't he go away? What does he want to prove by staying in Guraab?" No, he seems to be writing much of this to himself or for others after him, for others . . . not for me.

"It is finally over. Today was the second day after he lost his sixth life and escaped. I saw him when I left my room this morning. He was standing there under that same tree, panting and wagging his tail for me. Last night, when he was howling under the window, I wished I had a gun to kill him myself, so that I and the others would be rid of him, but someone yelled in the alleyway and again there was the sound of a gunshot and then there was silence, without a drop of blood on the earth . . . What did this animal want from me, standing there as though nothing had happened. He was staring at me, and I could see Sabz-Ali armed with a shovel, tiptoeing toward him from behind. I saw him one step away from the dog and he raised his shovel and the dog still stared at me. The shovel slid along his side and tore the skin off his backbone. He leaped toward me and ran into the alley. There, someone blocked his way and hit him with a club. He was foaming at the mouth. I am sure of this, and he no longer wailed. Wherever he went, someone appeared in front of him and then he attacked. He wouldn't have attacked if they had left him alone. The villagers had all poured out of their huts. Everyone was carrying something to beat the animal with. They pounded on his teeth. All I have written is merely the howls never uttered by that dog, and now I am at peace because I know that I am not real, and they are the ones that exist and I only observed them, all of them and the dog was evading their kicks and escaping to the hidden corners of the village. Froth and blood and pandemonium. The dog's eyes were searching for me. There was something in the gaze of the people as they screamed obscenities and chased him and beat him with their shovels and clubs with all their might, and there was something about their frothing mouths, and just then, out of fear, I lost consciousness. The secret of the carved image in the cavern was being revealed to me and I could see that the bare teeth on the stone were a sign of these same frothed teeth, and the man is the ancient spirit of this same rabid fury that I see and I ran back toward the cavern and amid the dust and the screams and the howling of the wind, the dog, lame and butchered, was still struggling to find an opening in the wall of flesh and blind blows. Just before reaching the hill top, I fell, and there I turned around and looked at Guraab.

"The helpless animal was lying on the ground, he had covered his eyes with his paws and the circle of flesh around him was getting tighter. Sabz-Ali approached him from the middle of the crowd and poured something on him. The animal did not move. Perhaps they thought he was dead and someone lit a match. Did that resounding wail not reach your ears? Consider that perhaps you heard it in the folds of the city's clamor, if you were sitting in the garden of your house that I once liked so much, and if the fountain in the reflecting pool was on and the water bubbles were popping and the green leaves of the orange tree shone on the water; perhaps you heard the dog's cry as he went up in flames and leaped up and broke the circle of people and ran. Ablaze and blind he ran into a wall, he stretched his neck back toward the flame around his middle and tried to bite at it and leaving smoke and smell in his wake he ran toward the wheat fields. I rolled down the stairs of the cavern and lit a match. This was it, this was why it persistently dragged me to its side, to keep me captivated. The magic of the carving is not in the images alone, it is also in its survival, and the man had plunged his dagger in the animal's head in such a way that it seems he had no other choice and his face was turned toward me and he was looking at me and from between his clenched stone teeth he roared something. His eyes, which were chipped at the corners and had taken on a beseeching look, said the same thing, 'Strike.' And I picked up a stone and struck it against his teeth, just what he had yearned for, for a thousand years. 'Shatter.' And I struck and struck again, stone against stone and the stone cracked and crumbled and then there was darkness and the terrifying sound of water.

"When I left the cellar, the world was also dark. Black smoke had enveloped Guraab and the plain. At the far end of the wheat fields, a few flames still rose amid the smoke. The people of Guraab, blackened, with singed hair and burned clothes, were on their knees here and there staring at the black earth and sky. No one wept, no one moved. Rostam had gathered a small stack of wheat where he had first shown me his thirteen seeds. He had cut them with his bare hands from in front of the fire and a woman held up her skirt, filled with stalks of wheat . . . seeds for next year. No one saw me coming toward my hut. Now I feel weak. It is night and the smell of smoke bothers me. When I look out the window, out in the dark plain ashes still glow. It is good fertilizer for the soil and I am thinking how am I going to seal this envelope, my mouth is so dry . . ."

It must be morning. He hasn't written anything else. This was it, the end of his last letter. I don't know, no one has any news of him. Early one morning someone left his few belongings behind our door . . . I no longer have much sleep or appetite. Just a few nights ago, when everyone was asleep, I went and turned on a water faucet so that water slowly dripped from it, and then I lay down. The sound of the water got louder and louder, and little by little I thought I was hearing other sounds . . . Sometimes I think, what if that dog, in that cellar, dug its teeth into his flesh. Then I say no, the dog was not rabid, an animal that docile could not have turned wild without reason . . . But why did he not want to understand that I was the one who was really there for him? After all that I have read to you, do you think I should wait for him? Do you think he will come one day, like he used to, or no . . . he has gone for good . . .

— *Translated by Sara Khalili*

Ghazi Rabihavi

Ghazi Rabihavi was born in 1956 in Abadan. After studying Persian literature there, he began writing short stories, novels, and plays. His publications include a novel, *Maryam's Smile* (1997), and a collection of short stories, *The Iranian Four Seasons*. His play *Look Europe!* (1997) is based on the abduction and imprisonment of the Iranian journalist and writer Faraj Sarkuhi. It was staged in London with Harold Pinter playing one of the characters. His other plays include *Voices, Fly,* and *The Stoning.* He has lived in London since 1995.

Rabihavi is among the younger group of writers who experiment with new narrative techniques. He often writes without familiar punctuation, and is creative with his use of time, place, and dialogue. His characters are often people who have been marginalized by official society, such as intellectuals in trouble, restless youth, prostitutes, and homosexuals. "White Rock," which is about the execution of a homosexual, was published in *Index on Censorship* in 1996, after Rabihavi had moved abroad. Founded in 1972 by Stephen Spender, the journal *Index on Censorship* focuses on censorship issues and charts free speech violations through the world.

WHITE ROCK

The photographer jumped down over the gallows and his three cameras flapped around with him. We were worried something might happen to them. The gallows were still lying on the back of the pickup truck. He dusted off his trousers and said, "Are you kids from around here?"

We looked at each other and one of us said, "Are you going to take pictures of us or the dead man?"

The photographer blinked nervously and asked, "Is he dead?" and ran, complete with his solid-looking black cameras, to the patrol car. It had arrived with three revolutionary guards carrying G-3 guns about an hour earlier. And one of us said, "I bet those guns aren't loaded."

Two of the officers threw their guns onto the backseat of the car and walked over to the pickup. And one of us said then, "I bet those guns *are* loaded."

They began to help take out the gallows posts from the truck and to set them up on either side of the white rock, where they had already dug two shallow holes to support them. Before they found the rock, one of the revolutionary guards had asked us, "Hey, you. Can any of you get us a stool?"

And one of us said, "He's going to be hanged, isn't he? Because you have to hang him."

But the other guy said, "Don't bother with a stool, this white rock will do."

A few local men were coming our way from different parts of the town. It was a good Friday morning for a hanging, only it would have been even better if it hadn't started to snow, or if we'd had gloves. They said if it snowed they wouldn't hang him. It wasn't snowing when they brought the dead man. When they brought him he was alive.

He came out of the ambulance and sniffed the air. He had pulled up the zipper of his gray and green jumper — or someone had done it up for him because his hands were strapped behind his back. The first snowflakes settled on his hair. A group of locals ran toward him. The photographer was checking his cameras. The headlights of the ambulance had been left on. The snowflakes were light and soft. They melted even before they touched the lights. One of us said, "Pity. I wasn't even born when they executed the Shah's guard."

One of us answered, "My brother was born then; my dad sat him up on his shoulders so could see the guy being executed. Bang! Bang!"

The truck driver said, "I'd love to stay and watch. It'd mean a blessing for me. But I've got to go to deliver this food for the troops."

The fat guard scratched his beard with the gun barrel and said, "Good luck."

The truck driver ran to the pickup, cursing the snow.

The prisoner was pacing up and down in the snow without any idea that he was moving closer and closer to the gallows. Sometimes he just stood there, with his long, thin legs, turning his head this way and that, sniffing the air. He wrinkled his nose and waggled his eyebrows, trying to shift the blindfold to find out where he was. But the blindfold was too tight. One of us said, "Shout out his name so he knows where he is."

Another said, "When I used to know his name he was a different person."

A couple of people were still working, trying to get the gallows firmly in the ground.

Only men and children could come to watch. One of the men, who had been given a leg up on the cupped hands of another, jumped down and said, "Where's the other one?" The prisoner turned his head and said, "Yeah. Where is he?"

We didn't know the other guy; he wasn't from our town. We only saw him once — no, twice — on the same night. It was the beginning of autumn. The sun was just setting when we saw him entering the gates. He had a long turtleneck sweater pulled down over his trousers. His clothes were black, like his hair. The officer at the gate was eating meat and rice. The stranger was carrying a bouquet of pink roses, and he was trying to hide a black plastic bag underneath it. He didn't like us watching him. But we did anyway and figured out that there were two bottles in the bag. He had the address of the prisoner but didn't know which way to go. So we showed him. At first we thought he was a rather tall boxer. He ran his fingers through his hair and lifted his head. Then he lowered his eyes. His eyebrows were shaved across his nose, where they should have run together, and he smiled at us. The sun trembling through the plane tree splashed his face with light and shade. He smiled and turned in the direction we had pointed. The security guy was washing his plate under the tap and asked us, "Who was that?" And we told him. He looked over at the prisoner's house.

People were moving closer to the gallows, gathering in front of it. The photographer was sitting in the ambulance having a smoke. The prisoner, walking toward the gallows, was still unaware of where he was. One of the guards took his arm and pulled him over to the rock. The photographer grabbed his cameras and jumped out of the ambulance. He was wearing one of those safari vests with lots of pockets. From one of them, he pulled out a wire contraption and hooked it onto the shoulder tabs. Then he got out some white cloth and stretched it over the frame he had made. Now the snow wouldn't bother him. With the umbrella that had just sprouted from his shoulder, he ran across the gallows.

None of the spectators was related to the prisoner; we didn't know if he had any relations. He was a loner; he built the wooden bodies for stringed instruments and twice a week went out of town. People said he had a wife and children somewhere whom he had abandoned. The grocer had said to him, "Give it another chance. You're only forty-five. It's actually the right time to get married."

The prisoner smiled and said, "Ah yes, the right time."

The guy holding the prisoner's arm was still looking at the hanging rope. Then he told the prisoner, "Stand on top of this stone, will you, pal. Just to test everything's okay."

The prisoner's feet searched for the stone. Found it. If we could have seen his eyes, we could have told if he was frightened or not. That midnight, in the autumn, when the guards attacked his house and arrested both of them, he pressed his face against the rear window of the car, his eyes searching everywhere for his lover. Then, his voice trembling, he yelled from behind the glass, "Leave him alone!" The car drove off; a crushed pink rose was still sticking to the back tire.

The prisoner asked, "Is it time?"

The revolutionary guard said, "No. The haji hasn't arrived yet.[1] We can't start without him."

---

[1] Haji: one who has been to Mecca; here, a cleric, a religious judge.

He said, "Then what?"

The officer said, "Take your shoes off. This is only a trial run."

The prisoner removed his feet from the loose-fitting canvas shoes and stood on them. His long, thin toes were red with cold. The guards had upended the white rock and were holding it in position; the slightest kick would topple it, leaving his feet dangling in space. The guard said, "Now climb up." He put one foot on the rock. It shifted, swayed, nearly fell over. The guard jumped forward and set it straight again.

"What's with you?" he said. "Are you in a hurry?"

Then he got up and, one by one, carefully placed the prisoner's feet on the stone. The prisoner stood on the stone and was raised up above the crowd. His shoes were left below, on the ground, and everything around him was white: the sky, the snow. The rest of the officers and the driver were standing under a big umbrella, like you have on a beach, next to the patrol car. It was a long way from the gallows. The photographer said, "What are you doing? The haji isn't here yet."

The guard said, "No, he isn't."

The photographer said, "Then come over here and have some saffron dates."

The guard said, "Only if you let me stand under your umbrella," and burst out laughing. The photographer looked up at his umbrella and said, "It's for the cameras," and walked toward the patrol car.

The spectators were not saying anything. They were just standing there, silent, looking at the prisoner. Hanging on to one side of the gallows, the guard pulled himself up next to him. If he hadn't been wearing boots, there would have been enough room for another pair of feet. The stone wobbled again, but didn't fall over. The guard grabbed the hanging rope and struggled to loop it around the prisoner's neck. The prisoner was trying to help, but couldn't see what the guard was doing. Then he jumped down and the rock stayed firm. He said, "Now you see how steady it is?"

In the distance a car was approaching. "Hurry up!" one of the revolutionary guards called out.

He looked at the patrol car and then at the prisoner.

"Try to get used to it," he said. "Then, when the time comes, you won't panic."

The only movement in the landscape was the distant car. We

could only just make it out, but because of the whiteness of the snow we could make out what type it was: either a Mercedes or a Hillman. Haji must have been lounging in the backseat.

"Make sure it doesn't work loose," the guard said. "I'll be right back."

The prisoner said, "What?"

But the guard had already moved off to the patrol car. From the weight in the backseat, the trunk of the approaching car sagged low to the ground. The guards were still eating their dates near the patrol car. Women were not allowed to watch because this was not their business; it had nothing to do with them. The prisoner tried to shift the rock with his feet. It refused to move. One of the spectators jumped forward but quickly froze to the spot. All of us were waiting for the approaching car. The revolutionary guards and the photographer were throwing the date stones into the snow. The snowflakes were melting as they hit the ground. The prisoner again tried to shift the rock. It moved but didn't fall. The silent spectators stood stock-still, as if they were frozen to the spot and it wasn't snowing. Our hands were red with cold. Red as the wine the guards found in the prisoner's house the night of his arrest. One of the bottles was empty, the other still half full. The guards also took the two long-stemmed crystal glasses. By now we could see the car. It was a Hillman. One of the officers threw the date box away. The rest quickly ate up what they had left in their hands. One of the revolutionary guards went to meet the car and the rest followed. The photographer glanced at the gallows. He started to move closer, but changed his mind and walked over to the ambulance instead. The prisoner was kicking at the rock with his feet. It tottered, fell down, and left his bare feet hanging in the air. His long, thin toes were searching for the stone. But by then it was too late. Then the movement stopped and his feet hung motionless. The car finally arrived, dazzling us with its headlights. We went to warm our hands at the headlights of the ambulance, because that was what the photographer was doing.

— *Translated by Neda Jalali*

Farideh Kheradmand

Farideh Kheradmand was born in Tehran in 1957. She studied drama and literature and worked as a playwright, director, and radio actor. Since 1992, she has devoted her time to writing. Her published works include several plays and children's books, as well as two collections of short stories, *A Bird Exists* and *Peace of Night*. She lives in Tehran.

PEACE OF NIGHT

Every night I sit in the pitch darkness of my room for hours, staring at one point.

On the window, my eyes fall on the cheerful profile of a clown projected through the needles of a pine tree. But I have closed the curtains for a while now, to shut out the clown. I no longer believe in his cheery smile.

Each and every night I stare at one point in the deep recesses of the room. Nothing is visible in the dark, and I find peace only when I hear that quiet chewing sound.

A hungry mouse slowly gnaws away at my papers and worthless notes, and I don't even move a muscle. I just listen to his mellow tune: the constant grinding of teeth on paper. It has a hum that entertains me.

Sometimes I think, "Which story is up now?" or "Which word is he working on?" And a sweet trance takes hold of me, the kind of trance that works best through self-delusion.

Last night, in the middle of the night, he suddenly stopped chewing. It worried me. I waited, but there was no sound. I yearned to hear the sound of the papers being chewed once again. "Maybe he's reached a plain white paper in the middle of my notes." He has a strange habit: he doesn't touch plain white paper. He only chews paper blackened with ink.

My anticipation grew. "He knows. He's just torturing me." A hatred rose inside me, but I did not let it seep out. Then I got worried that maybe something has happened to him. But I still couldn't turn the light on. My eyes had become accustomed to the dark. Any kind of light, no matter how faint, would have bothered me. I waited. And then another ploy: complete indifference. A while later, when I heard the sound of the nibbling, I smiled, without, of course, letting him know. And then my nightly serenity descended through me.

Sometimes I wonder, "How long does it take per word?" During these long nights, it has become clear to me that time is not something he squanders. All the papers and words that he deems superfluous, he simply ignores.

During the day, I write with the hope of hearing his whispers in the dark of the night. I write so he won't go hungry. And he is silent throughout the day as he sleeps and rests his jaws.

We have become accustomed to each other. During the day, he hears the whispers of the gnawing of my soul; and I, at night, the peaceful tune of the gnawing of papers and words.

— *Translated by Kuross Esmaili*

Poetry

INTRODUCTION

The relationship between poetry and the social context out of which it arises — and in which it must be seen as anchored — is complex and multifaceted. Trying to articulate it, partially and ever so tentatively, we grope for metaphors that can make it palpable — mirrors, road maps, models — knowing well that such images flaunt their inadequacy and difference more than their likeness or illustrative power. In the end, clinging to the certainty that poems, these concentrated sites of meaning, relate to the realities of a community's mind and life, we acknowledge that the exact nature and shape of a poem's "relevance" remains unknowable. An anthologist must then leave it to the reader's imagination to guess at the ways in which his offering may "reflect," "recall," or "reassemble" the social fabric in which it is etched.

For American readers of Persian poetry, the problem is compounded by misrepresentations, primarily based on information transmitted through the American media which not only simplifies but often deliberately distorts, crowding the mind with images that go against the grain of all art. No amount of pontificating on the ebb and flow of political events in Iran in the last two decades could even begin to account for the feverish mental activity of Iranian poets as they interpret their experiences or the emotions these have occasioned, not just for their immediate readers but for those outside their culture, as well as for posterity.

While to most Westerners the political events that have catapulted Iran to center stage of the world in the last two and a half decades may point to a historic retreat from modernity, Iranian poets, painters, and filmmakers are pulling at the sleeves of their muses to tell the world they not only have traversed all that is modern but are moving into the postmodern age (whatever that might mean) just as rapidly as they can. While to the outside viewer Iranian politics may appear to defy the linear logic of progress, Iranians see themselves as having passed the last twist in the winding spiral of their long, eventful history.

Witness the poems gathered here. In the midst of the turmoil and tumult associated with revolutions, wars, and an uneasy coexistence of a theocratic state with a society hungering for democracy, we have poems that still invite us, rather quietly, to contemplate the beauties of nature or to read the narrative of their maker's existence with greater empathy. The poets whose work is assembled here are actively revisiting those governing principles of writing and reading that, a revolution ago, dominated the lives of their forebears and role models. Code words of a generation — literary engagement, social symbolism, and socialist realism — are fast exiting the scene of Persian poetry, albeit on tiptoe, making way for pensive moods or undisturbed moments of attention to minutiae.

The new wise men and women of the Persian tribe are trying to assure us that culture, still very much bent on capturing beauty, is alive in their minds and their midst, if not on their streets. Witness also that the poets who are most instrumental in spearheading the new mood and mind — Royai, Atashi, Sepanlu — have begun to question the efficacy of the flat linear notions of literary history — all history, in fact — as it is expressed through the metaphors of the mirror or catchphrases like "literary engagement" and "commitment" to revolutionary change that dominated the scene in the 1960s. The stone that the carvers set aside has indeed turned out to be the cornerstone, to paraphrase a well-known psalm.

The way this is accomplished is remarkable, and most worthy of our attention, even though it may involve a momentary digression in the direction of certain perennial building blocks of early Persian poetry, established in eastern Iran and Central Asia over a millennium ago. It was there in the tenth and eleventh centuries, in the courts of Bukhara, Ghazna, and Samarqand, that Persian poets — men like Rudaki, Manuchehri, Ferdowsi, or Khayyam — conjured the first images of Persian poetry, describing the beauty of a hoopoe or a horse, commenting on a battle or a royal feast, raising their glasses well past midnight to life, youth, and the pursuit of joy. Recalling strong historical connections and a rich oral tradition, they gave Persian literary culture, perhaps even the world, a kind of concrete poetry that modern Persian poets like Atashi or Kiarostami link up with today.

Although the high clouds of mystical speculation that appeared on the horizon centuries later may have pushed heads upward or forced men inside the recesses of their airy imaginations, some sense of immediate wonder and joy, tied so much to time and place, continued to survive through the ages, eventually revivified by a new source of enrichment. When Persian poetry, always an elitist art, became too removed from the concrete concerns of the modern nation-states that had inherited the Persian aesthetic tradition, Romantic Europe contributed a much-needed midcourse correction. Still, in terms of Persian poetic modernity, this Romantic impulse was — or soon became — far more a return-to-nature movement than a wild-eyed fascination with the strange and the mysterious, or with the long ago and the far away. The grain of modern and modernist Persian aesthetics remained largely enmeshed in daily affairs and in its surroundings, be it in Iran itself, the new country of Afghanistan, or in Central Asia, dominated by the Russian culture and the Soviet ideology.

It was in response to the Iranian states' shallow and rootless push toward a Westernized project of modernity — first in the 1930s and again in the 1960s and early 1970s — that Iran's poets, recoiling from the pace far more than from the direction, formulated the notion of commitment that came to dominate aesthetic expressions of the time. Of course, the emergence in the last century of the Persian-speaking world's proximity to the Soviet Union, and the channeling of progressive impulses into Soviet-style communism, also played a crucial role. Iran's revolutionary movement, which began as an effort to return to the fountainhead of its native culture and ended up attempting to subordinate that culture to a religious ideology, brought intellectual Iranians back to the position they had traditionally occupied: visionaries positioned against a dogmatic power structure.

That is where I would situate many of the poems collected in this anthology. Doubts about dogma, pensive moods countering concentrated efforts in cultural engineering, fingers pointed toward life beyond politics — all combined with a newfound aversion to political revolutions — make up much of the fabric for the work found here. Above all, these poems radically rearticulate the past, both national and religious, and even the mythical past. The revolution is now in the text; it makes up the motive force of the creative mind behind it. No longer do we see nights of oppression automatically turn into the dawns of deliverance so prevalent in so-called Nimaic canon, or the mechanical and rather noisy clanking of the slaves' chains (as in young Shamlu's vision of future liberation), or retellings of ancient Iranian myths aimed at mobilizing our modern sense of patriotism (à la Akhavan). In their place is a new and often antithetical poetic impulse: a quiet invitation to view the soaring of a bird from underneath a turtle's shell, or ancient myths carved in stone which may be read as prophesying the ephemerality of modern myths of nationalism. Gone are noisy incantations of revolutionary marches, replaced by quiet meditations on youthful love, questioning the operations of memory as it tries to revive something of the past, as we found in Atashi's "A Woman out of Memory."

More radical departures are not uncommon. Royai, a poet always on the side of free rein of the imagination, is represented here by four poems from his collection *Seventy Tombstones*. In them he revises the lives of luminaries of the past, not as one might hear at a wake or read on a tombstone, but as depicted by an imagination freed from the shackles of celebratory rituals, shaped by received ideas. In a poem like "Martyr's Tombstone," he bestows immortality upon the martyred heroes of the revolution and war, at the same time registering his protest against the culture of death propagated by some revolutionary clerics. Beyond all relevancies that might accrue to various sorts of external referentiality, the poet thus demonstrates the possibility that poetry can be image centered and relevant at one and the same time.

In "Love Song," one of the earliest poems in our selection, Shamlu depicts a deeply dejected lover facing a joyful beloved, embodying a sense of abandon. In projecting love as a personage unable to speak, as if stifled by force into silence, the operations of the poem point to simultaneous and contradictory possibilities: love is there, but it cannot be consummated because it cannot be communicated. This is not unlike Sepanlu's depiction in "Miniature" of the confrontation between beauty's unstoppable urge to manifest itself and a restrictive social environment designed to banish all beauty.

Not surprisingly, the most radical visible trait separating the poetry written in the last quarter-century from the entire modernist canon, at least insofar as the centrality of the image to the idea is concerned, comes from the pen of a filmmaker. Abbas Kiarostami's poems in *Walking with the Wind* confirm the impression that he conceptualizes poetry and film as ontologically the same. His poetic personages—some making a single appearance, others quite ubiquitous—come from an array of contexts, the most evident being fauna and flora: the foal, the nag, and the horse; pigeons and doves and wild geese; butterflies and grasshoppers; a mosquito here, two dragonflies there, spiders everywhere; honeybees and worker bees and queen bees; lizards and snakes and turtles.

They appear as direct manifestations of specific states of being. The pine and the box tree, the sycamore and the oak, the mulberry and the cherry, the weeping willow and the towering cypress, all grow and decay side by side with the rattan, the cotton, the poppy, the violet, the begonia. Among these, nuns young and old move, seemingly directionless, mostly arguing and disagreeing, as small children play their games.

Finally, no twenty-first-century account of Persian poetry will be complete without taking note of the poetry produced by Iranian expatriates in the last two decades. In these, too, we witness a perceptible move toward a more image-conscious aesthetic. It seems as though the loss of the familiar territory we call home has in this case led to a new search for poetic expression, one marked by a relevance and coherence that together can make a poem universal as well as Iranian at the same time. While an inevitable sense of fractured ego may be most evident in more established poets like Nader Naderpur and Esmail Khoi, depictions of the mood of restorative nostalgia are on the ascendance. While in the works of early exile differences in the climate, the physical environment, and the nature of human relations are emblematic of the condition of exile and therefore a barometer of the speaker's mood, in more recent writings a genuine sense of wonder and appreciation often appears.

Younger expatriates even seem at times prepared to view their severance from the homeland more as a voyage of initiation. Far from rendering the speaker dysfunctional, the past is often recollected as a benign but not ideal point of entry to the present, thus allowing a pleasantly sad but not debilitating dialogue between the two. Summary rejections of the immediate environment, such as we are likely to see in texts of the older exiles, gives way to perceptible movements toward greater engagement with it. Often the presence of an interlocutor — a friend, a companion, a beloved child — acts to moderate the speaker's internalization of the environment. Here the backward glance tends to set up a model for creative inspiration and possible source of emulation for the world of the here and now. Establishing a link between the "self in present" and a remembered image of a "self in the past," the subsequent elevated mood plays a significant part in recovering the continuity of the individual and a modified sense of individual and collective identity.

Future historians of Persian poetry may well focus on the twentieth century as the time when it began to regain much of the glory it once possessed. The universal appeal of poets like Ferdowsi and Nezami, Attar and Rumi, Khayyam and Hafez, to nineteenth- and twentieth-century readers the world over may well have as much to do with the need in the recipient cultures to enrich or renew themselves with the aesthetics developed in the Persian-speaking world. It certainly owes a great deal to the creative and transformative strategies that their translators devised to make those texts their own. Similarly, the flourishing, at times feverish translation activity has played a decisive part in the evolution of the modernist poetic tradition, particularly in the manner in which this poetry has extended its appeal and social reach.

It is entirely possible to envision a future for Persian poetry in which it might be able to graft its newfound strength — in the ideas it proffers, its expressive strategies, and above all in the images it creates — to the eternal and universal human need for emotive expression. As a living and growing aesthetic tradition, it may well extend its domain further and wider than ever before. The outlook for Persian poetry appears bright at the dawn of the second millennium of its existence, just as it did when the grand epic *The Shahnameh,* the haiku-like *Rubaiyyat* of Omar Khayyam, or the dense lyrical expression of Rumi gave this poetic tradition its universal appeal.

AKH

Ahmad Shamlu

Ahmad Shamlu was born in 1925 in Tehran, but spent his childhood in various provincial towns. In his early youth he was a political activist who became a political prisoner under the Shah's regime. Later, like so many of his generation, he became a journalist, though his primary talent was as a gifted poet, taking on traditional Persian poetry with its set formulas of meter and rhyme. A follower of Nima Yushij (1897–1960), Iran's first modernist poet, Shamlu went on to develop his own distinct style, searching for new means to expand the metrical and verbal resources of poetry. He firmly believed that poetry should speak the language of the people and reflect their hopes and pains, yet Shamlu's poetry is effective because it mingles his intensely personal experience with his and other intellectuals' political and social concerns.

Shamlu published over twenty volumes of poetry. He translated Western poetry into Persian, including the work of Langston Hughes and Federico Garcia Lorca. He also edited and founded several artistic and literary journals, and translated both fiction and poetry from the French. For over thirty years, he collected the folk ballads, tales, games, and common street lore of the Persians, particularly natives of the capital city of Tehran, to form his *Dictionary of Street Language*. To date, his "Book of the Alley," along with much of his work, has never been published due to censorship. Shortly before the revolution, Shamlu lived in exile in the United States and England for almost three years, but returned to Iran early in 1979. Between 1979 and his death in 2000, he remained in Iran and continued to write poetry and criticism, despite severe pressure from the authorities. Along with many other writers whose work appears in this anthology, Shamlu was active trying to establish an independent Iranian writers' association, an effort that continues to evoke resistance from the state authorities even today. His accomplishments and the tremendous influence he has had on a younger generation of Persian-speaking poets made him one of the most revered literary figures in modern Iranian history.

IN THIS BLIND ALLEY

They smell your breath
lest you have said: I love you,
They smell your heart:
These are strange times, my dear.

They flog love
at the roadblock.
Let's hide love in the larder.

In this crooked blind alley, as the chill descends,
they feed fires
with logs of song and poetry.
Hazard not a thought:
These are strange times, my dear.

The man who knocks at your door in the noon of the night
has come to kill the light.
Let's hide light in the larder.

There, butchers
are posted in passageways
with bloody chopping blocks and cleavers:
These are strange times, my dear.

They chop smiles off lips,
and songs off the mouth:
Let's hide joy in the larder.

Canaries barbecued
on the flames of lilies and jasmines:
These are strange times, my dear.

Satan, drunk on victory,
squats at the feast of our undoing.
Let's hide God in the larder.

— *Translated by Ahmad Karimi Hakkak*

LOVE SONG

The man saying, "I love you,"
is a sad minstrel
who has lost his voice:
        if only love could speak.

A thousand happy skylarks
in your eyes
a thousand silent canaries in my throat:
        only if love could speak.

The man saying, "I love you,"
is the dark heart of the night
searching for moonlight:
        if love only could speak.

A thousand gleaming sunbeams with each step you take,
a thousand weeping stars
of my desire:
        if love alone could speak.

— *Translated by Ahmad Karimi Hakkak*

END OF THE GAME

The lovers
passed through, downcast,
disgraced by their untimely rhapsodies.
The alleys
were left with no murmurs and no sound of footsteps.

The soldiers
passed by, shattered,
weary
on scrawny horses,
faded rags of ousted pride
upon their spears.

What do you gain
boasting
to the world
when
every particle of dust on your cursed path damns you?

What do you gain from trees and orchards
when
you speak to the jasmine,
holding a scythe in your hand?

Where you have stepped,
plants
refrain from growing,
since you never believed
in the virtues of water and earth.

Alas! Our story
was the faithless ballad of your soldiers
returning
from the conquest of the harlots' fortress.

Wait for what the curse of the night shall make of you:
mothers in black,
mourning the most beautiful offspring of the wind and the sun,
have yet to lift their heads
from their prayer rugs.

— Translated by Arthur Lane and Firoozeh Papan

MORNING

Lukewarm and slow,
soiled water patterns of the summer rain
on charmless leaves of rose mallow
at five o'clock in the morning.

In the martyrs' graveyard
professional preachers
are still
asleep.

The hanging abyss of screams
in the air
is empty.

And those wrapped in bloodstained shrouds
turn over
in their tombs
weary.

Pockmarks of rain
trifle
on perfunctory tombstones
at five o'clock in the morning.

— Translated by Arthur Lane and Firoozeh Papan

Simin Behbahani

Simin Behbahani was born in Tehran in 1927. From the age of twelve she wrote poetry and published her first *ghazal*, a short lyrical genre in Persian poetry, when she was fourteen. She studied to become a midwife, but because she was suspected of belonging to the Tudeh, or Communist Party, initially she was not admitted to Tehran University. "From that time on," Behbahani writes in *A Cup of Sin: Selected Poems of Simin Behbahani*, "the purpose of my poetry has been to fight injustice. Whenever I could, I have portrayed it, revealed it. I have considered freedom the cardinal requirement of being a poet, and have never bowed my head to any power or office."

Behbahani eventually earned a law degree from Tehran University and taught literature in various high schools, meanwhile writing poetry for the rest of her professional life. She writes:

> I have worked mainly in the ghazal style. I began writing poems with ghazals and linked couplets. From early on, my poems have reflected my social milieu and conditions, though in effect these reflections have been reflections of my individual and emotional reactions to the society and conditions in which I have lived. . . . Reacting to and provoked by the outside world, I reveal the world within.

The advent of the Iranian revolution seems to have strengthened this dimension of Behbahani's work. In fact, her first post-revolution collection, titled "A Line of Speed and Fire," impressed the Tehran literary establishment as a book inspired by the revolutionary movement and replete with stunningly clear images of fleeting moments expressed in flowing rhymes not typical of the genre of the *ghazal* in modern times. It seemed as though the poet had internalized the tradition of the best imagistic utterances in Persian poetry and was combining it with uncanny intuitions and keen observations on the flow of events through a revolutionary moment.

For the past twenty years, I have tried to change the current meters of the ghazal by incorporating parts of natural, everyday speech, which in their natural setting may seem devoid of any obvious metrical design. By repeating and extending the meters of a beginning segment, I create a new pattern, free of the set patterns in traditional ghazals and free of the set themes and expressions associated with them. Thus I have created a new container ready for new contents.

In all, she has published fifteen volumes of poetry. The poems here are from *A Cup of Sin: Selected Poems of Simin Behbahani,* edited and translated by Farzaneh Milani and Kaveh Safa (Syracuse, N.Y.: Syracuse University Press, 1999).

A MAN WITH A MISSING LEG

A man with a missing leg
has one leg of his pants folded.
His eyes burn with anger
Is this a spectacle? they cry.
Though I turn my face away,
his image lingers:
his extreme youth, less than twenty, perhaps.
I pray he will not be like me,
having to endure another forty years.
Yet, the suffering that comes with existence
is impervious to such pleas.
Though my feet were quick,
the trail was difficult for me.
How will he manage with just one leg?

Tap, tap, he stamps the pavement with his cane,
though he needs no signature
to register his presence.
My tender smiles turned to thorns and daggers in his eyes.
Used to rough treatment,
he has no appetite for tenderness.
Lines of bitterness mark his cold, parched face.
As if, with his body diminished,
his spirit too had lost its resilience.
To help him persevere, I thought, I would offer him
some kindness and motherly advice.
But I realized it was more than he could bear.

I turned to him to start a conversation.
The spot where he stood was empty.
He was gone, the man with a missing leg.

— *Translated by Farzaneh Milani and Kaveh Safa*

I WRITE, I CROSS OUT

I write, I cross out, to find what I've lost,
to find words for turbulent thoughts.
I scratch the back of my skull
with a finger like an ivory dowel
to untangle braid by braid the tangled yarn.
In my mind filled with dust
the colors of your face have faded.
I close my tired eyes to contemplate
what remains.

I wanted to remember you. You changed into a cloud
on the far side of the sea.
How can I picture you in this scattered vapor?
Is this the tired wind breathing
or the sound of your voice in the streets?
Who is this and what is he saying?
I wish to know, that I may prepare an answer.
What is this turbulence
below the surface of my consciousness?
I am not the foam that breathes
with joy in the waves of the sea.
Your memories flee, and I have no remedy.
I cannot fold them in piles
like clothes in a closet.

You have asked what I want from you?
You *should* ask what I *wanted.*
Desires were drained from my heart
before I could desire.

— *Translated by Farzaneh Milani and Kaveh Safa*

IF THE SNAKE IS DOMESTIC

If the snake is domestic
I will give it shelter.
I will be fond of it still,
even if it does cruel things.

It slithered down the ceiling
with angry carnelian eyes
and a quick poisonous tongue,
and it coiled itself by my side.
People tell me, bring it salt:
as salt consumed will
make one beholden to its giver.
I will bring what is needed
from my poems: images like emeralds
formed in my lover's soul.
I shall lay them in front of it
and enumerate them, one by one.
Dazzled by the colors and light,
it will begin warming up to me.
It will move its head,
expecting me to scratch its back and neck.
Its fangs glistening like brass,
a snake intoxicated —
what need to destroy it?
Oh, this is a domestic snake.
You can't kill it in anger.
Even though it does cruel things,
I let it be.

— *Translated by Farzaneh Milani and Kaveh Safa*

AND BEHOLD

Do they not consider the camel, how it was created?

— From the Quran, Sura 88:37

And behold the camel, how it was created:
not from mud and water,
but, as if, from patience and a mirage.
And you know how the mirage deceives the eyes.
And the mirage knows not the secret of your patience:
how you endure thirst, sand, and salt marshes,
gazing at the immense presence with your weary eyes.
And behold how this gaze is marked with salt grooves
like the dry lines remaining on your cheeks after a stream of tears.
And behold the tears that have drained from you
all the means of consciousness.
With what nothingness should you fill this emptied space?
And behold in this emptied space the agitation of a thirsty camel,
made mad beyond the limits of its patience,
reluctant to meekly carry its heavy burden.
And behold its two incisors gleaming madly in a row of angry teeth.
Patience spawns hatred and hatred the fatal wound:
behold with what vengeance the camel
bites through the arteries of its driver.
The mirage lost its patience.
And behold the camel.

— *Translated by Farzaneh Milani and Kaveh Safa*

IT'S TIME TO MOW THE FLOWERS

It's time to mow the flowers,
don't procrastinate.
Fetch the sickles, come,
don't spare a single tulip in the fields.
The meadows are in bloom:
who has ever seen such insolence?
The grass is growing again:
step nowhere else but on its head.
Blossoms are opening on every branch,
exposing the happiness in their hearts:
such colorful exhibitions must be stopped.
Bring your scalpels to the meadow
to cut out the eyes of flowers.
So that none may see or desire,
let not a seeing eye remain.
I fear the narcissus is spreading its corruption:
stop its displays in a golden bowl
on a six-sided tray.
What is the use of your ax,
if not to chop down the elm tree?
In the maple's branches
allow not a single bird a moment's rest.
My poems and the wild mint
bear messages and perfumes.
Don't let them create a riot with their wild singing.
My heart is greener than green,
flowers sprout from the mud and water of my being.
Don't let me stand, if you are the enemies of Spring.

— Translated by Farzaneh Milani and Kaveh Safa

Mehdi Akhavan Saless

Born in 1928 in Mashhad in the province of Khorassan, Mehdi Akhavan Saless (a.k.a. M. Omid) began his career as a teacher. He became involved in politics in the 1950s and was imprisoned after the 1953 coup d'état. After his release, he worked at the Ministry of Education, and later as a literary commentator for Iran's radio and television organization.

His stature as a major modernist poet was established after the publication of his second volume of poetry, *Winter* (1956). Like so many others in the post–World War II generation of Iran's poets, Akhavan Saless was influenced by the modernist Nima Yushij's views on form, yet he never lost connection to the tone of the classical tradition. In his longer poems, Akhavan Saless brings together in a tight poetic structure the epic tradition of Ferdowsi, the dramatic qualities of Zoroastrian hymns, and themes from the simple folk ballads and tales of the Persian oral tradition. His shorter poems are sometimes cynical and sinister, sometimes playful and witty, and sometimes bitingly satirical. Akhavan Saless, a towering figure in contemporary Persian poetry, died in Tehran in 1990.

The following poem is a *qasida* — an important genre in classical and modern poetry — in praise of Iran as a nation. It has relevance in the context of post-revolutionary poetry, because with the establishment of the Islamic regime, the speech and actions of the leaders implied that they were more preoccupied with Islam than with Iran as a nation. In this poem, the speaker roams freely, first through Persian mythology and folklore and then through the history and geography of the land of Iran, expressing his abundant and unabashed love for it. Shortly after this poem was published, Akhavan Saless was summoned to the revolutionary court in Tehran and asked to declare his allegiance to the Islamic state, an episode that has stained the record of the Islamic Republic in its dealings with the country's leading intellectuals.

I LOVE YOU, ANCIENT HOMELAND

If I love anything in the world
I love you, ancient homeland

venerable aged one, ever so young
I love you, if I have ever loved

noble, antique Iran
I love you, precious pearl

eternal land of the grand
nurturer of the great, I love you

your mind shines forth like a work of art
and I am a lover both of your mind and art

I love your stories, myth or history
your traditions, accounts of your exploits

your scripts I love, let chisel be the pen
words inscribed on rocky pages of mount and hill

or be they recorded in books with black ink
with reed pens, or feathery plumes, I love it all

I admire your suppositions as if they were certainties
I love your declarations as if they were manifest

I worship your Ahura Mazda, your gods all
I love your divine glory, your splendor

with my life I love your ancient prophet
who is an old guide, beholder of light

I love the noble Zarathustra
more than all guides and prophets

man has not seen better than him nor will
I love that best of all humans

his three "goods"are the world's best guide[1]
I love maxims thus sweet and short

he was a leader, an Iranian superman
I love my leader to be Iranian

he neither killed nor ordered anyone killed
for that too I love him eminently

I love that true, ancient guide
be he gone beyond all legends

then that enlightened son of yours, Bamdad
bright-faced man of Nayshabur I love

and the glorious Mazdak I love in every regard
that eternal intelligence of all time

he gave his life bravely fighting injustice
man of justice with a lion's heart I love

he had an intellect universal and righteous
on that account I love him even more

With reverence I love Manes the worthy
both as painter and as prophet

that painter of superior souls I love
and the Arjang, his book of paintings

I love all your farms, dry or irrigated
your fields and pastures, your streams and brooks

---

[1] "Goods" refers to the prophet Zoroaster's guidance for a virtuous life: good thoughts, good
speech, good deeds.

I love your desert as well as your sea, dry and wet
your mountain as much as your forest, plain, hill

I love your discerning, life-offering martyrs
who were the pride of humanity

their souls, delicate as the breeze of dawn
and their steely courage I love

their thoughts as well I love
which have inspired revolutions of many ages

and their legacy, advice or admonishment
or even scattered tidings I love

I love those immortally memorable men
so many of whom have graced every century

your poets and their works I love
pure as the breeze of dawn

of Ferdowsi I love that palace of legends
which he built on the horizon of pride and victory

the rage and wrath of Khayyam I love
which forever works on the heart and the mind

and the pained burning and clamor of Attar
which ignites sparks in the soul, I love

and in Shams's lover the passion and fire
I love which sets the spirit aflame

and in Sa'di, Hafez and Nizami I love
the fervor, the poetry, and the tale

blessed be your regions, Rasht, Gorgan, Mazandaran
which I love as enormously as the Caspian Sea

blessed be the land watered by Karun
which I love as sweetly as its sugar

hallowed be your Azerbaijan the magnificent
I love that vanguard in the line of hazard

your Esfahan, known as "half the world"
I love better than the other half

blessed be Khorasan, the land that begets the select
that vast expanse I love with my soul and heart

glory to your Shiraz, peer of paradise
that cradle of talent and art I love

your land of the Kurd and the Baluch I love
as a tree bearing fruit of nobility

happy Kerman and the southern coast
which I love wet and dry, land and sea

I love the Afghans, a shoot of our common root
today in the claws of one worse than the Tartar

I love Sughd, Khwarezm and its desert
which the house of the Qajars lost

your Iraq and your Gulf I love
as much as Transoxania, gate to the Wall of China

I love Eran and our ancient Caucases
as a son loves the paternal abode

your legendary yesteryears and your dreamy morrows
both I love equally, with all my life

your legends I love for they let me
grow wings, more raptured than children

and I love your dreamy horizons, as forever
I have loved journeying through wondrous climes

like dreams and legends, your yesterday and tomorrow
I love both ends each in its place

but more than these I love your today
o living soul, o wealth at hand

you were at the zenith, in form, in substance
I love that zenith of prize and peril

rise up again to the zenith of substance
for I would love your new color, new forms

I love you, o homeland, to remain
neither western, nor eastern, nor Arab

may you be victorious so long as the world turns
may you be joyful and mindful and fruitful.

— *Translated by Ahmad Karimi Hakkak*

Esmail Khoi

Esmail Khoi is a leading Iranian poet living in exile. Born in 1938 in Mashad, he published his first volume of poetry when he was eighteen. Educated at Tehran Teachers Training College, Khoi went to England in 1961 for his graduate studies. Five years later, he received his doctorate in philosophy from the University of London. After his return from England, he published a second collection, *On the Galloping Stallion of the Earth.* In the 1960s and 1970s, as a founding member of the Writers Association of Iran, he opposed the restrictions on the freedom of expression under the Shah. After the Iranian revolution of 1979, Khoi found the conditions even more oppressive under the Islamic Republic. He went into hiding, and in 1983 left his homeland for England, where for the past twenty years he has been an outspoken opponent of the Iranian Islamic regime. Beyond politics, his poetry has attracted attention as an arena for the study of the aesthetics of exile, particularly as it relates to Iranian intellectuals. In his poems, exile appears as a condition disruptive to consciousness, evident in poetic settings where space and time cease to unfold predictably.

Khoi's publications in English translation include *Edges of Poetry: Selected Poems of Esmail Khoi* (edited by Ahmad Karimi Hakkak and Michael Beard, Blue Logos Press, 1995) and *Outlandia: Songs of Exile* (edited by Ahmad Karimi Hakkak and Michael Beard, Nik Publications, 1999).

LYRICAL

You are like the smell of a dove
like that clear silence
like the rainbow around her neck
like the warmth under her wings.

I long for no far-off flights
    not anymore
this piece of the sky for me
is enough.

My throat bears the marks
    of an eagle's claws.
May the balm of your fragrance
be sincere and plentiful.

And so
I shall become a woodpecker
building my nest
kiss by kiss
at the curve of your neck.

— *Translated by Ahmad Karimi Hakkak and Michael Beard*

OUTLANDIA

There's an essence to Outlandia,
it has everything your loving heart
                    might desire.
No, the air here is not that polluted
            and the water is wholesome.

What is more,
reason rules here, in all matters.
People abide by their laws

and the laws are made for the people:
Reflecting a combination
        of reason and experience,
and there are structures here
        open, flexible,
that resist underground tremors,
the trembling that warns of abrupt shifts and changes.

Not only its cities,
        its villages, too,
                are well cared for,
and its history:
rub off greed and blood, conquest and cruelty
                                        from its surface,
and it begins to reflect the human yearning for freedom.

Why is it then, O God,
that here, too, in this paradise,
happiness is still my forbidden fruit?

Over many years, in a place that is not mine,
I have learned a thousand points, as we say,
"finer than a hair,"
like the feeling that this land
would not let you be its master and lord,
that you cannot but be a beggar at its door,
not in those words, of course, but an uninvited guest,
seated at a table of condescending hospitality
where some helping hand
has invited multitudes of prideless outsiders,
                                stripped of self-respect.

I now see
as clearly as can be
that happiness is
witnessing your creation:
seeing the mark of your hand
                upon a door or a wall

on a rose petal,
          on a falling leaf,
                    in any paltry thing.

Nowhere in this paradise, though
                    need I say it,
have my hands planted or set anything in place
          not a rose bush
                    nor a brick or building block,
                              neither in a rose garden
                                        nor in a wall around a home.

I look around me
                    and I see
that no human edifice
standing in Outlandia
holds a mark from me.

And thus I decree:
          nothing
          here
          belongs to me.

Yes, Outlandia may be paradise on earth,
a place where no one minds what you do
yet, alas,
this is also the land
where none minds you!

And here
among these throngs so much minding
                    their work and their world
I find no mate for my soul
to whisper to her heart
          my wish for the hour
                    to say farewell
                              to this paradise

and to go back to my hell
my homeland.

— Translated by Ahmad Karimi Hakkak and Michael Beard

AN ALLUSION

Heaven forbid,
heaven
forbid,
that the dot, doodle, dot of the crows
on winter's blank page,
every one of them,
should be some sort of an allusion
to the impotence of the spring's
joy-soaked nature
to sing
the lyric of blossoming
with colored words.

— Translated by Ahmad Karimi Hakkak and Michael Beard

BAD BOY

They won't let you —
you see,
they won't let you rest
in your crib of loneliness,
far away from Mom's breath and the fragrance
of her kindness,
sucking on your fancy's pacifier

or play
with the talking doll of poetry
(a keepsake from your little sister)
and drive away fear,
the black bogeyman of fear,
        with the rattle of words
and be content,
like the remembrance of a pleasant dream
or a picture in a nicely carved frame
        with the mere fact
                of being.
                But
they won't let you,
no,
they won't let you.

Crouched, gingerly,
at God knows how much past midnight
from who knows what corner of this droning forest
        the bogeyman appears,
slashes the bad boy's throat,
opens up his chest,
takes out his desires,
carries them away,
        and eats them up raw.

— *Translated by Ahmad Karimi Hakkak and Michael Beard*

Nader Naderpur

Born and educated in Tehran, Nader Naderpur traveled to Europe upon completion of his secondary education and for the next five years lived in France and Italy, studying Western languages and literature. Upon his return to Iran, he translated poems and articles from the French, and published his first book of poetry, *Eyes and Hands,* followed by two other collections.

Naderpur's poetry, lyrical or otherwise, is rich in imagery and deeply embedded in the texture of the Persian language, occupying a poetic space between Behbahami and Shamlu. He experimented with such forms as *charpareh,* which slightly loosens the classical requirements of rhyme but remains well within the formal divisions of that tradition. After a few years, he began to experiment with freer forms in the style of Nima, Shamlu, and other modernists. What distinguishes his poetry is the polished language and meticulous observance of poetic diction as distinct from all that may appear prosaic and therefore without precedence in poetry. Many of his poems reveal a genuine, spontaneous feeling that drives through their diction and formalism. Naderpur has created masterpieces that have made him a most emulated poet, particularly among the Persian speakers of Afghanistan and Central Asia.

Naderpur left Iran in 1981. The experience of exile proved a powerful, if agonizing, source of inspiration for his latest works. In exile, Naderpur inhabits two places at once: an inner, remembered place, now evoked in ever-more-nostalgic images, and an outer, physical place where he dwells and spends his days. These places are separate but related.

Naderpur died in Los Angeles in 2000 and is buried there. His tomb has since become a focal point for those expatriate Iranians who see in his poetry reflections of their own situation as exiles unprepared for life outside their native environment. In all, he has published nine volumes of poetry.

A SPRING TALE

I said to myself, Well, man without a country!
Why have you turned away from the world?
What good did you gain in your own land
that you long for it so?

In this city of exile that is your home,
live the way you did where you were born,
and if the blood in your eyes is no less than tears,
don't shed another glance upon that bloody land!

If, as you see, fate did not favor you,
revenge yourself gallantly!
If you did not prevail in your own land,
reap what you desire from a foreign land.

Stroll out of your house at night,
sip wine the color of dusk!
Hand over the reins of wisdom to drink,
forget the grief of living!

The streets and lanes are thronging with beauties,
take one of them as a lover!
As our poets have declared:
"Get tangled up in the folds of her locks!"

Imagine that under the azure sky
you exist, and she exists, and there is no one else.
The whole world of the night is yours,
reveling and carousing your only tasks!

As my heart took in what I declared,
it abandoned despair and took courage.
The world now seemed a more gracious place,
time now seemed a more compassionate friend.

The sky was still light from the day
when I shaved my cheeks,
I taught my lips to smile,
and put on my best attire.

I left home with such joyous gait
the grief inside me recoiled in shame,
my copious hair windswept by
the drunken breeze that caressed me.

No more than two steps in the crowd,
an aged beggar blocked my way:
He wore an old sackcloth robe
and held an empty wine bottle in his hand.

He begged for a coin, I gave it to him.
He threw me a glance far from grateful.
Lost in thought, I wondered what
the unknown beggar was telling me with his eyes.

All of a sudden a spring cloud wept:
The earth soaked by God's pure tears.
I fixed my stare on that filthy old man,
he laughed at me with flashing teeth.

In the mirror of his eyes, my reflection
was wearing a sackcloth just like him.
Ahead or behind, I did not see
another soul but him and me.

He and I, two men lost and homeless:
One drunk, the other lucid,
our clothes dripping, weeping on our bodies,
as the spring sunset smiled.

As evening appeared from behind a cloud
instead of the old man, there lingered a thought.

Astounding! Instead of the sounds of the busy raucous street
there lingered the sad gurgle of a drainpipe.

I said to myself: Well, man without country!
Not even a shadow follows you.
Don't despair from this eternal exile,
as your future is not better than the present.

If you see no good in the past,
what can you expect from the future?
The evening was half alive, night was at hand:
With a bitter tear, the world laughed.

— *Translated by William L. Hanaway*

M. R. Shafi'i Kadkani

Mohammad Reza Shafi'i Kadkani was born in 1939 in Kadkan, in the province of Khorassan. He received his early schooling in Mashhad and later graduated from Mashhad University with a degree in literature. During his university years he became active in various cultural and literary societies, and his writings began to appear in various local publications. In 1953, together with a group of young writers, he founded a literary society dedicated to the promotion of modern poetry and short stories. He later moved to Tehran, earned a doctorate in Persian language and literature from Tehran University, and became a professor of Persian literature there. His dissertation, *Imagery in Persian Poetry*, marked a new epoch, both in introducing new literary discourses to the field of Persian literary studies in Iran and in broadening the scope of the academic study of Persian poetry. He has also been a visiting professor and researcher at Oxford, Princeton, and Harvard.

Shafi'i Kadkani is considered primarily an outstanding scholar of the classical tradition in Persian poetry. Numerous scholarly monographs and essays of his have been published in Iran and abroad. In 1998, his collected works were published again in two beautifully produced books, *A Mirror for Voices* and *The Second Millennium of the Mountain Deer*. In his compositions, he combines a taste for the experimental with an awareness of the old traditions, and employs simple lyrical language to express complex thoughts.

Shafi'i Kadkani has published over ten volumes of poetry as well as numerous other books on poetry and criticism.

POETRY—I

Splashing spring downpour
over the slumber of plain and desert
all giving, granting all over,
filled for an instant
with the wholeness
of itself, blossoming out,
containing the self,
folded in on itself,
flowing on the tongue of the vetch
sedge, soil,
full,
fresh,
fast.

Poetry
   arrives
      thus.

POETRY — II

Where then is poetry
    if it is not
where life resides?

Where then is poetry
    if it is not
where a handful of living words with a soul
     meet a human being
who needs them in life?

In vain we question this one and that
on its whereabouts,

people will point
in so many erroneous directions
from the alley of the imagination's language
to the crossroads of ambiguities
        to the circle of style, or texture.

Still, in the din of words
nobody will ever find
        where poetry resides.

And what is poetry — what, if not
that moment of cleaning dust
from the mirror in certainty's chamber,
that moment of seeing
in the blossoming of a rose
the liberation of the entire earth?

— *Translated by Dick Davis and Ahmad Karimi Hakkak*

PRAYER OF SUDDEN DREAD

Lo the Antichrist is coming, open the way for Christ,
Lo the day of resurrection is coming, sound the trumpets!
— Rumi

A dying voice between the East and the West,
once in a while it speaks:
I fear the comet that will loom on the eastern horizon.

Smoke-colored, it appears in mirrors.
It has cracked the arcades in the mosques
and in the synagogue of simple tuberoses,
it has left us respite
neither for joy nor for prayer.

Sunrise on the day of the Antichrist's coming!
The one who will prevent water from reaching the rose and the tulip,
Who locks up light
in felt boxes.

A hoopoe is praying
on the branch of the old walnut tree:
a prayer of sudden dread.
          What is it?
In the dawn sky, the dust and smoke of machine guns:
a full eclipse.

You too are accompanying the Antichrist,
          beware!
Think of the river
that flows, carrying the sky in its heart,
you are pure in spirit, yet
the city's air is unwholesome.

If one of the tulip's martyrs
— killed by the bullets —
should rise up from the earth,
he would tell the clouds,
would tell the wind
how filthy the air is, how low the sky.
And how, drop by drop,
Poison has emptied
the roses' veins of their flowing life-giving sap.

Standing by our windowsill,
you and I have by degrees
grown accustomed to the featureless dark.
Who knows
          What is passing outside
in the wind?
All windows are shut.

Caught in this dust,
you and I did not know
where the night is, and where the day —
or what the true colors of the sun, water and the flowers are.

They graft the trees one to another
so deftly
that you would see apples on the almond tree branches,
and indigo tulips
on the chamomile plant.

What generosity —
bestow it on water
and it will turn into a bubble!

You and I never found out
where they buried
the stout tree of light
         or where they may have taken it.

The clean clear crystal of words has grown so opaque
that the divine mission of the rose
has opened a way
to thornbushes, bugloss.

A dying voice between the East and the West;
once in a while it speaks:
I fear the comet,
The divine wrath it heralds.
Let us pray the prayer of pure dread.
The prayer of pure dread.

— *Translated by Dick Davis and Ahmad Karimi Hakkak*

Manuchehr Atashi

Manuchehr Atashi was born in 1931 in the southern city of Bushehr, where he received his primary schooling. He attended Shiraz University, and in 1954 returned to Bushehr to teach in high schools both in the city and surrounding villages. Later he attended Tehran University and in 1964 earned a degree in English language and literature. Following his career as a teacher, he joined the publishing arm of the National Radio and Television organization in Tehran as an editor. His poetry was first published in literary journals in 1951 and the first collection of his work, *Another Tune,* was published in 1959. Atashi's early poems were welcomed as a new authentic voice from the southern coast of Iran. The sun-soaked atmosphere of his native city, the austere yet untamed lifestyles of the southern nomads, and the overriding sense of belonging to the land depicted in his poems are among the formative elements in his compositions. In his later work, the active, angst-ridden atmosphere of the earlier compositions seems to give way to a brooding, contemplative mood. To date, Atashi has seventeen books to his credit. He has also worked on compilations of works by other prominent Persian poets, most notably *Poets of Peace,* which is to be translated in various languages under the auspices of UNESCO.

Atashi retired in 1980 and returned to Bushehr, where he dedicates his time to his poetry and other writings.

A WOMAN OUT OF MEMORY

A woman rises out of memory,
moves from behind the trees into the lagoon,
water rising up to her shoulders.
She moves the moon to ecstasy.

Behind the trees
a woman and the moon come together in the waters.

Loose and wet, a lock of hair
      floats forward on the waters.

A little red star twists in the fish's mouth,
a shepherd song rings in the valley,
and the river, whole, sinks back into memory.

— Translated by Ahmad Karimi Hakkak

VISITATIONS

What a beautiful day!
How thin the shadow next to the boulder!

I long for the droplets of your fingertips,
I long for your black eyes —
How shy their flowing waters!

I long for the privacy of my fancies —
what an exhausting peak!
Hiking up from zero to six thousand,
sitting here, at the top,
wading two tired blistered feet in the waters of the stream.

What lovely deer!
They arrive by the water, pause.
One, two, three — and where's the fourth,
soul mate of that young stupefied stag,
standing so sullen over there,
taking no fancy to the water?

I long for a smoke-filled chest, my own.
What ruthless days!
How crushed the silhouette under the boulder!

I long for your absent fingertips
for the distant memory of your black eyes.
How woeful their flowing waters!

— *Translated by Ahmad Karimi Hakkak*

Mohammad Ali Sepanlu

Mohammad Ali Sepanlu was born in Tehran in 1940 and began to publish his poems in the capital city's literary journals when he was twenty years old. During the 1960s, he published collections focusing on the darker corners of Iranian history. His fourth collection, *Sidewalks* (1968), snapshots of life as lived in Tehran's older quarters, marked him as a keen observer of everyday life and immediately captured the imagination of his audiences. It received much critical acclaim and went through several printings.

Before he graduated from Tehran University's Faculty of Law in 1963, Sepanlu had already begun a second career as a translator. His translations of Albert Camus and Jean-Paul Sartre helped make their work immensely popular in Iran in the 1960s. He has also written several film scripts and acted in a number of films.

Still, poetry remains central to his career. Over the decades, his poems have retained certain characteristics that are recognized as his trademark. In his use of language, he connects twenty-first-century readers of Persian to the parlance of their great-grandparents, which in itself is remarkable in view of the rapid changes in the Persian language in the twentieth century. However, the past infuses this seemingly peculiar idiom with considerable poetic significance, thus investing his compositions with an Old World beauty that casts its shadow over all modernist efforts. In mood, he broods over meaningful episodes that shed light on contemporary life by depicting scenes, images, or vignettes from the often forgotten corners of Iran's eventful history, both recent and ancient. *Turquoise in the Dust*, an anthology of Sepanlu's poetry published in 1998, best summarizes the poet's lifelong achievement in poetry.

MINIATURE

1

A bird without a season
is singing songs
through the women's foreheads.

A certificate of burial
is still
the reward for love,
and the invisible order
that has dragged down the city
and made the choice
mandatory for us all
awards a prize to love
and grants the soul a city.
The citizens, one and all, always
carry tiny iceboxes in their hearts.
In it, in one corner,
there's a cage with a silent canary inside,
in store for the spring (it might come!).
On the margins of
every schoolchild's notebook
there's a song scribbled in a script she cannot read
(she might learn it!),
and under her scarf every woman
hides a mourning dove in her hair.

2

Resurrection is in the nature of rain,
it's no surprise, in this land, for the rain
to pour after a delay of half a year,
We have yet to join those who have withered.

Like the seasonless bird
we are the youth of yesteryears.
Our ghosts, still young, still ride their bikes
back and forth before the coroner's office;
the windows are shut, of course,
but the purgatorial administration
still keeps its sojourners awake,
while suddenly from the loudspeakers
noontime salutes issue forth . . .

What consequences
flow from the firmament
of female foreheads
as they hit the alien air:
lightning sparks, sparks flash,
and the song of the mourning dove reverberates
amid the sparks and the wailing sirens.

The skies are rainy,
rain brings plenitude . . .

— *Translated by Ahmad Karimi Hakkak*

THE TERRACE OF DEAD FISHERMEN

Fog comes,
covers the heart of the world over,
and even after it passes
it lingers in my eyes.

There's a wedding on the other side of the dividing drape.
On this side, I gaze through an opaque mist,
give ear to whispers from the lost . . .

A narrow cobblestone pavement,
a tavern gate,
        a door opening on to the sea,
and some fishermen on the terrace,
their golden pipes
        lighting up the heart of the fog.

The smell of kerosene from the nearby lantern
comes studded with red dots.

I push aside the thin fog and ask:
"No fishing in the fog, ha?"
One answers back:
"We are after adventure;
you see strange things,
especially in the dark in the fog
there are treasures here,
I swear by this cup."

"Why not celebrate then, my friend . . .
Love is all there is!"

The wind picks up
shadows, mirrors, the fishermen's faces,
all drip through the fog's memory.

Rain in the noon of night
and a gray board over the gate:
The Café of the Lost at Sea.

                        — *Translated by Ahmad Karimi Hakkak*

THE GREEN BULL

A pretty green bull
is showing forth
out of the branches and leaves.

Pink butterflies loom up
on his henna-colored horns and short hair,
and the bull —
as he begins to eye a butterfly —
his whole form dissolves
into nonexistence.

(Ah, how very long must the sun and wind travel and twist
to remake the winged bull of green gold
        from the form of the foliage.
Even then, clearly
it would not turn out as it was at first.)

After his short-lived formation, the bull
breathes briefly, his form constantly changing.
He is now grazing in the gardens of Eden.
As he contemplates the columns of the Achaemenids,[2]
he imagines them to be
his own likeness in some mirror.

Adorn, O wind,
the twisting twigs of this apple tree.

— Translated by Ahmad Karimi Hakkak

---

[2]The Achaemenid dynasty (ca. 648 to 330 B.C.E.) was the first dynasty of the Persian Empire.

Yadollah Royai

Yadollah Royai was born in 1931. One of the most famous poets of the post-revolutionary period, he rose to prominence with the publication in 1967 of *Sea Songs,* a collection of terse, austere poems most notable for their formal features and rhetorical sophistication. Chief among a group of poets who steadfastly refused to accept the prevailing notion that poetry ought primarily to give expression to popular political discontent, Royai represents a contrarian tendency in modernist poetry. In the 1960s, he parted company with those poets who favored social commentary and launched what came to be known as "The New Wave" to privilege form over content and innovative use of language over preoccupation with contextual concerns. He believes that poetry tries to describe an ineffable realm of language and form.

In the early years of the Iranian revolution, Royai immigrated to France, where he has since published several new volumes of poetry, the latest of which is *Seventy Tombstones.* A literary critic, he is also a translator of French poetry into Persian.

MARTYR'S TOMBSTONE

A sketch of Zarathustra's smile upon the stone. A thin tablet (the vertical inscription on the tombstone) to be carved in the shape of a wave, from a marble different from that of the tombstone. Grass has grown all around the grave — and in the grass, a hatchet, upon the staircase to the altar down which he rolled, as he said under his soldier's blow: that we should not be is another form of our being.

You who on the front line
put your life on the line in front,
may my world be foam, a blade of straw, on your heaving forth!
And may your beauty forever
be the size of our lives!

— *Translated by Ahmad Karimi Hakkak*

TOMB OF MANICHAEUS

Like a tree
my death
begins
with a beginning
under thoughts of leaving
when thoughts remain above

Manichaeus wrote, "The most dangerous things are man's own thoughts." His disciple said: "Then thought is a thing," and asked that they place his book in his tomb. "Let them carve a small stream in the space of the following stone: with stone, filings below the water, and a fish that has the slightest contact with water. Decorative objects: A green vase with a yellow plant, a spinal column, a small bird, a few roots, and the fear of shears in Manichaeus, who said in his time of leaving: we turn on the perimeter of danger."

— *Translated by Haleh Hatami*

LABIAL VERSE 67

As I flee the din of voices,
ropes stretched in the wind
leave me baffled between help and helplessness.

The throat of help and helplessness,
a passageway for the wind to flee
remains the path for remembering you
when stretched ropes move next door to the throat.

— *Translated by Ahmad Karimi Hakkak*

LABIAL VERSE 181

Here, having landed, forever sits an eye
and like an eye, I
have landed here.

When my landing pauses,
waiting,

it knows with my other eyes,
forever waiting for a landing,
that a rising line
will turn my pause
into a perpetual stasis,
like the gone-before-come,
like the come-before-gone,
like the landing of an eye,
like me sitting down.

— Translated by Ahmad Karimi Hakkak

Reza Baraheni

Reza Baraheni was born in 1935 in Tabriz, the capital of the Azeri Turkish speaking regions of Iran. The experience of being a member of a linguistic minority infuses his work, both as a poet and as a notable fiction writer. He obtained his doctorate in literature from the University of Istanbul and in 1963 was appointed professor of English at Tehran University. He has also taught in universities in the United States, Britain, and Canada. In the mid-1960s, Baraheni entered Iran's literary scene through a series of extremely bold and highly controversial critiques of the Persian poets of the time. His early collections of poetry are seen as efforts to fit the discourse of Anglo-American modernists — poets like Eliot, Pound, Ginsberg, and Ferlinghetti — within the metric and imagistic patterns of Persian poetry. His collection *God's Shadow: Prison Poems* is based on a period of 102 days he spent in prison at the end of 1973, during the reign of the Shah. *The Crowned Cannibals,* a collection of prose and poetry about repression during the time of the monarchy, was published in the United States in 1977. Baraheni also spent time in the prisons of the Islamic Republic. He is also the author of several short stories and novels, including *Azadeh Khanum and Her Writer* and *The Hellish Life of Mr. Ayyaz.*

Still active in trying to promote democratic liberties in his country, he was one of the drafters of, and a signatory to, a 1994 open letter to the government of Iran calling for artistic freedom and an end to censorship. Baraheni now teaches at the University of Toronto. He is a former president of PEN Canada.

Although the following poem was originally written in English, we have included it here because it expresses the anguished state of mind of exiled intellectuals particularly well. It was published by the *Seneca Review* (volume 34, no. 1, Spring 2004).

IN THE NEW PLACE, OR EXILE, A SIMPLE MATTER

In the new place you don't speak of yourself
   your feet facing the front
     you tread backwards with needles in your throat
The etched plot was there before you suddenly stepped in
The old place walks ahead of you
    someone claps his hands and then you have two husbands
    one forgetting you, the other not remembering
The distance walks away with you
      both in the new country, and the old country
You gather the leaves, stuffing them into your ears
     and pull up the blindfold, fearing you will be raped in the
     eyes
You buy a new set of false teeth
     and write your brother at home to mail you a brand-new
     false mouth
Instead, he sends you *Discourses* of Shams of Tabriz, Rumi's
   mentor,
Because time is ripe to write the Third Script:
    The one neither the scribe nor the reader will understand
"Shines
in the mind of heaven God
who made it
more than the sun
in our eye.
Fifth element; mud; said Napoleon"
After the explosion into incomprehension
     the unimpossible beauty you might call it
       (two negations equaling not affirmation
       but running the whole gamut of endless negation)
Pound dissolves words into meanings, and Shams says:
                        don't, I say
But after the first four lines of Canto LI, Pound has already
   missed the point
    you hear him reading the rest of the poem
      four sets of false teeth blocking breath's rush to the

mouth,
    giving reference and preference to history,
        missing the point once again

You are after Walter Benjamin's fasting man
    but who is fasting here?
You want to tell someone or write somewhere
    that you find affinities between Shams and Benjamin too
both of them are pre-Adamite hermaphrodites in sudden
    languages
it hurts that no one knows
You buy a small bouquet of flowers
You're going to see your new boss
    Clinging to the precipice of his Imperial desk
And everyone is in search of something here
    they call it competence, and you call it
        the salad dressing of the new malady
They say you ought to have eye contact with everyone
        you have it with the beasts
    why not with humans?

And you are the new talk of centuries
        both the old and the new
        and you have hoisted both of them on your shoulders

All hurt minds of both dark hemis
            pheres
            broke down into exile
      at home or abroad, etching with broken wrists
    what Benjamin called "a charmed circle of fragments."
And your small bouquet of flowers laughs at your hypocrisy
    you toss it away and you watch
    until it gets tossed back at you

Suddenly the word "obfuscation" comes between you and the
    boss
    you see him sleeping while you are speaking,
    eye contacting And the birds in the yard

chirp away in frenzy, laughing at you
And you start telling your boss of the "fasting man
                    who tells his dream as if . . ."
You stop, the boss is sleeping and you are scared
        scared that he will suddenly snore
And you won't know what to do with the malady of both centuries,
The birds have stopped singing
    He wakes up as soon as you stop
    and says: "Don't, don't bother the snoring, if I snore,
    I'm still listening."
And he closes his eyes, and you tell him about the word "obfus-
    cation,"
To decipher the obliterated cipher of your being and his
And "the fasting man who tells his dream as if he were . . ."
He suddenly wakes up and says: "Be sure I'll do something
    about it,
        but competence, don't forget competence . . ."
And Walter Benjamin says: "a charmed circle of fragments."

I was not asking for money.
It soils the hand that gives
        and the hand that takes
        but I don't tell him, I need a job, a better job, for sure
And this is not the question. I'm trying to have the eye contact
    going
            And I gauge competence
For this you need a new sort of concentration
Like the one you had when you were being born
Passing through someone in blood and pus, deaf and blind
        the concentration of a solid constipation
            a towering, excruciating empire of constipation
And then somebody slapping you hard, screaming "obfuscation"
And you opening your eyes to the world, recognizing
                that the boss has no snoring habits

He has the unfortunate habit of sleeping soundly only, yes
    only . . .
        — this I won't tell you—but here it is anyway;

only, when a writer in exile speaks
You don't know the new country for sure
        and now you hardly know the old one either
And you start again, with your only strength in the argument:
    "The fasting man who tells his dream as if he were talking . . ."
And the boss wakes up: "Don't stop, I'm listening!"
    "But Sir, you're interrupting, I haven't stopped yet!"
I'm passing through mud and pus, deaf and blind
He sleeps now like a baby in a cradle
                on the grass on top of a cliff by the coast
    and the waves rolling with the white foam of their whales
        down there

"As I was saying . . ." I begin
And I stop in Benjamin's "charmed circle of fragments."
"I am not from this country, you know. I am just talking about
'the fasting man who tells his dream as if he were talking in his
    sleep.'
Comprenez? This is a country with two official languages!"
But there is some kind of innocence in this man's guilt
        as there is some kind of guilt in my innocence.

Now, I am all ready for action.
I put my left hand in my pocket
            slowly,
            sexually
            surreptitiously
Remember Benjamin: "Your strength lies in improvisation.
    All the decisive blows are struck left-handed."
I open the blade of my knife in my pocket as he sleeps
    take out the knife
    the baby, oh, the baby, in a cradle on the grass
    on top of a cliff by the coast, and the whales down there
        in the waves
I need a test: is he awake when he is awake?
            Is he asleep when he is asleep?
    Is he awake when he is asleep
    Is he asleep when he is awake?

Is he he?
So language tells you things that reality doesn't tell you
I decide: I'll wake him up by telling him a funny story:

The woman says you cannot do that here, it's impossible. She cannot
help laughing. The old man is holding something between his two
hands. Kids passing by don't notice it. It's only the shrewd eyes of the
old woman that notice the vein-stricken hands of the man holding it
between them. Then she says he shouldn't be ashamed of himself. He is
genuine. Artistic. Look at the young generation: they don't even know
how to hold it between their hands! She gets going, but after a minute
she turns back to tell him he can hold it like that for as long as he wants
to. But he has turned his back to her. And she doesn't find the hairy
back interesting at all. And then suddenly she sees the front and back of
the man at the same time, and her own face with all the wrinkles reflected in the mirror, facing both of them.

Is this the "charmed circle of fragments, Benjamin?" I scream
And when the boss wakes up to sneeze "obfuscation!"
        — dear reader or listener!
"Hypocrite lecteur! — mon semblable — mon frère!" —
        If you want to take a leak, please feel free to get up and
            go and do so
    This is not a practice in suspense poetry

I thrust the knife, with the same left hand
        drive it to the hilt into the heart
And fall supine before him, when he is rising
    not to call an ambulance,
        but to answer the telephone that started ringing
            a minute before I was dead.

Mohammad Mokhtari

Born in Mashad in 1942, Mohammad Mokhtari has published fourteen collections of poetry and numerous collections of essays on criticism. He was secretary of the Iranian Writers Association and played a major role in trying to revive it after the crackdown on civil liberties in the aftermath of the 1979 revolution, when its office in Tehran was closed by security forces.

Imprisoned under both the Shah's and the Islamist regimes, he established himself as a freelance poet and literary critic. Mokhtari also wrote about ancient Iranian mythology, which was his area of expertise. His last work, *Social Tolerance,* signals his undying interest in human rights, freedom of expression, and the establishment of the rule of law. Mokhtari was one of the authors of the 1994 declaration signed by 134 Iranian writers pleading for the right of free expression.

In October 1998, Mokhtari and his colleague Mohammad Jafar Puyandeh were summoned, together with four other prominent writers, to the revolutionary court and charged with attempting to establish an independent writers association. Mokhtari was last seen alive on December 3 going into a local shop. His body was found in a Tehran city morgue on December 9, 1998. Marks on his head and neck made it appear that he had been murdered, possibly by strangulation. Puyandeh's body was found a few days later. They were among the group of writers, journalists, and intellectuals murdered by the secret arm of the Iranian security service during the 1990s.

FROM THE OTHER HALF

Here I open my eyes to snow that has been falling
horizontally all morning.
There it must be midnight sharp, she is closing her eyes in salt,
a dream on the other side of the earth is pulling my train on this side,
as confusion fills my head.

When will it arrive?
How will it end —
this line drawn between two margins?
And this decrepit woman seated on my left, knitting incessantly
row after row,
the needle and her fingers bobbing up and down through salt and snow.

I turn toward the empty station where no one welcomes or waves
good-bye,
and the illusion of time is riddled with patches of outlandish
woods —
a white expanse pierced here and there, perhaps by a reed or a spear.

A temptation sparks my head, shines on my soul full force
in a dream seen on that side,
and a hand clips the edges of the dream with a pair of scissors.
Yet, as I close my eyes
I see on the blank page that her eyelids come together.

Sleep glitters from the depths of frozen lakes,
and the wind slaps her face every time it reappears through the salt
to mingle with the children
who have turned the icy surface into a festive playground,
a dance spiraling to the crystalline depth, to the noon of night
on the other side.

How has that figure remained afloat, with that inviting gaze?
Is it perhaps that everything lost on the other side
emerges here from the mouth of the ice,

witnesses the earth,
with its shining, shriveled face,
with earrings that glow, reflecting the scar on the corner of the
                                                                    mouth,
measuring the age of the scream in loneliness,
carving out a common fate all the way to this passenger heard by none
in a dream seen on the other side?

I should have paused as my lips stiffened,
this new cold hurts my right arm too.
Or, perhaps this restive blankness has tamed me.
It is as if something is freezing, or turning into salt, again.

Here nobody's gaze is clear.
For the visit, I must preserve my old eyes
and retract the dream to the point where it would wind down.

A white illusion runs over the body,
and at times a greenish black passes through the veins,
and the sights that rush in suddenly
        turn seeing into a horrid thing,
                even as they increase the temptation to look
over the expanse of this landscape dotted by white oaks,
        or mummies
        or faces of crystalline ice
        or bodies of crystal salt,
all tugging at your eye to transform them.
And this decrepit woman who is knitting her soul incessantly —
        and gazes only forward —
does she see what she is staring at? Can she see at all?

Outside this window there's a glance
        that has spread the darkness of its dawn
                over the light of this afternoon.
It shines on my right hand as it feels more and more numb,
and the shadows of my moving hand settle on the paper.

How much did I need to write for my eye to rest?
How wide did I need to open my eye for her to open hers, again?
And this decrepit woman is now stuck to the window . . .

My eyelids come together, my hand rests on the "t" in the word "yet."
And the snow must be falling, still horizontally,
against the window of the train, where it is dark by now.

— *Translated by Ahmad Karimi Hakkak*

Shams Langerudi

Shams Langerudi was born in 1951 in Langerud, a city on the coast of the Caspian Sea. He graduated with degrees in mathematics and economics and has worked as a teacher, journalist, and editor. He has published six collections of poetry, including *Notes for a Warden Nightingale* and *The Hidden Celebration*, a novel, a play, and an anthology of Iranian poetry. His very important work, a four-volume history of modern Iranian poetry, entitled *Analytical History of the New Poetry*, had been banned in Iran at one time, but is now in print there.

REQUIEM

I have come this long way
to see you.
I have seen the plowed land.

I have seen broken mud-bricks
and the half-hidden moon.

I have seen children astonished
and grass trampled.

I have seen shadows cast by soil
and flames arising from sighs.

I have seen the wind
but not you.

— Translated by Lotfali Khonji

BRANDS

Fiery brands, cooled,
burn even more.[1]

Poets!

Never did I wish to see you vagrant
among the flies

---

[1] In this stanza the poet uses the word *dagh,* which has several meanings: extreme heat, to scar, brand, or remorse. He couples this with the word *sard,* which means cold and also indifferent and nonchalant. He then claims that these words together can burn or hurt even more when combined. The word for scorch or burning, *soozan,* also means to hurt.

or in the United Nations' stained robes.
Never did I want your pens to disappear
in the locusts' frenzied storm.
But bread
was not a pretty word just for the page,
and freedom was not entrusted to people by birds.

Fiery brands, cooled,
burn even more.

Forgive us ancient poets!
Butterflies
have become spies in candle factories,
and sheep's eyes on the eve of slaughter
no longer speak.

Forgive us, Salahuddin![2]
Believe me, we imagined the Crusades ended,
that we had buried you in dust.

And you too, you
who do not know bombing games,
germ dolls or chemical smiles;
Swords are found only in museums.
Arise from your graves,
        O Afghan girls!
I know you are starved,
and your tired eyes, almond-shaped, do not calm your hunger.
You are thirsty,
and salty tears
only heighten your thirst.
Arise from your graves!
How readily you have succumbed
to slumber in your tiny tombs.

---

[2] Known in the West as Saladin, Salahuddin Ayyubi was a Kurdish general who united the Muslim forces and recaptured Jerusalem from the Crusaders in the twelfth century.

Fiery brands, cooled,
burn even more.

Oh, naked breeze who barefoot treads on bombs,
revere the sanctity of the dawn just past.
Amen.

You small winged dogs who bark in the skies,
guard Christ's lambs from the evils
of the scorched barefoot ones.
Amen.

O harlots of the Gulf!
You whom the world's banks have enriched,
shelter the children robbed of childhood.
Amen.

And O newspapers!
Let be the eternal weavers of dreams
in their small parcels of freedom.

Let them
make pens from bird feathers,
compose fragile poems about angels,
angels who have crashed to the ground
from hunger, and now stand on street corners
peddling cigarettes.

— Translated by Sholeh Wolpé

Partow Nuriala

Partow Nuriala, a poet and literary critic, earned a bachelor's degree in philosophy from Tehran University and a master of science degree from the University of Social Work in Tehran in 1978. She taught philosophy and worked as a social worker at Tehran University, but was forced to stop teaching by the Islamic regime. Later, with the help of two female friends, she opened Damavand Publications in Tehran, thus becoming one of the first independent female publishers in Iran. Within three years, the authorities shut down the press. In 1986, she and her two children came to the United States and began a new life in Los Angeles. Since 1988 she has worked in the Los Angeles County Superior Court (Jury Division) as a deputy jury commissioner while continuing an active literary career.

Nuriala has published four books of poems, numerous literary and cinematic reviews, a collection of short stories, and a play.

I AM HUMAN

Bow your form
in sight of the earth.
Hide your face
from the light
of the sun and moon,
    for you are a woman.

Bury your body's blossoming
in the pit of time.
Consign the renegade strands of your hair
to the ashes in the wood stove,
and the fiery power of your hands
to scrubbing and sweeping the home,
    for you are a woman.

Kill your word's wit:
ruin it
with silence.
Feel shame for your desires
and grant your enchanted soul
to the patience of the wind,
    for you are a woman.

Deny yourself,
that your lord
may ride in you
at his pleasure,
    for you are a woman.

I cry
    I cry
in a land where ignorant kindness
cuts deeper
than the cruelty of knowledge.

I weep for my birth
        as a woman.

I fight
        I fight
in a land where
the zeal of manliness
bellows in the field
between home and grave.
I fight my birth
as a woman.

I keep my eyes wide open
so as not to sink
under the weight
of this dream that others
have dreamed for me,
and I rip apart
this shirt of fear
they have sewn to cover
my naked thought,
        for I am a woman.

I make love to the god of war
to bury
the ancient sword of his anger.
I make war on the dark god
that the light of my name
may shine,
        for I am a woman.

With love in one hand,
labor in the other,
I fashion the world
on the ground of my glorious brilliance,
and into a bed
of clouds I tuck
the scent of my smile,

that the sweet smelling rain
may bring to blossom
all the loves of the world,
        for I am a woman.

My children I bring
to the feast of light,
my men
to the feast of awareness,
        for I am a woman.

I am the earth's steady purity,
the enduring glory of time,
        for I am human.

— Translated by Zara Hushmand

Mirza Agha Asgari

Asgari was born in 1951 in Asadabad, Hamadan. By the time he was eighteen, his poetry and other writings began appearing in various publications in Iran. He was twenty-four when his first collection of poetry, *Tomorrow Is the First Day of the World,* was published. In the early 1980s, his poetry, which often deals with freedom and politics, led to repressive actions against him by government authorities. As a result, he adopted the pen name Mani and continued to publish his works illicitly. In 1985, Asgari left Iran for West Germany, where he continues his cultural and literary activities, becoming the editor in chief of an Internet-based Iranian literary magazine on art and literature.

AMOROUS

We called love: one-half of existence;
a mad star in sanity's night sky.

And said:
Though love
    is the song of creation,
but it's two hearts' yearning
    and two smiles' allure
that brings it life.
Just as the flapping of wings
        make flight.

We bound love to red rose's name,
and said:
    — Enough this sojourn between silence and words,
for to be locked amid clarity and doubt
       is a kind of death, a grave affliction.
No escape for one who reaches the summit's edge . . .
        but to return or
          fly.

We tied love to a dove's wing
and said:
    — Why this hush?
One must unrobe
       each word.
Even though we think with forbidden words
it is other words we use
to portray ourselves!

— Translated by Sholeh Wolpé

Mina Asadi

Born in 1943 in Sari, Mazandaran province, Asadi began her career as a journalist at several well-known Iranian publications. Her political views and her opposition to the monarchical government led her to leave Iran in 1976 for Sweden, where she continues to live and work. Her poetry and essays often deal with oppression against children and women as well as protesting censorship. Since the early 1980s numerous collections of her poetry have been published in England and Sweden. She has also published various studies on Iranian children living in Sweden, and on immigrants and racism.

WEDNESDAY IN MARCH

Love goes up
        a breath-taking staircase.

Daffodils bloom
                from your hands.

And the dead goldfish
        caught in the glass jar
                inside the frame of the still-life painting
                        begins to swim again.

Love goes up
        the breath-taking staircase.
You
  blossom
    in my hands.

— Translated by Ahmad Karimi Hakkak

WAKEFUL REVERIES

These hands you caress so tenderly
have touched that lifeless form.

Not a nightmare,
not the illusion of a passing glance
through the shattered windowpane
of an abandoned morgue.

And you, too,
you who stroll through the garden

at night,
you, too, will hear the weeping,
the bursting open of hearts
and the stench of a thousand bodies
        torn asunder,
                stretched under the meridian sun.

— *Translated by Ahmad Karimi Hakkak*

Roya Hakakian

The author of two acclaimed volumes of poetry in Persian and most recently a memoir in English of post-revolutionary Iran, *Journey from the Land of No,* Hakakian left Iran in 1984 and a year later moved to New York, where she worked as a journalist, most recently at CBS on *60 Minutes II,* where she was an associate producer. She is also a frequent contributor to Connecticut Public Radio. In addition, Ms. Hakakian is a documentary filmmaker. *Armed and Dangerous,* her film about child soldiers, was screened at a special session of the United Nations. Ms. Hakakian is a recipient of the 2002–2003 Dewitt Wallace–Reader's Digest Fellowship.

I MUST BURY HIM

I must bury him
and not fear this pause in the past
and not turn into a pillar of stone
looking back.

I must pluck him
off the palm of my hand
and not let this knot in my throat
stop my breathing,
not let my spleen
swell in my temples.

I must bury him in a way
that would let me live,
that would leave me room enough for a smile
when remembering youthful memories.

He arrived
and I stood firm,
and grafted his wounded form
on to the slender stock of my youth
and I bore him on.

I did not love without him
and endured much with him,
and he laughed the same
in joy and when perturbed.

And it was for his sake
that I,
a pliant poet,
turned into a clown,
fonder than a fool,
and rode on a broom,
    calling out to the heavens.

With every laugh
I bought myself a piece,
not of love everlasting
but of my daily grain of friendship
from the fleet-footed vendor of vernal wares.

He always asked:
"And when will you write me a poem?"
not knowing that I can fool him,
can fool myself
but not my muse.

Now if I bury him,
even myself surviving,
tell me, for God's sake,
who am I
if not him stretched forth?

Tell me how, if you know,
I can wipe off the mirrors of so many days
the dust of his image
and not of my own.
And tell me, please, what to do
with all these songs
that constantly call me back to life
with the sun
that has leashed me with golden rays.

For God's sake tell me
to get up and walk away
from the tombstone of the memory
and wash my weary body once more
In the roaring rapids of life.

— Translated by Ahmad Karimi Hakkak

Ziba Karbasi

Ziba Karbasi was born in 1974 in Tabriz, the capital of Iranian Azerbaijan. She and her family fled Iran in the 1980s and sought asylum in Britain as political refugees. She now divides her time between London and Paris. Karbasi has published five volumes of poetry, all outside Iran. Many of her poems have been translated into several languages, and a volume of her poetry is being translated into English by Stephen Watts. She is the director of the Association of Iranian Writers in Exile.

THE REPUBLIC OF HATE

Hate is a train of dark horses
    carrying fire
        in their manes,
covering the city
    under their hooves
        in smoke and ashes.

Rancor is a tiger
    loose on the ridges of being.
Silence is the scorched larynx of a canary
    decreed not to sing
        even when the roses are in bloom.

Fear is the meeting of lovebirds
    who know
        and know well
that the twitter of their kisses
    will end for sure in death's voiceless cachinnation.

And love, alas, love!
    Goldfish in a cage of glass
        ceremoniously set
            on some mock
                New Year table.
It does remember though
    the spring in our homeland
        that never came to fruition.

— Translated by Ahmad Karimi Hakkak

Majid Naficy

Majid Naficy was born in Esfahan, Iran, in 1952. When he was only thirteen, his first poem was published in an influential literary journal, *Jong-e Esfahan.* His first collection of poems, *In the Tiger's Skin,* was published in 1969. In the 1970s, Naficy was politically active against the Shah's regime, but after the 1979 revolution, when the new regime began to suppress the opposition, his first wife and his brother were among those executed. He fled Iran in 1983 and, after spending time in Turkey and France, settled in Los Angeles. As an expatriate poet, Naficy has managed to combine the history and life, sights and sounds of his surrounding in exile with remembrances of his homeland, particularly Esfahan, this in spite of the fact that he is legally unsighted. His concern for women, the disabled, and the disadvantaged has resulted in a steady stream of compositions, which reflect the poet's will to work for social justice and effect positive change in class and gender relations. He has since earned his doctorate in Near Eastern languages and cultures from UCLA, and has published five collections of poems as well as two books of essays. His latest book, *Father & Son* (Red Hen Press, 2003), is a collection of poems about his son, Azad.

THE LITTLE MESSENGER

For Azad

You will tell your mother
  that yesterday afternoon
you went bicycle riding with me.

then you took a bath,
  studied the alphabet,
  ate dinner,
  slept well,
and in the morning,
with your bag on your back,
you took the number one bus
from my house to the kindergarten.

late afternoon your mother picks you up
and drives you home.
she opens your lunch box
and, from your leftovers,
she will gather what I cooked for you.

you play with your toy cars,
order your grandma around,
paint with your aunt,
then you fly
and, on your wings, come to me.

what do you take from me?
what do you give to her?
what do you take from her?
what do you give to me?

little messenger,
  I do not want you
  to fill this void;

to love someone
there is no need
    to share a roof.

— *Translated by Ardavan Davaran*

Abbas Saffari

Abbas Saffari was born in 1951 in Yazd, Iran, and moved to the United States in 1979. He was one of the first to write avant-garde, surrealist lyrics in Iran for the singer Farhad. He is the author of *Twilight of Presence* (Los Angeles: Tasveer, 1995), *Confluence of Hands and Apples* (Los Angeles: Kaaroon, 1992), and *Old Camera and Other Poems* (Tehran: Sales, 2002), and has been poetry editor of Iranian literary magazines in exile such as *Sang* (1997–2000) and *Cactus* (2000–2002). He has contributed poetry to the online *Poets Against the War* magazine.[1] He has translated into Persian the Japanese erotic poetry of Izumi Shikibu and Onono Komachi, as well as ancient Egyptian erotic poetry, and is currently translating a volume of ancient Chinese erotic poetry. He studied sculpture at Long Beach State University in California and now lives in Long Beach with his wife and two daughters. He is one of a handful of Iranian poets living outside of Iran whose work is published and read in Iran. In January 2004, *Old Camera and Other Poems* won Poetry Book of the Year in Iran.

---

[1] The "war" refers to the American invasion of Iraq. To date, over 9,000 poets worldwide have joined this grassroots peace movement.

SATURDAY NIGHT DINNER

The onion, I will grate
to keep my stream of tears from drying.
The potato, you peel
for your sleight of hand with skin.

Let Nusrat Fatah Ali Khan, the Sufi minstrel, play
for he opens us a window to Konya,[2]
a window adorned with narcissus, sleepy-eyed and languorous,
and a handful of homing pigeons.

If they call
from MasterCard
or the Internal I-don't-have-any-Revenue Service,
tell them he's gone to Kashmir
looking for the long-lost polo ball of King Aurangzeeb of India,
and it's unclear when he'll be back.

Don't laugh, my darling!
Cultural misunderstandings
dismiss the disturber
quicker than hollow conversation.

Now, while this aged Indian rice ripens,
put two glasses, lip to lip, near our hands
of our oldest vintage, four years old
and a reminder of a century past.
A sip of good wine
is enough to erase an entire
century from one's memory.
Sip after sip
we can backtrack so far
that after dinner

---

[2] Konya is the resting place of Rumi.

we can find ourselves in the moonlit
palm groves of Mesopotamia,
and around midnight
in a primordial place naked
and boundless.

— *Translated by Nilufar Talebi*

A BIRD IS A BIRD

When I draw open this curtain
a bent TV antenna
and often
a few red robins
decorate my morning.

But it is not a scarcity of windows
that has brought me here,
this rectangular blue
I could have had
anywhere else.
Birds, too,
all over the world
sit in such a way
that their velvety breasts
are within eye's reach.
Red robins or black crows,
what difference does it make?
A bird
is a bird.

To be honest, I don't remember
what I've come here for,
surely, there must have been an important reason.

One doesn't just
make a vagabond of oneself for no reason.
When I remember
I will finish this poem.

— Translated by Niluofar Talebi

Granaz Mussavi

Granaz Mussavi was born in 1974 in Tehran. She started writing professionally at *Donyaye Sokhan* magazine as a book review writer and literary critic. Her first poems were published in 1989, and she has continued writing poetry for various publications in Iran and other countries ever since. She earned a graduate degree in film studies from Flinders University of South Australia and has made four short films, one of which won the Best Director Award at Flinders. Her second book, *Barefoot Till Morning,* was the winner of the literary journal *Karnameh*'s Best Poetry Book of the Year Award in 2001 and is currently in its third printing.

THE AX

Part damp,
part moist,
on the ax's skin:
                Rain.
Part tree,
part metal,
on the tree's wet bone:
                The ax.
Part chill,
part wind,
on the tree's pain:
A cold hand
                Holding the ax,
Part sigh,
part loss,
it leaves
        on the forest base
                        a green line
                                of wet trees.

— *Translated by Sheida Dayani*

AFGHAN WOMAN

Far beyond my hands
a red sky
is about to crumble and fall.
The silent sound of feet
that do not run
carries the pines far away,
and the crow behind the window
no longer has a share in what is green.

Oh sun, you are a man,
you do not look at the world
through a veil's mesh,
carry away from the soil of my dreams
a wave wetter than the sea,
more naked than the forest.
Tell the wind to bring a leaf.

— Translated by Sholeh Wolpé

THE SALE

I wrap a scarf around the moon's head,
slip the world's bangles on her wrist,
rest my head on the gypsy sky's shoulders,
                    and say good-bye.

But I don't wish to look.
No,
I won't look
to see the radio and all its waves
            finally gone,
and the decorative plate, priced high,
not sold.
The bed was taken,
and the bedding — now asleep on the floor —
is full of fish without a sea.

Don't haggle — I won't let go
of my messy homework on the cheap,
and that book, *The Little Black Fish,* is not for sale.

"Always a few steps untaken.
The latecomer carries away nothing
but his own chaos and mess."

What remains is only a crow
in love, and never tamed.

You've come too late,
I gave my shoes to a cloud — a keepsake
to one who does not crush lovesick ants.

You're too late.
Nothing remains but a dress
invaded by vagrant moths.
Remember the gown that was home to tame butterflies?

Always a few steps untaken,
and so much time passes
that we begin to fear mirrors,
to stare at our childhood hair
that now plays a gray melody —
string by string.
We have forgotten our dance beneath this sky,
a sky dying of a black hacking cough.
It's time to leave.

In their letters they say the sky
is not this color everywhere.

The day my plane takes off with a sigh,
hand an umbrella to the clouds
to shield them from my tears.

If you see someone returning from night roads,
returning to seek her old bits and pieces;
if you see a girl who without a reason
whistles to herself and to the moon;

That would be me.

I'd be coming to gather the torn pieces of tomorrow,
to glue them together before it's time for dawn prayers.

That day, go to my house and water the geraniums;
perhaps spring will come
and then in five minutes I'll be there.
I'd close the door because
the moon always comes in through the window.

— Translated by Sholeh Wolpé

Abbas Kiarostami

Abbas Kiarostami is one of the most highly celebrated directors in the international film community. A graduate of Tehran University's Faculty of Fine Arts, Kiarostami was first involved in painting, graphics, and book illustration. He began his film career designing credit titles and directing commercials. He founded the film department of the Center for the Intellectual Development of Children and Young Adults (known as Kanun), where a number of high-quality Iranian films were produced. He ran the department for five years and directed his first film, *Bread and Alley,* in 1970. During the 1980s and '90s, at a time when the West had such a negative image of Iran, his cinema introduced to the world a humane and artistic face of his country.

Kiarostami is also a superb poet. In the selections presented here, he demonstrates a major stylistic break with the formal features of classical and modern Persian poetry, although thematically he relies substantially on the conventions that define the Persian lyrical tradition.

The wild cockscomb
bides its time
in the massed company of spring pansies.
*

Among hundreds of rocks
small and large
dawdles
a single turtle.
*

It sprouted
blossomed
withered
and fell to the ground.
Not a soul to see it.
*

Moonlight
thaws
thin ice on the old river.
*

A little nameless flower
blossoming alone
in the crack of a huge mountain.
*

Fearlessly
the village kids target
the scarecrow's tin head.
*

White-haired woman
eyeing the cherry blossoms:
"Has the spring of my old age arrived?"
*

Six short nuns
stroll
amid tall sycamores.
The shriek of crows.

The spider
stops
and takes a moment's break
to watch the sun rise.

*

Spring noon:
the worker bees
slow down.

*

As the wind rises
which leaf's turn is it
to fall down?

*

This time
the wild geese land
on cut reeds.

*

At summer noon
the scarecrow
sweats under its woolen hat.

*

The autumn sun
shines through the window
on the flowers of a carpet.
A bee beats its head against the glass.

*

How merciful
that the turtle doesn't see
the little bird's effortless flight.

— *Translated by Ahmad Karimi Hakkak and Michael Beard*

PERMISSIONS

PROSE

Abdollahi, Asghar: "A Room Full of Dust" (*Otagh-e por Ghobar*) from *Gardoon* 3 (1999), © 1999 by Asghar Abdollahi. Translated and reprinted by permission of the author.

Aghai, Farkhondeh: "A Little Secret" from *Raz-e Kuchak va Dastanha-ye Digar* (A Little Secret and Other Stories) by Farkhondeh Aghai. Tehran: Moin Publishers, 1994, © 1372 [1994] by Farkhondeh Aghai. Translated and reprinted by permission of the author.

Alizadeh, Ghazaleh: "The Trial" (*Dadresi*) from *Chahar Rah* (The Intersection) by Ghazaleh Alizadeh. Tehran: Zemestan Publishing, 1995, © 1373 [1995] by Ghazaleh Alizadeh.

Daneshvar, Reza: "Mahbubeh and the Demon Ahl" from the short story collection *Mahbubeh va Ahl* (Mahbubeh and Ahl) by Reza Daneshvar. Uppsala: Afsane Publishing, 1996, © 1996 by Reza Daneshvar. Translated and reprinted by permission of the author.

Daneshvar, Simin: "Ask the Migrating Birds" from the short story collection *Az Parandegan-e Mohajer Bepors* (Ask the Migrating Birds) by Simin Daneshvar. Tehran: Kanun Publishing and Now Publishing, 1998, © 1998 by Simin Daneshvar. Translated and reprinted by permission of the author.

Dayani, Behnam: "Hitchcock and Agha Baji" (*Hitchcock va Agha Baji*) from *Short Stories from Iran and the World*, edited by Safdar Taghizadeh and Asghar Elahi. Tehran: independently published, 1992, © 1992 by Safdar Taghizadeh and Asghar Elahi. Translated and reprinted by permission of Safdar Taghizadeh.

Dowlatabadi, Mahmud: "The Mirror" (*Ayeneh*) from *Haft Mard, Haft Dastan* (Seven Men, Seven Stories) compiled by Mozhgan Garmsiri. Tehran: Rahiyan-e Andisheh Publishers, 1998, © 1998 by Mahmud Dowlatabadi. Translated and reprinted by permission of the author.

Farrokhfal, Reza: "Ah, Istanbul" from the short story collection *Ah, Istanbul* by Reza Farrokhfal. Tehran: Esparak Publishing, 1988, ©

1988 by Reza Farrokhfal. Translated and reprinted by permission of the author.

Fassih, Esmail: "Sorraya in a Coma" from *Sorraya dar Eqma* (Sorraya in a Coma) by Esmail Fassih. Tehran: Alborz Publishers, 1984, © 1984. First published in English by Zed Books, Ltd., London, 1985. Reprinted by permission of author/translator and Zed Books, Ltd.

Golshiri, Hushang: "The Victory Chronicle of the Magi" (*Fathnameh-ye Moghan*) from *Kargahe-Qesseh* 1 (November–December 1980), 1–6. The English translation by M. R. Ghanoonparvar first appeared in *Iranian Studies* 30, nos. 3–4 (Summer/Fall 1997), 225–42. Revised translation reprinted by permission of Farzaneh Taheri, The Golshiri Foundation, M. R. Ghanoonparvar and *Iranian Studies*.

Mahmud, Ahmad: "Scorched Earth," from chapter 1 of *Zamine-Sukhteh* (Scorched Earth) by Ahmad Mahmud. Tehran: Moin Publishers, 1984, © 1361 [1984] by Ahmad Mahmud. Translated and reprinted by permission of Moin Publishers.

Khaksar, Nassim: "The Grocer of Kharzeville" from the short story collection *Baghal-e Kharzeville* (The Grocer of Kharzeville) by Nassim Khaksar. Utrecht: Nawid Publishers, 1988, © 1988 by Nassim Khaksar. Translated and reprinted by permission of the author.

Kheradmand, Farideh: "Peace of Night" (*Aramesh-e Shabaneh*) from the short story collection *Aramesh-e Shabaneh* (Peace of Night) by Farideh Kheradmand. Tehran: Negah-e Sabz Publishing, 2000, © 1378 [2000] by Farideh Kheradmand. Translated and reprinted by permission of the author.

Khorsandi, Hadi: "The Eyes Won't Take It" (*Chashmha . . .*) from *Asghar Agha* 18 (1996). English translation published by permission of Hadi Khorsandi and the translator, Lotfali Khonji.

Mandanipur, Shahriyar: "Shatter the Stone Tooth" (*Beshkan Dandan-e Sangi ra*) from *Mumiya va Assal* (*The Mummy and Honey*) by Shariyar Mandanipur. Tehran: Nilufar Publishing, 1996, © 1996 by Shahriyar Mandanipur. Translated and reprinted by permission of the author.

Modarressi, Taghi: "The Book of Absent People," from chapters 1 and 2 of *Adamya-ye Ghayeb* (Absent People) by Taghi Modarressi.

First English-language edition, New York: Doubleday and Company, 1986, © 1986 by Taghi Modarressi. Reprinted by permission of Anne Tyler and Russell and Volkening, Inc.

Nabavi, Seyyed Ebrahim: "First Love" from *Tehrangeles* by Seyyed Ebrahim Nabavi. Tehran: Rowzaneh Publishing, 2001, © 2001 by Seyyed Ebrahim Nabavi. Translated and reprinted by permission of the author.

Parsipur, Shahrnush: "Women Without Men," excerpt from *Zanan Bedun-e Mardan* (Women Without Men) by Shahrnush Parsipur. Tehran: Nashr-e Noghreh, 1989, © 1367 [1989] by Shahrnush Parsipur. First English-language edition published in 1998 by Syracuse University Press. This excerpt from The Feminist Press edition (New York: 2004). Reprinted by permission of The Feminist Press at CUNY and the author.

Pezeshkzad, Iraj: "Delayed Consequences of the Revolution" (*Avarez-e Deer-ras-e Enghelab*) from the short story collection *Rostam Solatan* (The Pretenders of Rostam). Los Angeles: Nashr-e Ketab, 2000, © 2000 by Iraj Pezeshkzad. Translated and reprinted by permission of the author.

Rabihavi, Ghazi: "White Rock" (*Sang-e Sefid*), first published in English in *Index on Censorship* 2 (1995), 127–32. Reprinted by permission of author and *Index on Censorship*.

Ravanipur, Moniru: "Satan's Stones" from the short story collection *Sangha-ye Shaytan* (Satan's Stones) by Moniru Ravanipur. Tehran: Nashr-e Markaz Publishing, 1991, © 1369 [1991] by Moniru Ravanipur. First published in English and translated by Persis Karim, Atoosa Kourosh, Paricher Moin, Dylan Oehler-Stricklin, Reza Shirazi, and Catherine Williamson in *Satan's Stones* by Moniru Ravanipur, edited with an introduction by M. R. Ghanoonparvar. Austin: University of Texas Press, 1996, © 1996 by University of Texas Press. Reprinted by permission of M. R. Ghanoonparvar and University of Texas Press.

Taraghi, Goli: "In Another Place" from *Jay-i Degar* (Another Place) by Goli Taraghi. Tehran: Nilufar Publishing, 2000, © 1379 [2000] by Goli Taraghi. Translated and reprinted by permission of the author.

POETRY

Akhavan Saless, Mehdi: "I Love You, Ancient Homeland" (*To ra ay ko-han bum-o bar dust daram*) first appeared in English in *Iranian Studies* 30, nos. 3–4 (Summer/Fall 1997), 244–47. Reprinted by permission of *Iranian Studies*.

Asgari, Mirza Agha: "Amorous" (*Asheghaneh*), translated by Sholeh Wolpé. Published by permission of Mirza Agha Asgari.

Asadi, Mina: "Wednesday in March" (*Chaharshanbeh-i dar esfand*), first appeared in English in *Parnassus: Poetry in Review* 25, nos. 1–2 (2001), 228. Reprinted by permission of Mina Asadi and Po-etry Review Foundation. "Wakeful Reveries" (*Roya-ye bidari*), translated by Ahmad Karimi Hakkak. Published by permission of Mina Asadi.

Atashi, Manuchehr: "A Woman Out of Memory" (*Zani az hafezeh*) and "Visitations" (*Didar*), translated by Ahmad Karimi Hakkak. Published by permission of Manuchehr Atashi.

Baraheni, Reza: "In the New Place, or Exile, a Simple Matter," from *Seneca Review* 34, no. 1 (Spring 2004), 16–20. Reprinted by per-mission of Reza Baraheni and *Seneca Review*.

Behbahani, Simin: "A Man with a Missing Leg" (*Mardi ke yek pa nadarad*); "I Write, I Cross Out" (*Minevisam va khat mizanam*); "If the Snake Is Domestic" (*Mar agar mar-e khanegist*); "And Be-hold" (*Va negah kon*), and "It's Time to Mow the Flowers" (*Vaght-e derow Kardan-e gol shod*) first appeared in English in *A Cup of Sin: Selected Poems by Simin Behbahani*, edited and translated by Farzaneh Milani and Kaveh Safa (Syracuse, N.Y.: Syracuse Uni-versity Press, 1999), © 1999 by Syracuse University Press. Reprinted by permission of the poet, the translators, and Syracuse University Press.

Hakakian, Roya: "I Must Bury Him" (*Bayad u-ra dafn konam*), trans-lated by Ahmad Karimi Hakkak. Published by permission of Roya Hakakian.

Karbasi, Ziba: "The Republic of Hate" (*Johuri-ye tars*), translated by Ahmad Karimi Hakkak, first appeared in English in *Parnassus: Poetry in Review* 25, nos. 1– 2 (2001), 229. Reprinted by permis-sion of Ziba Karbasi and Poetry Review Foundation.

Kiarostami, Abbas: "Selections from Walking with the Wind" (*Ham-

rah ba bad), translated by Ahmad Karimi Hakkak and Michael Beard, first appeared in English in *Walking with the Wind: Poems by Abbas Kiarostami* (Cambridge, Mass.: Harvard Film Archive Publication, 2001). Reprinted by permission of Abbas Kiarostami and Harvard Film Archive.

Khoi, Esmail: "Lyrical" (*Ghazalvareh*); "An Allusion" (*Kenayehvari*); and "Bad Boy" (*Bache-ye bad*) first appeared in English in *Edges of Poetry: Selected Poems of Esmail Khoi*, translated by Ahmad Karimi Hakkak and Michael Beard (Santa Monica: Blue Logos Press, 1995), © 1995 by Ahmad Karimi Hakkak and Michael Beard. Reprinted by permission of Blue Logos Press. "Outlandia" (*Bidarkoja*) first appeared in English in *Outlandia: Songs of Exile* by Esmail Khoi, selected and translated by Ahmad Karimi Hakkak and Michael Beard (Vancouver: Nik Publishers, 1999), © 1999 by Ahmad Karimi Hakkak and Michael Beard. Reprinted by permission of Nik Publishers and translators.

Langerudi, Shams: "Requiem" (*Marsieh*), translated by Lotfali Khonji, first appeared in English in *Index on Censorship*, no. 5 (1997), 39. Reprinted by permission of Shams Langerudi and *Index on Censorship*. "Brands" (*Dagh*), translated by Sholeh Wolpé, published by permission of Shams Langerudi.

Mokhtari, Mohammad: "From the Other Half" (*Az an nimeh*), translated by Ahmad Karimi Hakkak, first appeared in English in *Iranian Studies* 30, nos. 3–4 (Summer/Fall 1997), 363–65. Reprinted by permission of *Iranian Studies*.

Mussavi, Granaz: "The Ax" (*Tabar*), translated by Sheida Dayani, published by permission of Granaz Mussavi. "Afghan Woman" (*Zan-e Afghan*) and "The Sale" (*Haraj*), translated by Sholeh Wolpé, published by permission of Granaz Mussavi.

Naderpur, Nader: "A Spring Tale" (*Ghesseh-ye bahari*), English translation by William L. Hanaway, from *Iranian Studies* 30, nos. 3–4 (Summer/Fall 1997), 303–5. Reprinted by permission of the poet, the translator, and *Iranian Studies*.

Naficy, Majid: "The Little Messenger" (*Payambar-e kuchak*), translated by Ardavan Davaran, first appeared in English in *Literary Review* 40, no. 1 (Fall 1996), 201–2. Reprinted by permission of Majid Naficy and *Literary Review*.

Nuriala, Partow: "I Am Human" (*Man ensanam*), translated by Zara

Hushmand, first appeared in English in *Literary Review* 40, no. 1 (Fall 1996), 191–93. Reprinted by permission of Partow Nuriala and *Literary Review*.

Royai, Yadollah: "Martyr's Tombstone" (*Sang-e Shahid*); "Labial Verse 67" (*Labrikhteh-ha 67*); and "Labial Verse 181" (*Labrikhteh-ha 181*), translated by Ahmad Karimi Hakkak. "Tomb of Manichaeus" (*Sang-e mani*), translated by Haleh Hatami. Published by permission of Yadollah Royai.

Saffari, Abbas: "Saturday Night Dinner" (*Sham'e shanbeh shab*), first published in English in *Circumference* 2 (Summer/Autumn 2004), 40–42. Reprinted by permission of Abbas Saffari, Nilufar Talebi, and *Circumference*. "A Bird Is a Bird" (*Parandeh, parandeh ast*), translated by Nilufar Talebi, first appeared in English online, www.thetranslationproject.com. Reprinted by permission of Abbas Saffari and Nilufar Talebi.

Sepanlu, Mohammad Ali: "Miniature" (*Miniatur*); "The Terrace of Dead Fishermen" (*Café-ye mahigiran-e mordeh*); and "The Green Bull" (*Gav-e sabz*), translated by Ahmad Karimi Hakkak. Published by permission of M. A. Sepanlu.

Shafi'i Kadkani, M. R: "Poetry I" (*She'r I*); "Poetry II" (*She'r II*); and "Prayer of Sudden Dread" (*Namaz-e khowf*) first published in English in *Parnassus: Poetry in Review* 25, nos. 1–2, 226–28, © 2001 by Poetry in Review Foundation. Translated by Ahmad Karimi Hakkak and Dick Davis. Reprinted by permission of publisher and translators.

Shamlu, Ahmad: "In This Blind Alley" (*Dar in bombast*); "End of the Game" (*Akhar-e bazi*); and "Morning" (*Sobh*) first appeared in English in *Iranian Studies* 30, nos. 3–4 (Summer/Fall 1997). Reprinted by permission of *Iranian Studies*. "Love Song" (*Asheghaneh*), translated by Ahmad Karimi Hakkak.

SUGGESTED READING: MODERN IRANIAN LITERATURE IN ENGLISH TRANSLATION

PROSE

Alavi, Bozorg. *Her Eyes.* Lanham, Md.: University Press of America/Biblioteca Persica, 1989.

Amirshahi, Mahshid. *Suri & Company: Tales of a Persian Teenager.* Austin: University of Texas Press, 1995

Chubak, Sadeq. *Sadeq Chubak: An Anthology.* New York: Center for Iranian Studies, Columbia University, 1981.

———. *The Patient Stone.* Persian Fiction in Translation. Costa Mesa, Cal.: Mazda Publishers, 1989.

Daneshvar, Simin. *A Persian Requiem.* New York: George Braziller, 1992.

———. *Daneshvar's Playhouse: A Collection of Stories.* Washington, D.C.: Mage Publishers, 1989.

———. *Savushun: A Novel about Modern Iran.* Washington, D.C.: Mage Publishers, 1990.

———. *Sutra and Other Stories.* Washington, D.C.: Mage Publishers, 1994.

Fassih, Esmail. *Sorraya in a Coma.* London: Zed Books, 1985.

Golshiri, Hushang (Manuchehr Irani). *King of the Benighted.* Washington, D.C.: Mage Publishers, 1990.

———. *Black Parrot, Green Crow: A Collection of Short Fiction.* Washington, D.C.: Mage Publishers, 2003.

Hedayat, Sadegh. *The Blind Owl.* New York: Evergreen, 1969.

Khorsandi, Hadi. *The Ayatollah and I.* Columbia, La.: Readers International, 1987.

Miraftabi, Morteza. *Mystical Realities: Iranian Short Stories.* Bakersfield, Cal.: Favor Publishing, 1993.

Mirzadegi, Shokuh, *The Stranger Within Me.* Bethesda, Md.: Ibex Publishers, 2002.

Modaress-Sadeghi, Jafar. *The Marsh.* Costa Mesa, Cal.: Mazda Publishers, 1996.

Parsipur, Shahrnush. *Women Without Men: A Novella.* Syracuse, N.Y.: Syracuse University Press, 1998; Feminist Press, 2003.

Pezeshkzad, Iraj. *My Uncle Napoleon.* Washington, D.C.: Mage Publishers, 2000.

Ravanipur, Moniru. *Kanizu.* Persian Fiction in Translation, Series no. 5. Costa Mesa, Cal.: Biblioteca Iranica, 2004.

———. *Satan's Stones.* Austin: University of Texas Press, 1996.

Sa'edi, Gholamhoseyn. *Dandil: Stories from Iranian Life.* New York: Random House, 1981.

———. *Fear and Trembling.* Washington, D.C.: Three Continents Press, 1984.

———. *Othello in Wonderland and Mirror Polishing Storytellers / Two Plays by Gholamhoseyn Sa'edi.* Costa Mesa, Cal.: Mazda Publishers, 1996.

Sayyad, Parviz. *Parviz Sayyad's Theatre of Diaspora: Two Plays—The Ass and the Rex Cinema Trial.* Costa Mesa, Cal.: Mazda Publishers, 1993.

Taraghi, Goli, *A Mansion in the Sky and Other Short Stories.* Austin: University of Texas Press, 2003.

———. *Winter Sleep.* Costa Mesa, Cal.: Mazda Publishers, 1994.

POETRY

Baraheni, Reza. *God's Shadow: Prison Poems.* Bloomington, Ind.: Indiana University Press, 1976.

Behbahani, Simin, *Cup of Sin: Selected Poems.* Syracuse, N.Y.: Syracuse University Press, 1999.

———. *Wounded Rose: Three Iranian Poets.* Columbia, La.: Readers International, 1980.

E'tesami, Parvin. *A Nightingale's Lament: Selections from the Poems and Fables of Parvin E'tesami.* Costa Mesa, Cal.: Mazda Publishers, 1994.

Farrokhzad, Forough. *Another Birth: Selected Poems.* Emeryville, Cal.: Albany Press, 1981.

———. *Bride of Acacias: Selected Poems.* Delmar, N.Y.: Caravan Books, 1982.

————. *Remembering the Flight: Twenty Poems.* Vancouver: Nik Publishers, 1997.

————. *A Rebirth: Poems.* Costa Mesa, Cal.: Mazda Publishers, 1985.

Kianush, Mahmud. *Poems from a Persian Divan.* Ware, U.K.: Rockingham Press, 1994.

Kiarostami, Abbas. *Walking with the Wind: Poems by Abbas Kiarostami.* Cambridge, Mass.: Harvard Film Archive Publications, 2001.

Khoi, Esmail. *Edges of Poetry: Selected Poems.* Santa Monica, Cal.: Blue Lagos Press, 1995.

————. *Outlandia: Songs of Exile.* Vancouver: Nik Publishers, 1999.

Naderpur, Nader. *False Dawn: Persian Poems 1951–1984.* Literature East & West Series. Austin: University of Texas Press, 1986.

Naficy, Majid. *Muddy Shoes: Poems.* Venice, Cal.: Beyond Baroque Books, 1999.

Saffarzadeh, Tahereh. *Tahereh Saffarzadeh: Selected Poems, a Bilingual Edition.* Shiraz, Iran: Navid Publishing House, 1987.

Sepehri, Sohrab. *The Expanse of Green: Poems.* Los Angeles: Kalimat Press/UNESCO, Persian Series, 1988.

————. *The Lover Is Always Alone: Selected Poems.* Tehran: Sokhan Publishers, 2004.

Shamlu, Ahmad. *Love Poems.* Bethesda, Md.: Ibex Publishers.

Vajdi, Shadab. *Closed Circuit: The Poetry of Shadab Vajdi.* London: Forest Books, 1989.

ANTHOLOGIES

Ghanoonparvar, M. R., and John Green, eds. *Iranian Drama: An Anthology.* Costa Mesa, Cal.: Mazda Publishers, 1989.

Husain, Syed Akhtar, ed. *Tales from Iran: A Collection of Short Stories.* New Delhi: Syed Akhtar Husain, 1990.

Kapuscinski, Gisele, ed. *Modern Persian Drama: An Anthology/Bahram Beyza'I, Gowhar Morad, Abbas Na'lbandian.* Lanham, Md.: University Press of America/Biblioteca Persica, 1987.

Karimi Hakkak, Ahmad, ed. *An Anthology of Modern Persian Poetry.* Boulder, Col.: Westview Press, 1978.

Kianush, Mahmud, ed. *Modern Persian Poetry.* Ware, U.K.: Rockingham Press, 1996.

Moayyad, Heshmat, ed. *Stories from Iran: A Chicago Anthology, 1921–1991.* Washington, D.C.: Mage Publishers, 1992.

Paknazar Sullivan, Soraya, ed. *Stories by Iranian Women Since the Revolution.* Austin: University of Texas Press, 1991.

Shoshani, Shmuel, and Shmuri Shoshani, eds. *The Persian Nightingale in a Cage: Selected Persian Diaspora Poetry, Post-Islamic Revolution.* Chapel Hill, N.C.: Professional Press, 1997.

Southgate, Minoo, ed. *Modern Persian Short Stories.* Washington, D.C.: Three Continents Press, 1980.

Vatanabadi, Shouleh, and Mohammad Mehdi Khorrami, eds. *A Feast in the Mirror: Stories by Contemporary Iranian Women.* Boulder, Col.: Lynne Rienner Publishers, 2000.

———. *Another Sea, Another Shore: Persian Stories of Migration.* Northampton, Mass.: Interlink Books, 2004.

Yarshater, Ehsan, ed. *Hedayat: An Anthology.* Delmar, N.Y.: Caravan Books (Modern Persian Literature, series no. 2), 1979.

Yazdanfar, Farzin, and John Green, eds. *A Walnut Sapling on Masih's Grave and Other Stories by Iranian Women.* Portsmouth, N.H.: Heinemann, 1993.

Yazdanfar, Farzin and Franklin Lewis, eds. *In a Voice of Their Own: A Collection of Stories Written by Iranian Women Since the Revolution in 1979.* Costa Mesa, Cal.: Mazda Publishers, 1996.